Yoshitaka Okada (Ed.)

Struggles for Survival

Institutional and Organizational Changes in Japan's High-Tech Industries

Yoshitaka Okada (Ed.)

Struggles for Survival

Institutional and Organizational Changes in Japan's High-Tech Industries

Springer

Yoshitaka Okada, Ph.D.
Professor
Faculty of Comparative Culture
Sophia University
4 Yonban-cho, Chiyoda-ku
Tokyo 102–0081, Japan

Library of Congress Control Number: 2005936236
ISBN-10 4-431-28874-0 Springer-Verlag Tokyo Berlin Heidelberg New York
ISBN-13 978-4-431-28874-9 Springer-Verlag Tokyo Berlin Heidelberg New York

Springer is a part of Springer Science+Business Media
springeronline.com

Typesetting, Printing, and Binding: Kato Bunmeisha, Japan

Printed on acid-free paper

To Hideko Okada
With my deep appreciation

Preface

Globalization has, on the one hand, integrated markets throughout the world and stimulated the dynamic development of companies, especially multinational corporations. On the other hand, it has reduced the role of the government in each country. However, this general understanding of the changing role of governments is not quite applicable to high-tech industries, in which the governments of the United States, Japan, and European Union are said to be engaged in a "high-tech war." Indeed, international competition is actually expanding the role of national and regional governments in strengthening institutional supports for technological innovation by promoting cooperative learning among companies and technology-supporting organizations, disseminating technological information, and stimulating innovative activities. Each country or region is struggling to build a more effective system of innovation, introducing more market-oriented mechanisms, strengthening support systems, and mobilizing traditional institutions. When Japan faced economic difficulties in the 1990s, its traditional system of innovation came up against its own limitations, and Japan has been struggling to rebuild its system ever since.

I have been engaged in a research project titled "Fluidity of Japanese Institutions and Organizations in Advanced Technology Research: Search for a Fusion of Continuity and Change." This project attempts to determine how new mechanisms are introduced and how traditional institutions are effectively mobilized for further stimulating innovative activities in high-tech industries. This book, which is the outcome of this project, dissects what is a complex mixture of newly introduced mechanisms and existing institutions for innovation.

This project was developed as the cumulative outcome of a series of past research activities. My interest in Japan's high-tech industries began when I was involved in a United Nations University project titled "Japan's Self-Reliance in Science and Technology for National Development." Though my role was to examine the process of technology transfer from the U.S. to Japan in the semiconductor industry, I came to recognize the complexity of industrial development, which has involved not only market competition among firms, but also support from technology-supporting organizations, industrial associations, and governments. Effective support by technology-supporting organizations and governments was indispensable to Japan's success in technological innovation and the development of its semiconductor industry. I learned from this project the importance of a comprehensive approach to understanding systems of innovation and industrial dynamics.

I was in search of just such a comprehensive theory of industrial dynamics when I was invited in 1987 to be a visiting assistant professor in the Sociology Department at my alma mater, the University of Wisconsin-Madison. There I met Professor J. Rogers Hollingsworth, the former president of an international academic association, the Society for the Advancement of Socio-Economics (SASE). He introduced me to the fascinating field of institutional analysis and economic sociology and allowed me to participate in his project, "The Social System of Production." Through this project I became acquainted with a group of top-level scholars working in this field. Also, Mrs. Ellen Jane Hollingsworth and Professor Richard Whitley provided indispensable help to me by reading and criticizing my earlier book manuscript and encouraging my further research activities. Inspired by their scholarship and analysis, I began to develop the conceptual framework needed to identify the institutional dynamics of Japanese high-tech industries. A grant by Japan's Ministry of Education, a Grant-in-Aid for Scientific Research (B) (1990–1991), enabled me to start developing the concepts of "competitive-*cum*-cooperative inter-firm relations" and "techno-governance structure" to explain the dynamics of the Japanese semiconductor industry in the 1980s.

Another project, "Institutions and Policy Priorities for Industrial Technology Development," sponsored by the World Bank (1993–1995), also gave me a stimulating opportunity to understand the role of institutions in technological innovation. This was a seven-nation comparative research project to examine similarities and differences in the systems by which technology-supporting organizations stimulate innovative activities in the private sector. This project enabled me to further develop the concept of the techno-governance structure.

These three projects provided me with the basis for developing the present one, "Fluidity of Japanese Institutions and Organizations in Advanced Technology Research: Search for a Fusion of Continuity and Change." How is globalization affecting the traditional system of innovation for high-tech industries? How is this system changing with the decline of the Japanese economy in the 1990s? These were the initial questions I asked. Based on the concept of techno-governance developed in an earlier project, I placed the primary focus on the transformation of the innovation system under globalization, particularly examining institutional factors and techno-governance structures in three high-tech industries: semiconductor, telecommunications, and biotechnology. Factors included in my analysis as elements of the techno-governance structure extend to corporate organizations, strategies for innovation, inter-firm relations, technology-supporting organizations, and governments. I believe that such a comprehensive approach can shed some light on transformations in these three industries.

My strategy for this project was to bring together two institutional economists (including myself) and two corporate strategy specialists in innovation. I was extremely happy when Professors Yuzo Murayama, David T. Methé, and Kazuhiro Asakawa expressed interest in participating in this project. Professor Murayama, of Doshisha University, is an institutional economist specializing in the telecommunications industry. Professors David T. Methé, of Kwansei Gakuin University, and Kazuhiro Asakawa, of Keio University, specialize in corporate strategies for innovation in the semiconductor and biotechnology industries, respectively. I have employed institutional analysis to analyze the semiconductor industry. This was a team combining an unusual mix of excellent specialists, and the project was a stimulus for creative thinking by all of us. I am very grateful for the team members' active participation in and support of this project.

I also wish to express my sincere appreciation to the Murata Science Foundation and the Matsushita International Foundation for funding the library research and conceptual development of this project in 1999. Without timely funding at the empirical stage in the form of a Grant-in-Aid for Scientific Research (KAKENHI) (B) (12430011, 2000–2002) by the Japan Society for the Promotion of Science (JSPS), this project would never have been completed. Valuable contributions from many interviewees who spared their precious time and responded to our questions are also deeply appreciated. A Grant-in-Aid for Publication of Scientific Research Results (175256, 2005) by the JSPS has also been an indispensable help in publishing these research results. My appreciation also goes to Mr. Alan Gleason, who patiently edited the draft of this book and provided many valuable suggestions, to the staff members of Springer-Verlag Tokyo for their support in publishing this book, and to Ms. Miwa Higashiura and Ms. Kimiyo Akabane for administrative help in the recent JSPS projects. Above all, I am deeply indebted to my wife, Hideko Okada, who has patiently supported me throughout my academic career and who has developed the habit of working with me during my busy weekends.

Yoshitaka Okada
29 March 2005
Tokyo, Japan

Table of Contents

List of Tables

List of Figures

List of Abbreviations

ADI	Advanced I Strategy
ADSL	asymmetric digital subscriber line
AIST	National Institute of Advanced Industrial Science and Technology
ArF	argon fluoride
ARPANET	Advanced Research Projects Agency Network
ASET	Association of Super-Advanced Electronics Technologies
ASIC	application-specific integrated circuit
ASPLA	Advanced System-on-a-Chip Platform Corporation
ASRC	Advanced Semiconductor Research Center
ASUKA	Advanced System-on-a-Chip Through Collaborative Achievement Project
ATP	Advanced Technology Program
CAD	computer-aided design
CADD	computer-aided drug design
CD	compact disc
CD-ROM	compact disc read-only memory
CIM	computer-integrated manufacturing
CMOS	complementary metal oxide semiconductor
COE	center of excellence
COS	computer on silicon
CRADA	cooperative research and development agreement
CRT	cathode-ray tube
CVD	chemical vapor deposition
DARPA	Defense Advanced Research Projects Agency
DIPS	Dendenkosha information processing system
DNA	deoxyribonucleic acid
DOC	Department of Commerce
DOD	Department of Defense
DOE	Department of Energy
DOS	disk operating system
DRAM	dynamic random access memory
DSP	digital signal processor
DVD	digital versatile disc
EB	electron beam
EDA	electronic design automation
EIAJ	Electronics Industry Association of Japan

ERC	engineering research center
ERSO	Electric Research and Service Organization
ETL	Electro-Technical Laboratory
EUV lithography	extreme ultraviolet lithography
EUV-LLC	Extreme Ultraviolet Limited Liability Company
FCRP	Focus Center Research Program
FDD	floppy disk drive
FED	R&D Association for Future Electron Devices
FESTA	Femtosecond Technology Research Association
FIB lithography	focused ion beam lithography
FTTH	fiber to the home (glass fiber connections to houses)
GaAs	gallium arsenide
Gb	gigabit
GPRA	Government Performance and Result Act
GPS	global positioning system
HALCA	Highly Agile Line Concept Advancement
HDD	hard disk drive
IC	integrated circuit
ICOT	Institute for New Generation Computer Technology
IDM	integrated device manufacturer
IMEC	Interuniversity MicroElectronics Center
IMSI	Institute of Microsystem Integration
IMT2000 Protocol	International Mobile Telecommunications 2000 Protocol
IP	intellectual property
IPO	initial public offering
IPV6	Internet Protocol Version 6
ISEMATECH	International SEMATECH
IT	information technology
ITRI	Industrial Technology Research Institute
ITRS	international technology road map for semiconductors
ITU	International Telecommunications Union
JRDC	Japan Research and Development Corporation
JSBC	Japan Small Business Corporation
JSMEC	Japan Small and Medium Enterprise Corporation
JST	Japan Science and Technology Corporation
KAICRP	Kumamoto Area Integrating Cooperative Research Project
KAIST	Korean Advanced Institute of Science and Technology
Kb	kilobit
KSIA	Korea Semiconductor Industry Association
KTLO	Kansai Technology Licensing Organization
LAN	local area network
LCD	liquid crystal display
LLC	limited liability company
LSF	large-sized firm
LSI	large-scale integrated circuit

MARCO	Microelectronic Advanced Research Corporation
Mb	megabit
MCC	Microelectronics and Computer Technology Corporation
MCVD	modified chemical vapor deposition
METI	Ministry of Economy, Trade and Industry
MEXT	Ministry of Education, Culture, Sports, Science and Technology
MIA	Multivendor Integration Architecture Project
MIRAI	Millennium Research for Advanced Information Technology
MIT	Massachusetts Institute of Technology
MITI	Ministry of International Trade and Industry
MMI	Microelectronic Manufacturing Infrastructure
MoF	Ministry of Finance
MOS	metal oxide semiconductor
MOSIS	Metal Oxide Semiconductor Implementation System
MOTHERS	Market of the High-Growth and Emerging Stocks
MPT	Ministry of Posts and Telecommunications
MRAM	magnetic random access memory
mRNA	messenger ribonucleic acid
NASA	National Aeronautics and Space Administration
NCRA	National Cooperative Research Act
NEDO	New Energy and Industrial Technology Development Organization
NGL	next-generation lithography
NIST	National Institute for Standards and Technology
NMOS	n-channel metal oxide semiconductor
NSF	National Science Foundation
NSMP	National Semiconductor Metrology Program
NTTPC	Nippon Telegraph and Telephone Public Corporation
OS	operating system
PBX	private branch exchanges
PC	personal computer
PDA	personal digital assistant
PFC	perfluoro compound
PLD	programmed logic device
PMOS	p-channel metal oxide semiconductor
RISC	reduced instruction set computer
SBDD	structure-based drug design
SCOE	SEMATECH Center of Excellence
SEC	Securities and Exchange Commission
SELETE	Semiconductor Leading Edge Technologies Inc.
SEMATECH	Semiconductor Manufacturing Technology
SEMI	Semiconductor Equipment and Materials International
SETC	Semiconductor Technology Council
SIA	Semiconductor Industry Association

SIRIJ	Semiconductor Industry Research Institute Japan
SMF	small- and medium-sized firms
SoC	system on a chip
SRAM	static random access memory
SRC	Semiconductor Research Corporation
SSi	Super Silicon Crystal Research Institute
STARC	Semiconductor Technology Academic Research Center
STC	science and technology center
SVGL	Silicon Valley Group Lithography Division
TCAD	technology computer-aided design
TLO	technology licensing organization
TRI	Telecommunication Research Institute
TRON	the real-time operating system nucleus
TSIA	Taiwan Semiconductor Industry Association
TSMC	Taiwan Semiconductor Manufacturing Corporation
TSO	technology-supporting organization
ULSI	ultralarge-scale integrated circuit
UMC	United Microelectronics Corporation
VAD	vapor phase axial deposition
VDEC	University of Tokyo VLSI Design and Education Center
VLSI	very large-scale integrated circuit
VRML	Virtual Reality Modeling Languages
W-CDMA	wideband code division multiple access
WSC	World Semiconductor Council

Introduction

Yoshitaka Okada
Sophia University

Since the bursting of its bubble in 1992, the Japanese economy has been stagnating for more than a decade. The GDP growth rate fell from 3.1% in 1991 to 0.9% in 1992. Since then it has hovered around 1.0%, except when it went to 3.5% in 1996 and −1.1% in 1998.[1] This stagnation has occurred largely because domestic demand has drastically declined, while globalization has intensified international competition and has forced Japanese companies to relocate their production to low-production-cost countries. Even high-tech companies, such as those in the telecommunications and semiconductor industries, have had to confront changes in international industrial structures, since Japan has been lagging behind the United States in many fields of technological innovation and behind the European Union in several areas. Moreover, Korea and Taiwan are catching up with Japan in technology and engage in production with much lower labor costs and higher efficiency than Japan. Consequently, some Japanese industries have lost their world-leading positions.

This intensified international competition in technological innovation and business activity is putting pressure on Japanese companies to quickly change their management practices and become more flexible and open, while also forcing changes in the behavior of technology-supporting organizations (TSOs) and governments, and even in the nature of long-established practices and institutions. Institutions, understood as "rules, enforcement characteristics of rules, and norms of behavior that structure repeated human interaction" (North, 1989: 1321), have been the underlying, legitimizing, and sustaining elements of dynamic innovative behavior in Japan for many years.

Technology-related actors, such as companies, governments, and TSOs, are facing new and turbulent environments. Historically, the decline of industries is not a new phenomenon. The British textile industry lost its international competitiveness because of market-oriented specialization that split the vertical line of production into segments, in which rational decisions by each firm prevented their coordinated transformation for advanced technological development. Similarly, managerial innovations and specialized education not only sustained the rise of industrial capability in the U.S., but also ended up keeping research activities remote from product innovation and industrial development (Lazonick, 1992).

Weak coordinated efforts and an emphasis on rational decisions based on market movements seem to be persistent institutional characteristics of Great Britain, while specialization and a high R&D orientation are characteristics of the U.S. Partly owing to such characteristics, however, these countries are successful at generating radical innovations involving basic science in universities, risk-taking venture firms, and the growth of new industries. Evidence of this is abundant in the dynamic growth of the biotechnology and information technology (IT) industries in these countries. In other words, highly market-oriented institutional characteristics may become a hindrance to the dynamics of a particular industry, but they can also be the source of new growth and dynamics. What matters is whether existing institutions and global market conditions fit well with the particular industry and its practices. Alternatively, institutional transformation may create an environment suited to new global market conditions and the growth of a certain type of industry.

In Japan, cooperative learning—defined as the process of mutually increasing the exchange of rich technological information among partners, thereby promoting learning and advancing technological capability—has generated synergetic effects, facilitated goal attainment, produced positive long-term gains among partners, and played a very important role in generating industrial dynamics (Okada, 1999, 2001; Lundvall, 1988, 1992a, 1992b). However, the ease of facilitating cooperation in vertical relations between large-sized firms (LSFs) and small- and medium-sized firms (SMFs) confined benefits to the types of industries in which a division of labor was rather easily created, such as assembly-oriented industries (e.g., the electronics, automobile, and foundry industries), making Japan quite weak in knowledge-intensive industries such as chemicals, software, and biotechnology (Okada, 1999). Companies dynamically interacted through vertical inter-firm relations, though TSOs and governments functioned to support cooperation among competitors of similar sizes.

Vertical cooperation seems to be a persistent and institutionalized characteristic of Japanese inter-firm relations, one that became an important source of industrial dynamics in the 1970s and 1980s. However, existing industries moved their production facilities to foreign countries, weakening the mechanisms of vertical cooperation. Even Japan's leading technology position in the semiconductor industry was lost to the U.S., while a significant portion of its global market share was lost to Korean, Taiwanese, and U.S. companies. Technological innovation that would lead to the rise of venture firms and industrial transformation in such areas as the biotechnology and IT industries is not advancing quickly enough to replace the weakened existing industries. The biotechnology industry is basic-science oriented, while the IT industry requires innovative ideas from individuals. Crucial to both of these industries are a risk-taking attitude by venture firms and the advanced basic research capability of universities, both areas in which Japan seems to be lagging behind.

In the 1990s, Japanese companies faced three serious problems: (1) Japanese production was shifting to foreign countries, making innovations and risk-taking venture firms more needed than ever before; (2) the disintegration of vertical cooperation between assemblers and suppliers of parts and materials was reducing the dynamics of cooperative learning for improvements and innovation; and (3) the dynamic growth of new industries was coming from more idea- and basic-science-oriented activities, requiring a different set and level of TSOs and government policies. Japan has not yet made a successful transformation to such a support system.

Mechanisms and institutions that brought Japan prosperity in the 1970s and 1980s have become dysfunctional and less useful. Many nations and firms have historically coped with such difficulties and changes in market conditions by finding solutions and developing strategies for catch-up and industrial transformation. Technological innovation becomes especially crucial to industrial transformation, requiring each nation and company to identify new innovative areas for competition, sometimes by linking different segments within and between industries, reformulating inter-firm relations, reorganizing diverse TSOs for effective innovation, and even trying to change institutions. In the Japanese context such efforts often involve the role of national and regional governments, though they may be achieved without their involvement. How, then, are firms, TSOs, and governments presently trying to overcome the problems, changes in market conditions, and institutional restrictions they face, especially in relation to technological innovation as the key to industrial transformation? That is the basic question asked in this book.

Institutions function to restrict the range of choices for decision makers in determining the future direction of development, while they also function to encourage innovation within the confines of the institution. The old Japanese way of setting a company's goals and strategies promoted harmonious behavior within and between firms, while a good match between management practices and existing institutions provided a favorable environment for effective cooperative learning and industrial dynamics.

The Japanese situation in the 1990s (and in the mid-1980s in the case of the telecommunications industry) suggested that the old, traditional way of setting a company's goals and strategies and its relations with other firms, governments, and TSOs was not helping Japanese companies regain their international competitiveness. I shall use the term techno-governance to describe the way that companies, governments and TSOs harmonize their behavior in the interests of technological innovation, and shall refer to the resulting structure as a techno-governance structure. In other words, the old Japanese techno-governance structure not only failed to sustain the dynamics of Japanese industries, but also became a hindrance to dynamic development.

Japanese companies since then have been reformulating their organizational goals and strategies to cope with the new situation. They have been developing micro-level strategies to change intra- and inter-firm relations. But an individual company's attempts to change on its own are inadequate to create a favorable environment. Such attempts might create a bad image for the company by fomenting disharmony in the old techno-governance structure and violating institutional norms, while radical changes might make the company even more vulnerable against competitors.

Collective actions by companies may foster a favorable environment for implementing strategies for radical change if a significant number of firms follow suit. Since the late 1990s, Japanese companies have been collectively appealing to the national government and to regional governments for changes in policy and in the role of TSOs in supporting the companies' radical technological transformations. The outcome of such macro-level strategies often involves changes in institutions such as laws, education, the financial system, and social norms. Since existing institutions restrict industrial dynamics, institutional change becomes an important basis for widening decision options, forsaking routine decisions, and solving routine problems. This is especially so because institutions do a large amount of regular thinking on behalf of individuals (Rowe, 1989).

Hence, Japanese attempts to cope with the difficulties of the 1990s have involved two levels of strategy at the micro- and macro-levels. Changes in the behavior of technology-related actors, simultaneously influencing institutions, should thus be apparent in the techno-governance structure. Such macro-level strategies, along with those at the micro-level, may create a new way of harmonizing technology-related actors, transforming the techno-governance structure into one more suited to new types of technology and market environments, reestablishing the competitiveness of companies, and even assisting in industrial transformation.

This means that institutions and organizations co-evolve, mediated by changes in the techno-governance structure. To be specific, what seems to take place in this process of co-evolution is that technology-related actors reinterpret market conditions and historical incidents, analyze the existing techno-governance structure, search for new values and strategies, set targets for future competitive resource accumulation and products, influence institutional changes in regulations and policies, and reformulate the existing techno-governance structure. Such attempts may even come to stimulate changes in social norms.

Therefore the following questions can be asked in this empirical study. Have there been changes in the micro- and macro-level strategies of Japanese high-tech industries? Have micro-level strategies generated changes in corporate behavior and inter-firm relations? Have macro-level strategies generated changes in the behavior of governments and TSOs? How did institutions restrict such attempts to introduce changes? Have there been changes in the institutions themselves? If the result is a mixed outcome, what aspects of institutions are changed and what ones are not changed? What are the mechanisms of co-evolution between organizations as actors and institutions? What new form of techno-governance structure has arisen?

This book focuses on three high-tech industries in Japan: the semiconductor, telecommunications, and biotechnology industries. The Japanese semiconductor industry dominated the world market and became its technological leader in the 1980s, but ceded technological leadership to the U.S. and became less competitive in the world market in the 1990s. In contrast, the telecommunications industry was protected by the government until 1984 and remained less internationally competitive, while the biotechnology industry is considered quite weak, partly because of its science-oriented and knowledge-intensive nature and partly because of weaknesses in the university system in Japan. Are there differences among these industries in the micro- and macro-level strategies of companies, in the way the techno-governance structure is established, and in the way institutions restrict or promote innovative activities?

In Chapter 1, I develop this book's theoretical framework for analysis. Technology is understood as not simply machines and hardware, but as the embodiment of knowledge in people, suggesting the need for understanding institutional conditions to properly understand technological innovation. Among the theories of technological innovation, the national system of innovation is the first theory to incorporate institutional aspects. An examination of early, new, and contemporary institutional theories, however, suggests that the national system of innovation theory inadequately addresses the concept and role of institutions and the relations between organizations as actors and institutions. Attempting to create a more comprehensive framework that may be useful for analyzing the transformation of industries, I introduce the concept of the techno-governance structure, a harmonized pattern of interaction among technology-related actors for technological innovation. It consists of intra- and inter-firm relations and of companies' relations with governments and TSOs. The relations among these diverse actors change to cope with changes in institutions and non-institutional contingencies such as market conditions and historical incidents. Key tools for transformation consist of micro-level company strategies and macro-level collective strategies, in many cases initiated by companies, involving governments and TSOs.

Chapters 2, 3, and 4 focus on the semiconductor industry. In Chapter 2, I examine why the Japanese semiconductor industry lost its global competitiveness. I attribute this decline to the disintegration of the old techno-governance structure, which was locked into vertical inter-firm relations in which cooperative learning with a strong sense of commitment was exercised. While the government and TSOs extensively promoted cooperation among competitors in order to prevent lock-in into narrowly focused technological perspectives, this techno-governance eventually disintegrated, largely as a result of the U.S.-Japan trade disputes and the privatization of Nippon Telegraph and Telephone Public Corporation (NTTPC), which had led Japan's development of DRAM technologies. This disintegration weakened industrial dynamics in innovation, while the remaining vertical relations between semiconductor firms and equipment manufacturers entrapped them in outmoded perspectives. Meanwhile, cooperation through SEMATECH allowed U.S. competitors to take technological leadership away from Japan by developing the capability to place far more complex system designs (e.g., the microprocessor, digital signal processor (DSP), and logic circuit) on a chip—called the system large-scale integrated circuit (system LSI), or system-on-a-chip (SoC)—at the same line-refinement level as the more simply designed Japanese DRAM. This change resulted in Japan's loss of international technological competitiveness.

In Chapter 3, I analyze how Japanese semiconductor companies struggled to survive and rebuild their technological capability in the area of the system LSI.

The initial struggles took place amid poor market performances, attempts to maintain the institutional tradition of lifetime employment, and a firm belief in innovative capabilities based on the old techno-governance structure. Emphasis on the latter two factors delayed the introduction of changes and aggravated market performances to the point where changes in those factors were unavoidable. Semiconductor companies then introduced market-oriented strategies that resulted in terminating employees, dissolving vertical long-term relations, and dividing companies into independent units that could be sold or used to form joint ventures with competitors. This last strategy—modularizing company operations and dividing a company into separate units—unexpectedly resulted in the development of alliances with competitors in certain product areas while the same companies competed intensely in other product areas. This strategy thus generated "modularized competition."

Cooperation was also facilitated by government-subsidized research cooperatives that brought together competitors to share basic technologies, especially in the system LSI area where Japanese companies have been trying to integrate microprocessor, memory, DSP, logic, and other functional devices in one chip to leap past the U.S. technological level. The implementation of market-oriented strategies created diverse options for decision makers and resulted in their developing a far more complex mix of cooperation and competition, involving different partners in different product areas. This transformation is occurring with some old institutions remaining as a solid foundation for cooperative behavior, while newly introduced mechanisms and practices provide more openness and flexibility, possibly suggesting the rise of a new type of techno-governance.

Methé in Chapter 4 argues that institutions and agents (technology-related actors) co-evolve, and that agents' strategies become a key tool for change, since a wider array of options and choices increases the probability of coping with uncertain and turbulent conditions in the market. He separates the macro-level factors that influence and restrict agents' strategies into extra-institutional and institutional factors. The primary extra-institutional factor is techno-globalization, through which superior technology disseminates from one country to the rest of the world and restricts the range of technological innovation. In the case of the semiconductor industry, new technologies and production systems usually spread from the U.S. to Europe, Japan, Korea, and Taiwan. Institutional factors consist of local institutions that stimulate a particular way of innovating technology and advancing its capability in a local context, still confined within the restrictions of techno-globalization.

Methé also refers to the set of elements that stimulate technological innovation via techno-globalization as an innovation envelope. One element of this envelope is the complex interrelationship between semiconductor manufacturers and equipment companies. He argues that semiconductor inter-firm relations shifted from the system house to the integrated device manufacturer (IDM) and to a horizontal split between fabless design houses and foundry businesses. Future development may follow the direction of this horizontal split. In the process of techno-globalization, there still exists ample room for local institutions and an agent's strategies to exercise influence in a way that differentiates comparative advantages among countries as well as companies. One good example is Japan's comparative advantage generated from its effectiveness at vertical cooperation in DRAM production. When agents try to find a balance between the fragmenting forces of local institutions and techno-globalization, there occurs a complex co-evolution of local institutions, techno-globalization, and agents.

Murayama in Chapter 5 traces the development of the Japanese telecommunications industry, dividing it into three periods: closed, transition, and open. Tight governmental regulations during the closed period significantly determined what NTTPC could do, but the government came to ease restrictions during the transition period. Globalization, digitization, and privatization during the open period radically changed the institutional environment for NTT, the newly privatized successor to NTTPC. Despite this, the persistence of some restrictive institutions hampered NTT's dynamic development and led to its failure to advance into foreign countries. NTT's lack of global competitiveness also contributed to the failure of its major equipment suppliers in their own global market advancement.

In contrast, NTT DoCoMo, an offshoot of NTT, became a completely independent mobile telephone company and found a way to survive without NTT's help. Poor technology and severe competition in a small market forced the company to break away from institutional restrictions and develop an open management system for personnel, suppliers, resources, and even ideas. The consequence was DoCoMo's success in introducing i-mode, the world's first Internet-accessible mobile phone. DoCoMo's highly market-oriented and open approach notwithstanding, the philosophical basis of this new venture was the Japanese philosophy of *ba* (place), where interpersonal interaction and nurtured interpersonal relations provide a favorable environment for exchanging ideas and stimulating new ones.

In Chapter 6, Asakawa examines the Japanese biotechnology sector from the perspective of the theory of the national system of innovation. The Japanese pharmaceutical industry took a very different path of development from that followed by the semiconductor and telecommunications industries. It was more in-house R&D-oriented, with a much smaller R&D budget, because Japanese pharmaceutical companies were dependent on existing technology and not engaged in radical technological innovation. Universities remained indifferent to company activities, and companies engaged in collaborative research with universities mostly with the objective of producing well-trained students. Moreover, the government did not adopt the pharmaceutical industry as a policy target, unlike the electronics and machinery industries. Market-oriented inter-firm relations and weak cooperation with TSOs and the government characterized the old techno-governance structure of the pharmaceutical industry. With the advent of biotechnology research, however, the government began developing national-level innovation policies, while companies began developing micro-level strategies for radical innovation. Macro-level strategies by the government and micro-level company strategies have only recently started co-evolving.

Finally, in the Conclusion of this book I attempt to elaborate on the common characteristics of co-evolution among market conditions, historical incidents, institutions, and the techno-governance structure in the semiconductor, telecommunications, and biotechnology industries, and to suggest a new form of techno-governance structure that is possibly emerging at present.

Note

[1] http://www.mofa.go.jp/mofaj/gaiko/bluebook/2002/gaikou/html/siryou/sr_05_02_01_02.html and http://devdata.worldbank.org/external/CPProfile.asp?SelectedCountry=JPN&CCODE=JPN&CANME=Japan&PTYPE=CP

Bibliography

Lazonick, W. (1992) Organization and Technology in Capitalist Development. Edward Elgar, Hants, UK.

Lundvall, B-A. (1988) "Innovation as an interactive process: From user-producer interaction to the national system of innovation." In: Dosi, G.; Freeman, C.; Nelson, R.; Silverberg, G.; and Soete, L. (Eds.) Technical Change and Economic Theory. Pinter Publishers, London, pp. 349–369.

——— (Ed.) (1992a) "Introduction." In: National Systems of Innovation: Toward a Theory of Innovation and Interactive Learning. Pinter Publishers, London, pp. 1–19.

——— (Ed.) (1992b) "User-producer relationships, national systems of innovation and internationalization." In: National Systems of Innovation: Toward a Theory of Innovation and Interactive Learning. Pinter Publishers, London, pp. 45–67.

North, D. (1989) "Institutions and economic growth: A historical introduction." World Development 17(9):1319–1332.

Okada, Y. (Ed.) (1999) Japan's Industrial Technology Development: Role of Cooperative Learning and Institutions. Springer-Verlag, Tokyo.

——— (2001) "Cooperative learning and Japan's techno-governance structure: Exploratory case studies." Sophia International Review 23: 19–42.

Rowe, N. (1989) Rules and Institutions. Philip Allan, New York.

Web Pages

http://devdata.worldbank.org/external/CPProfile.asp?SelectedCountry=JPN&CCODE=JPN&CANME=Japan&PTYPE=CP

http://www.mofa.go.jp/mofaj/gaiko/bluebook/2002/gaikou/html/siryou/sr_05_02_01_02.html

Chapter 1

Institutions, Organizations, and Techno-Governance for Innovation

Yoshitaka Okada
Sophia University

How do we analyze the complex process of the decline and struggle for the survival of Japanese high-tech companies? Technological innovation itself is an important determinant of changes, but that is only a segment of a picture that covers a complex process involving diverse actors—not only companies, but also national and regional governments and such technology-supporting organizations (TSOs) as universities and technical colleges; associations; research consortia; national, regional and local technical institutes; consulting firms; and private contract laboratories. These actors develop a certain pattern of interaction in each country while drastic changes take place not only in environments, such as the competitive market, but also in institutions that function to restrict actors' behavior. In this chapter, I shall try to develop a framework of analysis that can comprehensively incorporate the aforementioned elements, reviewing some of the relevant theories.

1 Technology and Innovation

Technology is understood as a certain kind of knowledge that allows the adaptation of means for the production of goods. It is the collection of theoretical and practical knowledge, know-how, skills, and artifacts that individuals and organizations use to develop, produce, and deliver their products and services (Burgelman and Rosenbloom, 1997: 273). It is not simply mechanical information that is concretized in machines and hardware; it is also the embodiment of knowledge in people influenced by organizational history, diverse social backgrounds, culture, product-market conditions, social regulations, and quality of education (Tushman et al., 1997; Lundvall, 1992a; Burgelman and Rosenbloom, 1997; Mole and Elliott, 1987).

Technological innovation plays a major role in advancing the sophistication of knowledge that has a direct impact on the competitiveness of a company and on industrial development (Nelson and Winter, 1982). It comes from diverse levels of innovativeness. It can be derived from incremental innovations, involving imitation, innovative imitation, or application engineering, that rely on existing technology to be respectively copied, altered to be made suitable for the market, or applied to new areas. These innovations may be made based on internally accumulated knowledge in a company or a nation, though they may be new to others (Unger et al., 1999: 4). Technological innovation can also come from radical innovations or a new combination of existing technologies involving leveraged creativity or a state-of-the-art breakthrough. The former utilizes existing knowledge to create radically different technology, but the latter drastically changes the technological system and the industry (Okada, 2000; Crawford, 1983).

Identifying the level of innovativeness and the nature and sources of technological knowledge is important, but it covers only a small aspect of understanding technological innovation. That is because a new idea has to be turned into an invention, which then has to be used to develop a product, and finally a product has to penetrate the market. Such a process can be realized only when a company is well organized and effectively managed. Thus the importance of an innovation lies not in its ideas and inventiveness, but rather in its commercial viability and its ability to win a share of a market (West, 1992).

What further complicates our understanding of technological innovation is the importance of non-technology factors. Although product-market conditions are undeniably an important factor, innovation does not necessarily take place simply because market competition exists. Since technology is the embodiment of knowledge in people and since the importance of innovation is its commercial viability, diverse factors related to human behavior, such as product-market conditions, historical incidents, and institutions, influence technological innovation. Every institution, whether in the realm of law, education, industrial relations, or social customs, restricts and regulates the ways in which a system within that institution is operated, in which systems are related to one another, and in which individuals and organizations behave in recurrent situations within interrelated systems. Furthermore, institutional arrangements—the ways in which diverse institutions are linked and harmonized with each other—provide conductive or restrictive environments for idea formation, invention, product development, commercialization, and consequently the success of innovation.

Additionally, technological innovation is argued to be more effective when diverse technology-related actors, such as national and regional governments and TSOs, interact with one another, disseminate information, and stimulate innovations (Freeman, 1987; Dosi et al., 1988; Nelson and Winter, 1977, 1982; Lundvall, 1992a; Unger et al., 1999; Okada, 1999). In many cases they directly or indirectly contribute to companies' innovative activities, while their behavior is significantly supported, restricted, and influenced by institutional arrangements (Hage and Hollingsworth, 2000). This means that complex inter-organizational interactions among technology-related actors take place systematically or unsystematically for technological innovation. Whichever way they occur, such interactions require an environment that generates interdependence and harmony among technology-related actors. I use the term techno-governance to describe the way in which diverse technology-related actors are harmonized (Okada, 2000, 2001). Hence market environments, institutions, and techno-governance become important foci for understanding technological innovation.

2 The National System of Innovation and Its Limitations

An institutional perspective was introduced to the issue of technological innovation for the first time by scholars of the national system of innovation (Lundvall, 1992a; Nelson, 1993; Edquist, 1997). Lundvall (1985: 55) used the concept of the innovation system to capture interactions between a company's R&D laboratories and TSOs and their relations to the production system. The origin of the concept of the national system of innovation comes from Freeman's (1987) analysis of Japan. The key to this perspective is the recognition of innovation as an outcome of learning, searching, and exploiting, taking place in routines and feedback among diverse actors, and characterized by a certain power relation, trust, and loyalty in coordination and cooperation (Lundvall, 1985, 1988, 1992b; Lundvall and Maskell, 2000). Since learning among diverse actors necessarily involves human interaction, the focus of the national system of innovation is a social system, not a system of commodity exchange as found in neoclassical economics (Lundvall, 1992a).

Knowledge accumulation is an important prerequisite for innovation. Companies are understood to be highly effective at innovation because they can more easily accumulate and make use of knowledge than can individuals. Companies are key actors in innovation, and their role as innovators is considered more crucial to economic dynamics than their role in commodity exchanges in the market, which is an empty mechanism without knowledge accumulation. Therefore, how companies and other technology-related actors interact with one another in learning, searching, and exploiting becomes an important issue of inquiry (Lundvall, 1992a).

Who stimulates the creation of innovative ideas is also an important question. Empirical evidence identifies the importance of external sources: users in the scientific instrument sector (von Hippel, 1976); suppliers, big users, and research extension services in supplier-dominant sectors; intra-firm R&D departments and public organizations in science-based industries (Pavitt, 1984); and the suppliers of capital equipment and components in the U.S. (Nelson, 1982, 1985). Lundvall (1985) also emphasizes the importance of communication-intensive user-producer interaction, which could become costly if technology actors simply acted on the basis of self-calculation, market rationality, and opportunism. Thus inter-firm relations develop "organized markets" by incorporating elements of power, trust, and loyalty (Meeus et al., 1999).

But external to the market, Nelson (1993) argues that organizations related to science and engineering are important. Scientists in universities and engineers in firms, universities, and government agencies become key actors in technological innovation. This is because a new scientific finding often leads to many new technologies, and unaccountable experimental outcomes in engineering may also provoke thinking in the scientific community and the creation of new science. Universities and government research institutes engage in basic and applied research, but increasingly firms' R&D laboratories play an important role in linking inventions to innovations and to products. Government policies, education, and training also create differences. Packages of monetary, fiscal, and trade policies are also identified as important incentives to firms (Nelson, 1993; Kim and Nelson, 2000), while technology policies are not at all uniform among different countries and sectors.

Lundvall (1985) emphasizes the difficulty of separating the national system of innovation from the social system. He argues that since the national system of innovation is embedded in the social system, each nation needs to rely heavily on its social system to mobilize the necessary resources to stimulate technological innovation effectively and efficiently. Therefore each nation comes to develop a particular set of mechanisms to coordinate technology-related actors for the purpose of producing, diffusing, and exploiting economically useful knowledge, consequently generating differences in national economic performance.

Although its patterns and actors differ among countries and sectors, systematic interaction among technology-related organizations facilitates learning and stimulation, generating national disparities in technological innovation and industrial development. This is why the national system of innovation is argued to be important. And since such a system of innovation is immobile, embedded in the institutions and social systems of a particular nation, it remains a viable source of technological innovation and national performance even in the era of globalization.

Since technology is not simply mechanical information, but rather the embodiment of knowledge in people, influenced by such diverse factors as society, institutions, history, and environment, the theory of the national system of innovation provides us with a comprehensive approach to the issue of technological innovation. But because the focus of its research is on product innovation and related interactive learning, the range of actors and institutions covered in this research is limited. Its focus is too narrow to analyze the complex process of industrial transformation—the decline and reconstruction of industries—caused by historical incidents, technological paradigm shifts, changes in product-market conditions, and consequent changes in corporate strategies, inter-firm relations, and relations to other technology-related organizations.

There appear to be five areas of inadequacy in the national system of innovation argument that may be significant to our attempt to understand the current changes in Japan's high-tech industries. First, the argument provides a vague and confusing picture that fails to clarify the concept of institutions and relations between actors and institutions. The national system of innovation treats all non-firm factors, such as governments, universities, government laboratories, and social and cultural factors, as institutions without clearly separating them into institutions as rules of games and their enforcement (North, 1989), on the one hand, and technology-related actors (universities and governments, for example) on the other. Second, the restrictive nature of institutions and the national system and its impact on innovation are not adequately addressed. Third, the argument emphasizes the importance of intra- and inter-firm relations and "organized markets," but pays little attention to the involvement of different types of intra- and inter-firm relations in different situations and functions, formulated and changed by key decisions and strategies. Fourth, there are diverse mechanisms of coordination and control in each industrial sector, which play an important role in communicating tacit knowledge and generating a similar set of understandings, perspectives, and even consensus. The national system of innovation does not adequately cover these mechanisms. Finally, the argument fails to take into account changes in institutions and the national system, as well as the importance of micro- or firm-level and macro- or collective-level strategies, which alter the nature of linkages among diverse actors and generate changes in institutions and the national system. I shall briefly elaborate on these points and develop a framework that can be used for the analysis of Japanese high-tech industries.

2.1 Ambiguous Concept of Institutions and Relations between Actors and Institutions

Both Lundvall (1992a) and Nelson (1995) view the national system of innovation as socially embedded and strongly connected to social institutions. Nelson (1995), focusing particularly on scientists and engineers in diverse organizations, emphasizes the importance to technological innovation of non-firm organizations such as universities and government research institutes and their linkages to firms' R&D laboratories. Since the way scientists and engineers interact with each other is greatly influenced by such social institutions as the government, funding agencies, and educational and training institutions, Nelson interprets the national system of innovation in terms of the connection between firms' R&D activities and social institutions, both in general and specifically for technological innovation. Hence his concept of social institutions covers both non-firm technology-related actors, such as universities and government research laboratories, and general institutional characteristics, such as the rules of games enforced by educational and financial institutions.

Lundvall (1992a) argues that because interactive learning is a key element of technological innovation and is basically a social process, innovation is greatly influenced by relations between the structure of production indicated by intra- and inter-firm relations on the one hand, and the institutional setup, such as the role of the public sector, financial institutions, culture, ideologies, and government policies, on the other. As a result of their comprehensive perspectives, Nelson and Lundvall made a significant intellectual contribution in bringing to our attention the importance of the institutional setup to firms' technological innovations. But recent developments in institutional theory suggest that they have not effectively articulated the concept of institutions and the clear separation between institutions and actors.

The lack of separation seems to suggest that both of these arguments follow

Thorstein Veblen's concept of institutions. Veblen was an early institutional theorist who argued against the assumptions of neoclassical economics (Nelson and Winter, 1982; Johnson, 1992). He defined institutions as "settled habits of thought common to the generality of man" (Veblen, 1919: 239; Scott, 1995). An institution is a large set of routine behavior and an outgrowth of habit, generating various kinds of regularities in behavior (Johnson, 1992). Veblen argued that habit and conventions heavily influence the economic behavior of people. Individuals are both builders of and products of society and cannot become lone actors independent from other actors and society. Similarly, mutually dependent relations exist between individuals and the market. Changes in the market are reflective of collective actions to change the community's methods of material accounting based on changes in the community's collective thoughts on other related rules such as those governing property rights and resolution of conflicts (Veblen, 1919; Pessali and Fernandez, 1999). In Veblen's argument, actors and institutions were not clearly separated in a way that enables us to identify actors' roles in coping with their environments and changing institutions as well as institutions' roles in restricting and changing actors' behavior.

Focusing on more fundamental aspects of economic activity and borrowing a legal concept, John Commons, an early institutional theorist, argued that the basic element of economic activities is not exchange, but rather transaction, which is "two or more wills giving, taking, persuading, coercing, defrauding, commanding, obeying, competing, governing, in a world of scarcity, mechanisms and rules of conduct" (Commons, 1924: 7; Scott, 1995). For Commons, institutions are rules of conduct to solve conflicts of interest, construct a collective standard, and make market transactions under a scarcity of resources work effectively (Scott, 1995). Actors and institutions are clearly two separate entities. Although diverse options exist for actors in choosing which type of transaction to undertake, the process of transaction is, in general, embedded in and restricted by various institutions, legal, political, and cultural. Since institutions are a historical outcome of imperfect and pragmatic solutions to conflicts, they also expand and liberate individual behavior through countless numbers of routine and complementary transactions as well as collective movements to change standards.

Because of their emphasis on indeterminism and realism, the early institutional theorists focused mostly on case studies and descriptions, failing to develop a coherent theoretical framework. It was the theorists of the new institutional economics, such as Friedrich Hayek, Ronald Coase, Oliver Williamson, and Douglas North, who made a bold attempt to theorize about institutions. This group saw institutions as rules of games, identified by webs of interrelated rules and norms and by enforcement characteristics of rules and norms that structure repeated human interaction (North, 1989; Nee, 1998). Incorporating the rational choice concept (Olson, 1971), they argued that actors are given a range of choices and make a choice within the restrictions of institutions and environments. Thus they clearly separated organizations as actors from institutions and environments.

This separation came to be strongly emphasized by Friedrich Hayek. Focusing on the use of knowledge in economic activities, he stressed the importance of individuals' cognitive processes in their decision making and behavior in the market, clearly denying the condition of perfect knowledge that neoclassical economists assume. Individuals are different because of diversity in their knowledge and cognitive orientations and maps. They have different information sources and environments that contribute to a cumulative differentiation in individuals' knowledge, except that some part of their cognitive map is collectively and historically shared through socialization, imitation, and adaptation. Knowledge formation is not static, but it is evolving and dynamic with the constant acquisition of information from diverse sources. And the market is one of the important institutions that serve a cybernetic function to disseminate relevant information and stimulate knowledge evolution (Hayek, 1945; Langlois, 1995; Rizzello, 1997).

Hayek argued that there is some overlap in cognitive orientation between economic actors and institutions. The latter consist of collectively and historically shared knowledge that is largely the consequence of unplanned human action (Powell and DiMaggio, 1991). Individuals as economic actors are different from institutions. It can likewise be argued that each organization, as an economic actor, develops its own organizational culture and cognitive orientation, accumulates its own particular knowledge, and operates with organizational inertia, while organizations also have a knowledge base collectively and historically shared with other organizations (Tushman et al., 1997).

Thus economic actors, such as individuals and organizations, are different from institutions. The former have the freedom to make choices and influence other actors and institutions, while the latter are comparatively persistent, continuous, and slow and difficult to change. This distinction is fully recognized by other new institutional theorists such as Coase, Williamson, and North and by the contemporary institutional theorists. In this book, this separation between actors and institutions, and the complex interactions between the two, are treated as critical to explaining continuity and change in organizational behavior and institutions in Japanese high-tech industries.

2.2 Lack of Clarification of the Roles of Institutions in Restricting Actors' Behavior

The national system of innovation argument, in equating this system with the social system, does not treat institutions as a restrictive force that limits the range of options and choices for actors, and it also fails to understand that this restrictive force stimulates innovative behavior, generating idiosyncratic but highly effective developments within given institutional environments. Even thus restricted, economic actors can continuously engage in small actions that may generate minor changes in institutions, or in bold actions that overcome these institutional restrictions.

Contrary to Hayek, another new institutional theorist, Douglas North, more strongly emphasizes the importance and continuity of institutions and the path-dependent nature of institutional development. He defines institutions as "rules, enforcement characteristics of rules, and norms of behavior that structure repeated human interaction" (North, 1989: 1321). They are the rules of games in human interaction, consisting of informal rules (social norms, codes of conduct, customs, culture, etc.) and formal ones (constitutions, laws, etc.). By coercive, normative, and mimetic means (DiMaggio and Powell, 1991; Scott, 1995), institutions develop a model of mental constructs, become social scripts, guide or restrict individual and organizational behavior in a certain specified direction, and reproduce a repeated pattern of behavior (Schank and Abelson, 1977; Campbell, 1997; Nooteboom, 1997, 1999; Scott, 1995). Through such restrictions, institutions reduce uncertainty, solicit credible commitment to a set of behaviors, and minimize transaction costs (North, 1989, 1990, 1993).

North, despite his emphasis on the restrictive nature of institutions, identifies individuals and organizations as actors with open choices and decision-making capabilities that can influence and change institutions. But changes occur gradually, sometimes in a less conspicuous way. North argues that the restrictive nature of institutions has two effects: (1) confining decisions to a range of choices, resulting in a reproduction of the past; and (2) stimulating minor innovative activities within the restricted range of choices to generate gradual changes. Thus even the path-dependent nature of institutional development has its innovative and creative aspects, altering institutions little by little and attempting to reduce transaction costs.

Since institutions restrict the range of choices and behavior and since nations have different institutional settings, diverse ways of organizing economic activities exist. One group of contemporary institutional theorists, developing the varieties of capitalism argument, inquires what relations exist among diverse institutions within a nation and whether a pattern exists in their relations. This group focuses on national differences in the ways institutions—legal, financial, educational, industrial, and so on—complement one another, develop a nation's own configuration of institutional arrangements, and generate particular effects on economic performance (Crouch and Streeck, 1997; Hollingsworth and Boyer, 1997; Hall and Soskice, 2001).

These theorists argue that each national model pursues different objectives and makes use of quite different tools for coordinating economic activities (Hollingsworth and Boyer, 1997). Following the game theory assumption, they argue that institutions are determined by choice as in a game (Schotter, 1981) and consist of multiple equilibria generated by interactions among multiple economic actors who make choices from among diverse options (Hall and Soskice, 2001). Although the range of choice is restricted by shared understandings among actors and institutional environments within each model, the range of choice is still wide enough for individuals and organizations to generate some diversity and transformation in a national model. But in the course of responding to problems, each national model evolves based on a specific logic and continuity inherent in its own history and contingencies.

Several authors propose diverse national models, such as the liberal market versus the coordinated market economies (Hall and Soskice, 2001); German and Japanese models of coordinated market economies (Streeck and Yamamura, 2001); the market-based, meso-corporatist, European institution/public, and social democratic models (Amable, 2000); and three groups of different institutional complementarities for a technology-led regime: (1) the social democratic configuration, (2) the deregulated and science-pushed configuration, and (3) the leapfrogging configuration for lagging countries (Boyer, 2004: 18). In the German-coordinated market economy, corporate governance, education and training, inter-company relations, and industrial relations have their own coordinated logic, but in the U.S. liberal market economy, capital markets, education and training, strong competition policies, and a deregulated labor market show their compatibility. Even company strategies have their respectively different characteristics (Hall and Soskice, 2001).

The basic assertion in the varieties of capitalism argument is that even under globalization, there is no single best national model for optimum performance. Each model has its particular strengths and weaknesses. Hence, an understanding of the roles that institutions play in restricting options and choices as well as stimulating innovation within restrictions, along with some understanding of their compatibility with related institutions, is crucial to an understanding of technological innovation and is a focus of inquiry in this book.

2.3 Inadequate Attention to Types of Inter-Firm Relations and Company Organizations and Strategies

The argument of the national system of innovation emphasizes the importance of inter-firm relations and "organized markets," which differ according to companies' specializations. But when changes occur in their environments, companies with the same specialization tend to change their relations with other firms in a similar way, suggesting that changes in a company's environment influence a company's choice of the type of inter-firm governance—the way it harmonizes with other firms—that it employs. In many cases, such changes even trigger changes in organizational structure and company strategies. What is the relationship between, on the one hand, the types of inter-firm relations, organizational structure, and strategies of a company, and on the other hand the contingencies affecting a company? Do inter-firm relations change in the face of different contingencies? The national system of innovation lacks this perspective on changes in such relations, while transaction cost economics and the business system perspective emphasize this point. Moreover, by focusing on "organized markets," the national system of innovation tends to ignore the function of the market itself in generating diverse effects on innovative activities.

Ronald Coase (1937), a theorist of the new institutional economics, argued that the market involves such transaction costs as searching for information, writing up and enforcing contracts, preventing other transacting actors from cheating, and paying sales tax. Because of such costs in the market, firms internalize operations inside a hierarchy, but this is done only up to the point where the internalization (bureaucratic) cost becomes larger than the transaction cost in the market. Hence how efficiently the market works through contracts is very much determined not only by institutions, but also by the degree of internalization through which firms try to minimize the cost of market transactions as well as firm operation. Similarly, Oliver Williamson (1975, 1981, 1985, 1994) argues that higher market transaction costs are due to (1) a paired condition of bounded rationality and uncertainty, (2) a paired condition of opportunism and small numbers (monopoly, monopsony, or oligopoly), and (3) information asymmetry in the market. Thus a firm chooses among different types of inter-firm relations—namely, the governance types of market-based, bilateral-relations-based or trilateral-relations-based relations—or hierarchical intra-firm relations. If the choice of inter-firm governance—the means of harmonizing and coordinating inter-firm relations—fits well with the contingencies it faces, a company can cut both transaction and operational costs, achieve efficiency, and strengthen market competitiveness. Underlying these decisions on choices of governance type are company strategies, which allow a company to consistently pursue a set of goals. And what follows from these choices is an internal organizational structure that corresponds to the chosen governance type.

The business system approach, a contemporary institutional theory similar to the varieties of capitalism argument, also tries to explain the diversity in company organization and behavior among different countries. Instead of focusing on governance types, this approach argues that these differences are greatly influenced by culture and formal institutions, such as the role of the state, the financial system, the labor market, and dominant beliefs about trust, loyalty, and authority (Whitley, 1992, 1994, 1999; Whitley and Kristensen, 1997). These influences differentiate among the ways that economic activities and resources are coordinated and controlled in each nation, namely, the ways in which intra- and inter-firm relations are structured and in which the market operates. Certain combinations of these coordination mechanisms work quite effectively in certain social and institutional contexts. The characteristics of the coordinating mechanisms defined by Whitley, however, are so complex that they are not feasible for this comprehensive study of specific industries.[1] I shall therefore make use of the analytical framework of Coase and Williamson, who focus on the fit or match between types of governance and contingencies of operations.

2.4 Inadequate Attention to Diverse Mechanisms of Coordination and Control

Prior to the development of the varieties of capitalism argument, another contemporary institutional perspective on institutional arrangements provided important insights into how diverse types of mechanisms of actor coordination provide different outputs in economic activities and play a crucial part in formulating institutional arrangements (Campbell et al., 1991; Hollingsworth et al., 1994; Okada, 2000). Scholars adopting this perspective argue that the reason why nonmarket modes of coordination become important is simply because the market tends to be ineffective in communicating tacit knowledge and generating its dynamics (Hage and Hollingsworth, 2000). Lindberg et al. (1991) classified coordination mechanisms into market (spot market, auctions, venture firms, etc.), network (alliances, joint ventures, joint research, etc.), and hierarchy (companies, multinational operations, national research institutes, regional/local technical institutes, etc.), identifying the latter two as having important roles in coordinating economic activities along with the market. Hollingsworth, Schmitter, and Streeck (1994), focusing on the control and coordination of industries in several countries, also found diversity in institutional arrangements, especially state policies. But one consistent finding is that tightly controlled sectors perform better than loosely controlled ones.

Scholars of this institutional arrangements perspective recently shifted their focus to the issue of radical innovation, describing this approach in terms of idea innovation networks. They criticize the national system of innovation perspective for focusing on a limited set of technology actors and institutions, hence failing to examine how the modes of coordination in institutional arrangements (associations, various types of markets, the state, networks) and the structure of institutional sectors (e.g., financial markets, educational and research systems, industrial relations systems) are related to the innovation processes of firms (Hage and Hollingsworth, 2000; van Waarden et al., 1999). Nonmarket actors are considered vital for effectively communicating tacit knowledge, which is crucial to radical innovation. Hage and Hollingsworth (2000: 983) argue that radical innovations require "a variety of coordinated mechanisms to connect both firms and non-firms within and across arenas," including linkages outside of a nation, which the national system of innovation fails to address. They ask how the combination of modes of coordination and the structure of institutions at various stages of innovation in each industrial sector influence the way business organizations achieve radical technological innovation.

Therefore, following the arguments on institutional arrangements and idea innovation networks, this research adds diverse mechanisms of control and coordination to the narrowly focused technology-related actors in the national system of innovation.

2.5 Failure to Address Institutional Changes

The evolutionary growth theory (Nelson and Winter, 1982) views technological advancement and a country's technological competence in innovation as the key driving force in a country's economic performance. In reality, many inventors and R&D teams approach R&D differently, and winners and losers in competition are simply determined by ex post facto selection, making it impossible to predict winners. Thus the focus of the evolutionary growth theory has been on a historical description of technological change. But Nelson and Sampat (2001) and Nelson (2002) in their recent articles urge institutional theorists to focus on evolutionary institutional changes and to inquire into the role of routine social technologies to understand technology and technological change. A similar argument has been made by North, who has incorporated evolutionary concepts in understanding the transformation of the market. The relationship between institutional changes and technological innovation is becoming a new focus of recent research.

In this regard, another contemporary institutional theory, the resource orchestration perspective (Casper, 1999), argues that actors, especially with the help of governments, function to shift the place of resource allocation, orchestrate the coordination of necessary linkages within innovation networks, and overcome obstacles in existing institutions. National models of institutions and organizations first face a technology crisis; then governments, in cooperation with technology-related actors, develop a set of new policies, deregulate, and engage in new institution building. Actors in a national model cooperatively develop new systems for orchestrating resource allocations and nurturing organizational competencies as deemed necessary to innovate in particular sectors and to remove obstacles for technological innovation. These changes take place with some hybridization of a country's institutional framework.

Similar to the varieties of capitalism argument, the resource orchestration perspective emphasizes that institutional environments still remain critical determinants of organizational structure, while fine-tuning in sectoral reforms actually provides an environment for the evolution of the institutional framework. Such a perspective on changes in company strategies, government actions, and institutions becomes a vital element in explaining the decline and reformulation of Japanese high-tech industries.

Incorporating these criticisms of the national system of innovation, as identified by reviewing early, new, and contemporary institutional theories, I shall construct a framework for this research that I call a techno-governance perspective.

3 Concept of Techno-Governance Structure and Framework for Analysis

As the evolutionary growth theory (Nelson and Winter, 1982) argues, technological innovation is considered one of the leading factors in maintaining industrial development and competitiveness. But a simple understanding of the nature and source of technological knowledge is inadequate. Instead, an understanding of diverse factors involved in this complex process of technological innovation is required. These factors are (1) intra- and inter-firm relations; (2) companies' relations to technology-related actors that directly influence technological innovation; (3) companies' relations to diverse types of coordination mechanisms; (4) institutions that persistently restrict; and (5) product-market conditions and historical incidents that sporadically change companies' contingencies. Similar to the national system of innovation argument, the focus of this research is technological innovation by companies. But unlike the argument that treats TSOs and institutional characteristics simply as institutions, this book understands companies and TSOs as actors that develop a particular way of interaction among them and that may change this particular way in different contingencies. TSOs are actors, not institutions, and they may even influence institutions. For example, a university is an actor engaging in innovative activities, but the educational system is an institution, having a set pattern of rules for its operations. With this clear separation between actors and institutions in mind, I shall develop the concept of the techno-governance structure and the framework for analysis used in this book.

3.1 Intra- and Inter-Firm Relations

Accumulated knowledge is considered crucial to technological innovation, and companies are known for having capabilities in accumulating knowledge and information and in making use of these in products and sales superior to any other type of organization (Lundvall, 1992a). They can allocate human resources, develop organizational structures, and implement necessary strategies in research, product development, production, and marketing. Strategies are understood as the deliberate creation of defensive capabilities and advantages by allocating and coordinating diverse resources (Goodman and Lawless, 1994: 27). In other words, companies are key actors in technological innovation.

Von Hippel (1976), Pavit (1984), Nelson (1982, 1985), and Lundvall (1985, 1988) have all demonstrated the importance of inter-firm relations, especially with customers and suppliers, for technological innovation. Okada (1999: 12) found that Japanese companies view their most highly valued business partners in the descending order of customers with long-term relations, internal departments and laboratories, suppliers with long-term relations, and foreign investors and licensors. These relations involve intensive communications and interactive learning—which, as the national system of innovation approach argues, is the major source of innovation—and are hence valued higher than companies' relations with TSOs.

It is Willamson's concept of governance, i.e., the way diverse actors are harmonized in economic activities, that captures the importance of diverse types of inter-firm relations. His concept of governance focuses on the harmonizing mechanisms of companies' transactions as manifested in contracts, and he interprets market and hierarchy as two extreme forms of harmonizing company behavior. The market, at one extreme, has no internalized transactions, while hierarchy, at the other extreme, has all transactions internalized. An intermediate form, such as Japanese long-term relations, can be treated as a form that mixes the characteristics of both market and hierarchy. For some functions and some contingencies, a company may rely on internalized operations, and for other functions and contingencies, it may prefer to transact with other companies in the market.

The form of inter-firm relations a company uses may be determined by decision makers in order to minimize transaction costs based on the contingency of operations (Williamson, 1981). Using other forms in certain functional areas and contingencies increases transaction costs. Thus a company chooses and combines diverse types of inter-firm relations well fitted to its contingencies, which become sources of efficiency and positive performance. This harmonization of transactions and contingencies, along with coordinating mechanisms, is a primary characteristic of Williamson's concept of governance.

Williamson's focus on transactions based on contracts is, however, not adequate for an understanding of the technological changes taking place in Japan's high-tech industries. This is because the transacted portions of technology usually covered by patent and licensing contracts are quite small and because diverse organizations in Japan interact dynamically on the basis of long-term relations without contracts for technological development. As the national system of innovation perspective argues, interactive learning is among the most important aspects of technological innovation in Japan, so the focus of this research should be on interactive learning rather than on contracts. However, the market remains an option for decision makers who may choose to conclude a contract with a partner in the market when it has a specific value in certain contingencies.

Intra-firm interaction for R&D is clearly the most important hierarchical mechanism; it determines the organizational capability to mobilize internal resources, disseminate and exchange information, and stimulate innovation under effective monitoring, control, and coordination. Moreover, organizational control over information disclosure is vital for maintaining corporate secrets, which can be best secured under the hierarchical organizational form.

In contrast, the market, involving arm's-length transactions and short-term contracts, can be an important source of technological dissemination and change. Although the market cannot facilitate intensive interactive learning, its fluidity in inter-firm relations can be a vital source of flexibility and openness for technology-related actors, inducing quicker changes. The institutional arrangements argument emphasizes that the market is an important mechanism of actor coordination, especially in generating flexibility and choices in technology sales and purchases (Lindberg et al., 1991). However, the idea innovation networks perspective warns that the market can effectively facilitate transactions mainly when tacit knowledge is less involved (Hages and Hollingsworth, 2000). Nevertheless, because of the relative openness of entry and exit in the market, it may provide diverse options for a company's decision makers, enabling them to choose new information and expertise and to successfully influence the movements of other companies in competition (Metcalf, 1998). Differences and diversity in technological information among market actors under an initial set of conditions provide a rich ground for selections and changes, while competition forces other companies to assimilate or differentiate, creating convergent and divergent paths for technological development (Hayek, 1945; Rizzello, 1997; Groenewegen and Vromen, 1997). A repeated choice of market mechanisms by a company undeniably represents one type of repeated pattern in inter-firm coordination.

Inter-firm cooperation[2] can be another dynamic source of technological information and innovation, ranging in its interactions from function-specific, time-limited, repeated short-term contracts to comprehensive long-term relations. It covers diverse forms of cooperation from a level only slightly more structured than interaction in the market to a highly structured level very close to a hierarchy.

As Williamson argues, decision makers can choose types of inter-firm relations as they try to generate a fit between inter-firm relations and contingencies. But needs for consistency in behavior require companies to make such decisions as a part of company strategy and to develop proper organizational structures. The degree of fit between types of inter-firm relations and contingencies increases or decreases the costs and benefits of interaction and differentiates the companies' performances.

3.2 Companies' Relations to Technology-Related Actors and Other Types of Coordination Mechanisms

Technological innovation is argued to be more effective when diverse actors interact with one another, disseminate information, and stimulate innovation (Freeman, 1987; Dosi et al., 1988; Nelson and Winter, 1977, 1982; Lundvall, 1992a). Particularly, how inventions and innovations are diffused makes a drastic difference in the way an industrial sector or a firm develops its technological capability. Stimulating new ideas are often generated by a heterogeneity of ideas, which also requires a heterogeneity of technology actors. These characteristics of innovation suggest the importance of TSOs, directly and indirectly related to R&D activities, as effective and dynamic actors.

Government policies, funding agencies, universities, and national research institutes are often cited as important actors in developing an effective national system of innovation (Nelson, 1993). In descending order of importance, universities and technical colleges, regional technical institutes, and national technical institutes are valued highly by companies in Japan. Furthermore, various governmental measures to support R&D activities, such as research subsidies, tax incentives, and low-interest-rate loans, are also considered important (Okada, 1999). As the nature of innovation moves from incremental to radical, the roles of universities and the central government become especially important in generating new ideas and technology and in funding projects (Gibbons et al., 1994). This is partly because the university is the key institution for conducting research in basic science, partly because activities in basic research suffer from prohibitively high costs, risks, and uncertainty, and partly because exchanging and sharing information, which is vital for stimulating new ideas and technology, is something that competing companies tend to avoid.

Scholars of the institutional arrangements and idea innovation networks perspectives argue that diverse types of coordinating and control mechanisms compensate for the failure of the market in exchanging tacit knowledge (Hage and Hollingsworth, 2000). In the context of Japan, research associations where scholars and company researchers bring up diverse R&D issues for discussion are ranked as being more important than national/regional technology institutes, universities, and technical colleges, or research consortia that directly support companies' R&D activities. Academic and industrial associations that indirectly support these activities are also ranked important, just behind the directly supporting research consortia (Okada, 1999).

Whether a key innovation in a product is incremental or radical, companies' interactions with TSOs and governments, which have a different set of information, networks, capabilities, and funding sources, do much to differentiate companies in their ability to innovate. Some TSOs engage not only in innovation by themselves, but also in the diffusion and exchange of technological information, and consequently they stimulate innovation by diverse technology-related actors (Okada, 1999; Carlsson, 1994). How technological information is effectively and efficiently innovated, disseminated, and transformed into dynamic industrial activities is a process that undeniably involves national/regional governments and TSOs in Japan.

Hence, as Fig 1.1 shows, the focus of this research should be on interactions rather than transactions. These interactions take place in (1) intra- and inter-firm relations as argued in transaction cost economics; (2) companies' relations with national/regional governments and TSOs directly supporting R&D activities (e.g., national/regional technical institutes, research cooperatives, universities and technical colleges, private contracting laboratories, and consulting firms), as emphasized by the national system of innovation argument; and (3) companies' relations with TSOs indirectly supporting R&D activities (e.g., research, academic, and industrial associations), as emphasized by the institutional arrangements and idea innovation networks arguments.

When repeated interactions among companies, governments, and TSOs directly or indirectly related to technological innovation come to show a distinctive pattern, they form a techno-governance structure. Since governance is the way diverse organizations are harmonized and coordinated (Williamson 1975, 1981, 1985, 1994), a techno-governance structure is understood as a system, networked and harmonized among companies, governments, and TSOs, for allocating limited resources, disseminating technological information, stimulating innovation, and influencing the transformation of industry (Okada, 1989a, 1989b, 1990, 1999, 2001). Williamson defines governance as the way firms coordinate intra- and inter-firm relations, but in the present framework, the concept of techno-governance represents a system of harmonizing interactions, promoting interactive learning among companies, governments, and TSOs, and advancing technological development (Williamson, 1975, 1985). The capacity of a country to generate a competitive advantage in technology thus depends on its techno-governance structure and its ways of making use of social and institutional characteristics (Okada, 1999).

Such a harmonized structure, especially in Japan, with its constant promotion of interactive learning among companies and other participating organizations, enables TSOs and governments to offer improved technological services to firms, stimulate firms' technological competition, and effectively advance their

Figure 1.1 Techno-Governance Structures, Contingencies, and Path-Dependent Development of Institutions

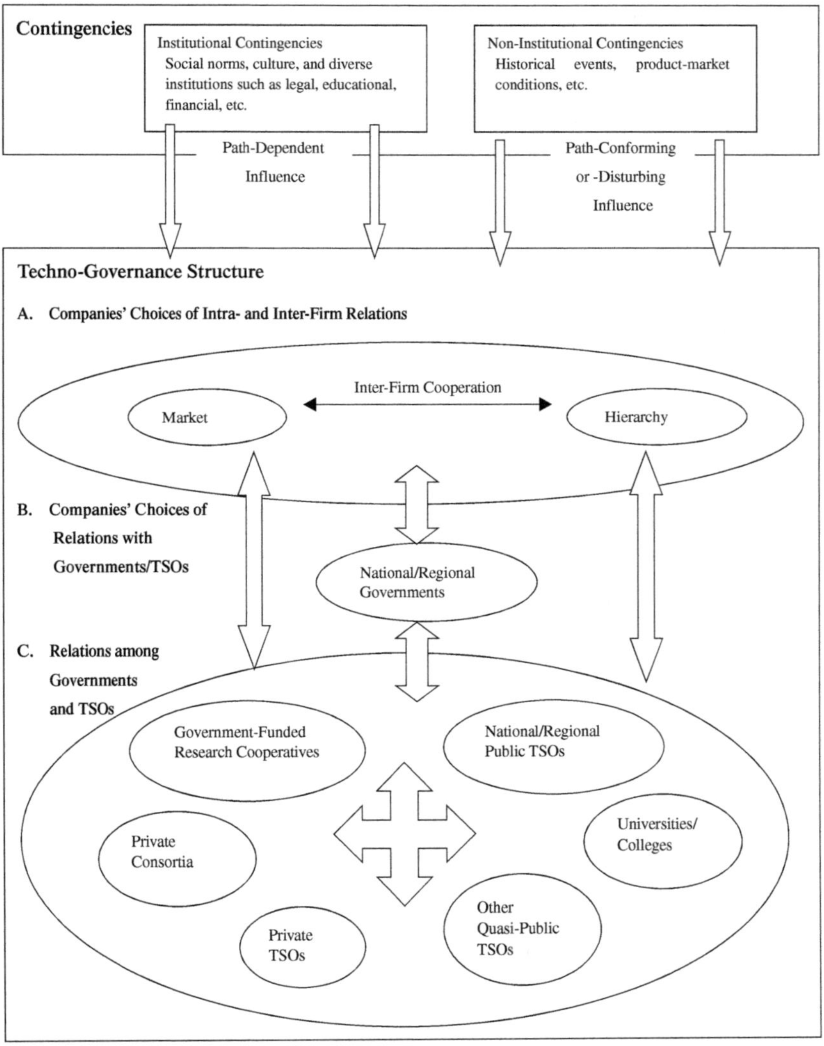

technological sophistication according to that nation's stage of economic development. But more important, the structure generates its own technological dynamics by (1) speeding up the flow of enriched technological information among actively cooperating firms; (2) stimulating technological innovation and improvement; (3) disseminating information to a wider body of firms, even including competitors and less dynamic firms through open channels; (4) preventing the monopolization of technological information; and (5) stimulating further market competition.

Therefore how companies choose to prioritize market, internal R&D, and/or inter-firm relations, how they interact with governments and TSOs, and how governments and TSOs interact among themselves to support companies in a repeated manner are all characteristics of a techno-governance structure. Furthermore, how well this structure—as a repeated pattern of interaction centered on companies—fits with contingencies will determine the companies' efficiency and effectiveness in technological innovation and their competitiveness in the global market.

4 Contingencies, Organizations, and Strategies

The fit between contingencies and the techno-governance structure thus becomes the key factor in technological innovation. What, then, are contingencies? Two types have a bearing on the techno-governance structure, i.e., the way companies, governments, and TSOs are harmonized. One type is institutional contingencies including social norms, culture, and diverse institutions such as legal, educational, financial, etc. As I pointed out earlier, the national system of innovation argument pays inadequate attention to the role of institutions in technological innovation. The other type consists of non-institutional contingencies, including historical events and product-market conditions (see Fig. 1.1).

4.1 Institutions as Contingencies

North defines institutions as the rules of games in human interaction, consisting of formal and informal rules (North, 1989). Adding more flexibility to his definition, this book defines institutions in a more game-theoretic way as "the way the game is played" (Schotter, 1981), so as to include actors' choices, the concept of multiple equilibria, and institutional transformation.

As Coase, Williamson, and North argue, individuals and organizations are not a part of institutions, but rather actors restricted under institutions and influenced by other non-institutional contingencies. Actors have the capacity to change as well as to maintain a set pattern of practices characterizing institutions. Still, institutions develop the cognitive orientation of individuals and organizations, restrict their behavior, and propagate a repeated pattern of behavior. They restrict the range of choices actors can select and the ways companies interact among themselves and with governments and TSOs. But institutions also stimulate new and innovative ideas, induce suboptimal solutions within the acceptable range of restrictions, create multiple equilibria, and contribute to gradual changes often not found in other types of institutional settings (Metcalf, 1998). Hence the path-dependent development of institutions remains important (Nelson and Sampat, 2001) and does not necessarily suggest that institutions are static.

4.2 Product-Market Conditions and Historical Incidents as Non-Institutional Contingencies

Among the most influential factors in a company's behavior are product-market conditions, since technological innovation without infiltration into the market cannot be properly considered an innovation (West, 1992). Failure to infiltrate into the market may threaten a company's survival. To infiltrate into the market with new products, companies must develop effective organizational structures and corporate strategies and operate efficiently. As Hayek argues, the market is an open space where diverse products and values can appear and where competition selects and generates changes, possibly in a certain direction. Movements in the market can send highly important signals to companies, sometimes forcing them to change their goals and products. Moreover, as complexity theory suggests (Groenewegen and Vromen, 1997; David, 1994; Arthur, 1988a, 1988b, 1989), certain historical incidents may generate a self-reinforcing and irreversible motion, forcing other companies and even competitors to follow blindly. This may lock in the direction of technological innovation and of the companies' survival.

4.3 Institutional and Non-Institutional Contingencies

Since the fit between contingencies and the techno-governance structure is understood as the very source of power and efficiency, as Williamson (1985) argues, two types of contingencies—institutional and non-institutional—become key factors in influencing the way a techno-governance structure is formulated. But these two sets of contingencies are opposite in their characteristics. Institutions are persistent and evolve very gradually. In contrast, product-market conditions and historical incidents are usually sporadic and inconsistent, and they fluctuate from period to period, though some historical incidents may generate lock-in effects in a way that influences even institutions. For example, alliances between Microsoft's disk operating system (DOS) and IBM's computer sales and between Microsoft's Windows operating system and Intel's microprocessor locked in the nature of computer market competition, and this institutionalization created a part of the economy that operated based on the law of increasing returns rather than the law of diminishing returns (Arthur, 1996). Generally, however, such poles-apart characteristic differences between the two types of contingencies, coupled with harmonized relations among technology-related actors, make the contingency/techno-governance structure relationship quite complex.

The path-dependent nature of institutions (North, 1989, 1990, 1993) becomes especially pronounced when the existing techno-governance structure fits well with these institutions and when non-institutional contingencies are highly favorable in their continuity. Routines, repeated relations, and continued company strategies become conspicuous, and they may blend more effectively with institutions than ever before. Conversely, forced changes in the techno-governance structure and in institutions arise, in many cases from extremely turbulent historical incidents and product-market conditions, especially when companies are losing their international competitiveness in the market. Companies may drastically change their relations with other companies, governments, and TSOs, and they may even be compelled to introduce new strategies and organizational structures for survival. These changes can conceivably result in altering the existing techno-governance structure and even institutions, though such alteration in a highly turbulent situation may still be limited because of the restrictive nature of institutions.

4.4 Path-Conforming and Path-Disturbing Influences of Non-Institutional Contingencies

Historical incidents and product-market conditions can be either favorable or unfavorable for a techno-governance structure. When they are favorable or less disturbing, companies accommodate those contingencies within a framework of well-functioning, path-dependent institutions. Therefore the non-institutional contingencies in this case have a path-conforming influence on a techno-governance structure, forcing it to make slight alterations (see Fig. 1.1). I refer to contingencies in this situation as path-conforming contingencies. When these contingencies are highly unfavorable and radically turbulent, however, they tend to generate enormous disturbances in the continuity of institutionally supported practices and behavior, thus having a path-disturbing influence on companies' decision makers and causing changes in the techno-governance structure and in institutions (see Fig. 1.1). I refer to such contingencies as path-disturbing contingencies.

How, then, do alterations in the techno-governance structure occur? To cope with changes in contingencies, companies develop strategies. They may decide not only to transform relations inside their firm and with other firms, governments, and TSOs through micro-level strategies, but also to transform the rules of games and norms of behavior formulated by institutions through macro-level collective strategies.

Micro-level strategies are much easier to decide and implement than are macro-level strategies, since they are a matter of decisions made by each company. However, particularly because of the narrow range of activities that a given company can influence, self-initiated micro-level strategies hold the risk of causing a company to antagonize internal and external actors and face institutional restrictions, which may allow competitors to take advantage of the company's vulnerability.

In contrast, macro-level strategies employ collective actions, which in many cases involve governments and various TSOs directly and indirectly related to technological innovation. These strategies influence government policies and the behavior of public and quasi-public TSOs. The resulting changes in government-

TSO relations eventually influence the ways in which companies interact with these organizations. Through collective macro-level strategies, companies try to transform institutional arrangements and idea innovation networks, and subsequently institutions, so that micro-level strategies become more effective and better supported by macro-level environments.

In a sense, micro- and macro-level strategies, if successful, take concrete form as changes in the techno-governance structure. Naturally, how and to what extent the old techno-governance structure is dismantled, deinstitutionalized, and replaced by a new emerging structure becomes important (DiMaggio, 1988). One group of scholars argues that individual- and organizational-level change precedes institutional change (Dacin et al., 2002; DiMaggio, 1988), and another group of scholars argues that institutions precede individual and organizational change (Lundvall, 1999). Denying unidirectional causation, Nelson (1993) argues for the co-evolution of institutions, firms, and technologies. Irrespective of uni- or co-evolution, the analysis of changes in these strategies brings insights into how companies are coping with historical events and product-market conditions, how they are overcoming institutional restrictions, and how companies, governments, and TSOs are trying to develop defensive capabilities and advantages through collective actions. However, the ways in which these micro- and macro-level strategies are used and combined differ according to whether contingencies are path conforming or path disturbing.

5 Institutions, Path-Conforming Conditions, and Strategies

When companies enjoy favorable institutional environments and path-conforming conditions in product markets and historical events, they find less need to change, continue old micro- and macro-level strategies, increase routine behavior, and reproduce a techno-governance structure that matches well with institutions (Nelson and Winter, 1982). Even under somewhat turbulent conditions, changes in strategies are likely to remain path dependent and to occur on the micro-level (North, 1989, 1990, 1993), since past decisions weigh heavily on existing institutions and techno-governance structures. Once investments are made in developing codes of communication and behavior, and once coordination among diverse related actors is well developed, it becomes costly and difficult to reverse the nature and direction of evolution (David, 1994, Arthur, 1988 a). Choices are very likely to follow an old pattern suitable for existing institutions, since the actors know that abandoning the existing pattern of behavior or relations may be too costly, that information on a new choice may be incomplete, or that decision makers may feel safe and comfortable in choosing an existing behavioral pattern (Magnusson and Ottosson, 1997).

Even in relatively unthreatening and fluid situations, companies may resort to preexisting choices path dependently. This is because institutions have their own internal dynamics for evolution. Path-dependent suboptimal practices are deliberately chosen by companies when (1) adaptive learning is expected to generate better efficiency than learning introduced through new practices (Winter, 1986); (2) increased use strengthens their belief in practices and creates higher expectations; (3) cooperation with external resources is expected to generate benefits; (4) large setup or fixed costs have prevented an alternative choice (Arthur, 1988 a, 1988b, 1989); or (5) existing values mixing with others, or a shifting emphasis in values, may create new ideas and movements for long-term evolution (Zajac and Olsen, 1993; Campbell, 1997).

Adaptive learning, rising expectations, cooperation with external organizations, and value shifts can still expand the meaning of shared values and information and can generate a long-term transformation within tolerable boundaries

Table 1.1 Micro- and Macro-Level Strategies and Dynamics of Techno-Governance Structures Under Path-Conforming and -Disturbing Conditions

		Macro-Level TSO Strategies		
		Continuity of old strategies	**Withdrawal of old strategies**	**Introduction of new strategies**
Micro-Level Intra- and Inter-Firm Strategies	**Continuity of old strategies**	Continuity of traditional company/ government/TSO dynamics effective for path-conforming conditions, but unfit for path-disturbing ones (1)	Continuity of traditional company dynamics effective for path-conforming conditions, but unfit for path-disturbing ones without government/TSO support (2)	Dysfunctional mismatch between company behavior and government/TSO support, ineffective for both path-conforming and -disturbing conditions (3)
	Withdrawal of old strategies	Lost company dynamics with mismatched government/TSO support, often as a transitional stage initiated by companies, but ineffective for both path-conforming and -disturbing conditions (4)	Disintegration of old techno-governance structure, as a breakdown of industrial dynamics or as a transitional stage in building a new techno-governance structure suitable for path-disturbing conditions (5)	Lost company dynamics with new, but still ineffective, government/ TSO support, often as a transitional stage initiated by governments and TSOs to cope with path-disturbing conditions (6)
	Introduction of new strategies	Lost company dynamics because of restrictive government/TSO support, ineffective for both path-conforming and -disturbing conditions (7)	New company dynamics without government/ TSO support, effective to some extent for path-disturbing conditions, or a transitional phase in building a new techno-governance structure (8)	Rebuilding of a new techno-governance structure, effective for path-disturbing conditions (9)

based on rule-following and routine behavior (Nelson and Winter, 1982; Winter, 1986; Rowe, 1989). Outcomes are evolutionary, sometimes by accident and sometimes by trial and error, though the transformation is very gradual and time-consuming.

Such evolutionary development enables techno-governance structures in different regions and nations to continuously and uniquely evolve and to cope with somewhat turbulent product-market conditions and historical events in their own ways. Consequently, evolutionary development generates variations in the pool of technology-related resources, in the effectiveness of information dissemination, in the direction and rate of technological evolution, and in the fit among patterns of interaction, institutions and non-institutional contingencies (Metcalf, 1998). Existing institutions, even when facing somewhat turbulent conditions, enable organizations to evolve based on nationally or regionally unique characteristics and to create new sources of dynamics out of their rule-following and routine behavior. As shown in Cell 1 in Table 1.1, such a gradual process of evolution is effective only when product-market conditions and historical events constitute path-conforming conditions, not path-disturbing ones, and when the continuity of micro- and macro-level strategies is still considered effective.

6 Institutions, Path-Disturbing Conditions, and Strategies

Historical events and product-market conditions can be quite turbulent and path disturbing, demanding an unpredicted pattern of behavior and radical alterations in relations inside a firm and with other firms, governments, and TSOs.

Although companies' micro-level strategies for intra- and inter-firm relations are much easier to decide and implement than macro-level strategies vis-à-vis governments and TSOs, enormous energy is still required to release them from initial self-reinforcing mechanisms and to reformulate mechanisms suitable to path-disturbing conditions, especially to a point where defensive capabilities and advantages can be adequately developed (Arthur, 1988b). Self-initiated micro-level strategies, however, have a very high risk of causing companies to antagonize internal and external actors, weakening their capabilities and advantages in the market and consequently aggravating their performance.

If leading and powerful companies adopt similar micro-level strategies and a significant number of others follow, those strategies may result in reformulating the techno-governance structure and reducing resistance against changes. But this becomes extremely time-consuming, and severe market competition may not give companies that much time to survive. Hence micro-level strategies require an understanding of delicate relations with institutions and other actors in the techno-governance structure and, needless to say, of the immediate product-market and historical conditions.

The solution to such a difficult situation often involves macro-level strategies and collective actions. If cooperative activities among related companies work effectively, they reduce the costs of obtaining information, technology transfer, trial and error, and fighting for standards (Arthur, 1988b), and they can change the techno-governance structure relatively quickly to provide a favorable environment for micro-level strategies. Also, governments and their related TSOs have historically made important contributions to stimulating and leading industrial transformations (Sable, 1994) and are often in demand under path-disturbing conditions. Collective actions may take some time to acquire shape, but the more turbulent the organizational contingencies are, the less time is required to develop such actions. If they are successful, macro-level strategies can change the ways in which companies interact with governments and TSOs, as well as the ways in which the latter organizations themselves interact to support the capability building of the former. They may even provide the initial push for changing the direction and speed of transformation in a techno-governance structure.

However, when TSOs are mostly privately owned and avoid collective approaches, macro-level strategies are difficult to formulate and often remain ineffective. Moreover, whether TSOs are privately or publicly owned, there is always a risk that strategies may be wrongly targeted and may not properly function to develop the defensive capabilities and advantages of companies and industries.

The development of micro- and macro-level strategies for changing a techno-governance structure requires technology-related actors to (1) reinterpret reality and reevaluate their innovative capabilities; (2) reformulate a cognitive map for coding and decoding information; (3) identify a range of choices; (4) make a selection based on a certain logic; (5) reformulate their goals and strategies; (6) dismantle existing interactive mechanisms and introduce new ones; (7) transform institutional arrangements by appealing to collective actions; (8) reestablish a techno-governance structure; and (9) attempt to change institutions. These efforts appear over the course of the continuity and withdrawal of old micro- and macro-level strategies and the introduction of new ones.

Table 1.1 shows the effects that diverse combinations of company strategies can generate, and it may provide some guidelines to this book's examination of the transformation of Japanese high-tech industries—specifically the semiconductor, telecommunications, and biotechnology industries—under the unprecedented path-disturbing conditions of the 1990s. As I have explained in the previous section, the continuity of old micro- and macro-level strategies opting for gradual evolution is effective only under path-conforming conditions (Cell 1). But when new micro- or macro-level strategies are introduced without respectively changing old macro- or micro-level strategies, the resulting mismatch between company behavior and government/TSO support makes the former ineffective under any conditions (Cells 3 and 7). The least dynamic situation occurs when companies withdraw both old micro- and macro-level strategies, resulting in the disintegration of the old techno-governance structure. If these disintegrated conditions persist, an industry loses its dynamics and the situation enters a transitional phase (Cell 5) of waiting for the introduction of new micro- and macro-level strategies (Cell 9).

When government/TSO support weakens, companies tend to withdraw their old macro-level strategies, while they may still enjoy the dynamics generated by old micro-level strategies. But they can remain somewhat dynamic only under path-conforming conditions, even as such a situation makes companies highly vulnerable to path-disturbing conditions (Cell 2). Conversely, the withdrawal of companies' micro-level strategies under continuing old macro-level strategies increases the probability that they will lose their dynamics while governments and TSOs provide mismatched and wrong support to them. Any attempt to introduce new micro-level strategies may face serious restrictions imposed by the continuing macro-level strategies. But it may also represent a transitional stage initiated by companies as they wait for the withdrawal of old macro-level strategies and the introduction of new micro-level ones (Cell 4).

The introduction of new macro-level strategies and the withdrawal of old micro-level strategies suggest that companies have lost their dynamics and have placed their hopes and expectations on government and TSO initiatives to develop a new techno-governance structure (Cell 6). In contrast, new micro-level strategies with the withdrawal of old macro-level strategies suggest that companies are regaining their dynamics through their own efforts, but the lack of government/TSO support may limit the continuity of dynamics or may represent a transitional phase in the development of new institutional support (Cell 8).

In the course of analyzing the semiconductor, telecommunications, and biotechnology industries of Japan, this book briefly introduces the nature and characteristics of the old Japanese techno-governance structure (Okada, 2001), but mainly it focuses on the withdrawal of old and the introduction of new micro- and macro-level strategies and provides insights into the possible development of a new techno-governance structure.

Notes

1 Business system characteristics specified by Whitley are (1) the degree to which private managerial hierarchies coordinate economic activities; (2) the degree of managerial discretion by owners; (3) the specialization of managerial capabilities and activities within authority hierarchies; (4) the degree to which growth is discontinuous and involves radical changes in skills and activities; (5) the extent to which risks are managed through mutual dependence with business partners and employees; (6) the extent of long-term cooperative relations between firms within and between sectors; (7) the stability, integration, and scope of business groups; (8) the dependence of cooperative relations on personal ties and trust; (9) the integration and interdependence of economic activities; (10) the impersonality of authority and subordination relations; (11) task, skill, and role specialization and individualization; (12) the differentiation of authority roles and expertise; (13) the decentralization of operational control and level of work group autonomy; (14) the distance between workers and managers; and (15) the extent of employer-employee commitment and the employment system (Lundvall, 1999).

2 Cooperation is understood as joint or collaborative behavior directed toward certain goals based on common interests and mutual expectations.

3 Although some individuals are also key actors in repeated interactions for technology

development, their roles are judged as relatively less important than organizations for purposes of identifying a techno-governance structure.

Bibliography

Amable, B. (2000) "Institutional complementarity and diversity of social systems of innovation and production." Review of International Political Economy 7(4, Winter): 645–687.

Arthur, W.B. (1988a) "Competing technologies: an overview." In: Dosi, G.; Freeman, C.; Nelson, R.; Silverberg, G.; and Soete, L. (Eds.) Technical Change and Economic Theory. Pinter Publishers, London, pp. 590–607.

——— (1988b) "Self-reinforcing mechanisms in economics." In: Anderson, P.W.; Arrow, K.J.; and Pines, D. (Eds.) The Economy as an Evolving Complex System: The Proceedings of the Evolutionary Paths of the Global Economy Workshop. Addison-Wesley, New York, pp. 9–31.

——— (1989) "Competing technologies, increasing returns, and lock-in by historical events." Economic Journal 99: 116–31.

——— (1996) "Increasing returns and the new world of business." Harvard Business Review 74(4, July/August): 100–109.

Boyer, R. (2004) "New growth regimes, but still institutional diversity." Socio-Economic Review 2(1): 1–32.

Burgelman, R.A. and Rosenbloom, R.S. (1997) In: Tushman, M.L. and Anderson, P. (Eds.) Managing Strategic Innovation and Change. Oxford University Press, Oxford, UK, pp. 273–286.

Campbell, J.L. (1997) "Mechanisms of evolutionary change in economic governance: Interaction, interpretation and bricolage." In: Magnusson, L. and Ottosson, J. (Eds.) Evolutionary Economics and Path Dependence. Edward Elgar, Cheltenham, UK, pp. 10–32.

Campbell, J.L.; Hollingsworth, J.R.; and Lindberg, L.N. (1991) The Governance of the American Economy. Cambridge University Press, New York.

Carlsson, B. (1994) "Technological systems and economic development potential: Four Swedish case studies." In: Shinoya, Y. and Perlman, M. (Eds.) Innovation in Technology, Industries, and Institutions: Studies in Schumpeterian Perspectives. University of Michigan Press, Ann Arbor, pp. 49–69.

Casper, S. (1999) "High technology governance and institutional adaptiveness: Do technology policies usefully promote commercial innovation within the German biotechnology industry?" Paper presented at Conference on National Innovation Systems and the Idea-Innovation Chain, held at The Netherlands Institute of Advanced Study in the Humanities and Social Sciences, Wassenaar, The Netherlands, 27–29 January.

Coase, R. (1937) "The nature of the firm." Economica 4(November): 386–405.

Commons, J.R. (1924) The Legal Foundation of Capitalism. Macmillan, New York.

Crawford, C.M. (1983) New Products Management. Richard D. Irwin, Inc., Homewood, IL.

Crouch, C. and Streeck, W. (Eds.) (1997) Modern Capitalism or Modern Capitalisms? Francis Pinter Publishers, London.

Dacin, M.T.; Goodstein, J.; and Scott, W.R. (2002) "Institutional theory and institutional change: Introduction to the special research forum." Academy of Management Journal 45(1): 45–57.

David, P.A. (1994) "Why are institutions the 'carriers of history'?: Path dependence and the evolution of conventions, organizations and institutions." Structural Change and Economic Dynamics 5(2): 205–220.

DiMaggio, P.J. (1988) "Interest and agency in institutional theory." In: Powell, W.W. and DiMaggio, P.J. (Eds.) Institutional Patterns and Organizations: Culture and Environment. Ballinger, Cambridge, MA, pp. 3–21.

DiMaggio, P.J. and Powell, W.W. (1991) "Introduction." In: Powell, W.W. and DiMaggio, P.J. (Eds.) The New Institutionalism in Organizational Analysis. University of Chicago Press, Chicago, pp. 1–38.

Dosi, G.; Freeman, C.; Nelson, R.R.; Silverberg, G.; and Soete, L. (Eds.) (1988) Technical Change and Economic Theory. Pinter Publishers, New York.

Edquist, C. (Ed.) (1997) Systems of Innovation: Technologies, Institutions and Organizations. Pinter Publishers, London.

Freeman, C. (1987) Technology Policy and Economic Performance: Lessons from Japan. Pinter Publishers, New York.

Gibbons, M.; Limoges, C.; Nowotny, H.; Schwartzman, S.; Scott, P.; and Trow, M. (1994) The New Production of Knowledge: The Dynamics of Science and Research in Contemporary Societies. Sage Publications, London.

Goodman, R.A. and Lawless, M.W. (1994) Technology and Strategy: Conceptual Models and Diagnostics. Oxford University Press, New York.

Groenewegen, J. and Vromen, J. (1997) "Theory of the firm revisited: New and neo-institutional perspectives." In: Magnusson, L. and Ottosson, J. (Eds.) Evolutionary Economics and Path Dependence. Edward Elgar, Cheltenham, UK, pp. 33–56.

Hage, J. and Hollingsworth, J.R. (2000) "A strategy for the analysis of idea innovation networks and institutions." Organization Studies 21(5): 971–1004.

Hall, R. and Soskice, D. (Eds.) (2001) "An introduction to varieties of capitalism." In: Varieties of Capitalism: The Institutional Foundations of Comparative Advantage. Oxford University Press, Oxford, UK, pp. 1–68.

Hayek, F.A. (1945) The Sensory Order: An Inquiry into the Foundations of Theoretical Psychology. Routledge and Keagan Paul, London.

Hollingsworth, J.R. and Boyer, R. (1997) Contemporary Capitalism: The Embeddedness of Institutions. Cambridge University Press, New York.

Hollingsworth, J.R.; Schmitter, P.; and Streeck, W. (Eds.) (1994) Governing Capitalist Economies: Performance and Control of Economic Sectors. Oxford University Press, New York.

Johnson, B. (1992) "Institutional learning." In: Lundvall, B-A. (Ed.) National Systems of Innovation: Toward a Theory of Innovation and Interactive Learning. Pinter Publishers, London, pp. 23–44.

Kim, L. and Nelson, R.R. (2000) Technology, Learning, & Innovation. Cambridge University Press, Cambridge, UK.

Langlois, R.N. (1995) "Do firms plan?" Constitutional Political Economy 6: 247–261.

Lindberg, L.N.; Campbell, J.L.; and Hollingsworth, J.R. (1991) "Economic governance and the analysis of structural change in the American economy." In: Campbell, J.L.; Hollingsworth, J.R.; and Lindberg, L.N. (Eds.) The Governance of the American Economy. Cambridge University Press, New York, pp. 3–34.

Lundvall, B-A. (1985) Product Innovation and User-Producer Interaction. Aalborg University Press, Aalborg, Denmark.

——— (1988) "Innovation as an interactive process: From user-producer interaction to the national system of innovation." In: Dosi, G.; Freeman, C.; Nelson, R.; Silverberg,

G.; and Soete, L. (Eds.) Technical Change and Economic Theory. Pinter Publishers, London, pp. 349–369.

——— (Ed.) (1992a) "Introduction." In: National Systems of Innovation: Toward a Theory of Innovation and Interactive Learning. Pinter Publishers, London, pp. 1–19.

——— (Ed.) (1992b) "User-producer relationships, national systems of innovation and internationalization." In: National Systems of Innovation: Toward a Theory of Innovation and Interactive Learning. Pinter Publishers, London, pp. 45–67.

——— (1999) "National business systems and national systems of innovation." International Studies of Management and Organization 29(2): 60–77.

Lundvall, B-A. and Maskell, P. (2000) "National states and economic development: From national systems of production to national systems of knowledge creation and learning." In: Clark, G.L.; Gertler, M.S.; Eldman, M.P.; and Williams, K. (Eds.) The Oxford Handbook of Economic Geography. Oxford University Press, Oxford, UK, pp. 353–372.

Magnusson, L. and Ottosson, J. (Eds.) (1997) "Introduction." In: Evolutionary Economics and Path Dependence. Edward Elgar, Cheltenham, UK, pp. 1–9.

Meeus, M.T.H.; Oerlemans, L.A.G.; and van Dijck, J.J.J. (1999) "Technological dynamics, interactive learning and organizational sets: An empirical specification of the relation between technological dynamics and interaction between multiple actors in a Dutch region." Paper presented at Conference on National Innovation Systems and the Idea-Innovation Chain, held at The Netherlands Institute of Advanced Study in the Humanities and Social Sciences, Wassenaar, The Netherlands, 27–29 January.

Metcalf, J.S. (1998) Evolutionary Economics and Creative Destruction. Routledge, London.

Mole, V. and Elliott, D. (1987) Enterprising Innovation: An Alternative Approach. Pinter Publishers, London.

Nee, V. (1998) "Sources of the new institutionalism." In: Brinton, M.C. and Nee, V. (Eds.) The New Institutionalism in Sociology. Russell Sage Foundation, New York, pp. 1–6.

Nelson, R.R. (1982) "The role of knowledge in R&D efficiency." Quarterly Journal of Economics 97: 453–370.

——— (1985) "Institutions supporting technical advances in industry." American Economic Review 75: 186–189.

——— (Ed.) (1993) National Innovation Systems: A Comparative Analysis. Oxford University Press, New York.

——— (1995) "Co-evolution of industry structure, technology and supporting institutions, and the making of comparative advantage." International Journal of the Economics of Business 2(2): 171–185.

——— (2002) "Bringing institutions into evolutionary growth theory." Journal of Evolutionary Economics 12: 17–28.

Nelson, R.R. and Sampat, N.B. (2001) "Making sense of institutions as a factor shaping economic performance." Journal of Economic Behavior and Organization 44: 31–54.

Nelson, R.R. and Winter, S.G. (1977) "In search of useful theory of innovation." Research Policy 6: 36–76.

——— (1982) An Evolutionary Theory of Economic Change. Harvard University Press, Cambridge, MA.

Nooteboom, B. (1997) "Path dependence of knowledge: Implications for the theory of the firm." In: Magnusson, L. and Ottosson, J. (Eds.) Evolutionary Economics and Path Dependence. Edward Elgar, Cheltenham, UK, pp. 57–78.

——— (1999) "Innovation, learning and industrial organization." Cambridge Journal of Economics 23(2): 127–150.

North, D. (1989) "Institutions and economic growth: A historical introduction." World Development 17(9): 1319–1332.

——— (1990) Institutions, Institutional Change, and Economic Performance. Cambridge University Press, Cambridge, UK.

——— (1993) "Institutions and credible commitment." Journal of Institutional and Theoretical Economics 149(1): 1–23.

Okada, Y. (1989a) "Technological development and growth of Japanese integrated circuit firms: An exploratory study." Working Paper at the Center for Japan-U.S. Relations, International University of Japan, Niigata, Japan.

——— (1989b) "*Nichibei handotai sangyo ni okeru shakai keizai tosei kozo no hikaku* (Comparison of socio-economic coordination structures in Japanese and U.S. semiconductor industries)." In: Marumo, A. (Ed.) *Kawariyuku Nihon no Sangyo Kozo* (Changing Japanese Industrial Structure). The Japan Times, Tokyo, pp. 52–98.

——— (1990) "*Nichibei handotai sangyo ni okeru gabanansu kozo no hikaku I & II* (Comparison of governance structures in Japanese and U.S. semiconductor industries I & II)." *Sekai Keizai Hyoron* (Journal of World Economic Review) (March): 40–53 and (April): 59–65.

——— (Ed.) (1999) Japan's Industrial Technology Development: Role of Cooperative Learning and Institutions. Springer-Verlag, Tokyo.

——— (2000) Competitive-*cum*-Cooperative Interfirm Relations and Dynamics in the Japanese Semiconductor Industry. Springer-Verlag, Tokyo.

——— (2001) "Cooperative learning and Japan's techno-governance structure: Exploratory case studies." Sophia International Review 23: 19–42.

Olson, M. (1971) The Logic of Collective Action: Public Goods and the Theory of Groups. Harvard University Press, Cambridge, MA.

Pavitt, K. (1984) "Sectoral patterns of technical change: Towards a taxonomy and a theory." Research Policy 13(6): 343–373.

Pessali, H.F. and Fernandez, R.G. (1999) "Institutional economics at the micro-level? What transactional theory could learn from original institutionalism." Journal of Economic Issues 33(2): 265–275.

Powell, W.W. and DiMaggio, P.J. (Eds.) (1991) "The iron cage revisited: Institutional isomorphism and collective rationality in organizational fields. In: The New Institutionalism in Organizational Analysis. University of Chicago Press, Chicago, pp. 63–82.

Rizzello, S. (1997) "The microfoundations of path dependency." In: Magnusson, L. and Ottosson, J. (Eds.) Evolutionary Economics and Path Dependence. Edward Elgar, Cheltenham, UK, pp. 98–118.

Rowe, N. (1989) Rules and Institutions. Philip Allan, New York.

Sable, C.F. (1994) "Learning by monitoring: The institutions of economic development." In: Smelser, N.J. and Swedberg, R. (Eds.) Handbook of Economic Sociology. Princeton University Press, Princeton, NJ, pp. 137–165.

Schank, R.C. and Abelson, R.P. (1977) Scripts, Plans, Goals, and Understanding: An Inquiry into Human Knowledge Structures. Lawrence Erlbaum, Hillsdale, NJ.

Schotter, A. (1981) The Economic Theory of Social Institutions. Cambridge University Press, Cambridge, UK.

Scott, W.R. (1995) Institutions and Organizations. Sage Publications, London.

Streeck, W. and Yamamura, K. (Eds.) (2001) The Origins of Nonliberal Capitalism. Cornell University Press, Ithaca, NY.

Tushman, M.L.; Anderson, P.; and O'Reilly, C. (1997) "Technology cycles, innovation streams, and ambidextrous organizations: Organization renewal through innovation streams and strategic change." In: Tushman, M.L. and Anderson, P. (Eds.) Managing Strategic Innovation and Change: A Collection of Readings. Oxford University Press, New York, pp. 3–23.

Unger, B.; Larson, C.; and Oosterwijk, H. (1999) "Innovative and economic performance evaluation." Paper presented at Conference on National Innovation Systems and the Idea-Innovation Chain, held at The Netherlands Institute of Advanced Study in the Humanities and Social Sciences, Wassenaar, The Netherlands, 27–29 January.

van Waarden, F.; Grade, E.; Schienstock, G.; and Unger, B. (1999) "National systems of innovation and networks in the idea-innovation chain in science-based industries." Paper presented at Conference on National Innovation Systems and the Idea-Innovation Chain, held at The Netherlands Institute of Advanced Study in the Humanities and Social Sciences, Wassenaar, The Netherlands, 27–29 January.

Veblen, T. (1919) The Place of Science in Modern Civilization and Other Essays. Huebsch, New York.

von Hippel, E. (1976) "The dominant role of users in the scientific instrument innovation process." Research Policy 5(3): 212–239.

West, A. (1992) Innovation Strategy. Prentice Hall International (UK) Ltd., Hemel Hempstead.

Whitley, R. (1992) Business Systems in East Asia: Firms, Markets and Societies. Sage Publications, London.

——— (Ed.) (1994) "Societies, firms, and markets: The social structuring of business systems." In: European Business Systems: Firms and Markets in their National Contexts. Sage Publications, London, pp. 5–45.

——— (1999) Divergent Capitalism: The Social Structuring and Change of Business Systems. Oxford University Press, Oxford, UK.

Whitley, R. and Kristensen, P.H. (Eds.) (1997) Governance at Work: The Social Regulation of Economic Relations. Oxford University Press, Oxford, UK.

Williamson, O. (1975) Markets and Hierarchies: Analysis and Antitrust Implications. The Free Press, New York.

——— (1981) "The economics of organization: The transaction cost approach." American Journal of Sociology 87(3): 548–577.

——— (1985) The Economic Institution of Capitalism. The Free Press, New York.

——— (1994) "Transaction cost economics." In: Smelser, N.J. and Swedberg, R. (Eds.) The Handbook of Economic Sociology. Princeton University Press, Princeton, NJ, pp. 77–107.

Winter, S.G. (1986) "The research program of the behavioral theory of the firm: Orthodox critique and evolutionary perspective." In: Gilad, B. and Kaish, S. (Eds.) Handbook of Behavioral Economics, Volume A. JAI Press, London, pp. 151–188.

Zajac, E.J. and Olsen, C.P. (1993) "From transaction cost to transactional value analysis: Implications for the study of interorganizational strategies." Journal of Management Studies 30(1): 131–145.

Chapter 2

Decline of the Japanese Semiconductor Industry: Institutional Restrictions and the Disintegration of Techno-Governance

Yoshitaka Okada
Sophia University

1 Introduction

In the 1980s, Japanese semiconductor manufacturers began to dominate the world market with three successive types of dynamic random access memories (DRAM): the 64 kilobit (Kb) (70% of market share in 1982), 256 Kb (90% in 1984), and 1 megabit (Mb) (90% in 1988). While the number of DRAM producers in the United States declined from 14 in 1970 to 3 in 1986,[1] Japan's world market share for all types of semiconductors first approached that of the U.S. in 1985, passed it in 1987 (48% Japan vs. 39% U.S.), and peaked in 1988 (about 51% Japan vs. about 37% U.S.) (Okada, 1989a, 2000). After that, as Fig. 2.1 shows, Japan's share of the world semiconductor market began to gradually decline.

Arguments are often made that the decline was largely due to the bursting of Japan's economic bubble in the early 1990s (Chon, 1997; Spencer and Grindley, 1993). But the effects of the bubble burst on the Japanese market started appearing only in 1992 (Fig. 2.2), and the decline had already begun in foreign markets long before then. Despite this, Japanese metal oxide semiconductor (MOS) memory production (in terms of units) continued to increase from 1982 to 1995 (Fig. 2.3), spurring false hopes for the revival of the memory market and continued Japanese domination, according to managers at Hitachi and Fujitsu Laboratories.

Forces underlying the decline of the Japanese share of the world semiconductor market were diverse, but each one contributed to a major structural transformation of the world market in the 1990s. The most important cause was the capacity of the semiconductor to house increasingly vast amounts of information on a small chip, which weakened demand for the expansion of storage capacity, reduced the speed of DRAM technology development, and changed the silicon cycle in the memory field.[2] This large storage capacity shifted the focus of semiconductor producers from function-specific semiconductors to the system LSI

Figure 2.1 World Semiconductor Market Share by Nationality of Producers

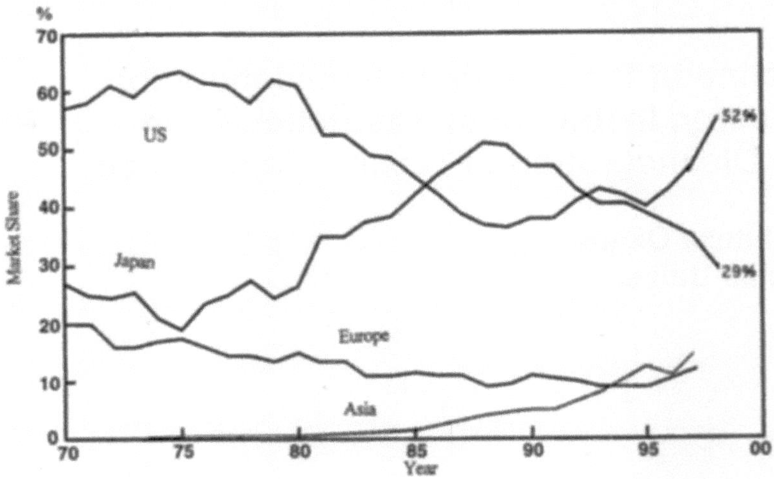

Source: Handotai Sangyo Kenkyusho (Semiconductor Industry Research Institute Japan), 2000.

Figure 2.2 Semiconductor Demand by Region

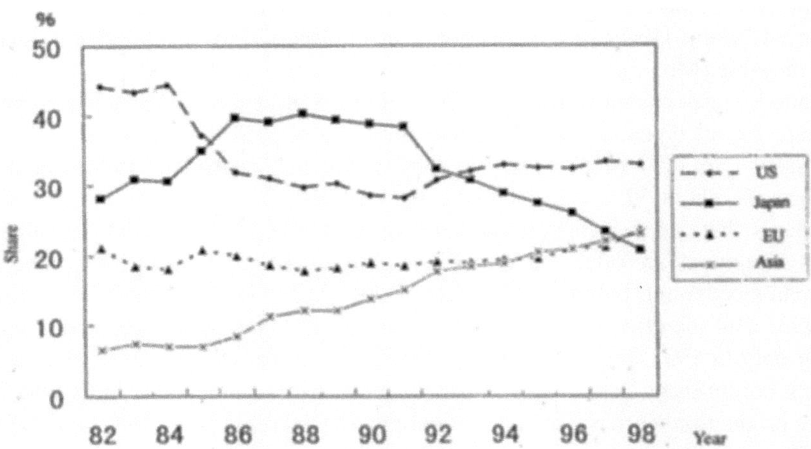

Source: Handotai Sangyo Kenkyusho (Semiconductor Industry Research Institute Japan), 2000.

(large-scale integrated circuit), which contains memory, a microprocessor, and other elements as parts of an integrated system, also known as the system-on-a-chip (SoC). This shift reduced demand for the stand-alone DRAM even as DRAM functions continued to be used in the system LSI. The increased use of flash memory also contributed to the reduction in stand-alone DRAM demand. Moreover, the development of more standardized production equipment permit-

Figure 2.3 World (in Bits) and Japanese (in Units) Semiconductor Production

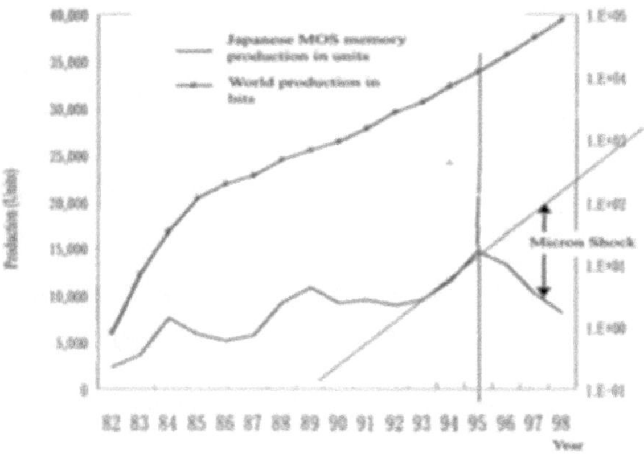

Source: Handotai Sangyo Kenkyusho (Semiconductor Industry Research Institute Japan), 2000.

ted easier entry into the semiconductor production business, enhanced competition among semiconductor manufacturers, and reduced prices, especially for memory.[3] Consequently, the size of the DRAM world market in terms of sales shrank from $40.8 billion in 1995 to $13.0 billion in 1998 (Handotai Sangyo Kenkyusho, 2000).

In the memory area, Korean companies rapidly developed their technological capabilities, became the leading producers, and started to dominate the high-end market. Samsung, for example, developed 16 Mb, 64 Mb, and 256 Mb DRAM technologies slightly behind Japanese companies (Okada, 2000; Fuji Sogo Kenkyusho, 1997a), but it became a leading producer of the 16 Mb DRAM (Press Journal, 1993, 1994) and even produced a sample 256 Mb DRAM ahead of Japanese companies (Press Journal, 1999). Samsung now dominates the high-end market, including the 256 Mb DRAM market.[4]

Meanwhile, Micron Technology of the U.S. began occupying the low-end market, such as the 64 Mb DRAM, providing half-generation-behind chips at a lower price and in a smaller size. This was made possible by incorporating some advanced technologies from chemical mechanical polishing[5] and by reducing the number of masks from 24 (as in Japan) to 16 for the 16 Mb DRAM.[6] As Fig. 2.3 shows, Micron's impact on Japan, known as the Micron Shock, became conspicuous in 1995.[7] The Japanese share of the world DRAM market dropped from 90% in the 1980s to 20% in 1998. Even the importance of DRAM production within a given company declined from an average of 28% in 1995 to 11% in 1998 (Handotai Sangyo Kenkyusho, 2000).

Another force that transformed the semiconductor industry was a shift in technological leadership from development of the DRAM to that of the system LSI. Japanese DRAM producers had taken the lead with advances in semiconductor technologies such as photolithography, wafer fabrication, and storage capacity expansion on the N-channel MOS (NMOS) until the early 1980s.[8] Then, in the 1980s, they led the transformation to the complementary MOS (CMOS) DRAM, which was operable with lower power consumption, a wider voltage margin, and a higher yield rate per wafer, hence lowering the cost of production.[9] Meanwhile, U.S. companies chose an alternative NMOS technology for their products and lost their market competitiveness (Langlois and Steinmueller, 2000). When they developed CMOS semiconductor capability in the 1980s and began competing against Japanese companies, the U.S. companies focused on more-complex ICs—microprocessors, logic, and the system LSI—instead of the DRAM and succeeded in developing chips with the same capacity as Japan's, but with an even faster transmission speed as demand for the system LSI increased. This factor is considered the key determinant of the Japanese decline in competitiveness.[10]

The standardization of semiconductor production equipment brought with it another change (Nishimura, 1996; Fuji Sogo Kenkyusho, 1997b), enabling less technologically sophisticated engineers and companies to engage in production of the semiconductor. For example, Applied Materials in the U.S. integrated diverse production processes with automatic software-controlled production adjustments. This equipment integration enabled less technologically sophisticated companies to produce semiconductors rather easily and to catch up with the leading companies over a shorter capability-building period. Because of such developments, Taiwanese companies, led by United Microelectronics Corp. (UMC) and Taiwan Semiconductor Manufacturing Corp. (TSMC), eventually dominated global foundry production for the system LSI through lower prices, punctual delivery, high quality, and open production information. The Taiwanese domination of foundry production made Taiwan's semiconductor specifications a global standard.[11] An increasing number of companies now follow this business model.[12]

Why were Japanese companies unable to detect these changes and respond promptly by taking a new direction in semiconductor development? This is the basic question asked in this chapter. To be more precise, why didn't Japanese companies recognize the weakening position of the DRAM in the semiconductor market, or the potential impact of dramatic improvements in information-processing capacity on the future of semiconductor devices, or the technological catch-up and lower prices of Korean and U.S. companies—or, especially, the shift of technological leadership from the DRAM sector to the system LSI? Why didn't they consider standardizing semiconductor production equipment to reduce R&D and investment costs, or even developing new business models, for example, as chipless makers, fabless makers, foundries, intellectual property (IP) vendors, or electronic design automation (EDA) vendors (Handotai Sangyo Kenkyusho, 1999)?

I would like to propose that the decline of the Japanese semiconductor industry that began in the late 1980s was primarily due to the institutionally and path-dependently restricted nature of the old techno-governance structure—the way diverse actors were harmonized in technology-related activities—and the disintegration of this structure without a clear alternative (Okada, 1989b, 1990,

1999, 2001). First I shall conduct an institutional analysis of techno-governance structures by comparing the old Japanese structure built up from the 1950s to the 1980s with the new U.S. structure developed since the 1980s. The purpose of this section is (1) to substantiate the importance of the techno-governance approach and its key factors in understanding industrial dynamics, and (2) to identify Japanese path-dependent institutional characteristics in contrast with those of the U.S. I shall then examine changes in the old Japanese techno-governance structure that gradually took place from the mid-1980s to the mid-1990s. I shall compare the governance structure of this period, which I call the Disintegration Period, with the old Japanese structure. Information from documents and from interviews with 28 companies (15 semiconductor producers and 13 semiconductor equipment manufacturers of various sizes) and 27 technology-supporting organizations (TSOs), covering almost all the key actors in the Japanese semiconductor industry, is expected to shed some light on the causes of the Japanese decline. I shall first explain the characteristics of the old Japanese techno-governance structure and conduct comparisons with the newly rising U.S. structure.

2 The Old Japanese Techno-Governance Structure: 1950s–1980s

2.1 Cooperative Learning and the Techno-Governance Structure

Market competition is undeniably an important stimulus of intra-firm R&D, and the dissemination of technological information to a wider body of related actors contributes greatly to stimulating technological and industrial advances. Technological information, however, is not very likely to flow easily to other actors in a highly competitive market, especially when it is considered one of the key competitive advantages for appropriation. Success in high-risk innovation could even result in monopoly, killing competition and diverse alternative approaches and reducing the speed and quality of technological advancement. In reality, many companies refrain from highly risky or uncertain R&D, while some free-ride or act opportunistically. These are just a few of many factors that may retard technological dynamics because of a lack of proper institutional development (Okada, 1999, 2001), suggesting that a market-oriented, "fragmented" or "disintegrated" approach is inadequate for dynamic technological transformation (Bolton et al., 1994; Macher et al., 1998; Chon, 1997).

The Japanese postwar developmental approach was to solve these problems by not only fostering a highly competitive market, but also by creating institutional arrangements to disseminate technological information to a wider body of technology actors, stimulate creativity, and ensure a diversity of approaches (see bottom of Fig. 2.4). Through these strategies, Japan tried to create "structured flexibility" in stimulating technological advancement (Florida and Kenney, 1990). The key means to this end were cooperative learning, fusion of ideas, and effective networking (Okada, 2001).

Figure 2.4 Old Japanese Techno-Governance Structure

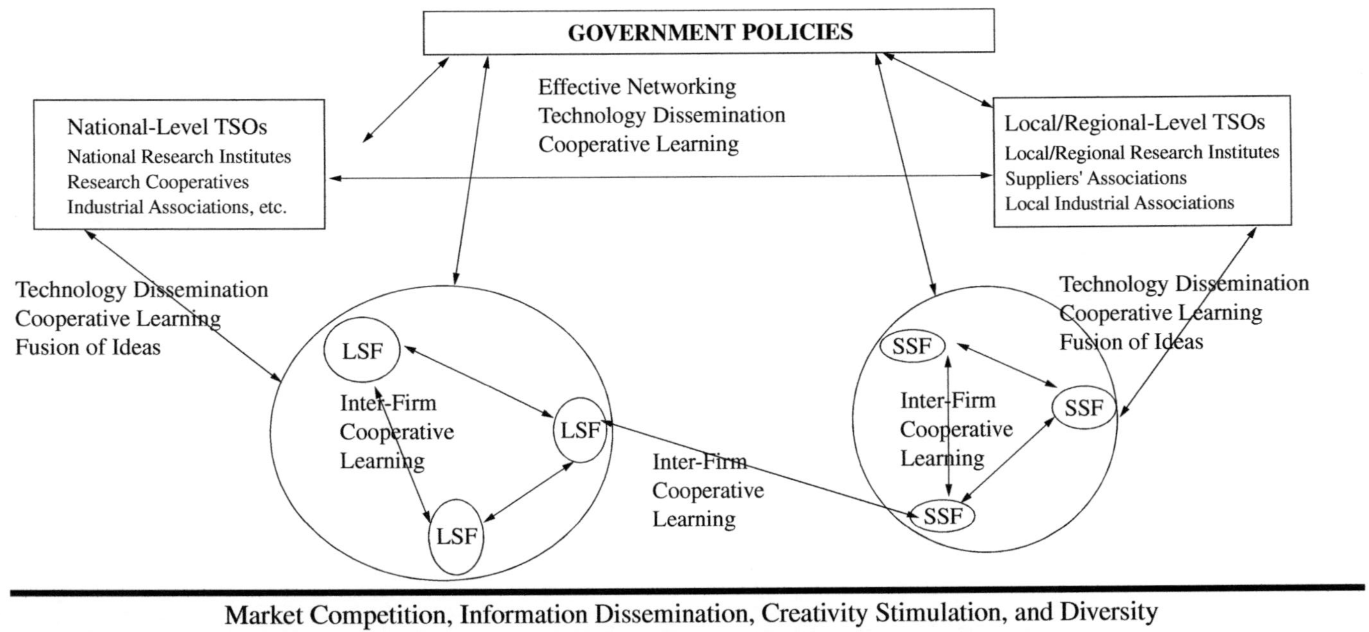

Amid market competition, there remained a traditional Japanese emphasis on cooperation that resulted in the development of highly enriched relations and learning among companies, governments, and TSOs. Cooperative learning is the process of mutually increasing the exchange of rich information among partners, promoting learning, and advancing capabilities. From the 1950s to the 1980s, this process successfully generated synergetic effects (Okada, 1993, 1995, 1999; Lundvall, 1988, 1992), facilitated goal attainment, and brought positive long-term gains to cooperating partners. It encouraged highly effective networking among organizational actors, and extended networks became an important means for disseminating information among partners and learning diverse technological approaches. It provided opportunities for companies and TSOs to fuse diverse technologies and ideas in the same as well as different industries, and it successfully stimulated innovation (Kodama, 1991). These means were especially effective when resources were limited.

At the core of the old Japanese techno-governance structure, four types of networks were developed (see Fig. 2.4). One was an exclusive inter-firm network among selected closely cooperating companies. A second was a freely accessible, open TSO-firm network that provided diverse services to companies. Another was a network between companies and governments that functioned to develop and implement government technology policies favorable to companies. Over these various company-linked networks existed a fourth type of TSO-government network, which became a major mechanism for distributing public funds to companies, implementing policies, and stimulating R&D activities by TSOs.

2.2 TSO and Governmental Roles in Information Dissemination and Creativity Stimulation

National and regional TSOs developed diverse ways of openly disseminating advanced technologies to companies. One way was not to impede job-hopping by their researchers. For example, the technological capabilities of Japanese semiconductor companies were dramatically improved when a large number of researchers moved to various companies from the Electro-Technical Laboratory (ETL)[13] and the Telecommunication Research Institute (TRI)[14] in the 1950s and 1960s (Okada, 1989a, 2000, 2001). The Japan Research and Development Corporation (JRDC) (presently the Japan Science and Technology Corporation, JST), a public corporation, was also established in 1961 solely for the purpose of disseminating technological information and promoting cooperative research (Kagaku Gijutsu Seisakushi Kenkyukai, 1990). Technical committees of industrial associations transmitted valuable information, especially from large-sized companies, to small- and medium-sized ones (hereafter referred to collectively as small-sized). And networks among public TSOs, governments, and specialists in those organizations, linked through the information exchange system as well as through training, cooperative research, and the advisory system, multiplied their assistance to companies (Okada, 2001).

Various R&D grants and subsidies were directly distributed to companies and private consortia, often in the form of matching funds from the Ministry of International Trade and Industry (MITI) (presently the Ministry of Economy, Trade and Industry, METI), JRDC, the New Energy and Industrial Technology Development Organization (NEDO), local governments, and the Japan Small Business Corporation (JSBC) (presently the Japan Small and Medium Enterprise Corporation, JSMEC). JRDC in 1981 also added a new goal of funding exploratory research conducted by individuals (Sigurdson and Anderson, 1991). The semiconductor industry was undeniably one of Japan's best-supported industries.

National and regional TSOs provided such support to companies as information services, problem solving and troubleshooting, education and training, contract R&D, collaborative R&D, and technology licensing. The national technical institutes were best known, apart from the universities—whose role in Japan was considered somewhat weak—for extensive research activities inclusive of both basic and applied research. For example, TRI and ETL were respectively the first domestic developers of the PN junction transistor in 1952 and of the solid-state circuit (a precursor of the integrated circuit) in 1960 (Okada, 2001). They were the key semiconductor-related TSOs to develop collaborative research with companies for the purpose not only of stimulating companies' innovative activities, but also of maintaining their own technological capabilities.

While the national technical institutes acted as innovation stimulators for large companies, the regional technical institutes, known as *kosetsushi,* served the same function for small-sized companies. Because of the less sophisticated nature of the smaller companies' technology and the consequent higher risk of opportunistic behavior by competitors, who could easily copy their technology and imitate their products, groups of small-sized companies often developed cooperatives among themselves to meet their R&D needs, supported by funding from governments, industrial associations, and JSBC (Maeda, 1999; see Fig. 2.4). The key to their success was bringing in highly motivated and competent company researchers and linking them to diverse sources of technological information (Okada, 2001). The networking capability of the *kosetsushi* was a critical factor in these endeavors.

2.3 Cooperative Learning in Exclusive Inter-Firm Networks

TSO-firm relations are vital, but basic industrial dynamics are determined by companies' intra- and inter-firm R&D capabilities. According to a World Bank survey (Okada, 1999) of 294 Japanese companies in seven industries,[15] long-term customers were the best stimulators of technological innovation; intra-firm laboratories and divisions and long-term suppliers followed as second and third in importance. As is well known, cooperating companies often developed vertical and horizontal *keiretsu*[16] relations (shown in Fig. 2.4 as groups of large- and small-sized firms linked to one another), though these relations were sufficiently numerous to ensure severe market competition. Intensive cooperation also took place among independent companies in the machine-tool industry, where such companies were predominant (Okada, 1999). Whether cooperative learning took place among *keiretsu* members or independent long-term partners, information flowed mainly among cooperating partners, making vital information unavailable to noncooperating companies and differentiating the benefits of interaction by types of relations and partners.

In the semiconductor industry, for example, Hitachi had strong vertical *keiretsu* relations with Kokusai and Shinkawa; NEC with Anelva, Kaijo Electric, and Ando Electric; Toshiba with Tokuda Seisakusho, Toshiba-Seiki, and Toshiba Machine; Fujitsu with Advantest; and Matsushita with Nihon Shinku Technics (Stowsky, 1989; Bolton et al., 1994; Chon, 1997).[17] Many of these semiconductor manufacturers also had internal equipment manufacturing capabilities (Chon, 1997). Each semiconductor company was also a member of a big horizontal *keiretsu* group and even had a large number of its own affiliates, though relations with vertical *keiretsu* companies and intra-group affiliates were considered much more vital for semiconductor technology development than with horizontal *keiretsu* groups.[18]

Within these exclusive inter-firm networks, new technological information was disseminated much faster and more effectively than in markets, since cooperative relations reduced the danger of opportunism and moral hazards. Companies in such relations enjoyed the benefits of sharing complementary technology, engaging in joint R&D, reducing the costs and risks of technological innovation, providing initial contracts to partners, delaying the opening of new technology to the market, and taking advantage of the lead time of innovative products (Goto, 1993: 75–78; Okada, 2000). They also benefited from transaction-cost cuts by exchanging business information, coordinating strategies, making joint purchases, and obtaining financial guarantees (Asanuma, 1985; Inoue, 1985; Imai, 1986). Above all, "stickiness" in information exchange permitted the cost-effective transfer of indispensable know-how and craftsman-type skills developed in the innovation process (von Hippel, 1994). This was especially important for the semiconductor industry, since a complex series of state-of-the-art manufacturing steps were often mastered at an experimental rather than a scientific level, and their outcomes were almost exclusively embedded in particular manufacturing equipment and not readily replicable with different tools and facilities (Bolton et al., 1994; Ham et al., 1998). Such complexity has historically required manufacturers to work closely with equipment suppliers to improve the performance of each tool. Thus Japanese-type cooperative relations were quite effective in stimulating innovative activities and improving various aspects of the semiconductor production process.

What enhanced "structured flexibility" in cooperative relations during the 1970s and 1980s were the intensification of cooperation among selected partners and the introduction of competition-generating measures in cooperative relations to an extent that did not jeopardize effective cooperation. These measures—such as evaluation, performance monitoring, grading, quality assurance, just-in-time delivery, the multiple-vendor system, strategic pricing, and flexible contracts—

introduced uncertainty and threatening environments, differentiated benefits into cooperative relations, and intensified pressure for stronger cooperation and learning (Okada, 2000; Asanuma, 1985). I refer to such relations that mix cooperation and competition as competitive-*cum*-cooperative relations (Okada, 2000). Commitment and trust in cooperative relations with strong mutual expectations to respond positively to competition-generating measures became the key to sustaining dynamic cooperative relations. It was only after lengthy unsuccessful mutual efforts to solve problems and meet mutual expectations that a partner could terminate such a relationship.

2.4 Problems of Exclusive Inter-Firm Networks and Corrective Mechanisms by TSOs

Cooperative learning within exclusive inter-firm networks tended, however, to isolate many companies from valuable technological information, generate an asymmetric flow of information, and differentiate the technological capabilities of companies inside and outside a group, though the degree of exclusivity differed with the types of relations and partners and the nature of the technology.

The advantages of cooperative learning could also become disadvantages. Because of their exclusivity, the more intensive these cooperative relations were, the more tightly the partners' technological perspectives were locked into narrowly confined relation-specific technological advances (Arthur, 1989). A solution to this problem often proposed for equipment manufacturers was to develop cooperative relations with multiple semiconductor manufacturers (Asanuma, 1989). Such cooperative relations were rather effective for incremental innovations, but not for generating or even recognizing radical innovations taking place outside those networks (Chon, 1997). Cooperative relations added another hurdle to the usual obstacles to bold technological change of high risk, cost, and uncertainty.

If Japanese companies had freely aligned themselves with multiple sources of diverse perspectives and technologies, this might have enabled them to shift their technological orientation more readily and become more innovative. A "simply flexible" market orientation is quite effective in generating fluidity in relationships and reformulating them. However, the lack of a strong sense of commitment endemic to the market does not necessarily guarantee better or more successful performance, even with a new technological perspective. A delicate problem here is that an open, flexible, fluid system may, on the one hand, facilitate the identification of diverse opportunities for technological change, but it cannot, on the other hand, effectively support the combining of complementary assets, quality assurance, technical improvements, marketing, distribution, and after-sales support. Rapid technological change seems to require an openness to new ideas, fluidity in relations, and flexibility in switching partners for technology acquisition. But it also requires faster integration, persistence, and the sustenance of newly introduced activities (Hobday, 1994). Japanese cooperative inter-firm relations were clearly inadequate for dealing with such a complex mixture.

A solution to these problems in the past was to develop networks of institutions, linking companies to national and regional governments and TSOs. The latter organizations functioned to (1) disseminate technological information to as wide a range of companies as possible; (2) provide channels of information acquisition to companies lacking in opportunities for cooperative learning; (3) create environments for exchanging different technological perspectives and developing multiple technological capabilities within a company; and (4) promote leading-edge technological development among companies and national or regional technical institutes to stimulate the transformation of industries.

Again, cooperative learning became a major means of realizing the above goals, but mainly as promoted by the government and neutral nonprofit organizations. The launching of the Japanese semiconductor industry is one of the best examples. Two university professors, several researchers from national technical institutes, and young engineers from eight electronics companies established a transistor study group in 1948, exchanged information intensively, and cooperated on various levels in the early study phase. With the help of government research grants to this study group, as well as the help of matching funds awarded to their companies, the eight young engineers successfully persuaded hesitant top executives to commence research activities and develop semiconductor production capabilities. The spread of vital information to all the relevant companies created a difficult situation for the top decision makers, since any delay on their part in developing technological capability meant a possible loss of future competitiveness (Okada, 1989a, 2000, 2001).[19]

Given the availability of low-cost help and various services by national/regional technical institutes and industrial associations, companies that could not enjoy the benefits of exclusive inter-firm cooperation aggressively made use of open TSO-firm networks. According to the aforementioned World Bank survey, in industries where *keiretsu* companies were predominant (e.g., auto parts, software, textiles), smaller *keiretsu* member firms engaged in intensive cooperation with larger ones. But independent companies made more extensive use of national research institutes and universities than did *keiretsu* members. In contrast, in the machine-tool industry where independent companies were predominant, they developed more inter-firm cooperative relations than did the smaller *keiretsu* companies, which made more use of regional technical institutes. This suggests that cooperative learning was a vital tool for dynamically operating companies, irrespective of *keiretsu*- or independent-firm-dominant industries. Firms that could not enjoy the benefits of cooperative relations relied extensively on public and quasi-public TSOs, which provided linkages to other TSOs, helped the firms obtain R&D grants, and organized collaborative R&D projects to promote inter-firm cooperative learning. In the semiconductor industry, for example, the Nagasaki Industrial Technology Center developed a collaborative project with a small semiconductor equipment company and a university, obtained a grant from JRDC, and developed wafer cutters that could cut wafers without dust, scratches, or cracks. This success led to the building of a factory next door to the institute (Chusho Kigyo Cho Gijutsuka, 1993; Okada, 2001).

Disadvantaged companies also made use of the benefits of agglomeration. One type was the *sanchi* (a local industry agglomeration), where a large number of specialized companies concentrated in one location and built their collective reputation as a production center specializing in certain products (Maeda, 1999).[20] Regional technical institutes, cooperatives, and industrial associations in these locations functioned to facilitate cooperation among small companies to raise their technological capabilities. In the "Japanese Silicon Valley" of Oita and Kumamoto prefectures, environments similar to *sanchi* have been developed where diverse public and quasi-public TSOs in cooperation with large-sized semiconductor companies help develop the technological capabilities of small-sized companies.

Government-sponsored research cooperatives, established by national technical institutes and major companies, functioned to solve the problem of narrowly confined technological perspectives associated with exclusive inter-firm cooperation by bringing together companies with diverse specializations and perspectives. They also stimulated high-risk and high-cost R&D and even disseminated vital technology to major, but technologically relatively weaker, companies.

Although each research cooperative was established in a different form, the Very Large-Scale Integrated Circuit (VLSI) Cooperative (1976–1979),[21] to take one example, allocated 15% to 20% of its funds to a joint laboratory (Okimoto, 1989; Fransman, 1990). But at this laboratory, difficulties in generating cooperation among competitors and a preference for developing multiple approaches over one targeted technology led Hitachi, Fujitsu, and Toshiba to develop electron-beam machines with three distinctively different design concepts. However, the exchange of reports among these three research teams at meetings held in the central laboratory stimulated innovative ideas among the participants, created a favorable environment for technological breakthroughs, and enabled each team to equip itself with multiple approaches, thereby reducing risks and uncertainty in the event that their own technology failed to reach a target or become commercially viable. In the development of photolithography technology as well, intensive cooperative relations were fostered between semiconductor companies and camera companies—Toshiba, Hitachi, and Fujitsu on the one hand, and Nikon and Canon on the other. Such intensive cooperation not only fused knowledge and ideas from two different industries, but also built a new industrial system for innovation and production in the photolithography field. Effective joint developments by ETL, Fujitsu, Hitachi, Mitsubishi, NEC, and Toshiba were also pursued in the fields of crystallography, diffusion, and etching (Fransman, 1990: 71–72).

Unlike the VLSI Cooperative, the Fifth Generation Computer Project (1982–1991), led by the Institute for New Generation Computer Technology (ICOT), for the first time in the history of Japanese research cooperatives placed all its research under the auspices of a single joint laboratory. This 100%-joint-research approach proved quite successful in assimilating internationally available knowledge, bringing together hardware and software specialists to generate synergetic effects, developing generic technology and testing capabilities, providing knowledge and skills to previously unrelated companies, jointly creating hardware among five companies through intensive cooperation, stimulating uninterested companies to actively enter this field, negotiating software standards, and diffusing developed software (Feigenbaum and McCorduck, 1984; Fransman, 1990).

Cooperative research can be established even when companies are very hesitant to cooperate with each other. For example, in the development of an optoelectronic IC with compound materials, the technology's close proximity to the market made companies, especially competitors, unwilling to share technology with one another, while a high level of uncertainty and cost also retarded companies' R&D activities in this field. A government-subsidized cooperative established by the Optical Measurement Project (1979–1985) under the leadership of ETL convinced related companies to participate in generic research on materials, material growth, and fabrication technology while the actual devices were developed by each member company. Despite their initial resistance to cooperation, the project succeeded in getting the member companies to jointly innovate and disseminate generic technologies and to build an optical communication system. This project thus successfully achieved a sharing of tacit knowledge and basic know-how without appearing to pose a threat to market competition among companies (Fransman, 1990: 108).

Even without a joint laboratory, the Future Electronic Devices Project (1981–1990), established to develop superlattice and three-dimensional devices through very generic research by each member company, brought about voluntary coordination in developing specific devices among companies in the Kansai region, while companies in the Kanto region remained independent. These differences also generated diversity in the ways member companies influenced one another and developed devices, though all members exchanged reports and information and shared tacit knowledge (Fransman, 1990: 185–188).

Cooperative relations among competitors, multiple approaches, government subsidies, opportunities to catch up with leading companies, and the availability of diverse expertise at research cooperatives helped to disseminate technological information to relevant companies, and solved the problems of asymmetric information flow and locked perspectives found in exclusive inter-firm relations. These cooperatives also reduced risks, costs, and uncertainty in leading-edge technology development, provided a base for fusing diverse ideas and perspectives, and consequently stimulated innovation. For leading companies, failure to join an R&D project meant the loss of technological advantages if the project succeeded in generating a significant advance in technology. Hence the joining of such projects functioned as insurance to keep up with technological changes by competitors (Goto, 1993: 105–110). But none of the post-VLSI Cooperative projects focused on the silicon-based semiconductor, the reasons for which will become clear later.

By making use of cooperative learning, the fusion of ideas, and effective networking while retaining market competition, the national government succeeded in transforming the R&D system from one of imitation in the 1950s, to incremental R&D in the 1960s, and to the development of self-reliant and indigenous technology in the 1970s and 1980s. This prevented the "maturation" of industries and raised the technological level of companies (Abernathy et al., 1983). Therefore TSOs advanced into new "techno-paradigms" (Freeman, 1987), enabling themselves not only to provide new technological information, but also to play the indispensable role of facilitating cooperative activities. Under the old Japanese techno-governance structure, however, universities and colleges did not effectively contribute to this transformation because of inadequate cooperation and communication among scientists and engineers, weak professional norms, and the lack of internal dynamics for improving research and education (Saxonhouse, 1986). The universities' weakness in generating radical innovations resulted in an emphasis on promoting research toward incremental innovations (Herbig and Palumbo, 1996).

Thus the old Japanese techno-governance structure generated its own dynamics by (1) speeding up the flow of enriched technological information through cooperative learning among diverse types and a wider range of companies, even including competitors and less dynamic firms; (2) stimulating technological innovation and improvement; (3) preventing the monopolization of technological information; and (4) further enhancing market competition. But the dynamics of this structure were effective only for incremental innovations, not for radical technological changes.

As Fig, 2.1 shows, the U.S. semiconductor industry made a remarkable comeback. Why was it so successful? Was it due to the development of a new techno-governance structure? If so, what are the key factors that characterize this structure and how different are they from those of the old Japanese techno-governance structure? The findings described in the next section substantiate the importance of the techno-governance structure and its key factors in understanding industrial dynamics. They also provide insights into institutional and techno-governance factors relevant to an understanding of the old Japanese and the new U.S. techno-governance structures.

3 Buildup of the U.S. Techno-Governance Structure: 1980s–1990s

To compete against Japanese technological leadership, the U.S. built up the research capabilities of its universities, established government-funded projects and consortia among companies, made use of national research institutes, and developed effective networks among companies, universities, national research institutes, and the government. The U.S. buildup took about 20 years, involving three periods: an Indirect Government Participation Period (1977–1987), a Direct Government Participation Period (1988–1995), and a Systematic and International Expansion Period (1996–1999). I shall briefly describe the characteristics of the newly developed U.S. techno-governance structure, comparing it with the old Japanese structure. Figure 2.5 depicts advances in the U.S. structure for all three periods.

Figure 2.5 New U.S. Semiconductor Techno-Governance Structure

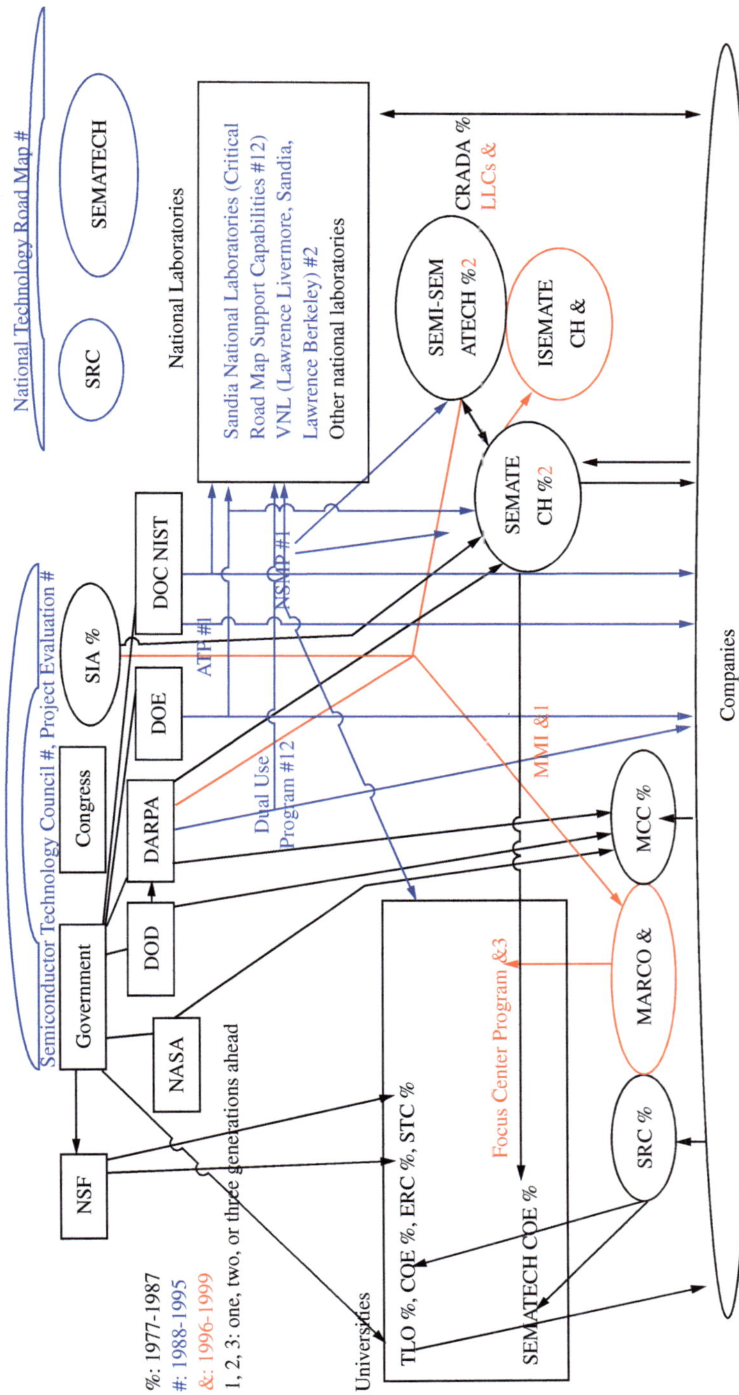

3.1 The Indirect Government Participation Period (1977–1987)

When the Japanese VLSI Cooperative succeeded in developing the 64 Kb DRAM in 1977, U.S. semiconductor manufacturers, fearing that the declining trend in the U.S. share of the semiconductor and equipment markets might be further aggravated, jointly established the Semiconductor Industry Association (SIA). The goals of SIA were to collectively develop macro-level strategies to obtain the U.S. government's assistance and to promote collective activities among companies to strengthen their competitiveness.

As a means of strengthening U.S. companies' technological capabilities overall, the government passed the Bayh-Dole Act in 1980 to promote the transfer of unused technologies from universities to companies. Although joint university-company research had been increasing since 1970, in 1980 only 5% of 30,000 patents generated in universities (patents owned by the federal government as a result of its funding of the research) were used for products (Matsushige, 1998; Tekuno Risachi Kenkyusho, 2000). The new law enabled universities and small firms (venture firms) to own the patents on technologies they had developed under federal-government-funded projects and to transfer university-owned technologies to private companies, especially small ones. This resulted in increasing the number of university patent acquisitions from about 250 per year before 1980 to more than 1,800 in 1995 (Matsushige, 1998). Many American universities established their own technology licensing organizations (TLOs) and engaged in sales of technology licenses. Thus two primary reasons for the U.S. loss of competitiveness, despite its rich resources and the world-leading research capabilities of its universities, were identified as a lack of technology dissemination capability and unfavorable legal conditions.

However, the Bayh-Dole Act was of little use to U.S. semiconductor manufacturers because academic research was mostly on the compound semiconductor, a field offering ample publication opportunities but having little economic significance (Gover, 1993). Research on the silicon-based semiconductor was mostly conducted within company laboratories. While the SIA pressured the U.S. government to make the closed nature of the Japanese semiconductor market an issue in U.S.-Japan trade disputes (Cortell, 1997; Macher et al., 1998),[22] 11 U.S. and Canadian semiconductor manufacturers established the Semiconductor Research Corporation (SRC) in 1982.

The goal of the SRC was to nurture semiconductor research capability at universities, target technology that would be usable one to two years ahead, and transfer it to private companies (Tekuno Risachi Kenkyusho, 2000). SRC designated six universities as Centers of Excellence (COEs) and conducted programs and projects at many universities in collaboration with companies and other organizations (Handotai Sangyo Kenkyusho, 1995; Gover, 1993).[23] SRC's efforts to nurture universities' research capabilities were continuous and extensive, covering many areas of semiconductor technology. By November 1983, SRC had

50 contracts with 30 universities, involving 100 faculty members and 125 graduate students (Bloch, 1983). Four phases of planning, initiation, performance and evaluation, and commercialization were closely monitored and carried out by SRC personnel, principal investigators, students, and operational and scientific industry representatives (Rea et al., 1997). Consequently, companies gained by (1) sharing research costs, (2) pooling talent, (3) reducing financial risks, and (4) sharing sophisticated and expensive equipment. Of SRC's performance, Intel cofounder Gordon Moore said, "The industry has probably leveraged more than two to three times the money it has invested in SRC, some $200 million over a 10-year period" (Rea et al., 1997: 50). But Randazzese (1996) found that such an outcome could be enjoyed only when each participating company committed a significant amount of resources and when SRC strongly encouraged job-hopping by university researchers, face-to-face relations, joint projects, and even student internships. The effects of journal papers, conferences, and general meetings were marginal by contrast. This suggests that the Japanese approach to human relations and cooperative learning is highly effective in technology transfer and creativity stimulation even in the United States. But unlike Japan, the involvement of universities in U.S. semiconductor research also helped turn some craftsman-type skills and knowledge from semiconductor manufacturing into science and universally applicable principles, creating a basis for the standardization and advancement of technologies.

SIA members also jointly established the Microelectronics and Computer Technology Corporation (MCC) in 1982 to conduct research funded by member companies, the Defense Advanced Research Projects Agency (DARPA), the Department of Defense (DOD), and the National Aeronautics and Space Administration (NASA). MCC functioned as a central research laboratory for its members. It once had about 400 researchers, but in the initial stages was not considered successful because of ambiguity in its objectives (basic research or product generation), attitudes of secrecy on the part of member companies, restrictions on technology transfer, and many other conditions imposed by the funding agencies (Gover, 1993; Beyer and Browning, 1999; Handotai Sangyo Kenkyusho, 1995; Gibson and Rogers, 1994). Cooperative research among companies was still a violation of U.S. antitrust law, so the MCC took the form of a joint venture, hiring its own researchers and receiving contracts from government agencies. The lack of involvement in its research activities by member company personnel impeded cooperative learning and the effective transfer of technology (Gover, 1993). MCC could not generate a sufficient return on investments, but it functioned well enough as an experiment in methods of cooperation and technology sharing (Gibson and Rogers, 1994), to which U.S. antitrust law was found to be a major obstacle.

Institutional developments favorable to effective cooperation among companies, universities, and national research institutes started gaining momentum when the National Cooperative Research Act (NCRA) made cooperative interfirm research legal with the permission of the Securities and Exchange Commission (SEC) in 1984. This permitted the involvement of government agencies and national research institutes in the capability-building process for private firms.[24] Given its contradictory nature vis-à-vis the principles of antitrust law, the NCRA has two unusual characteristics: One is that the NCRA interprets cooperation as legal when its benefits are proven to outweigh the threat to competition. The other is that whereas the plaintiff in a regular antitrust case can demand up to three times its actual loss, the NCRA approves only up to the amount of actual loss, thus reducing the risk of lawsuits in cooperative activities (Handotai Sangyo Kenkyusho, 1995). Therefore the U.S. eventually recognized the value of cooperative learning, and its perception started changing with the passage of the NCRA.

As a way of preserving U.S. core competency, President Reagan passed the Chip Design Law in 1984 and also called for the restoration of U.S. manufacturing competitiveness in 1985 (OhUallachain, 1997). Responding to his policy goals, in 1986 the National Competitiveness Committee (the Young Commission) cited the importance of cooperation among national research institutes, universities, and companies for pre-competitive technological innovation (Kikai Shinko Kyokai Keizai Kenkyusho and Nihon Apuraido Risachi Kenkyusho, 1994).

In 1986 and 1989, the Steven-Wilder Act was revised to allow national research institutes to cooperate with private companies—especially small firms (venture firms) and companies producing in the U.S.—by entering into a cooperative research and development agreement (CRADA). This allowed a company to benefit from public funds, personnel, facilities, equipment, intellectual property, and other resources found in national research institutes and even to pool resources scattered among several national institutes by developing a project team and a virtual research center. With a CRADA, a company joining such a project retained the exclusive right to its patents for five years and also benefited from a secrecy agreement on any patent-related technologies offered by the company (Tekuno Risachi Kenkyusho, 2000).

Hence, CRADAs allowed national research institutes to cooperate effectively with companies and with each other, creating unusually beneficial environments for the companies. The NCRA and the revisions to the Steven-Wilder Act provided the legal basis for cooperative learning, technology dissemination, and effective networking. They made U.S. national research institutes more openly and flexibly available and beneficial to companies while permitting the flexible formulation of project teams and virtual research centers. In contrast, patents generated from a Japanese government-funded project belonged to the government, with no exclusive rights granted to the company. Moreover, it was difficult to develop research projects in Japan involving different government ministries or even different national research institutes, to say nothing of developing virtual research centers.

Based on these legal changes, in 1987 fourteen U.S. companies and DARPA in DOD joined forces to establish the Semiconductor Manufacturing Technology (SEMATECH) consortium. According to managers at NEC and Hitachi, the goals of SEMATECH's members were to jointly develop and improve CMOS-based semiconductor process technology at a central facility (Langlois and Steinmueller, 2000) and to reduce R&D costs and improve semiconductor production capability (Irwin and Klenow, 1996). SEMATECH successfully developed process technology for an 0.8-micron line width on a 13-inch wafer in 1989 and for a 0.3-micron line width on an 18-inch wafer in 1993 (Denpa Shinbunsha, 1996). But there were two major problems: First, companies did not want to share with one another the tacit knowledge they deemed central to their competitive edge in research, and second, differences in specialization and levels of technological sophistication among companies generated conflicts over process technologies and over which products to develop (Spencer and Grindley, 1993).

These problems became apparent in one of the first attempts to jointly develop DRAM production capability. In 1989, SIA, backed by five semiconductor manufacturers and some U.S. electronics companies (Los Angeles Times, 1989), proposed the joint establishment of a DRAM manufacturing company, U.S. Memories, with the help of IBM's 4 Mb DRAM technology and SEMATECH's world-leading process technologies for 8-inch silicon wafers (Electronic News, 1989a). SIA also contemplated seeking government assistance in the form of guaranteed or low-cost loans. This project was considered important, since the American companies were dependent on Japanese products, and since the DRAM was the technology leader in process development (Electronic News, 1989a). But it raised serious antitrust issues, and Cypress Semiconductor criticized the project for competing against its own business. Similarly, Motorola, Micron Technology, and Texas Instruments, who were all producing their own DRAMs, expressed hesitation over joining this consortium (Los Angeles Times, 1989; Electronic News, 1989b). At the end of 1989, IBM suddenly announced it would license to Micron Technology and negotiate to license to Cypress Semiconductor the same technology that IBM was to provide to U.S. Memories. By then, the project was further clouded with uncertainty over its ability to raise needed funds (Washington Post, 1989).

Another underlying condition unfavorable to the targeting of a mass-produced DRAM was an emerging tendency toward industrial fragmentation and "simple flexible manufacturing" (Chon, 1997), a trend accelerated by the appearance of many venture firms. From 1957 to 1987, a total of 205 semiconductor start-ups were born worldwide, of which 193 (95%) were in the U.S.; 124 of them (64.2% of U.S. start-ups) were started from 1978 to 1987 (Angel, 1990). In Silicon Valley, high-technology venture firms sales grew by 60% to $24 billion, from $15 billion, from1982 to 1987, despite the worst recession of the region in 1985 and 1986 (Saxenian, 1991). Semiconductor-related start-ups captured the potential of the growing system LSI market and its involvement of diverse elements in complex operations. They specialized in an area requiring a limited range of high technology and served low-volume market niches with small-batch production methods, typically making use of computerized design and manufacturing equipment (Angel, 1990). Effectively exploiting the larger firms' high-level business threshold and their inability to develop small business activities around new technologies (Hobday, 1994), the start-ups capitalized on their flexibility and quick turnaround, responding quickly to market movements. Open and flexible networks of these specialists complementing and cooperating with one another made their existence highly significant, especially in new technology areas, and further stimulated the birth of new business models, such as chipless and fabless makers, foundries, and IP and EDA vendors. It was the existence of a highly effective market, along with a support system in the U.S. techno-governance structure—consisting of federal and state governments, universities, angel investors, venture capital firms, business incubators, and the high-tech stock market—that permitted the easy entry and exit of new entrepreneurs and provided opportunities for the growth of new ideas, technologies, and business models. The existence of an open and fluid market contributed greatly to the ability to move in new directions, and provided a rich environment in which even big businesses could choose and reformulate their business objectives by increasingly making use of venture firms technologies, engaging in mergers and acquisitions, and learning from new business models. Even so, profits were more often generated by large-sized semiconductor manufacturers who enjoyed scale-intensive capabilities, global market outlets, and ample financial resources (Hobday, 1994). Nevertheless, these new movements, along with specialization by existing large-sized semiconductor companies in such areas as the microprocessor, logic, digital signal processor (DSP), and programmed logic device (PLD) (West, 2000), were undeniably strong indicators of the development potential of the system LSI market.

The failure of U.S. Memories, the growth in venture firm activities, and the increasing specialization of the big semiconductor manufacturers suggested a need for SEMATECH to focus on areas applicable to diverse devices and on serving the varied interests of companies. SEMATECH shifted its focus to the improvement of vertical relationships between semiconductor manufacturers and equipment and materials suppliers (Spencer and Grindley, 1993), and to the development and evaluation of manufacturing equipment for the next-generation (one to two years ahead) system LSI, based on CMOS technology. SEMATECH began to (1) develop manufacturing equipment that could be installed into existing production lines; (2) provide future manufacturing equipment standards for joint development and risk reduction; (3) develop at least one U.S. manufacturing equipment company in each key equipment area; (4) formulate long-term strategic alliances for continuously providing key manufacturing equipment; (5) give free access to jointly developed equipment, systems, and materials; (6) develop a standard open architecture for computer-integrated manufacturing (CIM); (7) provide a place of open information exchange; and (8) stimulate company-university joint research by establishing SEMATECH centers (Denpa Shinbunsha, 1996).

In 1987, SEMATECH organized a consortium, Semiconductor Equipment and Materials International (SEMI-) SEMATECH, for equipment and materials manufacturers,[25] and implemented several projects. The Joint Development Program, which occupied about 60% of SEMATECH's program budget, provided research contracts for equipment and materials development with SEMI-

SEMATECH members and subsidized a third of the cost (Handotai Sangyo Kenkyusho, 1995). This program was followed by the Equipment Improvement Program, under which SEMATECH conducted equipment testing and certification (Spencer and Grindley, 1993). Special efforts were made in lithography and plasma chemical vapor deposition (CVD) technologies, which were considered keys to developing an advanced system LSI (Handotai Sangyo Kenkyusho, 1995, 1996). The Partnering for Total Quality Program also facilitated the sharing of information between manufacturers and equipment and materials suppliers, introduced continuous improvements, and fostered an understanding of the costs, strategies, and performances involved in total semiconductor production (Spencer and Grindley, 1993; Fuji Sogo Kenkyusho, 1997a). Based on these relations, SEMATECH discussed schedules or road maps for anticipated paths of technological innovation.

In cooperation with SRC, SEMATECH contracted with SEMATECH-designated Centers of Excellence (SCOEs) at 39 universities in 11 states and encouraged them to engage in intermediate- and long-range research on semiconductor technologies. National research institutes also joined in these research activities, making use of CRADAs.[26]

Although SEMATECH has often been criticized for favoring large-sized companies, segregating nonmember companies, and failing to generate a significant return on investment (Irwin and Klenow, 1996; Link et al., 1996), it has successfully generated enormous intangible benefits. SEMATECH (1) developed effective networks among companies, universities, national research institutes and the government, organizing about 200 meetings per year; (2) nurtured vertical cooperative relations between a group of semiconductor manufacturers and a group of equipment and materials manufacturers; (3) established a mechanism of technology transfer, relying heavily on person-to-person relations; (4) reduced the costs of equipment development and R&D duplication; (5) prevented the fragmentation of equipment design by standardizing equipment; (6) introduced total quality management for continued quality improvements, resulting in a higher yield rate; (7) developed a mechanism of information sharing on costs, quality, strategies, and performance; (8) reduced the costs of purchasing, operating, and maintaining U.S. equipment; (9) increased purchases of U.S. equipment; (10) achieved parity with Japan in circuit line width, applicable to diverse devices; and (11) strengthened the supply of complementary products and services by equipment and materials manufacturers (Link et al., 1996; Irwin and Klenow, 1996; Spencer and Grindley, 1993). The most significant successes of SEMATECH were to (1) develop vertical cooperative relations between semiconductor and equipment manufacturers; (2) standardize production equipment, which dramatically reduced the cost of equipment development and provided opportunities for integrating several types of equipment into one; and (3) focus on equipment usable for diverse devices, especially for the system LSI, which involved the most complex processes (Chon, 1997).

SEMATECH's success in creating an environment of cooperation and effective decision making may be partly attributable to the particular environment created by Robert Noyce, SEMATECH's first chief executive officer and Intel's co-founder. Noyce was gifted with a magnetic personality that combined friendliness, approachability, and seriousness with a sense of fun, and he had strong convictions, boundless energy, and outstanding abilities of all kinds (Beyer and Browning, 1999). He propagated a community of equals, with everyone having an equal right to actively participate and express an opinion, irrespective of official position or the section to which the person belonged. He frequently held meetings, constantly raised serious questions, solicited bold and risk-taking ideas, encouraged everybody to engage in the "constructive confrontation" of ideas, and discouraged any attitude of secrecy. But he made sure that once a consensus was reached, everybody was to follow an orderly pursuit of pre-set goals and engage in continuous improvements while quickly and openly learning from one another's mistakes. To generate order in a chaotic situation, he developed coordinating councils for cross-sectional coordination and implemented strict ethical and moral standards (Browning et al., 1995; Beyer and Browning, 1999).

Besides SEMATECH, the National Science Foundation (NSF) and most state governments worked together to develop research centers, called Engineering Research Centers (ERCs), whose goal was to conduct research by a pool of university researchers in areas that the private sector considered important.[27] In 1987, NSF also developed Science and Technology Centers (STCs) at universities, with each center intended to function for a duration of no more than 11 years, focusing on basic research directly related to national competitiveness building. In 1989, eleven STCs existed, some in cooperation with national research institutes.[28] All the centers that involved public funding faced strict periodic evaluations by professionals specializing in each area, in the case of STC at the third and eighth years (Handotai Sangyo Kenkyusho, 1995). The rise of U.S. entrepreneurship in new market- and technology-driven commercial enterprises is often attributed to the excellence of these centers and of American research universities (Gover, 1993).

Thus venture firms stimulated the transformation of the semiconductor industry by capitalizing on high technologies and creating diverse business models, and they provided large-sized companies with some alternatives and choices in technologies and business structures. In contrast to these developments in the market, SRC and NSF played key roles in nurturing semiconductor research capability at universities, which strengthened the scientific orientation of semiconductor technology development, while SEMATECH linked companies, national research institutes, and universities together. The ERC, STC, and SCOE centers that had been developed at the universities became important elements in effective networking with companies and national research institutes, while the universities' ownership of patents derived from federal government-funded projects encouraged them to take the initiative in linking with companies through TLOs. CRADAs allowed national research institutes to cooperate with companies and even among themselves quite openly and flexibly, providing unprecedented benefits for companies. Government funding, however, was restricted to consortia of companies, universities, and national research institutes and did not flow directly to individual companies, thus characterizing this period as one of indirect participation by the government. But government funding did introduce strict performance-oriented evaluations into these research activities.

Effective networks were developed among semiconductor manufacturers, equipment and materials suppliers, venture firms, the government, private company consortia, national research institutes, and universities. The development of long-term relations between equipment and semiconductor manufacturers, such as the intensive cooperation between Intel and Applied Materials, generated a drastic difference in the development of equipment. Networks and the mechanisms of cooperative learning, which had developed during this period according to principles similar to those operative in Japan, began stimulating creativity and disseminating technology.

Despite similarities in these American and Japanese principles of cooperation, however, there were five conspicuous differences: the U.S. (1) created many new business ventures based on new technologies and business models; (2) made very effective use of universities; (3) developed more open and flexible mechanisms; (4) implemented strict professional performance evaluations; and (5) created a structure with less need than in Japan for TSOs to correct the asymmetric flow of information. American universities played a key role in disseminating technological information and correcting the asymmetric flow of information through open and flexible relations with companies. Japanese universities were neither keen on serving the needs of companies nor on contributing to national competitiveness building. Besides, the Japanese government exercised very strict budgetary control and audits on government-funded projects, rather than strictly evaluating output and performance.

Failure on the part of SEMATECH to develop inter-firm cooperation targeting a specific device, the DRAM, and its extremely open and idea-generating period of constructive conflict led by Noyce, created a form of cooperative learning much more suitable to the United States, based on readily available strategic resources such as logic circuits and microprocessors. SEMATECH members cooperated to establish equipment standards for the next-generation system LSI, solicited cooperation among equipment manufacturers, and evaluated the performance of equipment. To develop standards, it was necessary to open up access to each company's information, engage in vigorous debate, and articulate logical reasons for decisions. Such exercises, along with input from university-based research, fostered greater information exchange, expanded perspectives and approaches, and forced members to think in a universal and scientific way.

Japanese reliance on human and vertical relations produced restrictions on the openness of perspectives and the direction of change, while difficulties in developing strong human relations in the U.S. resulted in an open, constructively conflictive, universal, and scientific approach to cooperative learning, which also opened the way to radical changes (Shimura, 1995). One consequence of such thinking and behavior in the U.S. was cooperation with equipment and materials manufacturers, something that could hardly be achieved when projects were vertically split among semiconductor manufacturers, as was the case in Japan with the VLSI Cooperative. Furthermore, to realize its goals, SEMATECH allocated ample human and financial resources for developing plans and strategies and administering them. American-style cooperative learning had a different value orientation from that of Japan.

3.2 The Direct Government Participation Period (1988–1995)

The U.S. government began directly subsidizing private companies' R&D during this period. Based on the Omnibus Trade and Competition Act of 1988, Congress passed a law to develop an Advanced Technology Program (ATP) administered by the National Institute for Standards and Technology (NIST) under the Department of Commerce (DOC). In 1991, ATP started to provide matching funds directly to companies' advanced research (Tekuno Risachi Kenkyusho, 2000), especially in semiconductor-related areas. Although ATP faced serious resistance from NIST administrators, who feared that their main work of standardization might be undermined, it became a major program of NIST under the Clinton Administration. NIST scientists and engineers at seven laboratories[29] evaluated proposals by themselves, while outside professionals were brought in to evaluate their business impact. This program succeeded in creating competition among its participants and solicited a large number of new, innovative ideas. The bottom-up process based on open competition contributed to developing an innovative environment.

Also in 1991, NIST started a program called the Semiconductor Initiative, which in 1994 officially became the National Semiconductor Metrology Program (NSMP). It often took the form of joint projects and involved a total of 23 semiconductor manufacturers, 46 equipment and materials manufacturers, 37 universities, 12 national research institutes, and 10 private consortia including SEMATECH and SEMI-SEMATECH (Kikai Shinko Kyokai Keizai Kenkyusho, 1999).

The open and flexible U.S. approach required a mechanism of coordination to make diverse research activities strategically focused. In 1992, SEMATECH, SIA, and SRC jointly established several subcommittees and developed a national technology road map for semiconductors with 179 scientists and engineers from industry, academia, government agencies, and national laboratories (Rea et al., 1997). They provided a long-term blueprint for U.S. semiconductor development that took into account the dual purposes of semiconductors for industry and defense. The road map was updated in 1994 with the participation of 240 scientists and engineers and has been continually updated to the present (Rea et al., 1997). To strengthen the road map's technological predictability, in 1995 SRC established a category of Science Area Members that included producers of complementary goods and IC purchasers. The road map functioned to coordinate diverse research activities at universities, national research institutes, government agencies including DARPA and NIST, semiconductor manufacturers, and equipment and materials manufacturers (Fuji Sogo Kenkyusho, 1997a). Since semiconductor production requires an enormous amount of equipment, parts, and materials, it was considered imperative to cut costs and duplication in research through such coordination, though this road map approach also brought with it the danger of technological lock-in, allowing competitors to go beyond or outside the road map.

In a corresponding effort, the federal government in 1993 established the Semiconductor Technology Council (SETC). Its goals were to (1) link assessments of future market and national security needs to opportunities for cooperative public and private investment; (2) seek ways to respond to technological challenges by promoting pre-competitive research cooperation; and (3) make assessments and recommendations from industrial and government R&D available for future rationalization and alignment (Rea et al., 1997). SETC provided effective coordination among the members of industry, Congress, and government (Handotai Sangyo Kenkyusho, 1995). Strategic approaches of this sort and cross-sectional coordination at any level of research are clearly missing in Japan.

From 1992, despite a big cut in the DOD budget resulting from the end of the Cold War, the Clinton Administration increased its budget for developing dual-use technology based on the national technology road map for semiconductors. DOD allocated its budget through partnership programs with companies and national research institutes. Those programs transferred dual-use military technologies to regional technology development programs and to private companies and promoted research on critical and general dual-use technologies, advanced defense-related manufacturing technology, high performance computer communication, agile manufacturing, and innovation in small businesses (venture firms) (Kikai Shinko Kyokai Keizai Kenkyusho and Nihon Apuraido Risachi Kenkyusho, 1994). Semiconductor technology, being the best example of dual industrial-military use, remained an important area of research focus in many of these programs.

Based on the road map and making use of CRADAs, the Department of Energy (DOE) also started promoting collaborative research between its laboratories and private companies. In 1992, a joint project was developed with computer manufacturers (Kikai Shinko Kyokai Keizai Kenkyusho and Nihon Apuraido Risachi Kenkyusho, 1994). Sandia National Laboratories, established in 1945 under the Manhattan Project to develop a nuclear bomb,[30] has built up critical road map support capabilities in lithography, 300 mm wafers, advanced interconnects, packaging, and design. Sandia developed centers for semiconductor equipment technology and contamination-free manufacturing, and it established an intensive partnership with SEMATECH for modernizing the technology base, enhancing the competitiveness of the U.S. semiconductor industry, and working directly with the industry to mutually develop optimum practices. The Sandia-SEMATECH partnership has developed a clearly defined division of labor and even an area of joint research, while SRC provides academic support to their activities (Gover, 1993). The partnership is considered one of the best examples of dual-use technology development and government-business collaboration in the semiconductor field (Nihon Denshi Kogyo Shinko Kyokai, 1996).[31]

To facilitate cooperative research among companies and national research institutes, a new form of organization for joint research, called the limited liability company (LLC), has been frequently used following changes in Internal Revenue Service regulations in 1994.[32] Investors have limited liability for an LLC and receive profits proportionate to investment, while an LLC itself pays no tax. LLCs avoided the complex and costly legal procedures required for establishing a company, made cost accounting simpler, could be used only for limited-term joint projects, and provided incentives for investors because they could receive profits directly. For example, to develop two-generations-ahead extreme ultraviolet (EUV) lithography technology,[33] Intel, Motorola, and AMD formed a joint venture, the EUV-LLC.[34] What is interesting is that the EUV-LLC concluded a CRADA with the Lawrence Livermore, Sandia, and Lawrence Berkeley National Laboratories (all under DOE) and strengthened its research capability by pooling specialists from these laboratories in a virtual national laboratory (Kikai Shinko Kyokai Keizai Kenkyusho, 1999). Thus the new combination of LLCs and CRADAs enabled companies and national research institutes to pool top-level researchers in the very important area of lithography. The LLC offered an attractive environment for cooperative research, flexibly opening up many different forms of cooperation. In Japan, where establishing a cooperative required voluminous documentation and legal clearance procedures, forms of cooperation were rather limited before 2002.

Pursuing the objective of "small government," the U.S. Congress passed the Government Performance and Results Act of 1993 (GPRA) to increase accountability and credibility in government funding, improve the administrative capability of funding agencies, and develop an auditing mechanism for Congress (Nihon Boeki Shinkokai, 1998). Consequently, many government projects for the semiconductor industry began to face severe review procedures.

The above findings suggest that the U.S. techno-governance structure had become well coordinated and further strengthened by (1) developing national technology road maps through private-sector initiative; (2) establishing direct government contacts with companies based on bottom-up project proposals; (3) increasing government support for companies' joint projects and their collaborative research with universities and national research institutes (e.g., NIST and DOE); (4) promoting military-industrial dual-use research by DOD; (5) establishing a division of labor for sustaining road-map capability as in the Sandia-SEMATECH partnership; (6) increasing ease and flexibility in project coordination with the use of LLCs and CRADAs; and (7) coordinating policy formulation (SETC) and intensifying evaluation by the government (GPRA).

The consequence was a revival of the international competitiveness of the U.S. semiconductor industry. In 1994, SEMATECH agreed not to receive any federal government funding from 1996 on and declared victory over Japan. U.S. semiconductor manufacturers regained 45.3% of the world semiconductor market, a higher percentage than Japan's, while U.S. equipment manufacturers held

53.6% of the world share in 1993. SEMATECH succeeded in producing equipment at a much lower cost than Japanese companies and improved its reliability as well (Handotai Sangyo Kenkyusho, 1995).

SEMATECH, with backing by SRC, MCC, NSF, NIST (ATP and NSMP), DOD, and DOE, had three major impacts on the U.S. semiconductor industry. First, its research activities and coordination of manufacturing equipment standardization turned the system LSI into the technology leader, whereas it had previously been produced using half- or one-generation-behind lithographic technology because of the device's complexity. Now, system LSI technology had caught up to the DRAM level and with better manufacturing equipment. Second, standardization allowed Applied Materials and other equipment manufacturers to expand operations into other equipment areas through mergers and acquisitions and to integrate previously separated operations with automatic software-controlled production adjustments. Intensive scientific research and software development allowed equipment manufacturers to transform craftsman-type complex adjustment skills into software automation. Third, this integration of manufacturing equipment made it easier for less technologically sophisticated companies to engage in semiconductor production. This was the very reason why Taiwanese companies succeeded in quickly establishing a foundry business, though now, after 10 years of success, they have accumulated technological capability, caught up with Japanese companies in terms of production capability, and started conducting their own internal R&D. The U.S. success should be attributed to the development of a highly flexible and dynamic techno-governance structure rather than to SEMATECH alone, though SEMATECH was indeed the initiator of movement in this direction.

U.S. advances in techno-governance during this period thus went far beyond those of Japan. The latter developed research projects for the purpose of catching up and gaining technological leadership. But Japan did not engage in strategic thinking for the continuous maintenance of leadership, which must be based on long-term technological forecasts and nationally coordinated research activities; these naturally require a very strong government role in coordinating and implementing policies through diverse agencies. In the U.S., government projects ensured that it would maintain its lead in semiconductor technology capability in diverse key areas by coordinating research activities through road maps, promoting cooperative industry-university-government projects, and developing means for making cooperation flexible, open, and attractive to companies. Flexibility, openness, and constructive conflicts that readily generate diverse and intensive creative stimuli were missing in Japan. This may be because cooperative learning was rather narrowly confined within vertical inter-firm relations, and because interactive dynamics were mistakenly measured and valued according to the intensification and refinement of relations. Such maintenance of trust, harmony, and vertical relations places priority on the nature of relations, not on their content and outcome, hence requiring strong normative restrictions to eliminate any behavior that would disturb harmony. In other words, Japanese cooperative learning in the past was culturally deeply embedded and institutionally and path-dependently restricted. Although a set of normative values for building up trust and harmony among cooperating partners undeniably remains crucial to any form of cooperative learning, it must be developed in a way that accommodates openness, flexibility, constructive conflict, and even incentives and benefits.

3.3 The Systematic and International Expansion Period (1996–1999)

When governmental support of SEMATECH was terminated in 1996, various government agencies started conducting semiconductor-related projects in a more systematic manner, even targeting 7- to 10-year long-term research.[35] During this period, ATP became the main government program, directly supporting innovative activities in the private sector (Tekuno Risachi Kenkyusho, 2000). Within ATP, the Microelectronic Manufacturing Infrastructure (MMI) Project became the biggest program in 1998, and most of the 1998 budget ($63.8 million) was used for developing semiconductor equipment manufacturing technology[36] in the form of matching funds to individual companies or a consortium of companies (Kikai Shinko Kyokai Keizai Kenkyusho, 1999).

Many of these projects took the form of LLCs and cooperative research. For example, KLA, Tencor, Du Pont Photomask, Photronics, Lucent Technologies, and EUV-LLC formed an LLC in 1998 to develop mask-pattern-defect testing equipment for EUV and electron beam (EB) SCALPEL masks. Micron Technology acquired LLC status for itself in 1998 to develop a mask-modifying system for non-gallium focused ion beam (FIB) lithography (Kikai Shinko Kyokai Keizai Kenkyusho, 1999).

Based on an earlier NSMP project on evaluating lens and mask materials for ArF (193 nm) lithography, the Physics Laboratory and the Electronics and Electrical Engineering Laboratory of NIST established a joint project on evaluating materials for F2 (157 nm) lithography. In coordination with this project, the Massachusetts Institute of Technology (MIT) Lincoln Laboratory, operated with DARPA funding, also developed a joint project with SEMATECH on evaluating materials for F2 lithography. Capitalizing on the next-generation technology developed by these F2 joint projects, equipment manufacturers and Intel established the Silicon Valley Group Lithography Division (SVGL) (Kikai Shinko Kyokai Keizai Kenkyusho, 1999), which merged with ASM Lithography, an EU company, on 22 May 2001.[37] Backed by a sudden increase in DARPA's lithography budget in 1999, the U.S. Navy established the Next Generation Lithography (NGL) Mask Center of Competency and has been conducting research on mask technology based on X-ray projection lithography in cooperation with Photronics and IBM (Kikai Shinko Kyokai Keizai Kenkyusho, 1999).

Lithography has been the key technology for advancing semiconductor capability, and national research institutes, the military, universities, and companies were all well coordinated in developing this technology. These key projects, established since 1998 along with many others by the MIT Lincoln Laboratory, NIST, ATP, and MMI, target the development of both next-generation (90–

70 nm) and two-generations-ahead (70–50 nm) lithography technologies. One exception is that SVGL is involved only in the next generation, and this may be a reason for its acceptance of a foreign takeover bid.

DARPA now focuses more on developing two-generations-ahead lithography. It funds EUV research by EUV-LLC, which closely cooperates with NIST national laboratories and semiconductor equipment manufacturers. It also funds research by Nikon and IBM on the PREVAIL method of electron-beam projection lithography and research by Bell Laboratories (Lucent Technologies) and equipment manufacturers on the SCALPEL method[38] (Kikai Shinko Kyokai Keizai Kenkyusho, 1997, 1999).

The main responsibility of DARPA, however, is to build up capability for the three-generations-ahead (50–25 nm) semiconductor, targeted at about 7 to 10 years ahead. The Ultra Electronics Project and the Nanoelectronics Project are trying to achieve 25 nm with electron-beam lithography.[39] DARPA's key program since 1997 has been the Focus Center Research Program (FCRP). SIA selected six crucial targeted technologies and plans to select six top-level research universities to be focus centers, which will also coordinate research activities with other universities, national research institutes, and more than 30 companies. The program commits to paradigm shifts, radical innovations, multiple approaches, and generic technologies in semiconductor production, nurtures future-oriented top-level researchers, and leads companies and other organizations in research activities, while keeping a close eye on the national technology road map for semiconductors (Handotai Sangyo Kenkyusho, 1998; Tekuno Risachi Kenkyusho, 2000). The program, funded jointly by SIA (50%), DARPA (25%), and SEMI-SEMATECH (25%), provides each center with $10 million per year with a commitment of 7 to 10 years (Kikai Shinko Kyokai Keizai Kenkyusho, 1997). The Microelectronics Advanced Research Corporation (MARCO) owned by SRC administers the program. In 2000, the University of California-Berkeley was selected as a focus center for semiconductor design and testing, and the Georgia Institute of Technology for interconnect technology. But they are to cooperate with other universities and develop virtual centers[40] (Kikai Shinko Kyokai Keizai Kenkyusho, 1999; Tekuno Risachi Kenkyusho, 2000). FCRP has fostered two significant networking developments that cannot be found in Japan. One is that even basic research at universities has started taking the form of cooperative research with companies and national research institutes. The other is that these projects consolidate scattered academic resources in virtual centers and provide valuable opportunities for academics to engage in cooperative learning.

Semiconductor production requires an enormous number of specialized skills and technologies, and it is no longer feasible to build up an innovative system inside one country alone. It was recognition of this fact by the U.S. that resulted in an expansion of research activities throughout the world. When the U.S.-Japan semiconductor disputes ended with a significant loss in Japan's share of the world semiconductor market, both countries recognized the need for international cooperation in the advancement of the semiconductor industry. The U.S.

and Japanese governments agreed to establish a World Semiconductor Council (WSC) in 1996. At the first council meeting, European and Korean semiconductor industry associations also joined. The stated goals of the WSC were to promote mutual understanding, free access to the market, and industrial development based on market principles. It also called for cooperation between suppliers and users in developing markets all over the world and among suppliers in the areas of standardization, environment, safety, intellectual property, and free trade and investment. The need for data analysis and the prevention of dumping was also emphasized. (Kikai Shinko Kyokai Keizai Kenkyusho, 1997).

One of the first tasks of the WSC to encourage supplier cooperation was to develop production standards for a 300 mm wafer among these countries. A cooperative project was necessary because the shift from a 200 mm to a 300 mm wafer was too costly ($10 billion for a 300 mm wafer in contrast to $1 billion for 200 mm), making the first such innovative company unprofitable and requiring radical changes and automation in equipment (Ham et al., 1998). A scheme for sharing costs and setting standards again was accepted as the solution, but now at an international level—a solution to which SEMATECH's experience proved extremely relevant. After negotiations, the WSC accepted the establishment of two U.S.- and Japanese-led consortia, but unified standards could not be achieved.

To coordinate domestic suppliers of the 300 mm wafer, the Electronics Industry Association of Japan (EIAJ) in 1996 established an organization called J300 for developing standards and organizing a private firm consortium, Semiconductor Leading Edge Technologies, Inc. (SELETE), that developed and evaluated equipment for the 300 mm wafer. Ten Japanese companies and one Korean company (the only firm outside Japan) joined.[41] SIA established a U.S. counterpart, the International 300 mm Initiative (I300I), for both standard setting and equipment evaluation, in which 6 U.S., 3 EU, 1 Taiwanese, and 3 Korean companies participated (Kikai Shinko Kyokai Keizai Kenkyusho, 1997). It was I300I that made U.S. companies recognize the need to bring in international expertise in some areas.

When SEMATECH was receiving government funds, it was not allowed to include foreign companies as members. While keeping itself closed to foreign companies, it established International SEMATECH (ISEMATECH) as a subsidiary, allowing foreign participation in only five limited areas (such as lithography, wafers, and manufacturing methods) where U.S. companies needed help from other countries. Other areas where U.S. manufacturers had already established superiority were excluded (Kikai Shinko Kyokai Keizai Kenkyusho, 1999). Although ISEMATECH was established for strategic reasons, U.S. companies were well aware of the need to make use of international resources and to develop cooperative relationships to strengthen their technological capabilities. In contrast, since Japanese companies had established SELETE and did not join I300I, they were excluded from ISEMATECH. The need to nurture their internal capabilities in critical technologies prevented them from joining a U.S. organization, resulting in their relative isolation from the rest of the semiconductor world. But an unwelcoming attitude from the U.S. side was also a factor, since SEMATECH had earlier received government funding, and serious concerns had often been expressed about leaking advanced technologies to Japan (Ham et al., 1998). Nevertheless, WSC and ISEMATECH succeeded in globalizing the U.S. national technology road map for semiconductors, now called the international technology road map for semiconductors (ITRS).

This period thus highlights a highly systematic, future-oriented approach to the development and international expansion of the U.S. semiconductor techno-governance structure. The privately funded SRC and MCC focused mostly on small projects, targeted one to two years ahead (Handotai Sangyo Kenkyusho, 1995), while NSF used the Engineering Research Centers at universities to academically support one- to two-year research activities. In coordination with the Focus Center Research Program, the SEMATECH Center of Excellence shifted its focus to a 3-to-5-year target (Kikai Shinko Kyokai Keizai Kenkyusho, 1997). Because of this shift, SEMATECH began increasingly representing the research interests of big semiconductor manufacturers.[42] Basic research targeted 7 to 10 years ahead was conducted at NSF's Science and Technology Centers at universities, while the Focus Center Research Program, funded by SIA, DARPA, and SEMATECH and conducted at universities, created a system for radical innovation and paradigm shifts in future semiconductor technologies. Diverse government and private-sector projects were all systematically linked to develop pragmatic technologies, especially in lithography, ranging from one-half to one, two, and even three generations ahead, and to target paradigm shifts, radical innovation, and multiple developments.

During this period, a clear shift took place away from a pragmatic-target-based approach toward a knowledge-stock-based one. At every level and in many areas of research, even beyond silicon technology, cooperation was well developed among companies, national research institutes, and universities and moreover became international in scope. According to a manager at the Association of Super-Advanced Electronics Technologies (ASET), the Japanese semiconductor industry had no comparable strategies for international cooperation, resulting in its relative isolation from the rest of the world. Yet despite the buildup of the U.S. techno-governance structure for cooperative learning, a weak tradition of cooperation among U.S. companies also reportedly hindered the orchestration of adequate synergetic effects.

The extensive participation of the U.S. government during this period can also be interpreted as a response to companies' needs to survive globalization. Up until the 1980s, semiconductor manufacturers took the form of integrated device manufacturers offering a diverse range of products and conducting their own R&D, design, manufacture, marketing, and sales. For example, Texas Instruments (TI) made its own processing equipment, silicon and chips, and packaged and shipped them. Intel developed many computer-aided engineering and layout tools in the 1980s (Nihon Denshi Kikai Kogyokai, 1999). When technological advances made it possible to put a system on a single chip, the content of a system itself became the basis for a company's competitiveness, while research on future devices and manufacturing equipment still remained important. However, the cost of R&D, now involving an enormous range of technological developments, became prohibitively high, and the global integration of markets put increasing pressure on companies to maintain good cash-flow management. The product cycle also became much shorter. Since basic research without immediate product applications weakens a company's cash flow, the 1990s saw U. S. companies shift their focus from basic to applied research, promote horizontal divisions of labor among firms, and create a multiplicity of business players and models such as chipless, fabless, foundries, IP vendors, and electronic design automation vendors[43] (Davidow, 1996).

For example, the Watson Research Center at IBM, known for its many Nobel-Prize-winning research projects, laid off 1,100 researchers out of 3,300 and dispatched the remainder to laboratories for applied research. The ratio of applied to basic research shifted from 4.5/5.5 in 1985 to 7.5/2.5 around 1998, and the proportion of concrete applications and solutions increased from 5% in 1992 to 30% around 1998. Lucent Technologies, which became independent from AT&T in 1996 and owns Bell Laboratories, introduced a stringent evaluation system and cut all research not leading to short-term outcomes. A significant portion of central research laboratory funding came from research contracts with manufacturing divisions, and researchers' performances were assessed by the amount of revenue generated, not simply by the number of patents. This weakening basic research capacity on the part of private companies was complemented by joint research with universities, national research institutes, and other companies (Saito, 2000; Tekuno Risachi Kenkyusho, 2000).

One of the best examples of the new form of laboratory is Intel's Microprocessor Research Laboratory in Santa Clara, established in 1995. It closely interacts with the manufacturing section located next door, invests in a variety of venture firms, takes a strong leadership position in SEMATECH, and participates in EUV-LLC with AMD, Motorola, and national research institutes (Tekuno Risachi Kenkyusho, 2000). To handle costly and uncertain basic research, Intel effectively makes use of government funding and cooperation with universities and other organizations. According to Gordon Moore, Intel's co-founder, "Intel ... limits internal basic R&D to what is needed to solve immediate problems" and "looks to universities for much of the basic research...." (Rea et al., 1997: 50). Thus the U.S. techno-governance structure functions not only to strengthen technological capability and national competitiveness, but also to respond to U.S. firms' needs to survive globalization.

We have found that the U.S. developed a far more effective techno-governance structure than Japan's, based on more open and flexible mechanisms through networks and fluidity in the venture firm market. But why was the old Japanese techno-governance structure unable to help its semiconductor manufacturers? Using an analytical scheme based on micro- and macro-strategies shown in Table 1.1, I shall analyze the Disintegration Period of the old techno-governance structure in Japan.

4 Technological Lock-In and the Disintegration of the Old Techno-Governance Structure

4.1 Technological Lock-In and Intra-Firm Cooperation

Japanese semiconductor manufacturers achieved international competitiveness by successfully developing NMOS DRAM technology to stabilize DRAM performance in 1968 (Okada, 2000), advancing production processes toward narrower circuit line widths and shifting to lower-power, higher-yield CMOS DRAM technologies in the early 1980s. According to a manager at Sony, these successes encouraged engineers to believe in the continuity of past practices in advancing process technology and in the value of making extra efforts to increase yield. They became perfectionists at treading past technological paths even as they strove to stay in the forefront of world leadership in DRAM development. If the DRAM had remained the lead product in the advancement of semiconductor technology, this micro-level strategy on the part of Japan's semiconductor manufacturers and their lock-in to a narrow technological perspective would have been quite helpful. But this was not the case.

This lock-in created five problems. First, it weakened the ability of the semiconductor manufacturers to recognize alternative paths within each company, even in DRAM production. Second, it prevented them from recognizing the potential of alternative devices that might replace the DRAM. Third, it fragmented the research activities most applicable to DRAM development and reinforced a strong sense of intra-sectional cooperation. Fourth, it prevented companies from keeping a close watch on overall technological and market movements and making changes accordingly. Fifth, a lack of worker mobility, while providing a favorable environment for nurturing a strong sense of intra-firm cooperation and high performance under the old techno-governance structure, also made it difficult to generate quick changes.

Japanese companies led with the world's first experimental production of the DRAM. In 1987 NTT announced the 16 Mb DRAM (Nihon Denshi Kogyo Shinko Kyokai, 1988); in 1990 Hitachi announced the 64 Mb DRAM (Nihon Keizai Shinbun, 1990); in 1993 NEC, Hitachi, and Toshiba announced the 256 Mb DRAM (Press Journal, 1993); and in 1995 Hitachi and NEC announced the 1 gigabit (Gb) DRAM (Press Journal, 1996).[44] Despite quick advances in experimental production, on the market Samsung became the world's largest producer of DRAMs in 1992 (Press Journal, 1994) and the leading producer of 16 Mb DRAMs in 1993, and it began sample production of 256 Mb DRAMs earlier than Japanese companies (Press Journal, 1999).[45] With negative growth in the DRAM market in 1992 and 1993, the 4-year silicon cycle began behaving erratically (Press Journal, 1993), and market shifts did not take place as expected. The shift to the 256 Mb DRAM in particular met with delays because of its high price, which made it cheaper to combine four 64 Mb DRAM chips instead (Press Journal, 1994).

Japanese engineers firmly believed that becoming the first producer of an advanced product was the key to success; this locked them into a race for DRAM advancement without their paying sufficient attention to the collapse of the silicon cycle and to changes in the market. As a matter of fact, world DRAM sales shrank from $40.8 billion in 1995 to $13.0 billion in 1998, and the DRAM's proportion of total semiconductor sales fell from 28% to 11% in those years. To further aggravate its position, Japan's share of the world DRAM market plunged from 80% in the late 1980s to 20% in 1998, and sales by its major producers fell from ¥1.9 trillion in 1995 to less than ¥1.0 trillion in 1998. The effects of global market shifts suddenly began to appear in 1995 (Handotai Sangyo Kenkyusho, 2000: 10).

One reason for this sudden decline of revenue was the "Micron Shock," as shown in Fig. 2.3. The narrow focus by Japanese engineers on advancing process technology for the DRAM even prevented them from developing more-attractive DRAM ICs at reduced prices and sizes, as Micron Technology and Korean companies had done. Micron Technology succeeded in reducing the number of masks (at $100,000/unit) in DRAM production by a third to a half, from 20, which shortened production process time and reduced costs enormously. It also reduced the size of a chip from 1 cm×1 cm to 7 mm×7 mm,[46] and at the same time it used a more expensive chemical-mechanical-polishing (CMP) process to improve the yield rate. These developments enabled Micron Technology to produce memory chips at a cost of about $4 per chip in 1995, while Japanese companies were producing them for about $6 each.[47] By lowering prices as well as production costs, Micron Technology also aimed to expand its market share rather than its profit rate.

Obsessed with the race for DRAM advancement, Japanese engineers also failed to recognize a big shift in the semiconductor industry. The growing capacity of the semiconductor increased demand for the system LSI, and SEMATECH's success in advancing CMOS process technology to narrow the line width of chips for the highly complex system LSI expelled the DRAM from its position as technology leader. Managers from Hitachi, NTT, and Sony share the view that Japanese companies were unable to predict these new movements in the semiconductor industry. The Hitachi manager expressed regret that the slow development of the earlier forms of system LSI made its emerging dominance difficult to detect and thus took Japanese companies by surprise.

This lack of awareness may be an unavoidable consequence of factional research activity that fosters a strong sense of cooperation within each section, enhanced by an organizational structure that separates production from design and sometimes design from algorithms and architecture. Managers at the venture firm MegaChips and the Joint Research Center for Atom Technology (JRCAT) even suggested that a concept like system LSI, which requires the amalgamation of many areas of specialization, would never have emerged from such an environment.

In Japan, work positions are rotated to promote open information exchange and to refresh the employee's motivation. But such rotation is often carried out without regard for a researcher's area of expertise, especially if his or her area is deemed a less important one. A researcher at one Japanese company developed a flash memory, a technology that would eventually replace the DRAM. He developed this technology when he was rotated from the Central Research Laboratory to a design section, where he conducted research on his own in addition to his regular work. Most of his colleagues did not believe in his work and ignored his research activity until he obtained a patent on a NOR-type flash memory. He was then sent back to the laboratory, where he developed a low-cost NAND-type flash memory (Press Journal, 1993). Because of the delay in his research activity, however, Intel had developed its flash memory sooner, and the Japanese company did not gain leadership in the market[48] until recently.[49] Without this individual researcher's enthusiasm and perseverance in working in isolation from the existing organizational structure, and without his company's admirable tolerance of such activities, this device might have never been developed, though stronger and earlier official support might have increased the speed of its development.

The above case represents one success in the face of adversity. Overall, the lack of worker mobility in the labor market tended to suppress opportunities for innovation. A manager of the venture firm Synthesis expressed his opinion that Japan's permanent employment system was important for developing intra-firm cooperation and generating dynamic interaction among employees, but it also prevented engineers from moving to companies where they could make the best use of their own skills. If one company stopped research in a certain field, its specialists were transferred to other sections to work on unrelated projects. If workers could have moved to companies where their expertise would be utilized, this technological know-how would not have been wasted. There were some cases of researcher mobility. For example, Sumitomo Electric Industries, a latecomer to the semiconductor business, succeeded in strengthening its technological capability by hiring five specialists from a company that withdrew from the development of a gallium arsenide (GaAs) IC. But such examples are very rare.

Hence, an obsession with the DRAM advancement race and a factional structure in research prevented Japanese engineers not only from paying sufficient attention to alternative paths in DRAM production and even alternative devices to the DRAM, but also from recognizing big changes in the semiconductor market.[50] The lack of worker mobility also reduced flexibility in solving the problems of technological lock-in.

4.2 Technological Lock-In and Inter-Firm Cooperation

In order to win the DRAM advancement race and obtain a higher yield from silicon wafers, Japanese semiconductor companies cooperated closely with equipment, parts, and materials manufacturers, nurturing the highly advanced craftsman-type technological capabilities of these manufacturers. It was the semiconductor companies that guided and coordinated the development of process technology, especially by equipment manufacturers. Semiconductor companies were the centers of new information and innovative stimulation as well as providers of expensive facilities for testing, particularly for the equipment manufacturers. Without strong cooperative relations with the semiconductor companies, equipment manufacturers faced enormous difficulties in technological innovation and development. Hence a set of equipment manufacturers cooperated with a particular semiconductor company and often developed highly relation-specific technologies, locking in their technological perspective to fit the needs of that company. The volume of an initial order, sometimes with a period of moratorium on sales as a condition for joint development, delayed the dissemination of equipment to other companies. But these locked technological relations generated their own successful dynamics when their locked-in characteristics matched well with the market.

Such relations, however, excluded new suppliers with innovative ideas from the Japanese supplier market, prevented the development of new markets by venture firms, and failed to allow suppliers to solve problems scientifically or generate diversity in products and approaches.

The exclusion of newcomers with innovative products was an especially serious problem. It is of interest that a number of Japanese technologies that made path-breaking impacts were first purchased by Western companies whose high evaluations then made Japanese companies recognize the value of these new innovations and products. For example, Sumitomo Electric Industries developed a high-quality GaAs wafer whose acceptance as a product by Japanese companies came only after an America device maker used the product and openly praised its quality. An entrepreneur who left Toshiba and established a venture firm, Thine Electronics, found his first opportunity to develop an analog/digital mixed signal system LSI in a joint venture with a foreign firm, not a Japanese one. An entrepreneur who was previously a researcher at NASA and established the venture firm SAMCO International developed thin-film CVD equipment in his garage in Kyoto, but he could not sell even one machine until an American buyer suddenly contacted him and purchased it. Immediately after this purchase, he succeeded in selling the equipment to Japanese companies.[51]

This intensive, vertically linked inter-firm system, based on a strong sense of cooperation and trust, left little space for newcomers to enter. The first hurdle they had to clear was the *yoshin* (credit) check conducted by the financial sections of many companies to investigate the trustworthiness of a potential business partner. Big companies requested evidence of past sales, tax records, and details of the company profile instead of evaluating the technology itself. Small firms without a substantive business record could not clear this hurdle and were thus forced to conduct business first with foreign companies. Long-term partners with a well-developed relationship of trust and cooperation enjoyed highly favorable positions and were granted priority in the development of any new equipment, thus excluding many new competitors from business opportunities.[52] Long-term cooperative relations narrowly limited the perspectives of researchers and managers and discouraged and excluded venture firms and newcomers.[53]

Vertical cooperative relations also hindered the development of software capability and of computer-aided design (CAD) technologies in Japan. When mainframe computers were dominant, software was considered an appendage to hardware. Software was usually customized to fit hardware and was developed by affiliated *keiretsu* companies, a situation that obstructed the development of a standardized software market (Okada, 1999). For similar reasons, Japan is now considered very weak in system design, a field currently dominated by U.S. ventures such as Cadence Systems and Synopsis (Nihon Denshi Kikai Kogyokai, 1999). But during the era of the mainframe computer, NTT had a highly competitive CAD system that it provided to its subcontractors free of charge, though it also sold a small number of systems at low prices. Unlike the U.S., where venture firms began selling CAD software for personal computers, in Japan subcontract relations, low-cost supply, and an unfavorable environment for venture firms precluded such developments.[54]

Japanese semiconductor manufacturers made an extra effort to raise the yield rate per wafer by introducing an extra circuit (*jocho kairo*) in the transistor. When a transistor did not function properly, this extra circuit was activated to correct the situation. The development of such mechanisms required manual adjustments of machinery and increased production processes and costs. Such complex operations and manual adjustments worked well under vertical cooperative relations, but clearly prevented the standardization of production processes through software adjustment. Nevertheless, the *jocho kairo* was an important approach that worked as a temporary solution until a scientific solution could be found to correct the basic problem, which Japanese engineers did not address properly.

Because of the development of the U.S. techno-governance structure, Applied Materials was able to automate production, integrate diverse operations, and sell equipment even to companies with limited technological capabilities (Kikai Shinko Kyokai Keizai Kenkyusho, 1999).[55] A manager from Sony contrasted the American and Japanese approaches as follows: Applied Materials analyzed production processes in a scientific way and created a uniform solution to mechanical adjustments, while Japanese technicians and engineers relied on experience and craftsmanship rather than scientific analysis.[56] The ease with which semiconductor manufacturers could implement minor adjustments within the framework of highly effective cooperative relations prevented them from seizing an opportunity to solve the basic problem of semiconductor failure in a scientific way.

Under Japanese vertical cooperative relations, the development of something like the Taiwan foundry business was unimaginable. UMC was established in 1979 and targeted the custom LSI market with system-design capability, a different specialization from that of Korea. In 1986, finding that it could not obtain enough business, UMC sold its system-design section and refocused on the foundry business (Kikai Shinko Kyokai Keizai Kenkyusho and Nihon Apuraido Risachi Kenkyusho, 1994: 269). It publicly disclosed its machinery specifications and approached system-design companies in Silicon Valley, offering free sample production and testing. Once sample production and testing were performed by UMC and the test results were acceptable to the customer, even fabless companies that bought system designs from chipless companies found it necessary to commit their production to UMC, since other production facilities might not have produced the same test results. Because they used advanced machinery and provided high-quality work, quick delivery, and low prices, UMC and TSMC both became centers of foundry production.[57] The sheer volume of production, especially by TSMC, resulted in making their production specifications a global standard, often called the "TSMC standard." The company makes this standard available through the Internet and even enables customers to track the production stage of their products.[58] Now TSMC has accumulated copyrighted system designs and intellectual property and has begun advancing into the EDA vendor market. If it succeeds in accumulating a sufficient amount of IP, it will soon become a competitor to system LSI producers.[59]

In similar fashion, another company in Taiwan began receiving orders from many big semiconductor producers to mount chips on circuit boards. It developed its own interface technology among varying devices, and then started to demand that the big semiconductor manufacturers follow its standard.[60] In Japan, such companies are classified as *shitauke* (subcontractors), an arrangement that makes them highly vulnerable to the bigger client companies and incapable of insisting on their own standards. Under Japan's vertical inter-firm relations, control by small companies over key technologies, exploitation of their own comparative advantages, and equality in bargaining—never mind an actual reversal of power relations—were inconceivable. The lack of openness and flexibility in Japanese vertical relations prevented the sort of transformation seen in Taiwan. The concept of bargaining power, rather than the maintenance of cooperative and trustful relations, allowed Taiwanese companies to reverse their relations when a shift in the distribution of resources altered the distribution of power.

Some managers attribute the relative inability of Japanese companies to create innovative ideas and produce paradigm shifts to Japanese culture, group orientation, and ethnicity. But there is ample evidence of Japanese creativity, adverse conditions notwithstanding. Findings suggest that when the maintenance of long-term relations became the primary goal of interactive behavior, vertical cooperative relations often suffocated new developments while encouraging locked-in technological developments. These relations worked as long as Japanese technological paths were in the mainstream. But once they were out of the mainstream, these relations became a hindrance, suggesting that vertical relations, systems, and the governance structure were the problem more than a lack of Japanese creativity.

Cooperative learning is a very important part of the semiconductor development process today, as the U.S. techno-governance structure has demonstrated. But the Japanese techno-governance structure, built as it is on rigid vertical cooperative relations, is poorly equipped to cope with radical change. Granted, sustainability and persistence in cooperation are also an important part of maintaining competitiveness in production, marketing, and sales (Hobday, 1994). But openness to alternatives, flexibility in practices, and acceptance of changes pointing to new cooperative relations have to be combined with sustainable relations. Cooperative values that are applicable to a mixed situation of openness and flexibility as well as sustainability and persistence must be developed, and they may be more egalitarian, constructive-conflict tolerating, and individual-initiative encouraging, as well as less structurally or sectionally restricted, than the cooperative values found in the Japanese old techno-governance structure. Cooperative relations should be able to tolerate constant, rigorous professional technical evaluations of performance, support risk-taking and entrepreneurial attitudes, and accept diverse forms of interaction having different goals and means. The nature of cooperation and its outcome, however, should remain one of the most important criteria of evaluation so that cooperative learning remains dynamic. In other words, long-term relations should be the outcome of cooperative, mutually constructive, open, flexible, and dynamic interactions, but should not be a goal in itself (Okada, 2000). Such an orientation is applicable to both intra- and inter-firm relations. Organizational structures that facilitate such behavior must also be encouraged. Usually, a decentralized structure is better suited to trying out a wide variety of approaches and achieving quick learning, and smaller independent organizations are speedier at realignment and recombination (Nelson and Winter, 1977; Langlois and Steinmueller, 2000). The existence of diverse organizational forms clearly increases choices and learning opportunities, suggesting that the promotion of venture firms and entrepreneurship is vital for such diversity. Even with these organizational forms, cooperative learning that links diverse approaches and organizations remains vital for dynamic interaction.

I have previously argued that lock-in to a narrow technological perspective occurs when a traditional and rigid system of cooperative learning persists in a company or when a technology-supporting system fails to stimulate technological change by a company. The findings cited here suggest that lock-in to a narrow technological perspective exists among Japanese semiconductor manufacturers. These findings fall under the category of "continuity of old strategies in micro-level intra- and inter-firm relations" common to Cells 1, 2, and 3 of Table 1.1 in Chapter 1. What, then, happened to Japanese companies' macro-level strategies of relations with technology-supporting organizations from the mid-1980s to the mid-1990s? If these relations had functioned properly, Japanese semiconductor manufacturers might not have been hit so severely. I shall examine this question in the next section.

4.3 Disintegration of the Old Techno-Governance Structure

4.3.1 Withdrawal of Old Macro-Level Strategies

Until the 1980s, TSOs and governments functioned as technological information disseminators and innovation stimulators to companies in Japan. They also corrected the asymmetric flow of information by nurturing the capabilities of companies not benefiting from cooperative learning and even brought competitors together to learn diverse approaches. Companies implemented macro-level strategies to take optimum advantage of the old techno-governance structure, which resulted in uplifting their technological capability, intensifying competition with more value-added products, and stimulating industrial transformation. In the 1980s, this supportive TSO/government environment disappeared.

4.3.1.1 Declining Role of National Research Institutes in Silicon-Related Research

In the early stages of Japan's semiconductor industry, ETL under MITI initiated the development of the industry. In 1951, TRI under the Ministry of Communication (Teishinsho) succeeded for the first time in developing a point contact transistor. And when Japan had difficulty advancing its technology from the transistor to the solid circuit, ETL succeeded in developing an experimental IC (Okada, 2000).

ETL and TRI researchers frequently job-hopped to private companies, especially when companies started establishing their own research institutes in the early 1960s. Both ETL and TRI also took the initiative in providing technological guidance and organizing government-funded cooperative research projects with companies. TRI continued such practices even after it became the research institute of a public corporation, the Nippon Telegraph and Telephone Public Corporation (NTTPC), in 1952 (Okada, 2000). From the 1950s, NTTPC nurtured the technological capabilities of its suppliers, such as NEC, Hitachi, and Fujitsu, by establishing extremely stringent standards, inspecting production processes, conducting joint projects, and giving technological advice (Okada, 1989a).

In the 1980s, when semiconductor manufacturers started enjoying large profits, manufacturing equipment became prohibitively costly for national research institutes to buy in order to continue silicon-based semiconductor research. For about 25 years, very few researchers moved from ETL to semiconductor companies, and lifetime employment at ETL hindered the hiring of young and energetic researchers. Such conditions stand in marked contrast to those at the Electric Research and Service Organization (ERSO) in Taiwan, where researchers stay for an average of only six years.[61]

A manager at ETL explained why ETL failed to maintain a leading role in the semiconductor industry. It was not simply due to costs and budgetary problems, but also to the laboratory's shift toward basic research, which created a wide gap between its research activities and the technological needs of companies (Fong, 1998). Another reason for ETL's failure was that it could not conduct any silicon-related research because, during the U.S.-Japan semiconductor disputes of the 1980s, the U.S. had pressured MITI not to engage in any research that might enhance the competitiveness of Japanese semiconductor companies in the immediate future. Management at the national research institutes was also problematic. These institutes lacked a clear separation between the work of researchers and of research assistants, allowing unqualified workers to engage in research activities while at the same time requiring highly qualified researchers to perform tasks normally conducted by research assistants. The equal allocation of research budgets between researchers and research assistants also effectively reduced the amount of research allowances allotted to more-qualified researchers. Moreover, hardly any financial incentive existed for excellence in research activities. Permanent employment was also criticized for preventing competition, openness, and flexibility (Toray Keiei Kenkyusho, 1997).[62]

Another serious problem often cited by critics was the lack of innovative activity at the national research institutes. The institutes were criticized for being uniform in their thinking and approaches and for lacking flexibility, due largely to tight regulations and restrictions imposed by the controlling ministries. The vertical split of research organizations under different ministries created redundancy in their research activities and prevented interdisciplinary exchanges, which were increasingly becoming an important factor in the success of newly emerging industries. The Japanese government's desire to deflect U.S. criticism of active state involvement in industrial activities further prevented it from developing visions and missions and from taking any strategic role as it relied increasingly on bottom-up industry pressure and lower-level bureaucrats' proposals (Fong, 1998).

These criticisms suggest that national research institutes contributed much to the techno-governance structure in the early catch-up phase, but are no longer dynamic actors in the semiconductor industry today. As they were diverted away from silicon-related research, focusing on basic research not closely related to companies' needs and lacking the stimulation to engage in innovative activities, semiconductor companies started finding their relations with these institutes less useful to their silicon-based semiconductor research, as the ETL manager had feared they would.

4.3.1.2 Withdrawal of Public Corporations from DRAM Research

In the 1970s, TRI at NTTPC established the LSI Research Liaison Conference with Japanese semiconductor manufacturers to help them catch up to the technological level of IBM and AT&T. TRI subsequently initiated the first VLSI joint development project with manufacturers (1975–1977) and succeeded in developing the world's first 64 Kb DRAM in 1977. It continued to improve DRAM technology with the world's first 128 Kb DRAM developed by TRI alone in 1978 and the world's first 256 Kb DRAM developed by TRI in cooperation with NEC and Toshiba in 1980. These advancements were a mixed outcome of the VLSI Cooperative (1976–1979) and the second VLSI joint project organized by TRI (1978–1980). Along with private companies, TRI continued to take the lead in technological developments through the third VLSI joint project (1981–1982), resulting in the world's first 1 Mb DRAM and 256 Kb SRAM in 1984 (Okada, 2000). TRI's last memory-related public announcement was about the experimental production of the world's first 16 Mb DRAM in 1987.[63]

DRAM contributions by TRI, formerly a research institute under NTTPC, suddenly ceased in 1987 (Okada, 2000) because of the privatization of NTTPC into a new company (NTT) in 1985. TRI withdrew from the memory area and shifted its research into the logic LSI, microprocessor, and automatic programming language areas, which were closely related to its own telephone business. Also, open bidding and competitive tendering replaced NTTPC's highly effective supplier-capability-building system. These practices enabled NTT to purchase lower-priced commodities, but NTT lost its family of suppliers, including NEC, Fujitsu, and Hitachi, to whom it used to transfer overall technology and productive capability. NTT now engages in the sale of patents without transferring technologies and know-how. Its role in disseminating leading-edge technological know-how ended with privatization. However, to retain world technological leadership, TRI continues to develop future technologies related to its own business area, since purchasing existing technologies does not guarantee leadership and since future products require leading-edge technologies.[64]

Privatization thus forced the leading contributor to memory development out of the old Japanese techno-governance structure and eliminated a highly effective system of concentrated research and technology transfer. These findings are not meant to suggest that the old NTTPC public corporation should be revived, but rather that these events undeniably weakened one dynamic source of technological innovation closely related to companies' needs and eliminated a key disseminator of industrially vital technologies.

4.3.1.3 U.S.–Japan Disputes Diverting Silicon-Related Government Projects to Non-Silicon-Related Basic Research

Government projects had been the key mechanism for soliciting cooperation among companies to conduct targeted research, expose companies to multiple approaches, stimulate their creativity, and lift them to a more advanced technological level. But with regard to the silicon-based semiconductor at least, such effects disappeared in the face of the U.S.-Japan semiconductor disputes, which began in 1977 but first reached a crisis in 1980 when Japanese IC exports to the U.S. exceeded imports (Okada, 2000). In 1981, the two governments agreed to establish a working group to address the issue, and in 1982 Japan agreed to make an effort to improve the situation by increasing its imports of U.S. semiconductors (Cortell, 1997).

In 1985, however, citing a lack of improvement in the trade situation, the SIA filed suit with the U.S. Trade Representative against Japan for dumping semiconductors.[65] In 1986, U.S. semiconductor manufacturers also filed a dumping charge against Japan with the U.S. Department of Commerce (Nikkei BP Sha, 1998). Consequently, the same year saw the signing of the first U.S.-Japan Semiconductor Agreement over the issues of Japanese market access and semiconductor prices in the U.S. and the third world—the so-called gray market. The next year, however, the U.S. levied a penalty, accusing Japan of dumping in the gray market (Tarui, 2000: 462). It was almost 10 years later, in 1996, that the dispute finally subsided with the decline in Japan's world market share to close to 30%, about 20% below its peak in 1987. In 1997, the two countries agreed to establish the World Semiconductor Council to continue discussing global semiconductor problems (Denpa Shinbunsha, 1997).

According to a manager at ETL, this dispute made a significant impact. First, Japanese government technology projects were shifted to basic research that was too remote from the companies' needs. Second, to make the situation worse, MITI forbade any government projects related to the silicon-based semiconductor. The word "silicon" was not allowed in any proposal.[66] The first project of this period, the Optical Measurement Project (1979–1985), focused on compound materials and developing a gallium arsenide semiconductor capable of transmitting optical signals and transforming them into electrical ones. ETL took the initiative to pursue research in an area on which companies were not focusing. But because of a limited government budget, the lack of company interest, and the lack of extra researchers to spare on this project, ETL became an organization that mainly conducted research with little help from private firms (Freeman, 1987).

Similarly, the Supercomputer Project (1981–1989) focused on the Josephson junction, the gallium arsenide field effect transistor, and the gallium arsenide high electron mobility transistor—in other words, on non-silicon-based semiconductors. Some of these innovative technologies became useful in recent years, but hardly any made a significant industrial impact (Stowsky, 1989). In the synchrotron orbital radiation project, X-rays were used only for evaluation purposes. Some companies requested that the government include basic research on X-ray lithography as a part of the project, but the government did not permit it for fear of aggravating the semiconductor dispute.[67] And research in the Future Electron Device Project (1981–1990) became more basic than ever, covering superlattices, 3-dimensional integration, superconducting electrons, and bioelectronic and molecular electronic devices.[68] Such projects were undeniably important for the future, and cooperative research produced some interesting results. But they should have been pursued only after the silicon-related technological needs of the industry were met.

When the Metal Oxide Semiconductor Implementation System (MOSIS) was established in the U.S. in 1982 to facilitate testing of military-related system LSIs for the Department of Defense, a consortium of universities requested the opening of the system to university researchers and succeeded in doing so in 1984. The consortium, located at the University of Southern California, placed multiple chip designs on a set of masks, produced sample chips, and tested their performance. It succeeded in reducing the cost of IC test production to a few hundred dollars per chip, compared to the usual $60,000 to $80,000 (Handotai Sangyo Kenkyusho, 1995).[69]

According to a professor at the University of Tokyo, in 1985 a group of Japanese national university professors, learning of this new U.S. movement, brought a proposal to the Ministry of Education to develop a system similar to MOSIS with CAD centers in Tokyo and Osaka and to establish a research group. This proposal was quickly rejected on the grounds that the U.S. might interpret this move as cutting into one of its areas of strength.[70] Although scholars were well aware of the need for Japan to develop system-design capability (currently a top-priority demand), a fear of aggravating the dispute with the U.S. prevented the development of CAD centers.

Even though the use of silicon as the base material for the wafers upon which semiconductor production processes are applied is presently predicted to continue for another 30 years,[71] the U.S.-Japan trade disputes forced the Japanese government to withdraw from funding silicon-related projects, and national research institutes became incapable of conducting such research. The privatization of the former public corporation NTTPC, the leading innovator in DRAM technology, forced it also to withdraw from DRAM-related research. In the 1980s, it was inevitable that Japanese semiconductor manufacturers would abandon their old macro-level strategies of working closely with the government and TSOs in silicon-related areas, while their old intra- and inter-firm relations remained unchanged. The nature of the techno-governance structure shifted to the status described in Cell 2 in Table 1.1, making semiconductor manufacturers incapable of coping with path-disturbing conditions without effective government and TSO support.

4.3.2 Persistent Lack of Dynamic Contributions from Academia

Though some companies intensively engaged in joint research projects with university faculty members, the latter's impact on silicon-based semiconductor technology was rather insignificant, as indicated by their exclusion from Fig. 2.4 as part of the old Japanese techno-governance structure. As was the case in the United States before 1977, a majority of Japanese university researchers focused on compound materials, not silicon (Gover, 1993). Despite this, companies engaged in joint projects with universities and maintained good relations with faculty members in order to exchange information, obtain advice whenever necessary, train their employees in research, and obtain graduates who had at least a basic knowledge of a specialized field (Watanabe, 1999).

Companies also had low expectations of universities in their training of students, since many Japanese universities were well behind the curve of technological advancement and neither forced their students to study hard nor tried to raise their level of research and teaching (Mitsubishi Sogo Kenkyusho, 1995). The academic world had been criticized for its inability to keep up with technological developments, conduct rigorous evaluations, utilize research budgets flexibly, make quick decisions, or strategically coordinate research activities among professors. Research facilities were substandard and were operated without research support staff. With regard to silicon-based semiconductor technology, the lack of specialists made for poor education and research that was fragmented and unattractive to students (Handotai Sangyo Kenkyusho, 2000). Such conditions may have been due in part to insufficient incentives for innovation and restrictions imposed by governmental regulations, while the lack of motivation, incentive, and open information exchange among university faculty members for better research and education also remained a serious problem.

In a techno-governance structure geared toward catch-up and incremental rather than radical innovation, national research institutes and their interactions with companies thus played a key role while university faculty members' contributions remained indirect and minor, making the knowledge stock necessary for a dynamic semiconductor industry relatively meager and difficult to accumulate in Japan.

4.3.3 Persistent Lack of Risk-Taking Venture Firms and Business Model Diversity

Diversity in ideas, business models, approaches, technologies, and organizations is often the key to generating opportunities for change as well as finding solutions to problems. The market may be the most effective mechanism for creating diversity, since it has open mechanisms with fluid relations and since individuals and organizations can enter and exit relatively freely. A rich diversity in technological information offering different options to a company's decision makers also makes a significant difference in their ability to cope with changes, as well as to build up core competencies suitable for a new environment (Metcalf, 1998).

The market, however, is only an empty mechanism for determining the allocation of resources. To provide substance, it requires two key elements: new technologies and entrepreneurs. The highly advanced research capability of universities is an important factor in generating new technologies. For instance, Stanford University played a key role in stimulating the development of Silicon Valley. In this sense, the weak role of universities in the old Japanese techno-governance structure was clearly a bottleneck, while lifetime employment at Japanese companies and the preference by the educational elite (winners of Japan's rigorous university entrance examination competition) for employment at stable large-sized corporations also discouraged the entrepreneurial spirit in Japan. The strong normative pressure for success and fulfilling mutual expectations, though very effective in group-oriented performance, also formed a psychological block against risk-taking activities (Kagaku Gijutsucho Kagaku Gijutsu Seisaku Kenkyusho, 1998). Intensive, sticky vertical inter-firm relations and inadequate support for start-ups from venture capital, high-risk-taking angel investors, the stock market, and business incubators also created a very difficult environment for entrepreneurs.

Despite this, among the venture firms that started up before 1991, some such as MegaChips and Thine Electronics managed to survive by developing consulting and software design businesses to maintain incoming cash flow,[72] while working to develop their own core competencies. In some cases, notably Thine Electronics and SAMCO International, foreign companies highly evaluated their products and core competencies, with some even becoming joint-venture partners,[73] since the Japanese *yoshin* system effectively prevented start-ups from conducting business with large-sized companies. To survive in this environment, Rohm opened a branch in the United States and constantly obtained new technologies from both Japan and the U.S. during the 1970s and 1980s, enabling the company to ride the semiconductor booms in both countries.[74] Thine Electronics operated as a fabless chipmaker for the analog/digital mixed-signal system LSI.[75] SAMCO International developed CVD technology in cooperation with a university professor at the outset, and Technos was established by spinning off from a parent company caught in internal disputes.[76] Tohken grew after surmounting two failures.[77] Strong core technologies and wise management enabled these ventures to survive.

Kyoto seems to have a tradition of giving birth to famous high-tech venture firms. Some rather unusual factors explain this phenomenon. First, Kyoto has one of Japan's leading universities, Kyoto University. But firms there also face serious limitations, one being that there are no large industries in the city. Hence they feel compelled to search for markets outside Kyoto—including the U.S. For Kyoto ventures, to seek an international market is not a rare undertaking, and many of the Kyoto firms interviewed for this project actually found their technologies, markets, and customers initially in the U.S. Because land is expensive in Kyoto, companies there tend to remain very small and specialized and to develop high value-added products. There is little incentive to move out of Kyoto because of the benefits of proximity to Kyoto University. But to compensate for their small size and specialization, the Kyoto firms have developed an extensive network among themselves and nurtured a strong spirit of cooperation, something that was already a well-institutionalized part of Kyoto's tradition as the *sanchi* of Japanese traditional clothes, *kimono*.[78] These cases suggest that pre-1991 ventures clearly faced marginal conditions and took more radical approaches for survival, initially working closely with foreign companies and expanding their markets in foreign countries. Yet they also made the best use of existing traditional cooperative relations to develop their positions within Japan. They benefited from the openness and flexibility of foreign companies and markets, which provided initial business opportunities and also required them to develop Japanese-type traditional cooperative relations. This suggests that the lack of openness and flexibility in Japanese companies and markets remained a serious problem for developing start-ups.

4.3.4 Withdrawal of Micro-Level Strategies: Disintegration of Inter-Firm Cooperation with Equipment Manufacturers

The loss of Japanese companies' markets in the mid-1990s further disintegrated the old Japanese techno-governance structure. Cooperative relations with parts and materials suppliers remained as intensive as before, since close cooperation for maintaining strict standards, the traceability of products through computer coordination, quick detection of the causes of problems, and information exchange for reducing production costs were indispensable to the maintenance of quality, a high semiconductor yield rate, and cost competitiveness.[79] In contrast, relations with equipment manufacturers were eventually severed. The reason was rather simple. Joint equipment development requires intensive exchanges of technology, information, and services, such as testing equipment in a production line. Cooperative work is indispensable, just as Applied Materials has worked closely with IBM and Intel (Chon, 1997).[80] However, when a joint partner does not have the capability to purchase equipment, its manufacturer has to sell newly developed equipment to competitors of the partner. In the 1970s and 1980s, ample orders and contractual agreements enabled Japanese semiconductor companies to delay the equipment manufacturers' sale of newly developed equipment to competitors for up to one or two years (Okada, 2000). But in the 1990s, equipment was sold to Taiwanese and Korean semiconductor companies almost immediately, or at most six months after development, because Japanese companies could no longer place enough orders to keep the equipment manufacturers occupied with production for the Japanese firms alone. This meant that semiconductor manufacturers, through joint equipment development, were giving their technological expertise away to their competitors even as they poured time and money into development.

NEC decided to purchase equipment through global competitive bidding and to no longer engage in joint equipment development with Japanese equipment manufacturers. NEC sold its shares of Ando Electric stock to Yokogawa Electric. Hitachi turned its internal equipment production sections into independent companies or sold them to other companies and drastically reduced its internal or joint development.[81] This was a general trend among semiconductor producers in the mid-1990s, the rare exception being the development of one or two key pieces of equipment.

For survival, a limited number of equipment manufacturers started to set up their own clean rooms and simplified mini-testing lines, which required costly investments. Many began to engage in close cooperation with Korean, Taiwanese, and U.S. companies instead of Japanese. For example, after losing its close cooperative relationship with NEC, Ando Electric developed intensive relations with Samsung, which needed such an arrangement to reduce its dependence on Applied Materials.[82]

Though a few large-sized monopolistic equipment manufacturers continued to operate independently (Okada, 2000), in the late 1990s, for the first time, even *keiretsu* companies had to face the severance of cooperative relations. Despite the importance of cooperative R&D in developing future equipment, semiconductor manufacturers were forced to withdraw their old micro-level inter-firm strategies. One of the key characteristics of the Japanese techno-governance structure for the semiconductor industry thus faded away. Compounded by the firms' earlier withdrawal of their old macro-level strategies with the government and TSOs in the mid-1990s and their layoff of employees and discontinuance of inter-firm cooperation with equipment manufacturers in the late 1990s, this led to the disintegration of the old techno-governance structure, as shown in Cell 5 in Table 1.1.

5 Conclusion

Since 1989, Japanese companies have faced a gradual decline in their world market share, brought about by Korean and U.S. firms' production of inexpensive and smaller-sized DRAMs, a shift in technology leadership from the DRAM to the system LSI, the development of integrated manufacturing equipment with software adjustment, and the expansion of Taiwan's foundry business into the system LSI area. Why were Japanese companies unable to cope with these changes, and why did the old techno-governance structure not help these companies?

Comparative analyses between the old Japanese techno-governance structure and the new U.S. one and between the old Japanese structure and the Japanese structure during the Disintegration Period suggest five key findings. First. the buildup of the new U.S. techno-governance structure caused changes in the global semiconductor market. Second, the U.S. techno-governance structure effectively combined both market mechanisms for creating venture firms and networks for systematically developing cooperation among technology-related actors. In contrast, the old Japanese governance was based almost exclusively on cooperative networks. Third, the U.S. networks operated on principles similar to those of the Japanese, which promoted cooperative learning, information dissemination, effective networking, and creativity stimulation. However, the U.S. networks seem to have placed less emphasis on the fusion of ideas and a diversity of approaches than did the Japanese networks. (For a diagram of these principles, see Fig. 2.4). Fourth, U.S. cooperative learning and coordination mechanisms differ significantly in nature from those of the Japanese, suggesting differences in the path-dependent institutional characteristics of the two countries. Fifth, various incidents that occurred from the mid-1980s to the mid-1990s strongly suggest that the old Japanese techno-governance structure had ceased to function in the silicon-based semiconductor sector, turning each semiconductor manufacturer into a lone player in the market without effective technological support, a situation very similar to U.S. conditions before 1977.

To advance CMOS processing technologies beyond Japan's level of capability was the goal of various U.S. research activities by SRC, MCC, and SEMATECH. Because of the varied interests and specialized devices of private U.S. companies, these research activities began to focus on developing manufacturing technologies applicable to any device, whereas their initial attempt to achieve technological superiority in a single DRAM device failed miserably. This more open approach inevitably led them to target the system LSI, which houses various devices on one chip. This focus also fit well with the newly developed "simple flexible manufacturing" scheme promoted by chipless and fabless companies as well as by IP and EDA vendors. SEMATECH also resolved conflicts of interest among its members by standardizing equipment specifications as well as offering them the benefits of drastically reduced costs for technology and equipment development, and it developed vertical cooperative relations with a consortium of equipment and materials manufacturers (SEMI-SEMATECH). One by-product of this standardization approach was Applied Materials' acquisition of several SEMI-SEMATECH members to integrate separate equipment with software control. Purchasing such integrated equipment enabled technologically less sophisticated companies to engage in system LSI production and to quickly become a new force in international competition. The prime examples of this were the Taiwanese companies that threatened Japan's international competitiveness in system LSIs. Meanwhile, Micron Technology and Samsung had also begun utilizing certain advanced technologies to squeeze Japanese DRAM producers out of the market. These changes, mostly stimulated by new technology developments in the U.S., do much to explain the Japanese decline.

The U.S. techno-governance structure was quite successful as a result of a combination, on the one hand, of using market mechanisms to turn new and advanced technologies into venture businesses, and on the other hand, of building cooperative networks among well-established companies, universities, national research institutes, and government. It is interesting to note that this governance structure fully appropriates new technologies generated by different types of technology innovators. Expensive and mass-production-suited advanced technologies necessary for the sustainability of large-sized manufacturers are developed collaboratively with TSOs, while new technologies with less-known market potential and below the business threshold for large-sized companies are tested in the venture firm market. Some entrepreneurs may even turn radical innovations into a full-blown industry, just as the semiconductor industry grew from venture firms into large-sized companies. The existence of such dual mechanisms enables the U.S. semiconductor industry to sustain international leadership in process technologies through effective networks, while the venture firm market fosters diversity and options for future development in products and processes. A clear difference in Japan is that networks remain the major mechanism for creating diversity and choices for future development, restricting the range of options and choices more than is the case under the U.S. techno-governance structure.

The U.S. technology-supporting system also allows large-sized companies to concentrate most of their resources on applied research for products close to the market, and the rest on small but key areas of basic research. Networks expose them to diverse technological areas, and joint projects with universities and national research institutes drastically cut the costs and risks of technology development. Consequently, the U.S. system also helps each semiconductor company to improve its cash-flow position, makes it more attractive to the stock market, and strengthens its competitiveness in the globalized market.

The U.S. techno-governance structure is a mixture of the traditional U.S. market orientation and elements transferred from the Japanese-type techno-governance structure. The latter aspect may be the reason why the U.S. techno-governance structure operates in part on principles and by means very similar to those of the Japanese structure. Both structures promote market competition, information dissemination, and creativity stimulation as indispensable conditions for advancing technological capabilities and industrial transformation. To achieve these ends, the U.S. structure uses such means as cooperative learning and effective networking.

Despite these similarities in principles and means, each country has experienced drastically different outcomes in behavior and performance because of the restrictions of path-dependently developed institutions. To generate mutual understanding and the sharing of disseminated information requires shared information-coding and -decoding capability. Such sharing can be most effectively achieved by relying on institutionally inherited behavioral patterns or practices, since technology is partly an embodiment of knowledge in people influenced by diverse social backgrounds, including culture and history. In the

Japanese case, a tradition of cooperation provided fertile ground for cultivating and sharing coding and decoding capability and stimulated industrial transformation and the building of technological capability. Cooperative learning affords partners a much deeper and richer exchange of information, cultivates a strong sense of mutual trust, and enables them to stimulate better performances in one another.

Until the 1980s, many state-of-the-art processes in Japanese semiconductor technology were mastered at an experimental level, not a scientific one, requiring complex expertise and craftsman-type experience in R&D and production. Cooperative learning between Japanese semiconductor and equipment manufacturers allowed them to develop and share this complex know-how quickly and intensively. The need for craftsman-type know-how also allowed companies to differentiate their products, making full use of their vertical cooperative relations.

As shown in Table 2.1, such relations were effective because partners interacted on the basis of relation-specific norms with particular skills in negotiation and less tolerance for constructive conflicts. These relations dynamically evolved within their own specific confines. Such involution, however, was also the source of certain problems—on the one hand creating an asymmetric flow of technological information between cooperating and noncooperating companies and preventing the entry of new ventures with fresh ideas and new technologies, and on the other hand locking partners into a relation-specific technological path. As a solution to these problems, the Japanese government and TSOs used cooperative projects to create networks for disseminating diverse technologies and multiple perspectives, fusing diverse ideas to prevent technological lock-in and stimulating new ideas as well.

However, even the cooperatives that formed among competing semiconductor companies suffered from vertical splits, making it necessary to develop several groups of competing companies grouped according to their past friendly relations and to divide equipment manufacturers on the basis of the tight vertical collaborative relations already in place between these manufacturers and specific semiconductor companies. To preserve harmonious relations in such a situation, the administrators had to be more cooperation-promoting and -enhancing than competition-stimulating. They had to employ a comprehensive approach with vaguely specified principles rather than a targeted approach with a specific set of principles, and to make evaluations more process-focused through budgetary auditing rather than output-focused through competition-triggering performance evaluations.

These characteristics of the old Japanese techno-governance structure were not necessarily negative vis-à-vis the development of DRAM technology, since dynamic vertical inter-firm cooperation was a key to advancing the technological and productive capabilities of semiconductor manufacturers, and since their relations were highly sustainable, based as they were on a strong sense of trust and commitment. Techno-governance based on Japanese path-dependent institutions created a favorable environment for DRAM development.

Table 2.1 Difference of Practices in Old Japanese and New U.S. Techno-Governance Structures

Characteristics	Japan	U.S.
(1) Cooperative Learning	More rigid, human- and vertical-relations oriented; more sustainable and normative	More open, functional, and interest-matching; less sustainable and more standardization oriented
(2) Incentives for cooperation	Intermediate	Strong
(3) Flexibility in the form of cooperation	More limited and rigid	More open, diverse, virtual, and evolving
(4) Negotiations	Interpersonal and relation-specific; less conflict and individual initiative tolerating	More open with universally applicable and logical reasoning; constructive conflict and individual initiative tolerating
(5) Linkages	Vertical split	Horizontal and vertical mixed
(6) Administrative coordination	Comprehensive approach with some vaguely specified principles	Specifically targeted approach with specific set of principles
(7) Supervision by the government and evaluation	Auditing and budgetary control; academic evaluation	Performance and professional evaluation
(8) Nature of research	Applied and pragmatic-target-based research	Applied and basic research, taking both pragmatic-target-based and knowledge-stock-based approaches, even targeting paradigm shifts
(9) Political coordination in semiconductor technology development	Coordination between MITI and industrial associations	Coordination among industrial associations, government administration, and Congress
(10) Technology transfer from universities to companies	Lack of infrastructure	Universities' patent ownership of government-funded projects and transfer to companies, especially small (venture) firms
(11) Universities' silicon-based semiconductor research capability	Weak; no capability building	Capability building by SRC, SEMATECH, and NSF
(12) National strategic coordination	Very weak	National technology road maps for semiconductors; division of labor, interface, and joint research on diverse levels and areas
(13) Systematic research structure	Very weak	Three layers, targeted at 1–2 years, 3–5 years, and 7–10 years ahead
(14) Research for promoting paradigm shifts and radical innovations	Only as part of government's general programs	Specific programs for semiconductor technology development
(15) Awareness of needs for international cooperation	Very weak and no strategy	Strong and highly strategic
(16) Use of internationally available resources	Very weak	Strategic
(17) Goals of techno-governance structure	Company-needs oriented; key technology capability building	Continuous, systematic, strategic technology capability building; favorable arrangement for companies to survive under globalization

Such techno-governance, however, was not conducive to the advance of the system LSI, which incorporates diverse devices and systems in one chip. SEMATECH's focus on the system LSI actually arose from its difficulty in achieving consensus among well-established semiconductor companies. To accommodate their disparate areas of specialization and system-design needs, SEMATECH found it necessary to develop next-generation manufacturing equipment with a more advanced CMOS process capability than Japan's, as well as a more complex system-design capability applicable to such diverse devices as microprocessors, DSPs, and logic. To achieve such a difficult goal and to regain its world leadership position in process technology, the U.S. government needed to develop a highly effective techno-governance structure following principles and means similar to those of Japan. This support system, with characteristics quite different from the support provided to market-oriented venture firms, catered more to the needs of large-sized companies, something for which SEMATECH was often criticized.

Despite similarities in the principles and means used to develop their respective techno-governance structures, the U.S. system clearly shows different characteristics from Japan's. The former involves (1) cooperation that is more open, flexible, functional, constructive-conflict tolerating, individual-initiative encouraging, and interest matching; (2) a strategic approach to developing future targets with standards and road maps; (3) heavier and more effective use of universities; (4) the introduction of strict performance-oriented evaluation; and (5) systematically developed capability and knowledge stock, covering a wide range of technologies and different future-target levels (1 to 2 years, 3 to 5 years, and 7 to 10 years ahead), including international alliances to strengthen areas of U.S. weakness.

To accommodate the diverse interests and needs of semiconductor manufacturers, SEMATECH had to develop cooperation both horizontally and vertically, engage in highly professional management to succeed with such complex coordination, and support its own and the manufacturers' activities with logical, scientific, and universally applicable reasoning. Developing standards and road maps while accommodating companies' complementary positions proved useful in establishing a base for cooperation and provided means for cutting each company's R&D costs. Moreover, as the U.S. techno-governance structure evolved with the dual rationales of defense and national industrial competitiveness building, an increasing number of government agencies, national research laboratories, universities, and companies gradually began to cooperate and share technologies. Standards, road maps, and political coordination also functioned to systematize a large number of R&D activities as well as to promote cooperation, to develop highly effective networks among the actors, and to prevent redundancies.

Standards and road maps were effective for domestic coordination, but to be internationally competitive, they had to be internationally dominant. Standardization also posed the hazard of technological lock-in, allowing other countries the opportunity to set targets beyond or outside the established path. To reduce such risks, ISEMATECH was established to strategically transform national technological road maps into international road maps, and to promote cooperation with other countries not only to strengthen weak U.S. areas, but also to keep other countries' technological developments on a similar technological path.

Regulations for CRADAs and LLCs made cooperation with diverse technology-related actors sufficiently attractive and beneficial to companies. Their open and flexible nature further stimulated the development of new types of cooperative activities, such as the systematized division of labor between SEMATECH and Sandia National Laboratories, as well as virtual centers for pooling scattered resources.

Although the SIA had to initially nurture the semiconductor research capability of U.S. universities, they became key centers for conducting both applied and basic research, training researchers, stocking technological know-how, and disseminating information. The universities turned craftsman-type semiconductor technology into universally applicable principles and science, providing a necessary foundation for standardization, software controls, and complex systems of cooperation. Through numerous joint programs, universities collaborated with companies, consortia, and national research institutes and played a vital role in openly disseminating technological information, stimulating a diversity of approaches, and preventing technological lock-in. They helped to solve the problems of asymmetric information flow and lock-in, although these problems were not as acute as problems found in Japan because of the open nature of learning among scientists and engineers in U.S. universities. The new U.S. techno-governance structure accommodated the diversity that was so necessary for developing system LSI capability and became dynamic, well-systematized, and well-structured. Despite this success, those same institutionally inherited American characteristics of market-oriented openness and flexibility also clearly resulted in weakening the sustainability, intensity of cooperation, synergetic effects, and possibly even the trust and commitment necessary for sustained and effective cooperative relations. Governmental policies and funding remain a key force in solving these problems and sustaining such cooperative relations. The U.S. system of cooperation requires different logic and supports from the Japanese system, primarily because of differences in the two countries' institutionally inherited behavioral patterns and practices—in other words, because of the path-dependent nature of institutional development.

While the U.S. techno-governance structure was being built up, Japanese companies were withdrawing from their relations with TSOs in silicon-related areas. Because of the Japanese universities' weak capabilities in basic research, TSOs were forced to engage in basic R&D, thus failing to respond to companies' needs in silicon-related applied research. Because of its privatization, Japan's leading innovator in semiconductor technology, NTTPC, withdrew from DRAM research activities and technology transfer. To make the situation worse, the U.S.–Japan trade disputes forced the Japanese government to withdraw all its support from silicon-related projects, which rendered national research institutes incapable of conducting costly silicon-based semiconductor research. Japanese semiconductor companies had to withdraw their macro-level strategies with the government and TSOs in silicon-related areas. The old Japanese techno-governance structure disintegrated, leaving semiconductor manufacturers vulnerable to path-disturbing conditions without a proper macro-level support system for cooperative learning and technology sharing. Finally, the withdrawal by semiconductor manufacturers from micro-level strategies involving joint development with equipment manufacturers decisively destroyed the old source of Japanese industrial dynamics based on vertical relations. An inadequate venture-firm orientation failed to provide semiconductor manufacturers with urgently needed options and choices in new technologies and business models. In short, the decline of the Japanese semiconductor industry is largely due to path-dependent institutional restrictions, while the disintegrating techno-governance structure lost its ability to either warn of or prepare for possible changes.

Cooperative learning and a dual economic structure of large- and small-sized firms have now become indispensable elements of global semiconductor development, as the U.S. techno-governance structure demonstrates. Ironically, these concepts are very familiar in Japan, and were even at one time sources of Japanese strength. In the past, the Japanese sense of cooperation strongly emphasized intensive vertical relations with little value attributed to market-oriented flexibility; this emphasis functioned well enough in sustaining dynamics on a predictable and fixed path. However, a period of rapid technological change, short product cycles, and high R&D costs and risks requires a less "sticky" mode of cooperation with more openness and flexibility.

How can we develop a new mode of cooperative learning that mixes openness, flexibility, and fluidity with sustainability and persistence? This is a key question that must be answered if Japan is to build a more effective techno-governance structure. Within an organization, an ambidextrous structure mixes and balances incremental innovation demands with discontinuous innovation requirements and combines paradoxical goals with integrated corporate goals (Tushman et al., 1997). The coexistence of heterogeneous systems within a techno-governance structure seems to be a possible answer. Different modes of systems can be introduced: one having a stronger orientation toward persistence and sustainability, and the other having more flexibility, openness, and fluidity, with both tied together by unifying goals. This dual structure can also be developed in two different modes: one for large-sized semiconductor manufacturers who must maintain and sustain leading semiconductor technologies and production, and the other for small-sized firms and start-ups. The latter organizations operate in a highly open and flexible way with diverse technological approaches, organizational forms, and business models in the more fluid environment of the market, creating options and choices for future potential changes in an industry. Existing small-sized firms need to be less averse to risk and more entrepreneurial, making full use of local networks as seen with the venture firms in Kyoto, while start-ups may also develop their own culture of cooperation as seen in Silicon Valley.[83] These organizations may also maintain some open and flexible but power-symmetric cooperative relations with large-sized firms.

Cooperative values in an open, flexible mode may need to be more egalitarian, constructive-conflict tolerating, individual-initiative encouraging, and less structurally restricted. Such relations may have to be substantiated by constant and rigorous professional technical evaluation, actual performance, entrepreneurial risk-taking attitudes, and the acceptance of diverse ways of interaction differentiated by goals and means. Even so, the traditional and institutionally inherited Japanese practices of cooperation with a strong sense of creative contribution, trust, commitment, and fulfillment of mutual expectations may still remain a key to promoting dynamic cooperative learning, though the meaning of cooperation needs to be transformed to accommodate a new phase of industrial development. Such complex characteristics may be realized through interactions among a large number of heterogeneous, small-sized, independent, and decentralized—but still collaborative and well-networked—organizations.

The path-dependent nature of institutions can become a hindrance to such developments. Companies, however, can try to change adverse institutional environments by effectively mixing micro- and macro-strategies and by forcing existing institutions to change in such a way as to better deal with path-disturbing conditions. Since the mid-1990s, Japan's government, companies, universities, and national research institutes have in fact been implementing diverse micro- and macro-strategies to cope with path-disturbing conditions. What, then, are the characteristics of this new Japanese techno-governance structure? Do they fit well with the new conditions of the market? Do they encourage the openness and flexibility in organizational environments that are necessary for system LSI development? How are path-dependent institutions contributing to or restricting these new developments? These questions are addressed in the next chapter.

Notes

1 In 1988, NEC, Toshiba, and Hitachi held the top 3 positions in the world semiconductor market in terms of sales, and 6 Japanese companies were among the top 10 (Okada, 2000: 79).

2 Information from managers at Sony, Hitachi, and Fujitsu Laboratories in Japan and Philips Semiconductors in the European Union (EU).

3 Information from managers at Sony, Hitachi, and Fujitsu Laboratories.

4 Information from a manager at NEC.

5 Information from a manager at Fujimi, a Japanese company specializing in the field.

6 Information from managers at NEC, Fujitsu Laboratories, Sony, and the Electro-Technical Laboratory (ETL) of the Ministry of International Trade and Industry (MITI).

7 The negative influence of this shock was strongly emphasized by managers at Mitsubishi, Fujitsu Laboratories, and Sony.

8 In the 1970s and early 1980s, Intel used the N-channel MOS (NMOS) for microprocessors, static random access memory (SRAM), and dynamic random access memory (DRAM), and the P-channel MOS (PMOS) was used for calculators. This fact suggests the superior performance of NMOS because it was used for more-sophisticated devices (information from a manager at Hitachi).

9 Information from managers at NEC, Hitachi, and Fujitsu Laboratories.

10 Managers at Hitachi, Sony, Tokyo Electron, and Philips Semiconductors strongly em-

phasized the importance of this factor.

[11] Information from a manager at NEC.

[12] For example, according to an NEC manager, a Taiwan circuit board maker developed a special interface to connect microprocessors, DRAMs, and other elements together on a board and started demanding changes in specifications from Intel and other major semiconductor producers.

[13] The Electro-Technical Laboratory (ETL, Denkishikenjo) of the Ministry of Communication (Teishinsho) was established in 1891 and was split into the Telecommunication Research Institute (TRI, Denkitsushin Kenkyusho) of the Ministry of Communication and the Electro-Technical Laboratory of the Ministry of Commerce and Industry (Shokosho) in 1948. The latter ministry became the Ministry of International Trade and Industry (MITI) and merged with the Trading Agency in 1949 (Johnson, 1982). The Denkishikenjo (ETL) was renamed the Denshi Gijutsu Sogo Kenkyusho in 1970, with its English name remaining the same, and was merged in April 2001 with 14 other laboratories to form the Sangyo Gijutsu Sogo Kenkyusho (National Institute of Advanced Industrial Science and Technology, AIST) (Okada, 2000; http://www.etl.go.jp/jp/gen-info/history/index.html).

[14] The Telecommunication Research Institute (TRI) of the Ministry of Communication (Teishinsho) came under the Ministry of Telecommunications (Denkitsushinsho) when the Ministry of Communication was split into the Ministry of Posts (Yuseisho) and the Ministry of Telecommunications in 1949. When Nippon Telegraph and Telephone Public Corporation (NTTPC) was established in 1952, TRI became a part of NTTPC and the Ministry of Telecommunications dissolved, transferring its telecommunications policy functions to the Ministry of Posts and Telecommunications (Yuseisho). With NTTPC's privatization in 1985, TRI also became a private entity (Okada, 2000; http://www.japanpost.jp/top/psa/).

[15] The World Bank survey covered the auto parts, foundry, polymer, textile, textile machine, and machine tool industries (Okada, 1999).

[16] A vertical *keiretsu* is a structure based on power-asymmetric inter-firm relations in which large-sized companies on the one hand and small- and medium-sized companies on the other closely cooperate with one another in business activities. A horizontal *keiretsu* is a structure based on power-symmetric inter-firm relations in which loosely affiliated large-sized companies of diverse complementary backgrounds cooperate with one another in business activities.

[17] Mitsubishi Electric also had some ties with Nikon Machine, JOEL, and Nihon Kagaku; Matsushita similarly did with JOEL (Stowsky, 1989: 251). But their relations were not as tight as those in other *keiretsu* groups.

[18] For example, NEC was in the horizontal *keiretsu* group of Sumitomo and had about 200 affiliates of its own in the early 1990s. Hitachi was in the horizontal *keiretsu* groups of Fuyo, Sanwa, and Daiichi-Kangyo and had about 800 subsidiaries, and Fujitsu was with the Daiichi Kangyo Group, Toshiba with the Mitsui Group, and Mitsubishi with the Mitsubishi Group (Ohsono, 1995; Gerlach, 1989). Matsushita did not belong to any *keiretsu* group, but it had more than 300 affiliates of its own (Ohsono, 1995).

[19] Another good example of disseminating technology to a wider body of companies is seen in the foundry industry of the early 1950s. The national government helped disseminate foundry technology, previously monopolized by leading companies, to as many small firms as possible through industrial associations. A few industrial associations became exclusive licensors of foreign foundry technologies and made highly advanced technology available to small firms at manageable costs (Kojima and Okada, 1997).

[20] MITI designated more than 400 locations, such as Kawaguchi and Kuwana as a foun-

dry *sanchi* and Tokamachi as a silk-weaving *sanchi*.

[21] For the beginning and ending dates of the VLSI Cooperative, see http://sangyo.kkc.or.jp/scripts/kkc_id/chrono_g.asp?kc_id=662 and http://unit.aist.go.jp/collab/ci/coordinator/jitanews0209.pdf.

[22] In 1981, the Semiconductor Industrial Association (SIA) hired Alan Wolff, the former deputy to the United States Trade Representative in the Carter Administration, and lobbied policy makers to the effect that the U.S.'s declining market share had been caused by unfair Japanese trade practices. The Reagan Administration accepted the complaint and in 1982 formed a U.S.-Japan high-technology working group to discuss the issue (Cortell, 1997).

[23] In 1990, the SRC consisted of 28 members, 4 associate members including 2 national laboratories under the Department of Energy (DOE), 26 affiliate members, and 7 U.S. government representatives including the Army, Navy, Air Force, Department of Commerce (DOC), and National Science Foundation (NSF). The U.S. government directly provided about 14% of the SRC research budget through SEMATECH in the same year (Gover, 1993).

[24] From 1984 until the end of 1995, a total of 575 consortia were registered under the National Cooperative Research Act (NCRA) in a variety of industries (Ham et al., 1998).

[25] The Semiconductor Equipment and Materials Institute was established in 1970 in the U.S. and was renamed Semiconductor Equipment and Materials International in 1987 when it became a partner organization to SEMATECH. Information from Semiconductor Equipment and Materials International Japan.

[26] To develop a Center of Excellence in contamination/defect assessment and control in the manufacture of semiconductors, the University of Arizona-Tucson closely cooperated with Sandia National Laboratories (under the Department of Energy); in metrology, Stanford University and the University of New Mexico-Albuquerque cooperated with Sandia National Laboratories; and in multilevel metals, the State University of New York-Albany, Rensselaer Polytechnic Institute, Colorado State University, and the University of North Texas-Denton cooperated with the National Institute of Standards and Technology (NIST, under the Department of Commerce) and Sandia National Laboratories. These universities cooperated with government agencies or national research institutes through cooperative research and development agreements (CRADAs) (Handotai Sangyo Kenkyusho, 1995).

[27] Of 511 Engineering Research Centers in existence in 1991, 56% (284) were developed from 1980 to 1990, and 86% were receiving funds from state or federal governments, covering about half their budgets. (Information is based on research conducted in 1991 by the Carnegie Mellon University Center for Economic Development, quoted in Tekuno Risachi Kenkyusho, 2000).

[28] Some of the Science and Technology Centers related to the semiconductor industry were the Center for Quantized Electronic Structures at the University of California-Santa Barbara; the Center for Parallel Computation at Rice University, California Institute of Technology, Argonne National Laboratory, and Los Alamos National Laboratory; and the Center for Discrete Mathematics and Theoretical Computer Science at Rutgers University (Handotai Sangyo Kenkyusho, 1995).

[29] Laboratories under NIST are the Electronics and Electrical Engineering Laboratory (EEEL), the Information Technology Laboratory, the Materials Science and Engineering Laboratory, the Physics Laboratory, the Manufacturing Engineering Laboratory, the Chemical Science and Technology Laboratory, and the Building and Fire Research Laboratory. Information from http://www.nist.gov/public_affairs/labs2.html.

[30] http://www.sandia.gov/history.htm

[31] http://www.sandia.gov/about.htm and http://www.sandia.gov/solution.htm

[32] Each state has its own regulations on limited liability companies (LLCs). For example, in the State of California, LLCs are regulated by the Beverly-Killee Limited Liability Company Act of 1994 (Kikai Shinko Kyokai Keizai Kenkyusho, 1999).

[33] Photolithography has advanced, making use of shorter wavelengths from g-line (436 nm) through i-line (365 nm) to KrF (248 nm), ArF (193 nm), F2 (157 nm), Ar2 (126 nm), Ne2 (80 nm), and extreme ultraviolet (EUV, 11.8 nm or 13.5 nm). Information is from a manager at Nikon.

[34] Information from a manager at Nikon.

[35] Information from a manager at Tokyo Electron.

[36] The Microelectronic Manufacturing Infrastructure (MMI) Project is aimed at developing equipment, materials, design tools, measurement and testing, and manufacturing processes for chip production, packaging, and board mounting.

[37] See http://www.asml.com/.

[38] Information from a manager at Nikon.

[39] Some of the organizations involved are IBM, the Oregon Graduate Institute, and the University of Texas.

[40] The University of California-Berkeley cooperates with nine universities: Stanford, MIT, Carnegie Mellon, Princeton, Michigan State, and four campuses of the University of California. The Georgia Institute of Technology cooperates with four universities: Stanford, Cornell, State University of New York-Albany, and Rensselaer Polytechnic Institute (Tekuno Risachi Kenkyusho, 2000).

[41] Information from Semiconductor Leading Edge Technologies, Inc. (SELETE).

[42] The top 6 semiconductor manufacturers of the present 10 SEMATECH members are IBM, Lucent Technologies, Intel, TI, Motorola, and AMD (Kikai Shinko Kyokai Keizai Kenkyusho, 1997).

[43] For example, some of the fabless and chipless companies lacking production facilities and engaged only in design are Cirrus Logic, S3, C-Cube Microsystems, and Sierra Semiconductor (Nihon Denshi Kikai Kogyokai, 1999). Two Taiwanese companies, TSMC and UMC, now dominate the foundry business of semiconductor production.

[44] Samsung announced the experimental development of the 256 megabit (Mb) DRAM in 1994 and the 1 gigabit (Gb) DRAM in 1996.

[45] Sample production of the 64 Mb DRAM was led by NEC in 1993, earlier than Korean companies (Press Journal, 1994).

[46] Information from a manager at ETL of MITI.

[47] Information from a manager at ETL.

[48] Information from an individual unrelated to this company and case.

[49] See http://nikkei.co.jp/sp2/nt20/20011017eini202717.html.

[50] Managers from NTT and Tokyo Electron made similar comments.

[51] Information from managers at Toshiba, Sumitomo Electric Industries, Thine Electronics, and SAMCO International.

[52] Information from a manager at the Venture System LSI Assist Center (VSAC) of the Japan Electronics and Information Technology Association (JEITA).

[53] Information from a manager at the Joint Research Center for Atom Technology (JRCAT).

[54] Information from a manager at NTT.

[55] Information from a manager at ETL.

[56] This comment from a manager at Sony.
[57] Information from a manager at Rohm.
[58] Information from a manager at NEC.
[59] Information from a manager at Seiko Instruments.
[60] Information from a manager at NEC.
[61] Information from a manager at ETL.
[62] Regional research institutes were also criticized for their lack of creative research capability, old facilities, and passive attitudes in solving client problems (Kikai Shinko Kyokai Keizai Kenkyusho, 2000).
[63] Information from a manager at NTT.
[64] Information from a manager at NTT.
[65] See http://www.hannan-u.ac.jp/~ida/2002sotsuron/kondou.pdf.
[66] Information from a manager at ETL.
[67] Information from a manager at ETL.
[68] Information from a pamphlet of the R&D Association for Future Electron Devices (FED).
[69] In 1986, the Metal Oxide Semiconductor Implementation System (MOSIS) was also opened to small- and medium-sized firms (Handotai Sangyo Kenkyusho, 1995).
[70] Information from a professor at the VLSI Design and Education Center, University of Tokyo.
[71] Information from a manager at the Super Silicon Crystal Research Institute (SSi).
[72] Information from managers at MegaChips and Thine Electronics.
[73] Information from managers at Thine Electronics and SAMCO International.
[74] Information from a manager at Rohm.
[75] Information from a manager at Thine Electronics.
[76] Information from managers at Technos and SAMCO International.
[77] Information from a manager at Tohken.
[78] Information from a manager at SAMCO International.
[79] Information from managers at Fujimi and Mitsubishi Materials.
[80] Information from a manager at the Semiconductor Industry Research Institute Japan (SIRIJ).
[81] Information from managers at NEC, Ando Electric, and Hitachi.
[82] Information from a manager at Ando Electric.
[83] Information from a manager at Rohm.

Bibliography

Abernathy, W.J.; Clark, K.B.; and Kanrow, A.M. (1983) Industrial Renaissance. Basic Books, New York.

Angel, D.P. (1990) "New firm formation in the semiconductor industry: Elements of a flexible manufacturing system." Regional Studies 24(3): 211–221.

Arthur, W.B. (1989) "Competing technologies, increasing returns, and lock-in by historical events." Economic Journal 99: 116–31.

Asanuma, B. (1985) "The organization of parts purchases in the Japanese automotive industry." Japanese Economic Studies (Summer): 32–53.

——— (1989) "Manufacturer-supplier relationships in Japan and the concept of relation-specific skill." Journal of the Japanese and International Economies 3: 1–30.

Beyer, J.M. and Browning, L.D. (1999) "Transforming an industry in crisis: Charisma, routinization, and supportive cultural leadership." Leadership Quarterly 10(3): 483–520.

Bloch, E. (1983) "SRC—The semiconductor industry draws on university resources." IEEE Spectrum 20(11): 56–57.

Bolton, M.K.; Malmrose, R.; and Ouchi, W.G. (1994) "The organization of innovation in the United States and Japan: Neoclassical and relational contracting." Journal of Management Studies 31(5): 653–679.

Browning, L.D.; Beyer, J.M.; and Shelter, J.C. (1995) "Building cooperation in a competitive industry: SEMATECH and the semiconductor industry." Academy of Management Journal 38(1): 113–151.

Chon, S. (1997) "Destroying the myth of vertical integration in the Japanese electronics industry: Restructuring in the semiconductor manufacturing equipment industry." Regional Studies 31(1): 25–39.

Chusho Kigyo Cho Gijutsuka (Small and Medium Enterprise Agency Technology Section) (1993) *Gijutsu no Suketto Kosetsushi* (Technology Helper *Kosetsushi*). Doyukan, Tokyo.

Cortell, A.P. (1997) "Centralization, access, and influence: The Reagan Administration and the semiconductor industry's trade complaints." Governance: an International Journal of Policy and Administration 10(3): 261–285.

Davidow, W. (1996) "The deconstruction of the semiconductor industry." Forbes ASAP (26 February): 70.

Denpa Shinbunsha (Denpa Publications) (1996, 1997) *Denshi Kogyo Nenkan* (Yearbook of Electronics Industry). Denpa Shinbunsha, Tokyo.

Electronic News (1989a) "Hear IBM offers DRAM group 4M chip; DRAM production consortium U.S. Memories Inc." 5 June, p. 1.

——— (1989b) "TI, Motorola, Micron will remain outside new group; outside of U.S. Memories Inc." 26 June, p. 58.

Feigenbaum, E.A. and McCorduck, P. (1984) The Fifth Generation: Artificial Intelligence and Japan's Computer Challenge to the World. Pan Books, London.

Florida, R. and Kenney, M. (1990) "High-technology restructuring in the U.S.A. and Japan." Environment and Planning A 22(2): 233–252.

Fong, G.R. (1998) "Follower at the frontier: International competition and Japanese industrial policy." International Studies Quarterly 42: 339–366.

Fransman, M. (1990) The Market and Beyond: Cooperation and Competition in Information Technology Development in the Japanese System. Cambridge University Press, Cambridge, UK.

Freeman, C. (1987) Technology Policy and Economic Performance: Lessons from Japan. Pinter Publishers, New York.

Fuji Sogo Kenkyusho (Fuji Research Institute Corporation) (1997a) "*Waga kuni handotai meka no aratana senryaku tenkai* (New strategic developments by Japanese semiconductor makers)." March. Fuji Sogo Kenkyusho, Tokyo.

——— (1997b) "*Waga kuni handotai seizo sochi sangyo no doko* (Trends in the Japanese semiconductor manufacturing equipment industry)." May. Fuji Sogo Kenkyusho, Tokyo.

Gerlach, M. (1989) "*Keiretsu* organization in the Japanese economy: Analysis and trade implications." In: Johnson, C.; Tyson, L.D.; and Zysman, J. (Eds.) Politics and Productivity: The Real Story of Why Japan Works. Ballinger Publishing Company, New York, pp. 141–174.

Gibson, D.E. and Rogers, E.M. (1994) R&D Collaboration on Trial: The Microelectronics and Computer Technology Corporation. Harvard Business School Press, Cambridge, MA.

Goto, A. (1993) *Nihon no Gijutsu Kakushin to Sangyo Soshiki* (Japanese Technological Innovation and Industrial Organization). University of Tokyo Press, Tokyo.

Gover, J.E. (1993) "Analysis of U.S. semiconductor collaboration." IEEE Transactions on Engineering Management 40(2): 104–113.

Ham, R.M.; Linden, G.; and Appleyard, M.M. (1998) "The evolving role of semiconductor consortia in the United States and Japan." California Management Review 41(1): 137–163.

Handotai Sangyo Kenkyusho (Semiconductor Industry Research Institute Japan) (1995) "*Handotai sangyo: Sozoteki kenkyukaihatsu e no chosen* (Semiconductor industry: Challenge toward creative research and development)." Nihon Denshi Kikai Kogyokai, Tokyo.

——— (1996) "*21 seiki ni muketa handotai gijutsu kiban no kochiku: Handotai sentan tekunorojizu no setsuritsu no teian* (Constructing the semiconductor technology foundation for the 21st century: Proposal for Semiconductor Leading Edge Technologies (SELETE)." Nihon Denshi Kikai Kogyokai, Tokyo.

——— (1998) "*LSI sekkeiryoku kyoka ni muketa kyodo katsudo no teigen* (Proposal for cooperative activities for strengthening LSI design capability)." Handotai Sangyo Kenkyusho, Tokyo.

——— (1999) "*ATLAS purojekuto no chosa kenkyu hokokusho* (Research report of the ATLAS project)." Handotai Sangyo Kenkyusho, Tokyo.

——— (2000) "*Teigensho: Nihon handotai sangyo no fukkatsu* (Proposal: Revival of the Japanese semiconductor industry)." Shinseiki Iinkai (Semiconductor in New Century Committee). March. Handotai Sangyo Kenkyusho, Tokyo.

Herbig, P.A. and Palumbo, F.A. (1996) "Innovation—Japanese style." Industrial Management & Data Systems 96(5): 11–20.

Hobday, M. (1994) "The limits of Silicon Valley: A critique of network theory." Technology Analysis & Strategic Management 6(2): 231–244.

Imai, M. (1986) *Kaizen* (Improvements). Random House Business Division, New York.

Inoue, M. (1985) "Competition and cooperation among Japanese corporations." In: Thurow, L.C. (Ed.) The Management Challenge: Japanese View. MIT Press, Cambridge, MA, pp. 139–159.

Irwin, D.A. and Klenow, P.J. (1996) "High-tech R&D subsidies: Estimating the effects of SEMATECH." Journal of International Economics 40: 323–344.

Johnson. C. (1982) MITI and the Japanese Miracle. Stanford University Press, Stanford, CA.

Kagaku Gijutsucho Kagaku Gijutsu Seisaku Kenkyusho (National Institute of Science and Technology Policy, Agency of Science and Technology) (1998) "*Daigaku nado karano gijutsu iten seiko jirei karano akuta bunseki* (Actor-based analysis of successful cases of technology transfer from universities)." Discussion Paper No. 6. Kagaku Gijutsucho Kagaku Gijutsu Seisaku Kenkyusho, Tokyo.

Kagaku Gijutsu Seisakushi Kenkyukai (Study Group on the History of Science and Technology Policy) (1990) *Nihon no Kagaku Gijutsu Seisaku shi* (History of Japanese Science and Technology Policy). Mito Kagaku Gijutsu Kyokai, Tokyo.

Kikai Shinko Kyokai Keizai Kenkyusho (The Economic Research Institute of the Japan Society for the Promotion of Machine Industry) (1997) "*Tenkan semarareru nichi bei ou sangyo gijutsu kyoryoku seisaku* (Challenges for transforming industrial technology cooperation among the U.S., EU and Japan)." Kikai Shinko Kyokai Keizai Kenkyusho, Tokyo.

——— (1999) "*Risogurafi taikei tenkanzen no handotai seizosochi gijutsu ni okeru hashi watashi kiki—handotai to seizo sochi no sangyo kyosoryoku ni hitsuyo na kohokiban no torikumi* (Transformation crisis in semiconductor production equipment technology, facing changes in lithography technology: Attempts to develop a support system for strengthening the semiconductor and semiconductor equipment industries)." Kikai Shinko Kyokai Keizai Kenkyusho, Tokyo.

——— (2000) "*Chusho seizogyo ni okeru sangakukan renkei katsudo no jittai to kadai: Chusho seizogyo shiengata sangakukan no jitsugen ni mukete* (Facts and problems about coordinated activities among governments, universities, and small- and medium-sized manufacturers: Toward the promotion of company-university-government alliances to support small- and medium-sized manufacturers)." Kikai Shinko Kyokai Keizai Kenkyusho, Tokyo.

Kikai Shinko Kyokai Keizai Kenkyusho and Nihon Apuraido Risachi Kenkyusho (The Economic Research Institute of the Japan Society for the Promotion of Machine Industry and the Japan Applied Research Institute) (1994) "*Kikai sangyo no gijutsu kyosoryoku no nichi ou bei hikaku ni kansuru chosa kenkyu* (Comparative research on U.S.-EU-Japan technological competitiveness in the machinery industry)." February. Kikaishinko Kyokai Keizai Kenkyusho and Nihon Apuraido Risachi Kenkyusho, Tokyo.

Kodama, F. (1991) *Haiteku Gijutsu no Paradaimu* (Paradigm in High Technology). Chuo Koronsha, Tokyo.

Kojima, S. and Okada, Y. (1997) "Catching up to leadership: The role of technology-support institutions in Japan's casting sector." World Bank Technical Paper No. 384. The World Bank, Washington, DC.

Langlois, R.N. and Steinmueller, W.E. (2000) "Strategy and circumstance: The response of American firms to Japanese competition in semiconductors, 1980–1995." Strategic Management Journal 21 (10–11): 1163–1173.

Link, A.N.; Teece, D.J; and Finan, W.F. (1996) "Estimating the benefits from collaboration: The case of SEMATECH." Review of Industrial Organization (11): 737–751.

Los Angeles Times (1989) "Struggle seen for new chip venture." 23 June, p. 1.

Lundvall, B-A. (1988) "Innovation as an interactive process: From user-producer interaction to the national system of innovation." In: Dosi, G.; Freeman, C.; Nelson, R.; Silverberg, G.; and Soete, L. (Eds.) Technical Change and Economic Theory. Pinter Publishers, London, pp. 349–369.

Lundvall, B-A. (Ed.) (1992) "Introduction." In: National Systems of Innovation: Toward a Theory of Innovation and Interactive Learning. Pinter Publishers, London, pp. 1–19.

Macher, J.T.; Mowery, D.C.; and Hodges, D.A. (1998) "Reversal of fortune? The recovery of the U.S. semiconductor industry." California Management Review 41(1): 107–136.

Maeda, Y. (1999) "Textile industry." In: Okada, Y. (Ed.) Japan's Industrial Technology Development: The Role of Cooperative Learning and Institutions. Springer-Verlag, Tokyo, pp. 177–198.

Matsushige, K. (1998) "*Jisedai no sangyo sosei kyoiku to sangaku renkei kenkyu shisutemu no arikata ni kansuru chosa kenkyu* (Survey research on ideal forms in education for next-generation-industry creation and an industry-university cooperative research system)." Kyoto University, Kyoto.

Metcalf, J.S. (1998) Evolutionary Economics and Creative Destruction. Routledge, London.

Mitsubishi Sogo Kenkyusho (Mitsubishi Research Institute) (1995) "*Wagakuni ni okeru kenkyu kaihatsu katsudo no genjo oyobi shorai tenbo ni kansuru kiso kenkyu* (Research on current conditions and future prospects of R&D activities in Japan)." Kikai Shinko Kyokai Keizai Kenkyusho, Tokyo.

Nelson, R.R. and Winter, S.G. (1977) "In search of useful theory of innovation." Research Policy 6: 36–76.

Nihon Boeki Shinkokai (Japan External Trade Organization) (1998) "*Beikoku seifu no kenkyu kaihatsu soshiki ni okeru gyosei kaikaku oyobi sono jiko hyoka ni kansuru chosa* (Research on administrative reform of U.S. federal government's R&D organizations and their self-evaluation)." Kikai Shinko Kyokai Keizai Kenkyusho, Tokyo.

Nihon Denshi Kikai Kogyokai (Electronic Industries Association of Japan) (1999) "*Handotai shin jigyo keitai ni kansuru chosa kenkyu hokoku* (Research report on the new semiconductor business model)." Report by Handotai Iinkai, Handotai Shinjigyo Keitai Chosa Kenkyukai (Semiconductor Committee, New Semiconductor Business Model Survey Research Group). Nihon Denshi Kikai Kogyokai, Tokyo.

Nihon Denshi Kogyo Shinko Kyokai (Japan Electronic Industry Development Association) (1988) *Denshi Kogyo Shinko 30 nen no Ayumi* (Thirty-Year History of Electronics Industry Development). Nihon Denshi Kogyo Shinko Kyokai, Tokyo.

——— (1996) "*Beikoku seifu dyuaru-yusu gijutsu kaihatsu purojekuto to kokuritsu kenkyusho no yakuwari: Handotai o chushin to shite* (U.S. government's dual-use technology development projects and roles of national research institutes: Focusing on the semiconductor)." Kikai Shinko Kyokai Keizai Kenkyusho, Tokyo.

Nihon Keizai Shinbun (Nihon Economic Newspaper) (1990) "*64M DRAM shisaku seiko* (Success in the experimental development of the 64M DRAM)." 8 June.

Nikkei BP Sha (Nikkei Business Publications) (1998) *Denshi Kogyo 50 Nenshi* (Fifty Years of the Electronics Industry). Nihon Denshi Kikai Kogyokai, Tokyo.

Nishimura, Y. (1996) *Handotai Sangyo no Yukue* (Future Directions in the Development of the Semiconductor Industry). Maruzen Publishing Co., Tokyo.

Ohsono, T. (1995) Charting Japanese Industry. Cassell plc, London.

OhUallachain, B. (1997) "Restructuring the American semiconductor industry: Vertical integration of design houses and wafer fabricators." Annals of the Association of American Geographers 87(2): 217–237.

Okada, Y. (1989a) "Technological development and growth of Japanese integrated circuit firms: An exploratory study." Working Paper at the Center for Japan-U.S. Relations, International University of Japan, Niigata, Japan.

——— (1989b) "*Nichibei handotai sangyo ni okeru shakai keizai tosei kozo no hikaku* (Comparison of socio-economic coordination structures in the Japanese and U.S. semiconductor industries)." In: Marumo, A. (Ed.) *Kawariyuku Nihon no Sangyo Kozo* (The Changing Japanese Industrial Structure). The Japan Times, Tokyo, pp. 52–98.

——— (1990) "*Nichibei handotai sangyo ni okeru gabanansu kozo no hikaku I & II* (Comparison of governance structures in the Japanese and U.S. semiconductor industries I & II)." *Sekai Keizai Hyoron* (Journal of World Economic Review) (March): 40–53 and (April): 59–65.

——— (1993) "Institutional arrangements and the Japanese competitive-*cum*-cooperative system of production." Paper presented at a conference on the Comparative Market Economies Project held at St. John's College, Cambridge University, 23–26 September.

——— (1995) "Interactive learning and technological development in Japan." Paper submitted to the World Bank for the Policy and Institutional Priorities for Industrial Technology Development Project.

——— (Ed.) (1999) Japan's Industrial Technology Development: Role of Cooperative Learning and Institutions. Springer-Verlag, Tokyo.

——— (2000) Competitive-*cum*-Cooperative Interfirm Relations and Dynamics in the Japanese Semiconductor Industry. Springer-Verlag, Tokyo.

——— (2001) "Cooperative learning and Japan's techno-governance structure: Exploratory case studies." Sophia International Review 23: 19–42.

Okimoto, D. (1989) Between MITI and the Market: Japanese Industrial Policy for High Technology. Stanford University Press, Stanford, CA.

Press Journal (1993–1999) *Nihon Handotai Nenkan* (Japan Semiconductor Yearbook). Press Journal, Tokyo.

Randazzese, L.P. (1996) "Exploring university-industry technology transfer of CAD technology." IEEE Transactions on Engineering Management 43(4): 393–401.

Rea, D.G.; Brooks, H.; Burger, R.M.; and LaScale, R. (1997) "The semiconductor industry—Model for industry/university/government cooperation." Research Technology Management 40(4): 46–54.

Saito, F. (2000) *"Kenkyu" to "Kaihatsu" o Kangaeru* (Thoughts on Research and Development). NEC Creative, Tokyo.

Saxenian, A. (1991) "The origins and dynamics of production networks in Silicon Valley." Research Policy 20(5): 423–437.

Saxonhouse, G.R. (1986) "Industrial policy and factor markets: Biotechnology in Japan and the United States." In: Patrick, H. (Ed.) Japan's High Technology Industries. University of Washington Press, Seattle, pp. 97–136.

Shimura, Y. (1995) *Handotai Sangyo Shin Jidai* (New Age of the Semiconductor Industry). Nihon Noritsu Kyokai Management Center, Tokyo.

Sigurdson, J. and Anderson, A.M. (1991) Science and Technology in Japan. Longman Group UK, Ltd., Essex, UK.

Spencer, W.J. and Grindley, P. (1993) "SEMATECH after five years: High-technology consortia and U.S. competitiveness." California Management Review 35(4): 9–32.

Stowsky, J.S. (1989) "Weak links, strong bonds: U.S.-Japanese competition in semiconductor production equipment." In: Johnson, C.; Tyson, L.D.; and Zysman, J. (Eds.) Politics and Productivity: The Real Story of Why Japan Works. Ballinger Publishing Company, New York, pp. 241–274.

Tarui, Y. (2000) *Nihon Handotai 50 Nenshi: Jidai o Tsukutta 537 Nin no Shogen* (Fifty-Year History of the Semiconductor in Japan: Testimony of 537 People Who Made the History). Sangyo Times and Handotai Sangyo Shinbun, Tokyo.

Tekuno Risachi Kenkyusho (2000) "*Wagakuni no sangyo gijutsu doko ni kansuru chosa kenkyu* (Survey research on recent movements in Japanese industrial technology development)." Kikai Shinko Kyokai Keizai Kenkyusho, Tokyo.

Toray Keiei Kenkyusho (Toray Management Research Institute) (1997) "*Kenkyu kaihatsu shisutemu no seibi ni kansuru kiso chosa: Kenkyu shien taisei no saikochiku ni mukete* (Basic survey on reorganizing the research and development system: Rebuilding technology supporting institutions)." Kikai Shinko Kyokai Keizai Kenkyusho, Tokyo.

Tushman, M.L.; Anderson, P.; and O'Reilly, C. (1997) "Technology cycles, innovation streams, and ambidextrous organizations: Organization renewal through innovation streams and strategic change." In: Tushman, M.L. and Anderson, P. (Eds.) Managing Strategic Innovation and Change: A Collection of Readings. Oxford University Press, New York, pp. 3–23.

von Hippel, E.A. (1994) "Sticky information and the locus of problem solving: Implications for innovation." Management Science 40: 429–439.

Washington Post (1989) "Future of joint chip venture now in doubt." 10 November, p. 1.

Watanabe, S. (1999) "Polymer industry." In: Okada, Y. (Ed.) Japan's Industrial Technology Development: The Role of Cooperative Learning and Institutions. Springer-Verlag, Tokyo, pp. 133–176.

West, J. (2000) "Institutions, information processing, and organization structure in research and development: Evidence from the semiconductor industry." Research Policy 29: 349–373.

Web Pages

http://nikkei.co.jp/sp2/nt20/20011017eini202717.html

http://sangyo.kkc.or.jp/scripts/kkc_id/chrono_g.asp?kc_id=662

http://unit.aist.go.jp/collab/ci/coordinator/jitanews0209.pdf

http://www.etl.go.jp/jp/gen-info/history/index.html

http://www.hannan-u.ac.jp/~ida/2002sotsuron/kondou.pdf

http://www.japanpost.jp/top/psa/

http://www.nist.gov/public_affairs/labs2.html

http://www.sandia.gov/about.htm and http://www.sandia.gov/solution.htm

http://www.sandia.gov/history.htm

Chapter 3

Institutional Changes and Corporate Strategies for Survival in the Japanese Semiconductor Industry

Yoshitaka Okada
Sophia University

1 Introduction

Japan has developed its business system by making heavy use of its inherited traditions (Whitley, 1992). Instead of simple-mindedly focusing on such neoclassical concepts as profit, price, cost, and quantity to achieve allocating or accounting efficiency, Japanese companies and the government have strongly emphasized non-allocative or production efficiency, promoting worker participation, long-term relations, cooperative learning, and capability building[1] (Leibenstein, 1987; Dore, 1987; Porter, 1990; Ettlinger, 1991). Institutional arrangements[2] and various systems were developed to enhance this Japanese heritage, especially by promoting cooperation among economic actors and orchestrating harmonies in industrial, inter-firm and government-business relations, which consequently functioned well to achieve an effective mix of allocative and non-allocative efficiency (Abegglen, 1958; Dore, 1973, 1986; Aoki, 1984; Iwata, 1977; Tsuda, 1984; Imai, 1988a, 1988b; Johnson, 1982; Kitschelt, 1991).

This system of production was quite helpful in advancing the R&D and production capabilities of Japanese semiconductor companies, the main product of which was the dynamic random access memory (DRAM). On the one hand, lifetime employment, worker participation and commitment, and harmonious labor-management relations created a favorable environment for accumulating craftsman-type skills and for promoting dynamic interactions and cooperative learning among researchers, engineers, and workers. On the other hand, long-term inter-firm relations, especially between semiconductor and equipment manufacturers, involving a strong sense of trust and commitment to the continuity of relations, created a similar environment for improving production capability, jointly developing leading-edge equipment, and achieving a higher yield rate of semiconductors. It was their craftsman-type improvement of advanced basic technologies in lithography and etching that enabled Japanese companies to overcome competition in the global market in the 1980s (Okada, 2000). Consequently, Japan achieved the world's largest share of the semiconductor market, about 14% higher than that of the U.S. in 1988 (about 51% for Japan vs. about 37% for the U.S.) (Okada, 1989, 2000).

Japanese shares of foreign markets, however, began to gradually decline from 1989, long before Japan's own economic bubble burst in 1992.[3] Several forces contributed to a major structural transformation of the world semiconductor industry in the 1990s: (1) the capacity of the semiconductor to house voluminous information on a small chip weakened demand for the expansion of memory capacity[4] (Handotai Sangyo Kenkyusho, 2000); (2) Korean semiconductor manufacturers began to dominate the high-end market, such as the 256 megabit (Mb) DRAM market;[5] (3) Micron Technology in the U.S. started occupying the low-end market, such as the 64 Mb DRAM, with lower prices and smaller size;[6] (4) technological leadership shifted from the DRAM in Japan to the system large-scale integrated circuit (system LSI, also often called system-on-a-chip) in the U.S., which includes such devices as memory, microprocessors, digital system processors, and other elements as parts of an integrated system;[7] and (5) the standardization of semiconductor production equipment, particularly led by Applied Materials in the U.S., enabled technologically less sophisticated engineers and companies to engage in semiconductor production, examples being United Microelectronics Corporation (UMC) and Taiwan Semiconductor Manufacturing Corporation (TSMC) (Nishimura, 1996; Fuji Sogo Kenkyusho, 1997a, 1997b). (For an analysis of the Japanese decline, see Chapter 2.)

The above factors suggest that the centers of semiconductor industry dynamics and technological advancement have shifted from Japan to the U.S., Korea, and Taiwan, and that long-term relations based on craftsman-type improvements and technological advances are no longer a factor in product differentiation and international competitiveness. The Japanese heritage institutionalized in the old techno-governance structure is no longer a force for enhancing competitiveness in the market. How, then, do Japanese semiconductor manufacturers cope with this difficult situation? How does the institutionalized heritage of the old structure hinder or help companies in formulating their strategies for survival? These are the questions asked in this chapter.

To be more precise, based on the concepts of technology, institution, techno-governance structure, and corporate strategy developed in Chapter 1, I shall ask the following questions. How did the old techno-governance structure restrict and delay changes in the corporate strategies of Japanese semiconductor companies? What led to the disintegration of inter-firm relations under the old structure? What were the means used to create fluidity, flexibility, and decision making options in a company and to speed up the disintegration of intra-firm relations, including lifetime employment? What types of macro-level strategies in inter-firm and government-business relations were used, and with what consequences? What strategies were being employed to develop the missing vital factors for new industrial dynamics? What are the consequences of these struggles and the characteristics of the newly developed techno-governance structure? Does the new structure create openness and flexibility on the one hand, and generate persistence and sustainability on the other, as I have suggested in the conclusion of Chapter 2?

2 Decline of Market Share and Disintegration of the Old Techno-Governance Structure

2.1 Indecisive Dual Strategy and Withdrawal from All-Purpose DRAM Production

Japanese companies were slow to recognize changes in the international industrial structure and to adjust their corporate strategies accordingly. In the 1980s, the semiconductor sales of Japanese manufacturers grew an average of 15 % annually, and the amount invested in facilities was much larger than in any other country (see Fig. 3.1; Handotai Sangyo Kenkyusho, 2002: 26). In 1992, however, sales figures plunged by 12.4% from 1991 (Press Journal, 1993: 30), largely because of the loss of cost advantages vis-à-vis Korean companies who benefited from a depreciated won (Nihon Keizai Shinbun, 1993a). This negative growth in sales forced NEC and Toshiba to reduce their facility investments by 20% from 1991, Hitachi by 25%, Fujitsu by 57% and Mitsubishi by 44% (Press Journal, 1993: 33), putting them on a par with U.S. companies in the amount of investment but still above Asian companies (see Fig. 3.1).

Japanese companies then began emphasizing the importance of non-DRAM

Figure 3.1 Semiconductor Investment by Region

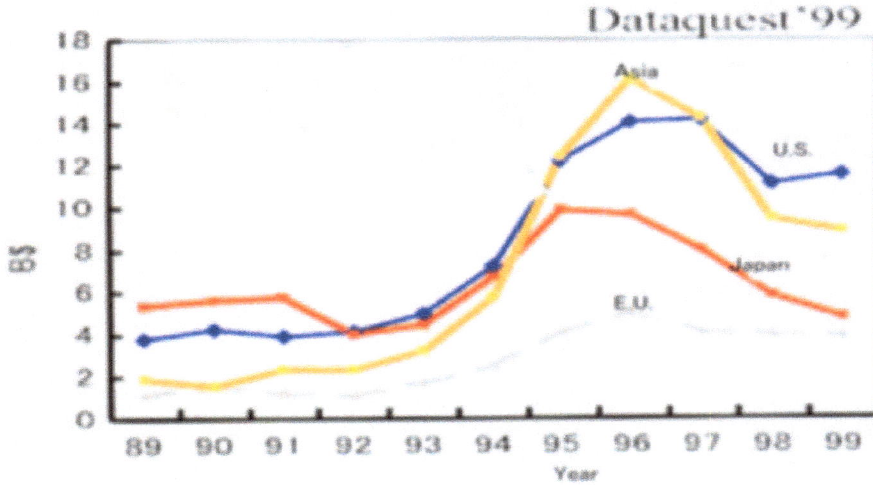

Source: Handotai Sangyo Kenkyusho (Semiconductor Industry Research Institute Japan) (2002) "SoC *bijinesu moderu no tenkai* (Development of business models for SoC)," Gijutsu Iinkai, ATLAS, June, Handotai Sangyo Kenkyusho, Tokyo, p. 26.

Table 3.1 Disintegration of the Old Techno-Governance Structure

Year	Withdrawal from all-purpose DRAM production	Layoffs	Termination of long-term inter-firm relations	Organizational reform
1985				Toshiba established a system LSI R&D section.
1990	NTT			
1992			NEC started to purchase equipment from companies outside of Japan.	NEC established the System LSI R&D Institute.
1993			Hitachi sold away ion implantation and stepper equipment sections.	NEC developed an IC with logic and memory combined. Hitachi announced its shift to system LSI. Sony concentrated system designers in the LSI Product Development Center.
1994				Sony introduced an in-house company system.
1995				Hitachi introduced a group system for more independent operations by each unit.
1996	Mitsubishi IBM Japan			NEC established the System LSI Divisional Headquarters.
1997	Nippon Steel Oki Electric			Matsushita introduced an in-house company system and strengthened its system LSI R&D capability. Toshiba established the Computer on Silicon Center.
1998		Toshiba and Hitachi announced the transfer of 6,000 and 4,000 workers, respectively, within two years.		Hitachi introduced an in-house company system, reorganized semiconductor production, and strengthened its system LSI design capability. Fujitsu shifted its main product focus from DRAM to the system LSI. Mitsubishi introduced system LSI strategies.

1999	Fujitsu Matsushita Hitachi NEC	NEC announced the reduction of 15,000 workers over the next three years. Hitachi announced the reduction of 6,500 workers. Mitsubishi announced the reduction of 14,500 workers within two years.	Hitachi sold a wafer production section to Shinetsu Chemical and a photomask production section to Dai Nippon Printing.	Toshiba introduced an in-house company system. Fujitsu concentrated on the system LSI and chemical compound ICs. Sony introduced an in-house network company system. Mitsubishi strengthened its system LSI capability. Matsushita dissolved Matsushita Electronics and concentrated resources in system LSI development within Matsushita.
2000		Toshiba announced the reduction of 9,000 workers.	NEC terminated relations with Ando Electric and Minato Electronics. NEC announced it would purchase equipment globally on a bidding basis. Toshiba announced it would reduce the number of long-term partners.	NEC introduced an in-house company system and set up a fund for M&A. Toshiba concentrated more engineers in research laboratories and centers under corporate headquarters to crosscut R&D over diverse in-house companies. Hitachi set up a fund for M&A. Mitsubishi led in multi-chip packaging technologies.
2001	Toshiba	Toshiba announced the reduction of 12,000 workers. Hitachi announced the reduction of 14,700 workers. Mitsubishi announced the reduction of 1,000 workers.		Sony reorganized in-house companies. Hitachi spun off its semiconductor equipment business. Mitsubishi spun off its information system business.
2002		NEC increased its planned reduction to 14,000 workers, from 4,000. Hitachi requested 4,000 voluntary retirees, resulting in 9,000 workers leaving. Mitsubishi announced the reduction of an additional 2,100 workers. Fujitsu announced the reduction of 21,000 workers.		Matsushita introduced an in-house company system and reorganized businesses into seven in-house companies. NEC spun off its semiconductor division as an independent company. Hitachi spun off its home appliance and industrial equipment businesses.

areas, the flash memory and the system LSI. Yet, still confident of their DRAM capability, they continued to struggle to recover their leadership in this area, though they were well aware of the risks of relying on the investment-heavy DRAM. To jointly develop the 256 Mb DRAM, for example, Toshiba contracted with IBM and Siemens in 1992; Hitachi with Texas Instruments (TI) in 1993; and NEC with AT&T in 1993 (Press Journal, 1994: 52) and Samsung in 1994 (Nihon Keizai Shinbun, 1994). In 1995 Toshiba contracted with IBM, Siemens, and Motorola to develop the 1 gigabit (Gb) DRAM (Nikkei Sangyo Shinbun, 1997a). Japanese companies pursued this dual-edged strategy because of their reluctance to give up the high-profit, high-risk DRAM business, but this only made any new strategy ineffective for recovery, given their heavy losses in the DRAM.

Meanwhile, Korean companies started taking the lead in DRAM production, while Micron Technology in the U.S. began selling DRAMs at much lower prices than the Japanese in 1995, a development referred to in Japan as the "Micron Shock." Then, to make matters worse for the Japanese companies, computer prices plunged in 1996, further suppressing 4 Mb and 16 Mb DRAM prices (Press Journal, 1997: 45). The Korean companies coped with such price movements by making risky large-volume investments to benefit from the economies of scale and reduced production costs, which further reduced DRAM prices on the market (Nihon Keizai Shinbun, 1995). The Japanese companies' indecisiveness finally caught up with them as they were forced to face serious consequences.

In 1996, most Japanese companies began withdrawing from all-purpose DRAM production, while they continued to produce high-value-added special-DRAM products. Mitsubishi decided to shift its domestic DRAM production to the U.S. and Germany in 1996, and even to withdraw from the U.S. in 1998. IBM Japan announced it would halt its Japanese DRAM production, other than high-value-added products, in 1996. Nippon Steel withdrew from DRAM production in 1997 and from the semiconductor business altogether in 1998. Oki Electric gave up building a new DRAM factory in 1997 and made the 128 Mb DRAM its last all-purpose product in 1998. Fujitsu stopped its European DRAM production in 1998 and domestic production in 1999. Matsushita halted DRAM production in 1998 and dissolved Matsushita Electronics in 1999 (Nihon Keizai Shinbun, 1996, 1998a, 1998b, 1999a; Nikkei Sangyo Shinbun, 1999). (Table 3.1 summarizes the movements of Japanese semiconductor companies that led to the disintegration of the old techno-governance structure.)

Although Toshiba was the only company that struggled to continue all-purpose DRAM production, in 1998 it had to dissolve the 1 Gb DRAM joint development project with Siemens and IBM that had begun in 1995, and instead tried to develop a DRAM joint venture with Infineon Technologies. The failure of these negotiations finally pushed Toshiba out of all-purpose DRAM production in 2001 (Nihon Keizai Shinbun, 2001a), even dissolving a Fujitsu–Toshiba 0.13 micron 1 Gb DRAM project that had started in 1998 (Press Journal, 2002: 176–177). In 1998 Hitachi sold the ownership of its U.S. joint venture to its partner, TI, dissolved its 1997 technical agreement for developing a 1 Gb DRAM with the same company, and concentrated its DRAM production in Singapore and Japan (Nihon Keizai Shinbun, 1999b). Even so, in 1999 difficulties in the DRAM business further pushed Hitachi to merge its DRAM division with NEC and jointly establish Elpida Memory, the only remaining Japanese all-purpose DRAM producer (Press Journal, 2000: 211–212). Old competitors found themselves compelled to cooperate for survival.

Consequently, the Japanese share of the world DRAM market dropped from 90% in the 1980s to 20% in 1998, and even the DRAM's share of total production within each company drastically declined from an average of 28% in 1995 to 11% in 1998 (Handotai Sangyo Kenkyusho, 2000). All Japanese semiconductor manufacturers, except one, withdrew from all-purpose DRAM production.

2.2 Disintegration of Lifetime Employment

Permanent employment, which fit well with the Japanese value orientations of harmony and commitment, had been one of the most important factors in keeping Japanese management effective. Its prevalence in practice gave it the weight of a social contract. Hence, instead of laying off employees, Japanese companies in financial difficulties would resort to reductions of salary, working hours, and days, or the temporary dispatch or permanent transfer of workers to other companies. Layoffs were considered the last resort when a company's survival was at stake.

The decline of semiconductor sales in 1992 was not damaging enough to alarm Japanese managers, but it triggered various efforts to cut operating costs. Hitachi cut the salaries of executives, postponed raises in the basic salaries of 9,000 managers, and dispatched 60 workers to Hino Motors (Nihon Keizai Shinbun, 1992a, 1992b). Fujitsu reduced its recruitment of university graduates to two-thirds of the 1991 level and stopped hiring directly from the labor market (Nikkei Sangyo Shinbun, 1992). NEC increased work by internally developing software previously subcontracted out and shifting production workers to sales (Nihon Keizai Shinbun, 1993b).

By 1993, however, the president of Toshiba was already citing the limitations of the aforementioned measures in reducing operating costs and the need for more drastic measures, such as withdrawing from, selecting, or concentrating on certain production areas, a type of restructuring that many Japanese companies had not experienced in the postwar period (Nihon Keizai Shinbun, 1993c). Despite their awareness of the situation, Japanese semiconductor companies sat on the fence and continued all-purpose DRAM production. This was partly because the decline of DRAM demand was not yet at a devastating level and partly because the big electronics companies had a strong concern for the welfare of their workers and were sensitive to the social contract of permanent employment. Even amid the later devastating drop in semiconductor sales in 1998 and subsequent worker layoffs, the presidents of Hitachi and NEC declared that it was a company's responsibility to maintain employment (Nihon Keizai Shinbun, 1998d; Nikkei Sangyo Shinbun, 1998a, 2001). These institutional concerns were a significant factor in decision making, causing a slow, delayed response to pressures to cut personnel costs (Nikkei Sangyo Shinbun, 1998d; Asahi Shinbun, 1998a).

However, the withdrawal of Japanese semiconductor companies from all-purpose DRAM production without an alternative product that could absorb surplus employees finally forced them to engage in drastic restructuring, resulting in layoffs of a large number of employees in their domestic and global operations and making them incapable of maintaining their commitment to the social contract of permanent employment. In 1998, Toshiba announced the transfer of 6,000 workers within two years, and Hitachi announced the transfer of 4,000 workers in a year to their group companies and 60 workers to Honda, with a temporary suspension of annual base-pay raises for managers (Asahi Shinbun, 1999a). Such practices were exercised and accepted in Japan as one of the companies' last resorts in the face of unfavorable market conditions. In contrast, NEC, Fujitsu, and Mitsubishi maintained their positions without employee reductions.

The market situation in 1999, however, further aggravated company positions, forcing NEC to reduce its workforce by 15,000 (9,000 within Japan) over the next three years, out of which about 6,000 were actual layoffs not covered by reduced hiring, early retirement, or dispatch to other companies (Nihon Keizai Shinbun, 1999c). And in 2002, the last year of this three-year reduction plan, a scheduled reduction of 4,000 had to be increased to 14,000 (8,000 in Japan) because of the closure and sale of production and sales facilities (Nihon Keizai Shinbun, 2002a; Asahi Shinbun, 2002a)[8].

For Toshiba, the two-year reduction of 6,000 employees did not improve its position after 1998, and in 2000 it had to announce 9,000 additional reductions within two years (Asahi Shinbun, 2000). Despite these measures, Toshiba had to once again announce a reduction in 2001 of 17,000 employees within Japan by eliminating 25 group companies (Nihon Keizai Shinbun, 2001b). It also told 12,000 workers to stay at home, paying them 90% of their basic salary (Asahi Shinbun, 2001a).

Hitachi announced a reduction of 6,500 employees in 1999 (Asahi Shinbun, 1999b) and 14,700 in 2001 (Asahi Shinbun, 2001b). But even this effort was not sufficient. Hitachi then requested 4,000 volunteers to take early retirement in 2002, resulting in 9,000 employees leaving the company (Nihon Keizai Shinbun, 2002b).

Similarly, in 1999 Mitsubishi announced a reduction of 14,500 employees within two years (8,400 in Japan, of which 3,000 were retirees, and 6,100 outside Japan) (Asahi Shinbun, 1999c), and additional reductions of 1,000 employees in 2001 and again 2002 (Press Journal, 2002: 174–175). Mitsubishi actually ended up laying off 2,100 employees in 2002 (Nikkei Sangyo Shinbun, 2002a). Fujitsu, which had been trying to avoid reducing its workforce within Japan, announced the reduction of 16,400 (11,400 outside Japan and 5,000 in Japan) in 2001 and another 4,600 employees later the same year (Asahi Shinbun, 2001d; Nihon Keizai Shinbun, 2001c).

The shock of the burst economic bubble in 1992, and even the industry's mass withdrawal from the DRAM market, initially did not spur any major change in employment practices. But since 1998, Japanese semiconductor manufacturers have been coping with their loss of market competitiveness by making employee reductions an annual event. As the experience of the Japanese semiconductor companies cited above suggests, frequent occurrences of employee reduction signaled the disintegration of lifetime employment and overall worker-oriented commitment, which had been a key component of the Japanese management system. Given the need for fluid, flexible, and open organizations to stimulate innovation and to generate new and internationally competitive products, this disintegration of core management practices functioned to create an environment offering more options for decision makers.

2.3 Disintegration of Long-Term Inter-Firm Relations with Equipment Manufacturers

The poor performances of Japanese companies in the mid-1990s further disintegrated one of the key dynamic elements of the Japanese semiconductor industry. Cooperative relations with parts and material suppliers remained as intensive as before, since maintaining strict standards, the traceability of products through computer coordination, quick detection of the causes of problems, and information exchange to reduce the cost of production was indispensable for quality maintenance, a high yield rate of semiconductors, and cost competitiveness.[9] By contrast, however, relations with equipment manufacturers disintegrated.

Since custom-made equipment requires testing on a semiconductor company's production line, it involves intensive exchanges of technology, information, and services; hence, for example, Applied Materials works closely with IBM and Intel (Chon, 1997).[10] However, when a partner cannot purchase a sufficiently large volume of equipment to cover a significant portion of development costs, its manufacturer has to sell new products to competitors of the partner. In the 1970s and 1980s, ample orders and contractual agreements enabled semiconductor companies to delay equipment manufacturers' sales to competitors by as much as one or two years (Okada, 2000). In the 1990s, newly developed equipment was sold to Taiwanese and Korean companies almost immediately or at the latest six months after development, in effect giving the technological expertise of Japanese semiconductor manufacturers away to their competitors.

Facing such a situation, Japanese semiconductor companies began to criticize their long-term relations with equipment manufacturers for creating a lax environment and failing to force the manufacturers to take self-initiative in technological advancement. Cooperative relations reduced pressures for improvement and innovation, spoiled *keiretsu* companies insofar as they themselves did not have to watch for changes in the market or take any self-initiative, and locked both the semiconductor companies and the *keiretsu* equipment manufacturers into relation-specific technological approaches. The *keiretsu* companies became extremely vulnerable, especially when a parent company faced financial restrictions and could not help them (Nikkei Sangyo Shinbun, 2000a, 2001). Inter-firm relations thus hemmed in the perspectives of both partners and spoiled them, with both sides failing to keep up with changes. These institutional restrictions were the very reason for the failure of the equipment manufacturers.

Hitachi withdrew from manufacturing high-voltage ion implantation equipment and steppers in 1993 (Nikkei Sangyo Shinbun, 1993a), spun its internal equipment production off into independent companies and sold it to other companies, and drastically reduced in-house or joint development. Hitachi sold its wafer production business to Shinetsu Chemical and its photomask production business to Dai Nippon Printing in 1999 (Press Journal, 2000). In 2000, NEC decided not to conduct joint equipment development anymore and instead to purchase equipment based on global competitive bidding. Consequently, NEC sold its share of Ando Electric stock to Yokogawa Electric, finding no need to continue owning a company that produced testing equipment. Its affiliate, Minato Electronics, was to merge with Ando Electric, but the failure of the merger also forced the former out of the tester business (Nikkei Sangyo Shinbun, 2000a). From the mid-1990s on, semiconductor companies increasingly withdrew from internal or joint equipment development, except for developing one or two key items of equipment—suggesting that, for the first time, even *keiretsu* companies had to face a severance of relations. The old Japanese-type inter-firm relations entrapped both semiconductor manufacturers and their *keiretsu* members on the DRAM technological path and made one of the key dynamics of the Japanese semiconductor industry obsolete.

The old techno-governance structure, less fluid and deeply embedded institutionally, thus limited the strategic choices of semiconductor companies to the pursuit of dual technological paths and the traditional personnel practices of temporary relief. The consequences were a delay in restructuring and poor market performance. Discontinuing old institutional practices became the only available means of survival, and companies began attributing their failures to the old techno-governance structure, thus providing the impetus for its disintegration.

3 Struggles for Survival

What products should Japanese companies produce in order to regain their competitiveness? What sort of corporate structure will enable them to cope with market changes and the pressures of globalization? How can they strengthen their technological capability? Is there any need for collective activities that will compensate for the weaker areas of that capability? These were questions frequently raised and discussed by companies in the mid-1990s. The first three concern companies' micro-level strategies, and the last question pertains to their macro-level strategies.

3.1 New Micro-Level Strategies

3.1.1 Semiconductor Companies' Initiatives

3.1.1.1 Shift to the System LSI (System on a Chip) and Organizational Restructuring

In the past, small differences in DRAM structure and in manufacturing skills and techniques produced differentiations among firms in semiconductor performance and silicon wafer yield. This Japanese firm-specific craftsman-type approach to manufacturing demanded constant improvements in in-house technological capability, supported by intensive cooperation with equipment manufacturers. The firm-specific approach allowed an initial mover into the market with a three-month lead time to enjoy market leadership and appurtenant advantages (Okada, 2000).[11]

To compete against Japan for technological leadership, U.S. semiconductor manufacturers took a contrasting approach in the 1980s. They developed a cooperative venture, the Semiconductor Manufacturing Technology (SEMATECH) consortium, and shared the costs and risks of developing next-generation equipment in cooperation with Semiconductor Equipment and Materials International (SEMI-) SEMATECH. This new attempt created a foundation for inter-firm cooperation as well as an open space for innovative business models. A standardization of semiconductor manufacturing equipment was quite acceptable to semiconductor companies, because each one was attempting to differentiate its products at the chip design and system levels rather than with the semiconductor device itself.[12] SEMATECH succeeded in standardizing semiconductor manufacturing equipment and cutting R&D costs drastically by spreading risks and costs among member companies, and, because of regained technological leadership in the complex LSI field, it put U.S. semiconductor companies in a stronger position in their respective markets vis-à-vis foreign, particularly Japanese, competitors (for details, see Chapter 2).

Now that integrated, standardized manufacturing equipment with software adjustment capability could produce high-quality, low-cost semiconductors, Japanese craftsman-type manufacturing became too costly and less competitive. Japanese companies needed to develop a new device and method of production to add value to their products. They focused on the fact that Japanese companies by themselves produced diverse devices, including DRAM, microprocessor, logic, DSP, and analog devices, while Korean (DRAM), U.S. (logic LSI), and EU (analog LSI) companies usually specialized in certain limited areas and devices. Japanese companies set as their strategic focus the development of the system LSI, which houses a combination of the aforementioned semiconductor devices on one chip. Such a device would maximize the use of the in-house capabilities of Japanese companies and still differentiate their products by developing the technology to integrate devices previously produced separately, since companies from different countries were not very likely to align in this manner to integrate their individual specialties in one product.

The following issues, however, remained problematic. (1) What types of system LSI should Japanese semiconductor companies produce?[13] (2) Would it be feasible costwise?[14] (3) Would Japanese companies prove capable of designing an entire system? With their focus shifting from "how to make" a DRAM to "what to make" with the system LSI,[15] many Japanese companies, other than those that had been producing consumer goods, continued to have difficulty figuring out "what to make."

Japanese companies had actually begun building up their system LSI capability early on. For example, in 1985 Toshiba established its LSI Technology Development Department, which conducted R&D on a microcomputer unit for a local area network (LAN) and the real-time operating system nucleus (TRON) (Nikkei Sangyo Shinbun, 1993b). In 1992 Fujitsu announced a regular chip combined with a Josephson device (Asahi Shinbun, 1993). In the same year, NEC announced it would augment its R&D on a system-on-silicon at the newly established Ultra Large-Scale Integrated Circuit (ULSI) System Development Institute and the ULSI Device Development Institute (Nikkei Sangyo Shinbun, 1994). In 1993, NEC announced a combined logic and memory chip as one of the first products for the system LSI. That same year, Sony also strengthened its design capability for the system-on-silicon at its Shinagawa LSI Product Development Center, while Matsushita established a research laboratory for the application-specific integrated circuit (ASIC) (Nikkei Sangyo Shinbun, 1995).

However, it was not until NEC's 1996 withdrawal from all-purpose DRAM production that it officially established a System LSI Divisional Headquarters, and in 1997 it developed a semiconductor combining DRAM and virtual channel memory. In 1996, Toshiba tried to do away with a vertically split R&D structure focusing on a specific device, such as the DRAM or microprocessor, by establishing an Advanced I Strategy (ADI) Divisional Headquarters[16] that would gather all related researchers for product development under one roof. In 1997, Toshiba also established a Computer-on-Silicon (COS) Development Center for strengthening research on the reduced instruction set computer (RISC) (Nikkei Sangyo Shinbun, 1997b). In 2000, it developed a system-on-a-chip (SoC) project team for mobile telephones at this center, with 80% of its researchers coming from research laboratories and centers under the corporate headquarters of Toshiba and 20% from research sections of "in-house" manufacturing companies, a ratio that had previously been 40% vs. 60%, respectively (Nihon Keizai Shinbun, 2000b). (The meaning of corporate headquarters and in-house companies will be clarified in the next section). Despite an early start on R&D, because of the dual strategy pursued by Japanese companies, their resource concentration on the system LSI lagged behind that of the U.S., particularly in the development of standardized production equipment for the complex LSI.

Mitsubishi quickly shifted its resources from memory to the development of ASICs and 32-bit RISC-type microprocessors in 1996 (Nikkei Sangyo Shinbun, 1996). Although it was well behind NEC and Toshiba in developing an organizational structure for the system LSI, Mitsubishi's embedded memory and system LSI strategies began generating some hit products in 1998. Because of its incremental R&D strategy for developing a system LSI, which led some companies to claim that Mitsubishi's products were not true system LSIs.[17] Mitsubishi emerged in 2000 as the world leader in embedded random access memory (eRAM) technology and packaging with a large number of pins (Nikkei Sangyo Shinbun, 2000b). Two other giants, Hitachi and Fujitsu, suffered from a lack of hit products, despite Hitachi's strong microprocessor tradition and its announcement of stronger research and product development for the system LSI in 1993 (Nikkei Sangyo Shinbun, 1993b) and Fujitsu's increased concentration on the chemical compound semiconductor (Nikkei Sangyo Shinbun, 1998b).

Difficulty in developing a true system LSI was understandable. The integration of all devices into a system LSI generated problems of increased production cost and lower yield,[18] though it functionally improved performance. Technological barriers remained high. Until a solution was found to these problems, a special mounting technology was used to place, for example, a DRAM on a logic LSI. Mitsubishi was successful in this respect with its embedded memory products.[19]

Another problem was system-design capability. For many years, hardly any educational or training courses on system design were available in Japan. As with the software industry, the Japanese were considered weak in abstract and systematic thinking. To make the problem more complex, some companies developed an organizational structure for designing a system LSI within a limited time, concurrently mobilizing about 1,000 people within and outside the company. Since this required the ability to coordinate a very large number of people not necessarily linked by hierarchical power positions or human relations, it became a new challenge for managers to organize system-design operations. A manager at Matsushita Electronics, which was dissolved in 1999 and then revived in 2000 as a semiconductor section focusing on the system LSI inside Matsushita Electric, expressed his fear that few Japanese were talented at such complex management tasks (Nihon Keizai Shinbun, 2000a).

The biggest problem still remaining was what to produce. It was predicted that the proportion of personal computer (PC)-related equipment[20] in the semiconductor market would decline from 50% in 1998 to about 30% in 2003, while the proportion of information technology (IT)-related equipment would increase from about 37% in 1998 to 65% in 2003 (Handotai Sangyo Kenkyusho, 2001: 2–8). IT-related equipment includes digital cellular telephones, smart cards, fax machines, portable compact discs (CDs), silicon audio, liquid crystal display (LCD) monitors, digital versatile discs (DVDs), digital TVs, routers, digital cordless telephones, local area network (LAN) switches, modems, screen telephones, car navigation devices, car audio systems, anti-lock brake systems, airbags, telephone switching systems, and personal digital assistants (PDAs). New devices, such as TV telephones, global positioning systems (GPS),[21] and Internet protocol telephones with Internet Protocol Version 6 (IPV6),[22] are expected to further boost system LSI demand (Handotai Sangyo Kenkyusho, 2001: 2–6; 2002; Jiyu Kokuminsha, 2002). Further infrastructure development will also take place, since the use of asymmetric digital subscriber lines (ADSL),[23] the Bluetooth protocol,[24] and the international mobile telecommunications (IMT2000) protocol[25] were predicted to start a rapid increase from 2003 to 2005 and glass fiber connections to houses (FTTH)[25] around 2010. The future, it is said, will be a "ubiquitous society" in which all equipment and household appliances are digitally connected and networked.

Preparing for such developments, NEC, Hitachi, Matsushita, Fujitsu, NTT,

ARM, and 16 other companies in 2002 established the T-Engine Forum to jointly develop the old Japanese TRON operating system for future digital home appliances (Nihon Keizai Shinbun, 2002c). The focus is clearly on the use of the system LSI in IT-related equipment. In a sense, the Japanese strategy is to target next- or even next-next-generation semiconductor technologies and future products.

3.1.1.2 New Alliances

Unfavorable market conditions did not wait for Japanese semiconductor companies to solve their product, organizational, and technological problems. The companies were forced to reduce payrolls and increase their organizational flexibility. Beginning in the mid-1990s, Sony (1994), Matsushita (1997), Hitachi (1998), and Toshiba (1999) introduced a new "in-house company" system for separate units within these corporations (hereafter referred to as parent companies), each with its own independent decision-making authority, personnel system, and cash-flow accounting, primarily with the objectives of cost efficiency and management flexibility (Nikkei Sangyo Shinbun, 1997c, 2000c; Nihon Keizai Shinbun, 1998e). An in-house company remains as a unit inside a parent company despite its organizational autonomy, while the controlling entity over an in-house company is usually referred to as the corporate headquarters.

Meanwhile, however, several revisions of Japan's Commerce Law led to the propagation of another organizational system, "the company separation system." The government revised the law to facilitate mergers and acquisitions (*gappei seido*) in 1997, stock exchanges and transfers (*kabushiki kokan/kabushiki iten seido*) in 1999, and the breaking up and spinning off of companies—known as the company separation system (*kaisha bunkatsu seido*)—in 2001. A spinoff company remains under the control of the parent company through stock ownership and representation on its board of directors. Technically, however, spinoff companies are no longer part of the original parent company, as opposed to in-house companies that exist within the parent company but operate semi-independently under the control of corporate headquarters.

Both the in-house company system and the company separation system created a basis for generating organizational flexibility (Nagase, 2004: 146–156).[27] Making use of these systems, Sony (1999, 2001), NEC (2000, 2002), Hitachi (2001, 2002), Mitsubishi (2001), and Matsushita (2002) divided their companies into several units, separating them organizationally and modularizing them by business focus and operations into in-house companies, some of which they later spun off as subsidiaries (*bunshaka*) for more efficient and independent financial performance through independent fund-raising, stock issues, investments, and other means (Nagase, 2004: 133–136; Yoshikawa, 2002: 2–42; Nihon Keizai Shinbun, 2001f, 2001g, 2002d; Nikkei Sangyo Shinbun, 2000d; Asahi Shinbun, 2001 f, 2002d). (For a history of these organizational structural changes, see Table 3.1).

The in-house company system and the company separation system modularized company operations and introduced more market-oriented relations among corporate headquarters, in-house companies under headquarters, and spun-off subsidiaries, creating a fluid situation within each corporation and providing organizational flexibility as well as fluidity.[28] Some of the units then separated under the company separation system were sold to, or formed joint ventures with, other companies, especially competitors, and some were retained inside the original group.

Such spinning off of in-house units in favor of the parent company did not, however, occur without some resistance from traditional institutions. It was feared that the company separation system could be easily abused for quick and unnecessary downsizing of the parent company, threatening the lifetime employment of its employees. In 2001 the government enacted the Labor Contract Succession Law, which requires that a parent company: (1) provide its labor union with details on existing labor contracts to be guaranteed in a newly spun-off company; (2) guarantee, in principle, the same labor contracts as with the parent company and such conditions as including the period of employment at the parent company in calculating paid holidays and retirement allowances; (3) not shift unrelated employees to the separated unit for the purpose of laying them off; and (4) allow the parent company union and the employees selected for transfer to object to unfair practices (Araki, 2005).[29] This law in principle tries to guarantee employees the continued practice of lifetime employment even in spun-off companies, though such guarantees may change when those companies are sold. Thus while the parent company was provided with greater fluidity and flexibility, it still remained under pressure to retain the institutional heritage of lifetime employment. This is one clear indication that some elements of traditional Japanese institutions were sustained and combined with the newly introduced market orientation, despite the contradictory nature of these elements relative to the new system.

The smaller size of the modularized and separated units, however, also reduced each unit's financial and technological capabilities, rendering them too weak to compete internationally, a condition that unexpectedly increased their mobility, creating opportunities for these units to be divested or merged with, acquired from, or aligned with other companies, especially competitors. Japanese companies' preferred partners were Japanese, partly because they often had problems with and did not gain much from the international alliances of the 1980s,[30] and partly because technologically they had become less attractive to foreign competitors.

In 1999, NEC and Hitachi established Elpida Memory, a 50–50 joint venture, to preserve production capability in the all-purpose DRAM area in Japan. Past successes in Japanese inter-firm cooperation usually involved a vertical relationship between a big producer and a small-sized supplier, with unequal power distribution and complementary specialization. This new alliance, however, involved two partners of equal power, both of whom boasted advanced technological capability as well as strong employee pride in and loyalty to their respective parent companies. Naturally, the alliance suffered from conflicts and difficulties in decision making regarding the location of factories within Hitachi or NEC, basic technologies, and the sales system. These conflicts delayed the planning and development of a competitive product (Daiyamondo, 2002). Finally, in 2002 the company decided to bring in a president from outside, hoping to resolve its internal conflicts. Here, within a new framework of horizontal cooperation, the old habits of vertical cooperation interfered with the decision making and daily operations of the joint venture. Again, this example indicates that the institutional persistence of old concepts of cooperation delayed decisive corporate action.

Sony, which had direct connections to the consumer market and placed less emphasis on semiconductor production and traditional long-term relations, was one of the most active companies to cooperate with other companies on the system LSI early on, as well as to switch partners quickly as alliance conditions changed. It aligned with Oki Electric in 1996 to develop a DRAM-embedded system LSI with a line width of 0.25 micron, and in 1998 with Fujitsu to develop and test an 0.18 micron DRAM-embedded system LSI (Nikkei Sangyo Shinbun, 1998c). But in 1999 Sony switched partners from Fujitsu to Toshiba to develop a 0.10 micron 128 Mb central processing unit (CPU) for the PlayStation II, establishing a joint venture with 51% owned by Toshiba (Press Journal, 1999). Then in 2001, Sony announced alliances with Toshiba and IBM to develop next-generation system LSI process technologies (Asahi Shinbun, 2002b) and with Toshiba to develop next-generation design technology (Asahi Shinbun, 2001c). New projects served as insurance for the future continuity of these alliances. In the liquid crystal display sector, Sony chose Samsung as a joint venture partner in 2003; this could result in the transfer of advanced technologies to one of its most threatening competitors in the market. Sony enhanced its semiconductor capability by carefully choosing the right partners for each period and for each product. In the past, the frequent switching of partners in this manner was not really an accepted practice of Japanese inter-firm relations. But amid the present semiconductor crisis, unstable inter-firm relations of this type became a common phenomenon.

Mitsubishi switched its system LSI partner from TI to Matsushita in 1998 (Asahi Shinbun, 1998b). This partnership successfully developed a hit product, an embedded system LSI, and advanced to the point of joint development in 1999 of 0.15–0.10 micron system LSI process technologies and of joint production in 2000 (Press Journal, 2000). Despite its success with Matsushita, which provided a direct link to consumers, Mitsubishi switched partners again, this time to Hitachi, with whom it merged its system LSI business and established a company called Renesas Technology (Asahi Shinbun, 2002c). The position of Matsushita is not clear, but some predict a very strong alliance among Hitachi, Mitsubishi, and Matsushita, since Hitachi and Matsushita also jointly developed home appliance digital network technologies and system LSIs, one of the key technologies of the "ubiquitous society" (Nihon Keizai Shinbun, 2001d).

Despite Fujitsu's loss in its battle with Toshiba to maintain an alliance with Sony, an old alliance with Toshiba to develop a 0.13 micron 1 Gb DRAM (1998–2001) facilitated a renewal of relations (Press Journal, 2002). In 2002, Fujitsu announced an alliance with Toshiba for system LSI development and production, and even suggested the possibility of integrating their system LSI businesses to compete against the Mitsubishi–Hitachi alliance. Meanwhile, NEC made its semiconductor division an independent company in 2002 (Nikkei Sangyo Shinbun, 2002b).

Hence, as shown in Fig. 3.2, the Japanese system LSI sector now has three key groups: Hitachi–Mitsubishi–Matsushita, Toshiba–Fujitsu–Sony, and NEC, though Matsushita's position in the alliance is not clearly defined. Unaligned NEC may affiliate with the Mitsubishi–Hitachi–Matsushita group, since Mitsubishi sold its high-value-added DRAM section to Elpida Memory in 2002 and since NEC and Mitsubishi merged their display businesses and established NEC Mitsubishi Visual Systems (Asahi Shinbun, 2003).

Such movements in the system LSI sector describe a clear picture of reformulation of the Japanese semiconductor industry, separating cooperators and competitors. The reality, however, as shown in Fig. 3.3, is far more complex than what is depicted in Fig. 3.2. And the predictions about Matsushita and NEC may be quite wrong if the movements depicted in Fig. 3.3 prove more predominant than the simple separation of cooperators and competitors shown in Fig. 3.2.

In 1998, Mitsubishi and Sharp agreed to collaborate on semiconductor standardization (Nihon Keizai Shinbun, 1998c). In 1999, Toshiba collaborated with Matsushita and San Disk to develop a flash memory (Nihon Keizai Shinbun, 1999d). In 2001, Toshiba and Matsushita together established Toshiba Matsushita Display Technology to jointly produce a liquid crystal display (Asahi Shinbun, 2001e), and in October 2004, Toshiba joined with Matsushita and Hitachi to establish IPS Alpha Technology for joint production of an IPS-system liquid crystal display.[31] In 2001, Toshiba integrated its satellite business with NEC and agreed to jointly produce a magnetic random access memory (MRAM) (Nikkei Sangyo Shinbun, 2002c); in 2002, it joined with Mitsubishi to develop a third-generation mobile telephone (Nikkei Sangyo Shinbun, 2002d) and establish an integrated transformer and electronic distribution business (Asahi Shinbun, 2001g). Meanwhile, NEC had already formed an alliance with Matsushita to develop a third-generation mobile telephone in 2001 (Nihon Keizai Shinbun, 2001e).

Hitachi also exhibited a penchant for complex inter-firm relations. It collaborated with Fujitsu and Sanyo on a joint venture for mobile telephone music delivery, competing against a Sony–Matsushita alliance; with NEC on DRAM production (Elpida Memory); with Mitsubishi on system LSIs (Renesas Technology); with IBM on hard disk drives; with Fujitsu on plasma digital displays (Fujitsu Hitachi Plasma Display); with Fuji Electric and Meidensha on power semiconductors; and with Toshiba in the nuclear fuel business (Asahi Shinbun, 2003; Daiyamondo, 2002; Nihon Keizai Shinbun, 1999e).

Independent decision making by each separated company, their weak financial and technological capabilities, and severe market pressures increased the mobility of the separated companies, introducing a fluid market-like environment within a group of companies and creating diverse ways for a parent com-

Figure 3.2 New Inter-Firm Alliances in the DRAM and System LSI Areas

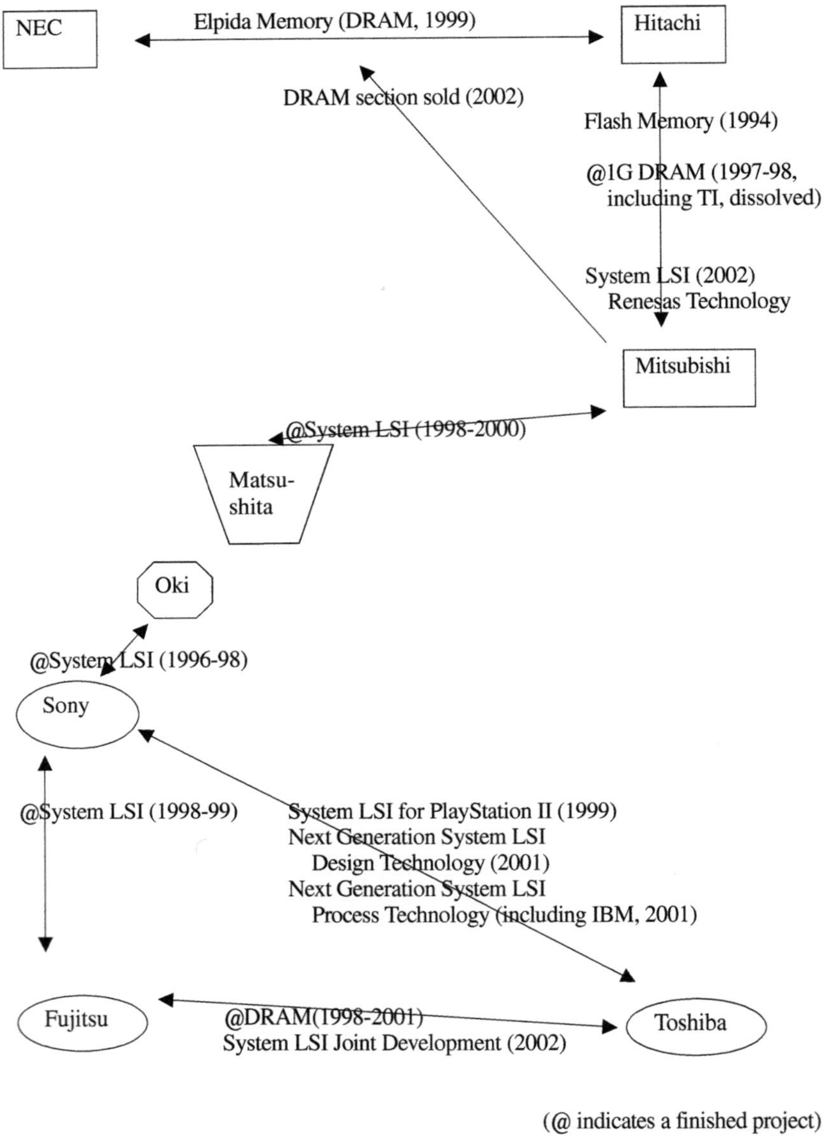

Figure 3.3 New Inter-Firm Alliances in Other Areas

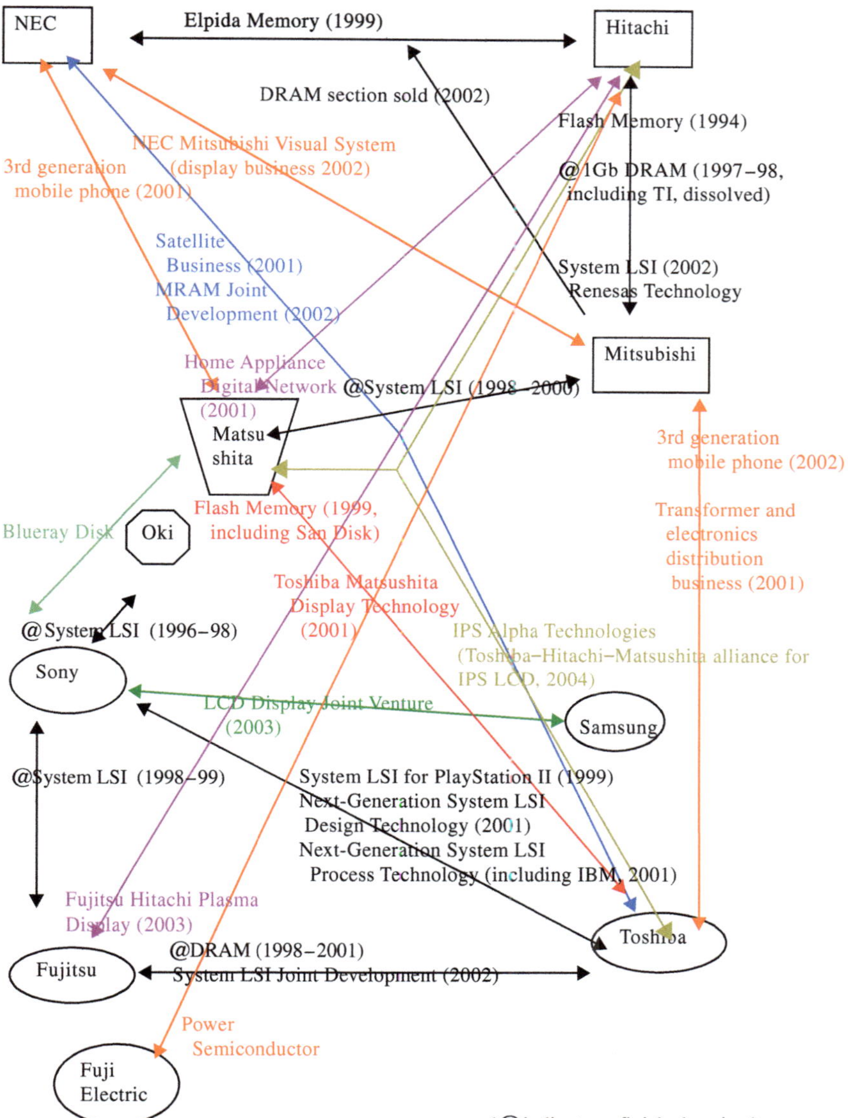

(@indicates a finished project)

pany to reorganize these modularized and separated companies. Market-oriented relations among the parent company, its in-house companies, and spun-off subsidiaries introduced fluidity in their relations and dramatically increased the decision-making options available to managers, allowing them to choose and preserve the seeds of next-generation technologies and to develop strategies for survival in highly competitive markets (Asahi Shinbun, 2003).

Alliances and joint ventures with diverse partners, including nearly all of a given company's competitors, resulted in the development of highly complex macro-level networks for cooperative relations, even suggesting the existence of a uniquely Japanese type of network that might be called a "loosely-networked circle." Such a phenomenon can occur only when network members share a common sense of harmony and cooperation, as these Japanese companies clearly do. This does not at all suggest the rebirth of "Japan Inc.," since intense product -level competition, which I call "modularized competition," exists among different networks and since the picture of collaboration is so complex and fluid that no clear separation between collaborators and competitors can be identified, at least not by generally known company names such as NEC, Hitachi, and Matsushita.

One set of companies competes with other networks of companies in certain product areas, while a different set of companies cooperates in certain other product areas. A company may be a cooperating partner in one product area and a competitor in another product area. This is quite different from the U.S., where the venture firm market itself functions to create a truly fluid situation for generating new ventures and creating options and choices for future development, and where cooperators and competitors are, in general, clearly separated. In Japan, however, market-like relations among separated company units introduced fluidity, while those units themselves started developing their own particular cooperative relations based on their needs and who they identified as their competitors. This survival strategy thus created a complex mixture of cooperation and competition among semiconductor companies. This mixture seems to be a newly evolving extension of Japanese competitive-*cum*-cooperative business behavior (Okada, 2000), which functions to preserve cooperation among a parent company, its in-house companies, and spun-off subsidiaries, as well as to maintain the legitimacy of lifetime employment by guaranteeing jobs for employees in severed units.

Inter-firm relations in the Japanese semiconductor industry are in a period of extreme flux, but one thing clear is that these changes are destroying the old way of thinking in inter-firm relations. Conflicts in some joint ventures such as Elpida Memory hint at a recognition of the limitations inherent in the traditional concept of cooperation. A search for more effective and rational forms of cooperation has begun, though at present the problems are more conspicuous than any successful examples of constructive rebuilding. Disintegration, decentralization, and market orientation are triggering changes, but cooperation unconstrained by traditional values is becoming one of the key strategies for survival. In this sense, the culture of cooperation persists in Japan, but it is evolving into a more complex network-like form.

3.2 New Macro-Level Strategic Initiatives

The culture of cooperation makes itself apparent in collective efforts to share costs and risks in developing next- and next-next-generation processing technologies. Just as the Very-Large-Scale Integrated Circuit (VLSI) Cooperative (1976–1979) had fostered technological advances that enabled Japanese semiconductor companies to become world leaders in technology, once again they resorted to collective undertakings to rebuild their capability. (For a summary of new consortia for macro-level strategies, see Table 3.2.)

3.2.1 Private-Firm Initiative for Collective Solutions

Facing difficult market conditions from the early 1990s, twelve semiconductor producers established a think tank, the Semiconductor Industry Research Institute Japan (SIRIJ), in 1994. Since then, SIRIJ has been conducting research on prospects for long-term technology development, international cooperation, social contributions by the semiconductor industry, and problems and needs associated with the development of future technologies and the revival of the industry. The organization has developed a variety of proposals and schemes for collective solutions.

According to a manager at SIRIJ, the establishment of this organization signified a big shift from the past, when the Japanese government had played a dominant leadership role. Under restrictive pressure from the U.S.–Japan trade disputes and expectations for a more limited role by governments in the era of globalization, the Japanese government adopted a rather negative attitude about subsidizing the semiconductor industry in the early 1990s. Disappointed by this lack of support,[32] semiconductor manufacturers established the SIRIJ without government help.

3.2.2 Private Consortia as Substitutes for Inter-Firm Cooperation in Equipment Development

Although cooperative relations between semiconductor and materials producers remained intact, the breakdown of intensive cooperation between semiconductor and equipment manufacturers, especially with small- and medium-sized companies, created a serious problem. Even though NEC stated its intention to buy the best equipment on the global market, the actual solution to this problem by the semiconductor industry in general was to establish a private-firm-based consortium that jointly designed standardized manufacturing processes and developed equipment. The reason the SIRIJ took the lead in developing such consortia was this. If there are to be continuing advances in semiconductor devices, it must be the semiconductor producers, not the equipment manufacturers, who take the lead in technological development and support the capability building of the equipment manufacturers. The solution—particularly when pre-competitive technology development is too costly, and insofar as it does not contribute to conflicts of interest among semiconductor manufacturers—is to develop technology

Table 3.2 New Consortia for Macro-Level Strategies

Name	Goals	Members and other information
A. Private consortia		
Semiconductor Industry Research Institute Japan (SIRIJ, established in 1994)	Think-tank, lobbying, long-term technology development, international cooperation, collective problem solving and needs identification, and reviving the semiconductor industry	12 (11 Japanese and 1 U.S.) semiconductor manufacturers Established by the initiative of the private sector, motivated by a lack of governmental support for the industry
Semiconductor Technology Academic Research Center (STARC, established in 1995)	To engage in contract research, technology dissemination, consulting, human resource development in the semiconductor industry, and semiconductor-research-and-design capability building in universities	11 Japanese semiconductor manufacturers Capitalization of ¥110 million obtained by pooling their donations to universities; with an annual budget of ¥3 billion Company-based research targets, conducted at universities with company researchers' guidance
Semiconductor Leading Edge Technologies, Inc. (SELETE, 1996–2000)	Cooperative evaluation and development of 300 mm-wafer-based semiconductor production equipment and materials in 250 nm and 180 nm line widths Basic research on 130 nm lithography and other processes	10 Japanese semiconductor manufacturers; with 170 employees Participation of Samsung as a contract research partner Capitalization of ¥5 billion with ¥10 billion annual budget Consortium with only private firms No inclusion of equipment manufacturers Similar to the multiple vendor system at Toyota and Nintendo Cooperation among semiconductor manufacturers and competition among equipment manufacturers For semiconductor manufacturers, the benefit of low cost; for equipment manufacturers, the benefit of a large number of customers via one competition
Advanced System-on-a-Chip through Collaborative Achievement Project (ASUKA, 2001–2005)	To develop 100 nm and 70 nm next-generation system-on-a-chip equipment for multiple-product and small-quantity operations Lithography, mask, and other process technologies Technology computer-aided design (TCAD)	11 Japanese semiconductor manufacturers Joint operation of STARC and SELETE (¥76 billion for five years, 340 researchers) Private firm consortium
B. Government subsidized consortia (Research cooperatives)		
Super Silicon Crystal Research Institute (SSi, 1996–2001)	To develop crystal growth technologies for 400 mm wafer, to be marketed around 2010	7 Japanese companies Reaction to SEMATECH's move Total budget was ¥13.3 billion, funded by the government (51.1%) and 7 Japanese companies (48.9%)
Association of Super-Advanced Electronics Technologies (ASET, 1996–2001)	To develop two-generations-ahead technology, especially lithography technology for 130 nm and 100 nm with multiple approaches	41 companies, including Intel, IBM, TI, and Samsung, involving 550 researchers (200 in the central laboratory and 350 at corporate laboratories) ¥51 billion for five years with about ¥2 billion from companies More open and cooperative than the VLSI Cooperative, but with good legal protection Trying to create global standards

Millennium Research for Advanced Information Technology (MIRAI, 2001–2007)	To develop 45–65 nm material and process technologies jointly with ASET and the Advanced Semiconductor Research Center (ASRC) of the National Institute of Advanced Industrial Science and Technology (AIST)	24 companies; 120 researchers in three central research laboratories Industry-government-university alliance ¥25.2 billion Tsukuba Super-Clean Room funded by the government Budget ¥3.480 billion in 2001, ¥4.310 billion in 2002, ¥4.364 billion in 2003
Highly Agile Line Concept Advancement (HALCA, 2001–2004)	To develop 130 nm system LSI production equipment and systems that are 60% energy efficient Multiple-product and small-lot production equipment with 1/10 of investment cost	11 semiconductor companies, one university and one national research institute Total government and private fund of ¥8 billion
Advanced System-on-a-Chip Platform Corp. (ASPLA, 2002–2004)	To develop standardized processing technology for the 90 nm next-generation semiconductor and to test new systems-on-a-chip	11 Japanese companies and 1 national research institute Capital of ¥1.85 billion provided by 10 companies Government fund of ¥31.5 billion for initial facility building Government initiative to overcome firm-specific technology, possibly promoting stronger alliance Research budget of ¥8.7 billion a year

collectively and inexpensively, and if possible to make it a part of the next-generation global standard to achieve economies of scale.

Learning from the experiences of SEMATECH in the United States, 11 Japanese semiconductor manufacturers, following a proposal submitted by SIRIJ, established a private-firm-based consortium, Semiconductor Leading Edge Technologies (SELETE) (1996–2000). SELETE developed semiconductor equipment and materials for 300 mm wafers; advanced lithography technology, encompassing argon fluoride (ArF) excimer laser lithography, advanced mask technology, and electron beam direct-writing lithography; technology computer-aided design (TCAD); and perfluoro compound (PFC) emission reduction technology. In 2000, SELETE had approximately 170 employees with an annual budget of 10 billion yen. Its 1999 annual report clearly states that its goal is inter-firm cooperation in pre-competitive areas where risks and uncertainties are high (Handotai Sentan Tekunorojizu, 1999). Given the disintegration of inter-firm cooperation in equipment development and the withdrawal of semiconductor producers from company-specific production processes, the development of standardized manufacturing equipment and materials does not interfere with competition among semiconductor companies.

Although a SELETE manager expressed hope that the consortium's results would become a global standard, a proposal for cooperation with the U.S. project I300I did not materialize, and only one foreign company, Samsung, joined as a research contractor. Samsung's participation did not help much in terms of generating a global standard, but the collective solution was still the only available recourse for Japanese semiconductor companies, other than purchasing U.S. and European equipment without developing their own technological capability.

The U.S. SEMATECH, which was the model for SELETE, established a consortium of equipment and materials manufacturers, SEMI-SEMATECH, as its partner. U.S. equipment manufacturers took a collective approach, responding to the demands of SEMATECH. By contrast, SELETE did not demand a collective approach from equipment manufacturers. Instead, it operated in a manner rather similar to Toyota's multiple vendor system or Nintendo's software development system, an approach more familiar to Japanese managers that makes use of competitive pressure among equipment manufacturers. SELETE provided basic specifications to any interested equipment manufacturers in every field, who then competed on the basis of development speed and quality. From the early stages of the competition, a group of engineers from the various participating semiconductor producers evaluated manufacturing equipment prototypes submitted by equipment manufacturers on a test line set up by SELETE, providing criticism and comments on equipment performance. This feedback, however, was kept strictly confidential to ensure that the competition remained fair. Although any equipment manufacturer could bring in its equipment for evaluation, SELETE purchased only two sets, the fastest in development and the best in quality. Needless to say, the purchased equipment tightly adhered to the provided specifications, met very high quality standards, and cleared every demand or comment voiced by the SELETE evaluators. A manager at SELETE stated that the consortium's demands and the competition among equipment manufacturers created an extremely rigorous environment. Although SELETE was a copy of U.S. SEMATECH, it made use of the existing Japanese multiple vendor system, introducing market-like competition in vertical cooperative relations, but with more open, fairer, and tougher relations than were found in the existing Japanese system.

For equipment manufacturers, this was a very good sales opportunity, since by winning one tough competition they could sell their equipment to all Japanese semiconductor manufacturers. If they failed, however, the consequences were serious. For each of the 10 participating semiconductor producers, the development cost was only 10% of the cost of independent development. SELETE not only cut its costs drastically, but also raised equipment standards by meeting the demands of all member companies.

Recently, in cooperation with the Semiconductor Technology Academic Research Center (STARC), which aims to build universities' semiconductor research and design capabilities, SELETE transformed itself into the Advanced System-on-a-Chip through Collaborative Achievement (ASUKA) Project (2001–2006) and targeted the development of 100 nm and 70 nm next-generation equipment for multiple products and small-quantity operations. The ASUKA Project has a budget of 76 billion yen for five years jointly financed by SELETE and STARC, with the involvement of 340 personnel.[33] The project mainly focuses on the development of lithography and mask technologies, advanced process technologies, and TCAD (Handotai Sentan Tekunorojizu, 1999, 2002).

The establishment of SIRIJ, SELETE, and the ASUKA Project is indicative of both new and old characteristics. As they did under the old techno-governance structure, Japanese companies continue to resort to a collective approach. However, the private-sector initiative undergirding these collective activities suggests that Japanese companies have become more flexible, open, and rational in identifying their mutual interests and cooperating without an external mediator. Under the old techno-governance structure, government subsidies were a key mechanism to solicit cooperation and mediate interests among competitors in a consortium. SELETE also introduced market-oriented competition among equipment manufacturers, replacing the old vertical cooperation arrangement between semiconductor and equipment manufacturers. By using the multiple vendor system, with which Japanese manufacturers were well acquainted, competition could be introduced among equipment manufacturers, and cooperative relations between semiconductor and equipment manufacturers could be maintained through the media of criticism and commentary in a more tougher and competitive environment (Okada, 2000).

3.2.3 Creation of VLSI Cooperative-Type Organizations Among Competitors with Government Subsidies

3.2.3.1 Cooperative for Maintaining World Leadership in Wafer Technology

To develop the basic technologies for producing 400 mm silicon wafers, Japanese companies established a new cooperative modeled after the old VLSI Cooperative. The silicon wafer is one of the few sectors in parts and materials production where Japan still holds a large share of the world market (63% in 1999). Reacting to SEMATECH's 1992 attempt to develop a large-sized wafer with a German company,[34] in 1996 Japanese wafer companies, with the help of a government subsidy, formed a new cooperative, the Super Silicon Crystal Research Institute (SSi) (1996–2001).

Advancement in wafer technology is vital not only for maintaining leadership in wafer production, but also for reducing the cost of semiconductor production. For example, a 200 mm, 300 mm, or 400 mm wafer can respectively yield 20, 50, or 100 4-Gb chips with a size of 25 mm by 40 mm. Thus the yield per wafer increases drastically as wafer size increases. The total budget of the SSi consortium was 13.3 billion yen, funded jointly by the Japanese government (51.1%) and seven Japanese wafer manufacturers (48.9%). SSi succeeded in producing a single silicon crystal weighing 438 kg for the first time in the world. It also aimed at making its technology the future global standard and invited two major foreign wafer producers to join, but they declined.[35]

Since Japanese wafer producers had never engaged in any collective undertakings, the chief manager of SSi feared that competition among them might hinder cooperative activities and waste the enormously high cost of SSi's silicon crystal production experiments (10 million yen per experiment). At the beginning, SSi faced difficulties soliciting the participation of company-dispatched researchers in pre-experimental discussions and simulations. However, once the wafer producers began to recognize one another's relative strengths and weaknesses, an environment conducive to cooperation developed as they found ways to complement one another. Nevertheless, it took about two years before their cooperative relations fully matured.[36]

SSi faced a far more difficult situation than did the VLSI Cooperative. First, SSi had to foster cooperation among participants who were all competitors in the same industry, instead of dividing participants into three groups of already-collaborating semiconductor and vertically-cooperating equipment manufacturers, as the VLSI Cooperative had. Second, its chief manager was from a private company and relied on the government-dispatched executive director of SSi only as a last resort to settle conflicts, whereas the VLSI Cooperative was managed by a national research institute researcher dispatched by the government. Third, the SSi chief manager relied heavily for advice on highly capable university professors, a rare arrangement in Japan. Fourth, as a way of soliciting frank and honest opinions, he made use of secret ballots and then engaged in open discussions based on the voting results.[37]

The success of SSi is indicative of some recently emerging characteristics of government-subsidized cooperatives. Competitors are increasingly willing to cooperate with one another, with less need to rely on the government's authority than in the past, though government subsidies clearly remain an indispensable incentive for cooperation. Once members find a sound and convincing basis for participation under proper management, they willingly engage in open, serious, face-to-face discussions. Even within the traditional framework of a research cooperative, innovative approaches enabled SSi to solicit participation and cooperation among competitors. This constitutes a rather new style of cooperation in the Japanese context.

3.2.3.2 Cooperatives for Maintaining Leadership in Semiconductor Technologies

To acquire international competitiveness in next- and next-next-generation semiconductors, Japanese companies set up the Association of Super-Advanced Electronics Technologies (ASET) with a government subsidy (1996–2001). ASET involved 550 researchers: 200 at a central research laboratory who were transferred from participating semiconductor companies, and 350 at the company laboratories of equipment manufacturers. Its total research budget was about 51 billion yen for five years. Although 41 companies dispatched researchers and shared operating costs of about 2 billion yen, funding took the form of a research contract with the New Energy and Industrial Technology Development Organization (NEDO), a government organization. ASET mainly focused on lithography technologies,[38] based on ArF, electron-beam direct writing, X-rays, electron-beam mask writing, and superfine synchrotron radiation, as well as extreme ultraviolet lithography.[39] The level of lithography was to reach 130 nm line width within three years and 100 nm within five years.[40]

One key aspect of ASET in which it resembled the old VLSI Cooperative was an approach that involved multiple paths for lithography. When the future direction of advancement in semiconductor technology is highly uncertain, it is quite risky to focus on only one or two lithography technologies. Multiple paths must be taken, with a concomitantly tremendous increase in R&D costs and risks. ASET not only stimulated innovation in basic technologies and reduced risks and research costs, but also allowed companies to equip themselves with multiple approaches, thus preparing them to cope with sudden changes in lithography methods. The reduction of information asymmetry among participating members has been an essential function of publicly funded research consortia like ASET.

To facilitate the above goal, ASET established one central laboratory to enable all company-dispatched researchers to work together and share information. They were more open and cooperative than those who were in the VLSI Cooperative, which had had to establish three groups of friendlier companies in the central laboratory.[41]

IBM, TI, and Samsung joined ASET and dispatched researchers there, while one German company conducted contract research at its own laboratory.[42] This foreign participation, which might appear rather unusual insofar as EU and U.S. national projects are not open to foreign companies, was partly to prevent an image of Japanese closure to foreign countries and partly in the interests of developing future global standards. ASET tried to be as open with information as possible—at the same time protecting this information with patents—in hopes of turning its technologies into global standards in the future and bringing back customers for advanced semiconductors and foundry businesses from elsewhere in the world. Indeed, ASET-developed technologies have in fact become global standards in electron beam and mask writing.[43] ASET also took the initiative to establish the International Forum for Semiconductor Technology in cooperation with SEMATECH, the Interuniversity MicroElectronics Center (IMEC) in Belgium, and other foreign and Japanese organizations. Openness and information dissemination coupled with good legal protection have become an important part of Japanese companies' key strategies.

In terms of management, ASET had no means to offer financial incentives to researchers, since each participating company paid its dispatched researchers' salaries based on that company's internal criteria. The only means available to ASET managers to stimulate better performances were to frequently interact with the researchers, encourage individual initiative, and allow them freedom, while also strictly implementing tough criteria for evaluation based on technological and strategic implications. For the first time, the estimated strategic value of a newly developed technology in a potential future market became a key criterion of evaluation, since technology by itself does not provide an adequate advantage without taking its strategic implications into account.[44]

ASET developed a virtual organization, Millennium Research for Advanced Information Technology (MIRAI) (2001–2007), in cooperation with the Advanced Semiconductor Research Center (ASRC) at the National Institute of Advanced Industrial Science and Technology (AIST). MIRAI tries to develop new materials and to process technologies for next-generation semiconductors with 65 to 45 nm line widths, involving about 120 researchers at three central research laboratories. While MIRAI emphasizes the development of indigenous technologies through industry-government-university alliances, it maintains an open and transparent stance toward international cooperation. A contract with NEDO provided 9.36 billion yen for the first two years.[45]

One area of success by U.S. SEMATECH was the development of standardized equipment used by most semiconductor manufacturers. Although this approach was also attractive to Japanese companies as a means of cutting development costs, some found it difficult to enter into agreements with competitors and felt uneasy about cooperating in the development of close-to-the-market equipment. This reluctance was partly because in the past, cooperation among competitors had been achieved through negotiations by a neutral party, the government, with the added incentive of subsidies. Consequently, standardization efforts vis-à-vis close-to-the-market equipment also began to require the involvement of the government, but often with the addition of complex features to differentiate Japanese equipment from the rest of the world and thereby to justify government subsidies.

The first project of this type was the Highly Agile Line Concept Advancement (HALCA) (2001–2004), which developed 130 nm system LSI processing equipment with such features as multiple-product and small-lot production and 60% energy efficiency. HALCA used the same 130 nm line refinements as ASET's first project, which started in 1996. In a sense, the HALCA project was a sequential stage in developing standardized production equipment following earlier lithography development, but with complex features added to gain international competitiveness; this was a type of equipment development that had previously been left to vertical inter-firm relations. Eleven semiconductor companies, one university, and one national laboratory participated, with joint funding from the government and the companies totaling 8 billion yen over a three-year period.[46]

Although HALCA placed more emphasis on developing new mechanisms of multiple-product and small-lot production suitable for the system LSI, the establishment of the Advanced System-on-a-Chip Platform Corporation (ASPLA) (2002–2004) had a clear target of developing 90 nm standardized processing technology for next-generation semiconductors and testing new systems-on-a-chip, the basic technology for which was apparently developed by the ASUKA Project (70–100 nm). Whereas HALCA offered additional attractive features to induce companies to join, ASPLA had a specific goal of overcoming the industry's firm-specific orientation and standardizing process technologies for the system LSI with a government subsidy in hopes of laying the groundwork for future alliances. ASPLA was incorporated in July 2002 with 10 companies investing a total of 1.85 billion yen and the government providing a 31.5-billion-yen clean room at ASRC in AIST. The participants consisted of 11 companies and one national research institute. ASPLA has now successfully completed the development of 90 nm process technologies and has begun to offer testing of customer-provided systems-on-a-chip. Five of its member companies—Fujitsu, NEC, Toshiba, Renesas Technology, and Tresenti Technologies—were scheduled to begin mass-producing ASPLA-tested systems-on-a-chip in May 2005.[47]

Thus the tradition of inter-firm cooperation with government subsidies served, as it did with the VLSI Cooperative, to drastically reduce the firm-by-firm costs of developing new technologies, in this case for next-generation wafers and semiconductors, and to standardize process technologies for the system LSI.

3.2.3.3 Cooperative for Nurturing Regional Semiconductor Capability

A new type of government-subsidized regional cooperative also appeared during this period. In the semiconductor industry, applied research was mainly conducted on test lines that were usually near research laboratories under corporate headquarters around Tokyo or Osaka. When financial difficulties forced semiconductor companies to use regular production lines for both testing and production, they shifted their applied research activities to locations near the production lines. This led to a proliferation of advanced applied research activities in the Kumamoto and Oita areas of Kyushu, collectively called the Japanese Silicon Valley. Since local industries were not capable of supporting such activities, the Kumamoto Area Integrated Cooperative Research Project (KAICRP, Kumamoto Chiiki Kesshugata Kyodo Kenkyu Jigyo) was established in 1999 for a period of five years with 1.8 billion yen in funding from the Agency of Science and Technology and 1.5 billion yen from private companies. The purpose of the project was to develop a regional Center of Excellence, coordinated by Kumamoto University and the Kumamoto Technopolis Foundation. Although it is very unusual to find a university at the center of a national project in Japan, Kumamoto University was the only place with advanced semiconductor research capability in that region.

KAICRP involved 4 major semiconductor producers, 8 major equipment manufacturers, 8 companies outside the region, and more than 100 local companies that were divided into seven groups led by Toshiba, Mitsubishi, NEC, Tokyo Electron, Toppan Printing, Saga Prefecture, and Kumamoto Technology. The project focused on ultra-precision sub-100 nm measurement technology used for testing. Its four areas of research were (1) electron beam three-dimensional measurement and depiction (with Toshiba and Kumamoto University as core members); (2) wafer/circuit high-speed testing (Mitsubishi and Toppan Printing); (3) resist and etcher development (Tokyo Electron and NEC); and (4) ultra-precision high-speed stage and hybrid measurement equipment (Kumamoto Technology and Kumamoto University).[48]

A group led by Kumamoto University established a company, Kumamoto Technology, to promote cooperative research. It is owned by 30 local and outside companies who received research contracts and will own all patents developed by the group. Any machine developed within this group will be sold through Kumamoto Technology, and each member company will serve as part of the sales force. Since most members are medium-sized companies reluctant to divulge their own technological expertise and new ideas, interaction and cooperation among them did not initially take place. The leader of the group searched for a mechanism to protect each member's proprietary ideas and decided to use patent applications for this purpose. Each member wrote a patent application, then brought the idea to a meeting. Discovering that their expertise was largely complementary in nature, the members started exchanging information and contributing to the improvement of their respective ideas, leading to more sophisticated and refined ideas suitable for patent applications. For example, one equipment company found an idea submitted by a materials company to be of great interest. Immediately, the companies began cooperating on improving the idea and performed experiments at the university with the help of graduate students, who played a key role in conducting the experiments, acquired essential know-how, and subsequently found jobs at the member companies. The growing number of graduates who find jobs in related businesses in this manner has become a key mechanism of technological and business information exchange and collaboration in Japan.

Many local companies have good ideas, but often do not make the effort to bring them to fruition. To push them into action, one company from the Tokyo area was asked to invest in the Kumamoto area. Kumamoto University subsequently started a joint project with that company independent of KAICRP. These activities immediately generated a strong reaction from the other member companies, helping stimulate competition and an acceleration of their efforts at innovation.

Transparency is extremely important. All e-mail communications on accounting, procurement, and so on, other than actual patent applications, were opened to all members. Before this policy was implemented, the lack of transparency created distrust and skepticism among members, generated several complaints, and interfered with project advancement. After the opening of e-mail communications, this skepticism gradually faded, encouraging more open information exchange and cooperation. Besides this open communication, university technical assistants and graduate students played a vital role in providing information, soliciting communications among members, and linking diverse companies and organizations together. One important case also contributed to reducing skepticism among members. A well-known semiconductor manufacturer had a rather embarrassing technological problem and initially did not want to make it known to the other members. Convinced of the importance of openness, however, this company brought the problem to the attention of the group in the form of a patent application. This prompted the others to bring up ideas of their own and discuss solutions, resulting in the manufacturer's development of a new machine with many parts developed by other members of the group. This experience showed the group's members the importance and effectiveness of cooperation.[49]

The above six examples of government-subsidized cooperatives—SSi, ASET, MIRAI, HALCA, ASPLA, and KAICRP—suggest that a traditional research cooperative model is still in active use. These cooperatives have functioned to stimulate innovation, disseminate technological information, cut R&D costs, reduce risks, generate synergetic effects, and solve the problem of asymmetric flow of information by offering multiple approaches to each member. They have developed cooperation by emphasizing openness, transparency, flexibility, fluidity, evaluation, and speed. The open attitude at ASET even allowed foreign competitors to participate in national projects, not only to bring in new and stimulating ideas, but also to establish global standards. With similar objectives, ASET also launched an international forum for cooperation with foreign semiconductor research organizations. Internally, it relied on traditional face-to-face relations, but actively encouraged individual freedom and creativity with a strict evaluation of technological and strategic values. SSi used secret ballots to assess the views of its members and cautiously established an agenda for intensive discussions to determine cooperative work. KAICRP, on the other hand, made use of the patent system, an open flow of information, the joint development of machines and sales, competition, and transparency as a means of effectively developing cooperative relations among its members. These three cases strongly suggest that a cooperative approach to the development of advanced technology still remains very effective in Japan, though management practices and strategies have changed somewhat in their implementation to fit with researchers' interests and the strategic needs of technologies.

3.2.4 Creating Previously Missing Links with Universities

When Japanese companies withdrew from basic research in the 1990s, their managers expressed serious concerns about who would be building up Japan's technological capability 10 years into the future. Because of their traditional weakness in basic research activities, Japanese universities were not considered a substitute.[50] Consortia of the sort described above would last only up to five years. Among the few exceptions were the long-term R&D projects conducted by the R&D Association for Future Electron Devices (FED). Funded by government research contracts, FED had been conducting basic research on heterostructure and superlattice devices, bioelectronic and molecular electronic devices, high-temperature superconducting electron devices, quantum function devices, and hard photon technology.[51] FED was playing a very important role, substituting for the universities in semiconductor-related basic research. But in 1999, even this organization was forced to shift to more short-term R&D activities that would contribute to the buildup of system LSI capability. This policy change put FED's management in a very difficult position, forcing it not only to cover both basic and applied research, but also to accommodate the diverse needs expressed by project members dispatched by companies with disparate specialties vis-à-vis system LSI production.[52]

Even Japan's most prominent semiconductor-related national research institute, the Electro-Technical Laboratory (ETL), was merged with 14 other laboratories into a single research organization, the Sangyo Gijutsu Sogo Kenkyusho (National Institute of Advanced Industrial Science and Technology, AIST) in April 2001 (Okada, 2000).[53] This organization included both applied research centers and basic research sections, but its primary emphasis was on applied research.[54] In the 1990s, activities at national research institutes shifted dramatically toward applied research without providing an answer to the key question,

"Who is conducting basic research in Japan?"[55] Would basic research conducted by national research institutes be sufficient? Would universities be capable of conducting basic research that would meet future corporate needs? These questions became a very serious issue for SIRIJ from the moment it was established in 1994.

One of SIRIJ's first projects was to set up another organization, STARC, jointly funded by 11 major semiconductor producers in 1995 with a capitalization of 110 million yen. The goal of STARC was to nurture the research capabilities of universities in company-needs-based future semiconductor technologies through industry-university collaboration. In the past, the goals of company-university relations had not been at all clear. Corporate funding of joint research was viewed as little more than a donation, with hardly any useful outcome for the companies, since university professors simply conducted research based on their own interests. Companies provided significant amounts of money to universities simply for the purposes of gaining information, training researchers, and hiring qualified graduates. The 11 members of STARC decided instead to pool this "donation" money to fund projects selected through competition. In 2000, the odds of a project application winning this competition were about one in four. For each project, one senior fellow from STARC and two to four mentors from member companies who specialized in the project area would monitor the research to make sure the project moved forward. University researchers had to present their proposals in front of company representatives and convince them of the originality and value of the project, and a minimum of two company representatives had to express a willingness to serve as mentors.[56]

STARC also partially sponsors the University of Tokyo VLSI Design and Education Center (VDEC), which gives users access to computer-aided design (CAD) software and valuable up-to-date information through branches at nine national universities. The center also reduces the enormous cost of test-producing system VLSIs by pooling diverse designs into one wafer.[57] STARC's introduction of market-oriented and competition-based mechanisms and its funding of a new facility for open academic use brought about a big change in Japanese university-company relations, resulting in more effective research activities that proved their merit in meeting company needs.

Despite its original emphasis on future technology and concerns about a lack of basic research, however, STARC's recent research goals tend to be more applied than basic. Examples include technologies for improving design productivity, especially through automation; reusing and sharing existing intellectual property; and increasing the added value of systems-on-a-chip through design.[58] Concerns about basic research capability remain unabated, though this organization has undeniably helped stimulate the advancement of university research.

The integration of diverse devices into one system LSI chip requires highly sophisticated mounting and packaging technologies, the importance of which is not as well recognized as other challenging areas such as lithography and mask technologies. In 1997, twenty-four companies established the Institute of Microsystem Integration (IMSI) to pool their donations to university professors and to develop projects that would mandate intensive interaction between the professors and company researchers.[59] Like STARC, IMSI helped shift university-company alliances from traditional long-term relations toward more open and more competition-based arrangements.

Universities are also making efforts to link their research activities to companies. In 1998, the Ministry of Education passed the Technology Licensing Organization (TLO) Law to promote the transfer of patents and special rights not owned by the national government to companies from universities, technical high schools, university joint organizations, and national research institutes (Kenkyu Sangyo Kyokai, 1999: 66–67). By August 2000, fifteen TLOs had begun operations based on this law.[60] However, many TLO officials simply rely on market responses to new technology information. They refrain from evaluating or taking strategic actions for the effective sale of new technologies,[61] suggesting a lack of expertise in evaluating technology in specialized fields or in effectively transferring technologies.

As a way of promoting research capability and personnel fluidity at Japanese universities, in 1996 the government revised the Temporary Staff Dispatching Law to allow universities to hire temporary researchers and research support staff, and in 1997 it revised the Law on Employment Terms of University Faculty Members to permit universities to employ teaching and research faculty for a limited term at their own discretion. A labor market for temporary employment was thus introduced to improve university research capabilities.

To promote university-business joint research, in 1997 the Ministry of Education issued an ordinance allowing university faculty members to conduct research at private companies and revised a law to allow national university faculty members to take leaves of absence without negatively impacting their retirement pay. That same year, the government granted companies the exclusive right to patents obtained from their joint research with national research institutes and universities (Kenkyu Sangyo Kyokai, 1999: 55–56). These regulatory changes prompted the establishment of various organizations within universities to engage in joint development projects.

One of the closest links between companies and a university can be found at Ritsumeikan University, where faculty members in the natural sciences engage in intensive and extensive joint research with private companies, and those in the social science and business faculties engage in consulting activities. Because of this new orientation, a very successful company in the system LSI sector, Rohm, donated a center for system LSI design, research, and education to Ritsumeikan University.[62] Deregulation has introduced flexibility in university behavior and created new options for corporate decision makers.

The weakness of universities and national research institutes in silicon-based semiconductor research forced companies to form a consortia, STARC and IMSI, and to play a leading role in rebuilding the capabilities of the universities and institutes. These consortia may serve an important function at present in fostering university-industry cooperation and pursuing basic research tailored to corporate needs. But this trend has not yet generated a significant impact on the industry because the consortia are lacking in cumulative experience, and the institutionalization of this trend has not yet taken hold. How effective can company-led efforts to raise the capabilities of universities and institutes be? The U.S. TLOs have worked very effectively, simply because the long-term accumulation of creative capability at U.S. universities has generated new technologies and ideas. In 1995, the Japanese government passed the Science and Technology Basic Law to improve the scientific research environment at Japanese universities and further stimulate innovative activities. But when the cause of the Japanese semiconductor industry's failure is understood to lie in paradigmatic shifts not only in technology, but also in business models, these important questions need to be answered: How can the creativity required for these shifts be stimulated at universities? How effectively do universities use their research funds to stimulate radical innovations? Despite increased budgets for scientific research, these questions have never been seriously discussed in Japan. This Japanese limitation leaves the effective development of venture firms as one of the industry's last remaining options for success.

3.2.5 Promoting the Growth of Venture Firms

The number of venture firms, financial schemes, angel investors, and venture capital companies has been increasing in Japan. Since November 1999, the Tokyo Stock Exchange has been operating a market called MOTHERS (Market of the High-Growth and Emerging Stocks), and since 2000, the Osaka Securities Exchange has been operating NASDAQ Japan (renamed Nippon New Market—Hercules in 2002). They provide funds to venture firms with potential future growth as well as diversified opportunities for investors.[63] In 2000, the Japan Semiconductor Venture Association was established to represent the interests of venture firms in the semiconductor industry and to promote the development of infrastructural support for them. At the time, it had about 120 members.[64]

Venture firms usually face difficulties keeping themselves alive in the market at the outset. Many of these firms subsist by running consulting and software design businesses to maintain cash flow into their companies[65] while they work to develop their own core competencies. This situation is exacerbated by the Japanese *yoshin* credit system, which relies on a track record of past sales and in many cases prevents the venture firms from selling their products to large-sized Japanese companies. In some cases, it is foreign companies who first recognize a Japanese venture's core competency at an early stage,[66] and its subsequent record of sales to a foreign company then opens the door to sales of products to Japanese companies. For example, Rohm, initially a small electronic parts company, faced difficulties selling its products in Japan and, for the sake of survival, established a U.S. branch in 1970. This turned into a blessing when Rohm's U.S. sales enabled the company to clear the Japanese *yoshin* hurdle; its U.S. branch also obtained new American technology more quickly than many of its Japanese competitors, thus positioning the company to ride the Japanese semiconductor boom of the 1980s.[67] SAMCO International is another example of a firm that faced difficulties selling its products in Japan. SAMCO developed chemical vapor deposition (CVD) technology in cooperation with a Kyoto University professor, but could not sell its product until a U.S. company purchased it and publicly praised its quality.[68] Thine Electronics and Real Vision are examples of companies who survived initial difficulties by designing software and doing consulting work while they accumulated competence as fabless makers in 3D graphics and analog/digital mixed-signal system LSIs.[69] Technos spun off from a parent company caught in a family dispute among its owners and survived by developing testing devices based on its core technology.[70]

Surprisingly, some of Japan's most famous venture firms were born in Kyoto, the ancient capital of the country but not well known for industrial activities other than traditional textile production. Kyoto firms face serious restrictions, one being that small firms there cannot find big companies to buy their products. Hence it was common for venture firms in Kyoto to seek out markets and even technology in foreign countries. Another restriction is expensive land, which forces Kyoto firms to remain very small and specialized and to focus on high-value-added, high-tech products. Some advantages they do enjoy are the presence of the prestigious, Nobel Prize-winning Kyoto University and the existence of highly effective networks among producers based on a strong institutionally-inherited sense of cooperation. These institutions are a good fit with the Kyoto venture firms' focus on high technologies and their small size of operation. This complementarity between geographic restrictions and institutional environments has created conditions that both nurture venture firms and compel them to search for foreign markets.

Rohm itself is an example of a very successful Kyoto venture. Rohm was forced to align itself with small- and medium-sized competitors in Kyoto to compensate for missing elements in the early developmental stage of its system design chips. These companies developed intensive long-term cooperative relations, but they also strictly evaluated one another, exchanged information openly, searched for areas of synergetic gain, made quick decisions to avoid project delays, and resolved their conflicts quickly through top-level negotiations. Such relations continue to the present. These long-term relations are undeniably based on the traditional Japanese model with a strong sense of trust, mutually accepted interests, and frequent interactions involving all levels, from top to bottom. However, unlike older Japanese-type relations, these companies are quite open with their arguments and criticism while sharing visions, ideas, and enthusiasm with one another.[71] Their interaction is rich and synergetic, but it is also built on tough mutual evaluation, openness, conflict tolerance, and speed.

With no other effective mechanism to stimulate paradigm-shifting innovations in Japan, venture firms are considered a source of some hope. But reality may be much harsher than many anticipate; so far, new ventures are creating little change in the semiconductor industry, and the old techno-governance structure still restricts the advancement of venture firms. As a matter of fact, venture firms have been around since the early days of Japanese industrialization. For the sake of survival, they operated very rationally, going beyond the boundaries of Japan to market their products and to obtain technology. This does not mean, however, that such firms developed more market-oriented organizational relations. To overcome their small size and specialization, they found horizontal cooperation with other firms to be crucial; this involved traditional Japanese-type trust-based, long-term relations, albeit with a high level of tolerance for conflict and criticism. In the early stages of postwar industrialization in Japan, such firms had already developed a more rational type of cooperation with greater openness, flexibility, and enthusiasm—the type of cooperation that well-established semiconductor manufacturers are presently struggling to develop. Extremely unfavorable domestic market conditions drove the small Kyoto ventures into the rough waters of international competition while forcing them to rely heavily on traditional existing institutions of cooperation in Japan, but the firms achieved this by transforming these traditional relations into a more rational form of horizontal cooperation.

4 Conclusion

Institutions guide or restrict individual and organizational behavior in a specific direction and induce repeated patterns of behavior. Japanese companies have been known for developing their own business system, emphasizing non-allocative or production efficiency, and promoting worker participation, long-term relations, cooperative learning, and capability building. Lifetime employment, long-term subcontracting relations, and an emphasis on trust, commitment, and cooperation became an important part of the rules of the game in Japanese business activities. The craftsman-type approach to DRAM development was dynamic because highly cooperative vertical inter-firm relations between semiconductor and equipment manufacturers and the internal accumulation and improvement of know-how afforded by lifetime employment provided the basis for dynamic interaction, cooperative learning, capability building, and synergetic effects. These characteristics of Japanese production and management systems became comparative advantages for Japanese companies. In a sense, the Japanese business system was eminently suited for DRAM production, and the Japanese techno-governance structure successfully harmonized diverse actors, leading to world leadership in the semiconductor field. Once such a business system is institutionalized and the techno-governance structure is well established, they not only restrict companies' strategic choices, but also stimulate innovation within the institutional framework.

Even though cooperation is one of the most important characteristics of the Japanese business system, it was more highly developed in the vertical relations between semiconductor manufacturers and parts, materials, and equipment suppliers, whereas the semiconductor manufacturers themselves competed fiercely with one another in the domestic and foreign markets. Horizontal cooperation among competitors was possible only in pre-competitive leading-edge research areas with the help of significant government subsidies and efforts to engineer this cooperation. Such horizontal cooperation became possible partly because the companies alone could not cope with the high risks and costs of basic research, partly because their exposure to multiple approaches to the development of targeted technologies provided insurance against future unexpected, rapid technological changes, and partly because the targeted technologies would not immediately differentiate the companies' relative market competitiveness. Since the benefits derived from cooperation in basic research remained far higher than the costs, cooperation among competitors with government subsidies remained viable. However, under the extremely turbulent market conditions of the 1990s, even this institutionally-embedded form of vertical and horizontal cooperation among companies, governments, and TSOs changed. But this change came only after a period of hesitation and resistance to the point where it became untenable to sustain the old practices; moreover, change took place in a way that altered the institutional heritage rather than abandoning it.

When Japan's semiconductor technology orientation began shifting from the DRAM to the system LSI, and when market demand for Japanese DRAMs radically declined, institutional restrictions not only delayed the awareness of changes in the industry, but also generated false hopes that Japanese semiconductor manufacturers would regain their dominant position simply by continuing with institutionalized practices. The excellent fit between the Japanese business system and DRAM production created organizational inertia that led to a continued emphasis on the DRAM and made it difficult for the semiconductor manufacturers to shift their technological focus and make tough decisions to abandon some of their production and management systems. Even when future prospects for the DRAM became quite dim, false hopes encouraged the Japanese companies to adopt a dual strategy, delaying a radical shift to the system LSI or other devices.

A social commitment to lifetime employment, long-term inter-firm relations, and a value orientation toward continuity, cooperation, and trust prevented Japanese companies from quickly reorganizing their production. Even when the reduction of demand created surplus employees, the commitment to lifetime employment reduced the opportunities for a semiconductor company to shift its financial resources from poorly performing areas to new technological innovation and production. Long-term inter-firm relations ended up impeding the innovative capabilities of both semiconductor and equipment manufacturers by locking them into narrow old perspectives. Some companies even continued to nurture weaker companies, believing in the past successful method of mutual capability building. When new ideas and technologies were needed, the companies' emphasis on long-term relations, trust, and the *yoshin* system prevented venture firms and entrepreneurs from entering the Japanese market, reduced business opportunities for innovative products, narrowed the range of strategic choices for a company to make, and discouraged entrepreneurial spirit and motivation. Such institutional restrictions failed to make use of the fluidity found in the venture firm market, preventing changes and sustaining the old techno-governance structure.

Whether a company takes a more fluid and open market-oriented approach or a more internally controllable hierarchical approach is very much up to the decision makers of that company. In a period of crisis, especially in a country where institutional restrictions are strong, where the emphasis is on cooperation and collective behavior and where a leader's role is relatively weak, it is risky for a company's top decision makers to forcibly displace workers, terminate cooperative relations, and restructure a company unilaterally, because such actions are quite likely to generate a legitimacy problem for the decision makers and adversely affect employee morale. In such a situation, layoffs targeting a certain quota tend to result in a larger number of more competent workers leaving a company, creating further problems in maintaining even a minimum level of profitable operations.

It was the introduction of market-oriented mechanisms that allowed Japan's top decision makers to implement restructuring without generating a serious legitimacy problem. For example, a semiconductor manufacturer could terminate its long-term relations with equipment manufacturers by telling them to engage in market competition and prove themselves as viable producers. Even though there was in fact little prospect of reestablishing cooperative relations, this approach to termination left open the possibility of resuming relations after adequate improvements. Similarly, worker layoffs were more easily accomplished by dividing up a company into several units and making those separated units operate independently of the main unit, with some to be sold to outside companies, some to form joint ventures, and some to be kept inside. Under this modularization of product areas and functions, an organizationally separated unit becomes either an in-house company or a spun-off subsidiary according to its degree of independence. Fearing that companies would abuse the separation system by spinning off separated units for quick and unnecessary reductions of their payrolls, the Japanese government passed a law trying to guarantee, in principle, the continued practice of lifetime employment in spun-off companies, though such guarantees might change when those companies were sold away. This was an attempt to maintain the traditional institution of lifetime employment under turbulent economic conditions. Yet despite the legal protection extended to affected employees, modularization and separation are basically a way to eliminate surplus employees while incurring minimal legitimacy and morale problems within the Japanese context of strong traditional institutions. Permanent employment can be guaranteed, but only as long as a spun-off subsidiary operates profitably or a future owner successfully manages an acquired unit. While the in-house company system and the separation system allowed companies to introduce a highly market-oriented approach, the employment guarantee law functioned to prevent the disintegration of the Japanese management system. It preserved an element of the old source of Japanese industrial dynamics while modularization and separation allowed companies greater fluidity and flexibility. The sales of separated units also served to generate revenue for financially hard-hit companies.

Besides the above employee-reduction effect, modularization and separation serve as a very effective and convenient means of organizational restructuring. Dividing an organization into independent units helps to formulate a clear focus on products, goals, and strategies in each separated unit as well as the corporate headquarters within a parent company. Smaller-sized, independent operations also make each separated unit more flexible, open, and manageable and encourage them to develop market-like relations with one another. Moreover, the organizational dismantling inevitably weakens each unit financially, managerially, and technologically so much that it threatens the survival of the individual units and creates an opportunity for corporate headquarters to sell them, merge them, or use them to form joint ventures with other companies' separated units, especially those of competitors. Some examples of competitor collaboration of this sort are the establishment of Elpida Memory by NEC and Hitachi and of Renesas Technology by Mitsubishi and Hitachi. They are examples of a successful merging of specific competencies of competitors into one company. Modularization and separation clearly created more open and fluid environments, allowing semiconductor companies to remain flexible in their decisions and behavior.

In a highly market-oriented economy with a less institutional orientation toward cooperation, such as the U.S. economy, alliances and mergers are very likely to occur with a clear demarcation between cooperators and competitors. A similar tendency is found in alliances and mergers among Japanese system LSI producers (Fig. 3.2). But once we start looking at other product areas, the distinction between alliance partners and competitors becomes quite ambiguous (Fig. 3.3). One company may cooperate closely with another in one product area while it competes fiercely against the same company in other product areas. Modularized competition among Japanese semiconductor manufacturers is a newly emerging and unique phenomenon of Japanese networks, where alliances and cooperation, involving nearly all competitors of a given company, occur whenever needs and interests match, no matter the companies involved. Such networks may therefore be characterized as "loosely-networked circles."

This new form of Japanese alliance suggests that for semiconductor companies, a market-oriented approach serves as a means of breaking up rigid traditional forms of cooperation and creating organizational fluidity so that resource advantages can be reclaimed by generating a new set of cooperative relations and networks with competitors. The Japanese institutional heritage of cooperation persists in a new form, and the less accepted concept of market orientation functions rather as a means of introducing changes and creating fluidity in rigid traditional forms of cooperation.

An important point here, however, is that cooperation is not what it used to be. The know-how of cooperation cultivated in vertical relations fits poorly with and creates conflicts in the currently prevalent form of horizontal cooperation. Japanese companies have also become more calculating and flexible in switching partners as situations change. To stabilize cooperative relations and generate synergetic effects from cooperative learning, they prefer to align with partners offering attractive technological capability as well as sharing fundamentally similar rules of cooperation, on the basis of which they can bargain and negotiate the details of the means to achieve this cooperation. This may be why Japanese semiconductor companies still choose Japanese partners. Given the stronger emphasis on vertical cooperation in the past, this new form of horizontal cooperation would never have arisen from the domestic context without the threat of foreign competitors and devastating market conditions.

The need to rebuild their technological capacity with limited financial resources compelled Japanese semiconductor producers to revive the traditional system of the research cooperative and to engage in joint technology development, either with or without government subsidies. The government provided subsidies to projects developing next-next-generation, high-risk, high-cost process technologies, while private consortia focused on developing next-generation equipment and jointly establishing test lines. But even in the development of close-to-the-market standardized equipment, the government would provide subsidies if there were signs that an inter-firm agreement was facing some difficulty. This is not much different from what SEMATECH did with U.S. semiconductor manufacturers. Because of Japan's long history of organizing research cooperatives, such collective collaboration among Japanese competitors with new management methods evolved rather quickly and effectively.

The long-standing Japanese institution of cooperation thus provided the foundation for alliances among Japanese semiconductor companies, but newly emergent conditions made their approach to cooperation more open and flexible, accepting horizontal cooperation among competitors and even a complex mix of competition in some product areas and cooperation in others. Fluidity in intra- and inter-firm relations is now becoming the major means of change in Japan, whereas in the West fluidity is more effectively created by the venture firm market. In other words, cooperative competition through a multitude of complex networks is becoming a primary strategy for survival by Japanese semiconductor manufacturers. Surprisingly, venture firms in Kyoto had already developed such networks of cooperation among themselves as early as the 1970s, mainly because they were excluded from the dominant techno-governance structure. Japanese venture firms who were initially forced to seek out non-Japanese markets often engaged in an open, flexible, and fluid type of cooperation with Japanese and foreign companies. Their success in foreign markets allowed them to reenter the Japanese market.

The above findings suggest that the old techno-governance structure restricted the ways in which business activities could be organized in Japan and that companies who did not follow its game rules were excluded from the Japanese market. But recent changes also suggest the possibility of transforming the old techno-governance structure into a new form with flexibility, fluidity, openness, transparency, evaluation, and speed, yet still based on the institutional heritage of cooperation that emphasizes the importance of synergetic benefits. These changes suggest a complex mixture of contradictory practices of cooperation and competition and the coexistence of multiple techno-governance structures, which may provide alternative strategic choices for decision makers to choose from while creating a "loosely-networked circle of competitive-*cum*-cooperative relations." The current changes in Japan's semiconductor industry appear to be moving in the direction of developing these complex new conditions.

Notes

[1] Efficiency is understood as generating a maximum total value of outputs from any given set of inputs (Shepherd, 1997) and is an outcome of a combination of both allocative and non-allocative efficiency. The former is accomplished by allocating resources to maximize the output most effectively achieved by introducing competition and rewarding a winner in a market, and the latter is determined by other factors such as developing group dynamics, soliciting commitment, and stimulating motivational drives.

[2] An institutional arrangement is a set of interrelated systems that regulates inter-system relations and the behavior of individuals and organizations in recurrent situations in a society.

[3] Some scholars (Chon, 1997; Spencer and Grindley, 1993) argue that the decline of the Japanese share of the world market was largely due to the burst of the economic bubble in Japan.

[4] Information from managers at Sony, Hitachi, and Fujitsu Laboratories in Japan and Philips Semiconductors in the European Union (EU).

[5] Information from a manager at NEC.

[6] Information from managers at NEC, Fujitsu Laboratories, Sony, and the Electro-Technical Laboratory (ETL) of the Ministry of International Trade and Industry (MITI).

[7] Managers at Hitachi, Sony, Tokyo Electron, and Philips Semiconductors particularly emphasized this factor as the key determinant of the Japanese decline in competitiveness.

[8] To obtain the layoff record of each company was not easy, leaving newspapers as a valuable information source.

[9] Information from managers at Mitsubishi Materials and Fujimi.

[10] Information also from a manager at the Semiconductor Industry Research Institute Japan (SIRIJ).

[11] For example, the leading producer of the 64 kilobit (Kb) DRAM was Hitachi; the 256 Kb, 1 megabit (Mb), 4 Mb, and 16 Mb DRAM market leaders were NEC, Toshiba, Hitachi, and Samsung respectively (Press Journal, 1993, 1994). Market leaders differed for each product because each company tried to benefit from initial mover advantages. Companies failing to enjoy initial mover advantages quickly shifted their focus to winning advantages with the next-generation product.

[12] For example, Intel was specializing in the microprocessor and its periphery large-scale integrated circuit (LSI), Lucent Technologies in the communication LSI, and Texas Instruments in the digital signal processor (DSP) (Nihon Denshi Kikai Kogyokai, 1999).

[13] Information from managers at Mitsubishi, NEC, Hitachi, Fujitsu Laboratories, Sony and Matsushita Electronics.

[14] Information from managers at Fujitsu Laboratories, Sony, and Matsushita Electronics.

[15] Information from a manager at Hitachi.

[16] The "I" in "I strategy" stands for information, intelligence, and integration.

[17] An opinion expressed by a manager of a company competing with Mitsubishi in the system LSI field.

[18] The cost structure of the system LSI, including even the lowest-cost device, must be calculated on the basis of the most expensive device. For example, a DRAM chip costs ¥300, and one logic LSI costs ¥10,000. When these two devices are integrated into one semiconductor, the cost of producing the DRAM also approaches ¥10,000. The yield rate for the system LSI also worsens, since a good DRAM may end up having a bad logic LSI.

[19] Information from a manager at the Institute of Microsystem Integration (IMSI).

[20] PC-related equipment consists of such products as desktop and notebook computers, hard disk drives (HDD), compact disk read-only memories (CD-ROM), cathode-ray tube (CRT) monitors, printers, and floppy disk drives (FDD) (Handotai Sangyo Kenkyusho, 2001: 2–6; Jiyu Kokuminsha, 2002).

[21] The global positioning system (GPS) assists in identifying a location.

[22] Internet Protocol Version 6 (IPV6), which provides for 128-bit IP addresses, increases the number of available addresses from the present 3×10^9 with the 32-bit IPV4 to a maximum of about 3×10^{38}. It can thus assign addresses to a virtually limitless number of commodities, making it possible to install a chip in any supermarket product, give it an address, and tally sales instantly (Handotai Sangyo Kenkyusho, 2001: 2–36; Jiyu Kokuminsha, 2002).

[23] The asymmetric digital subscriber line (ADSL) is a method of high-speed data transmission using existing telephone lines.

[24] Bluetooth is a short-distance, high-speed wireless connection protocol developed by Nokia, Ericson, Intel, IBM, and Toshiba.

[25] International Mobile Telecommunications 2000 (IMT2000) is a third-generation mobile telephone protocol, making use of about 2000 MHz bandwidth, standardized by the International Telecommunication Union (ITU). NTT DoCoMo proposed Wideband Code-Division Multiple-Access (W-CDMA) as a global telecom system for IMT2000, and started official W-CDMA operations under the commercial name FOMA in October 2001. See http://www.umtsworld.com/technology/japan_wcdma.htm and http://www.nttdocomo.co.jp/info/new/release.html.

[26] The Fiber To The Home (FTTH) project aims to connect houses via glass fibers for communications.

[27] Also see http://www.moj.go.jp/MINJI/minji20.html and http://www. nri.co.jp/opinion/r _report /m_word/syohokaisei.html.

[28] Information from managers at Mitsubishi, NEC, Hitachi, Fujitsu Laboratories, Sony and Matsushita.

[29] http://www.mhlw.go.jp/general/seido/toukatsu/gaiyou.html

[30] Information from managers at NEC and Hitachi.

[31] http://panasonic.co.jp/corp/news/official.data/data.dir/jn041029-1/jn041029-1.html

[32] Information from managers at Fujitsu Laboratories and Dainippon Screen Manufacturing.

[33] http://www.jeita.or.jp/eiaj/japanese/press/pre80.htm

[34] Information from a manager at the Super Silicon Crystal Research Institute (SSi).

[35] Information from a manager at SSi.

[36] Information from a manager at SSi.

[37] Information from a manager at SSi.

[38] In the U.S., research in this area utilizes the forms of the limited liability company, the cooperative research and development agreement (CRADA), and the consortium, in which diverse participants jointly develop targeted technologies. The EUV Limited Liability Company conducts research on extreme ultraviolet (EUV) lithography. E-litho conducts research on electron beam projection solutions, and SEMATECH conducts research on F2, electron beam projection, and extreme ultraviolet lithography. In Europe, the Interuniversity MicroElectronics Center (IMEC) conducts research on F2. The information is from a manager at ASET. (For details on limited liability companies, CRADA

and SEMATECH, see Chapter 2.)

[39] Though one company proposed the inclusion of electron projection lithography, the consortium rejected this proposal because of the technology's closeness to the market.

[40] Other focus areas were magnetic storage, full-color reflective liquid crystal displays, next-generation LCD processing, semiconductor process equipment, and electronic system integration. The information is from a manager at the Association of Super-Advanced Electronics Technologies (ASET) and an ASET pamphlet.

[41] Information from a manager at Hitachi.

[42] Information from a manager at ASET.

[43] Information from a manager at ASET.

[44] Information from a manager at ASET.

[45] http://www.miraipj.jp

[46] http://www.semiconductorportal.com/GSC/shodescr.cfm?nm=HALCA

[47] http://release.nikkei.co.jp/detail.cfm?relID=70921 and http://www. semiconductorportal.com/GSC/shodescr.cfm?nm=ASPLA as well as information from the Advanced System-on-a-Chip Platform Corporation (ASPLA).

[48] Information obtained from a professor at Kumamoto University who is a leading figure in the Kumamoto Area Integrated Cooperative Research Project (KAICRP).

[49] Information from the professor at Kumamoto University.

[50] Information from a manager at Toshiba.

[51] Information from a pamphlet of the R&D Association for Future Electron Devices (FED).

[52] Information from a manager at FED.

[53] See http://www.etl.go.jp/jp/gen-info/history/index.html and http://www.aist.go.jp/index_en.html.

[54] Information from a manager at FED.

[55] Information from managers at FED, the Electro-Technical Laboratory (ETL) of the Ministry of International Trade and Industry (MITI), and the Femtosecond Technology Research Association (FESTA).

[56] Information from a manager at STARC.

[57] Information from a pamphlet of the VLSI Design and Education Center (VDEC), University of Tokyo.

[58] Information from a pamphlet of the Semiconductor Technology Academic Research Center (STARC).

[59] Information from a manager at IMSI.

[60] Information from a manager at the Kansai Technology Licensing Organization (KTLO).

[61] Information from managers at KTLO and the Tohoku Techno Arch.

[62] Information from the Ritsumeikan University Liaison Office.

[63] See http://www.tse.or.jp/english/mothers/index.html.

[64] Information from a manager at Thine Electronics.

[65] Information from managers at Synthesis, Thine Electronics, and MegaChips.

[66] Information from managers at Thine Electronics and MegaChips.

[67] Information from a manager at Rohm.

[68] Information from a manager at SAMCO International.

[69] Information from managers at Thine Electronics and Real Vision.

[70] Information from a manager at Technos.

[71] Information from a manager at Rohm.

Bibliography

Abegglen, J.C. (1958) The Japanese Factory. The Free Press, Glencoe, IL.

Aoki, M. (1984) The Co-Operative Game Theory of the Firm. Clarendon Press, Oxford, UK.

Araki, T. (2005) "Corporate governance reform, labor law developments, and the future of Japan's practice-dependent stakeholder model." Japan Labor Review 2(1, January): 26–57.

Asahi Shinbun (Asahi Newspaper) (1993) "*Josefuson soshi to handotai o ittaika, Fujitsu-ken, fukugo soshi kaihatsu ni seiko* (Fujitsu Laboratories succeeds in combining Josephson device and semiconductor)." 13 February.

——— (1998a) "*Kaikaku semarareru Mitsubishi Denki, sengo hatsu no akaji e, risutora okure jakutaika* (Mitsubishi Electric pressed for reform, first postwar deficit due to delayed restructuring)." 12 February, morning, p. 11.

——— (1998b) "*Matsushita–Mitsubishi Denki ga teikei, jisedai handotai o kyodo kaihatsu* (Matsushita and Mitsubishi Electric align to jointly develop next-generation semiconductor)." 19 December, morning.

——— (1999a) "*Hitachi, gyoseki o kaho shusei, kanrishoku no shokyu mo teishi, 30 nenmae no rieki suijun* (Hitachi reduces estimated earnings and stops annual salary raise for managers, faces profit rate as low as 30 years ago)." 11 February, morning.

——— (1999b) "*Hitachi Seisakusho, kon nendo 6,500 nin sakugen, shin shacho ga kaiken* (Hitachi plans to reduce 6,500 employees this fiscal year, new president announces)." 26 May, morning.

——— (1999c) "*Mitsubishi Denki, 14,500 nin sakugen e, akaji bumon wa bunsha ya baikyaku* (Mitsubishi Electric reduces 14,500 employees, sections in red are to be separated or sold)." 1 April, morning, p 12.

——— (2000) "*Toshiba handotai bumon chushin ni 9,000 nin sakugen hoshin, 2002 nendo mokuhyo* (Toshiba plans to reduce 9,000 employees by FY2002, mainly in semiconductor division)." 18 March, morning, p. 1.

——— (2001a) "*12,000 nin ichiji kikyu handotai jigyo de kongetsu gejun kara Toshiba* (12,000 employees in semiconductor production temporarily remain home from late this month at Toshiba)." 7 November, morning, p. 8.

——— (2001b) "*Hitachi 14,700 nin sakugen e, gurupu zentai no 4.3%* (Hitachi reduces 14,700 employees, 4.3% of its group)." 1 September, morning, p. 3.

——— (2001c) "*Toshiba to Sony, LSI kaihatsu de teikei e* (Toshiba and Sony to align for LSI development)." 21 May, evening, p. 2.

——— (2001d) "*Fujitsu 16,000 nin no jinin sakugen e* (Fujitsu reduces 16,000 employees)." 20 August, morning, p. 3.

——— (2001e) *Daiyoryo e kaihatsu ryoku kyoka, teikei zen hoi jidai ni, Toshiba–Matsushita, ekisho togo* (Toshiba and Matsushita integrate liquid crystal divisions to strengthen R&D capability for large volume storage, aligning with any capable partner)." 18 October, morning, p. 13.

——— (2001f) "*Shanai kanpani sei, tenurukatta sogo denki wa bunsha ga jiryu* (Slack electronics companies find separation by in-house company system to be recent trend)." 20 October, morning, p. 9.

——— (2001g) "*Toshiba–Mitsubishi Den, henden haiden bumon o togo e, raishun nimo shin kaisha* (Toshiba and Mitsubishi Electric merge transformer and distribution sections, to establish new company next spring)." 19 December, morning, p. 1.

——— (2002a) "*NEC ga 14,000 nin sakugen, gyoseki ohaba akka de* (NEC reduces 14,000 employees due to poor performance)." 8 February, morning, p. 3.

——— (2002b) "*Handotai no shisutemu LSI—4 sha ga kyodo de seizo kotei kaihatsu* (System LSI semiconductor—four companies jointly develop production processes)." 3 April, morning, p. 11.

——— (2002c) "*Handotai senryaku no kaku ni shisutemu LSI de Hitachi–Mitsubishi Denki jigyo togo* (Hitachi and Mitsubishi Electric merge system LSI divisions as key semiconductor strategy)." 19 March, morning, p. 10.

——— (2002d) "*Ashinami midare roso komatta, 'kigyonai de kotonaru chingin'* (Unions find difficulty coordinating due to 'different wage system at each in-house company')." 8 February, morning, p. 3.

——— (2003) "*Handotai saihen de mirai ni tane* (Planting future seeds by reorganizing the semiconductor industry)." 19 January, morning, p. 7.

Chon, S. (1997) "Destroying the myth of vertical integration in the Japanese electronics industry: Restructuring in the semiconductor manufacturing equipment industry." Regional Studies 31(1): 25–39.

Daiyamondo (2002) "*Hitachi dai jigyo saihen* (Hitachi makes drastic reorganization)." 8 June, pp. 42–48.

Dore, R. (1973) British Factory-Japanese Factory: The Origins of National Diversity in Industrial Relations. University of California Press, Berkeley, CA.

——— (1986) Flexible Rigidities. Stanford University Press, Stanford, CA.

——— (1987) Taking Japan Seriously. Stanford University Press, Stanford, CA.

Ettlinger, N. (1991) "The roots of competitive advantage in California and Japan." The Annals of the Association of American Geographers 81(3): 391–407.

Fuji Sogo Kenkyusho (Fuji Research Institute Corporation) (1997a) "*Waga kuni handotai meka no aratana senryaku tenkai* (New strategic development by Japanese semiconductor makers)." March. Fuji Sogo Kenkyusho, Tokyo.

——— (1997b) "*Waga kuni handotai seizo sochi sangyo no doko* (Trends in the Japanese semiconductor manufacturing equipment industry)." May. Fuji Sogo Kenkyusho, Tokyo.

Handotai Sangyo Kenkyusho (Semiconductor Industry Research Institute Japan) (2000) "*Teigensho: Nihon handotai sangyo no fukkatsu* (Proposal: Revival of the Japanese semiconductor industry)." Shinseiki Iinkai (Semiconductor in New Century Committee). March. Handotai Sangyo Kenkyusho, Tokyo.

——— (2001) "*SoC bijinesu moderu no kento* (Examining business models for SoC)." Gijutsu Iinkai (Technology Committee), ATLAS. May. Handotai Sangyo Kenkyusho, Tokyo.

——— (2002) "*SoC bijinesu moderu no tenkai* (Development of business models for SoC)." Gijutsu Iinkai (Technology Committee), ATLAS. June. Handotai Sangyo Kenkyusho, Tokyo.

Handotai Sentan Tekunorojizu (Semiconductor Leading Edge Technologies) (1999) "*SELETE 1999*." Annual Report. Handotai Sentan Tekunorojizu, Tokyo.

——— (2002) "*SELETE seisan gijutsu kenkyubu saishu hokoku* (SELETE manufacturing technology research department final report)." 26 March. Handotai Sentan Tekunorojizu, Tokyo.

Imai, K. (1988a) "Network industrial organization in Japan (first part)." Gestion 2000 (1): 91–115.

——— (1988b) "Network industrial organization in Japan (second part)." Gestion 2000 (2): 19–31.

Iwata, R. (1977) *Nihonteki Keiei no Hensei Genri* (Principles of Japanese Management). Bunshindo, Tokyo.

Jiyu Kokuminsha (2002) *Gendai Yogo no Kiso Chishiki 2002* (Encyclopedia of Contemporary Words 2002). Jiyu Kokuminsha, Tokyo.

Johnson, C. (1982) MITI and the Japanese Miracle. Stanford University Press, Stanford, CA.

Kenkyu Sangyo Kyokai (Japan Research Industries Association) (1999) "*Sangyo kagaku gijutsu no kiban seibi no arikata ni kansuru chosa kenkyu hokokusho* (Research report on how to maintain a basic infrastructure for industrial and scientific technology development)." March. Kikai Shinko Kyokai Keizai Kenkyusho, Tokyo.

Kitschelt, H. (1991) "Industrial governance structures, innovation strategies, and the case of Japan: Sectoral or cross-national comparative analysis?" International Organization 45 (4, Autumn): 453–493.

Leibenstein, H. (1987) Inside the Firm: The Inefficiencies of Hierarchy. Harvard University Press, Cambridge, MA.

Nagase, N. (2004) *Kaisha-Ho* (Company Law). Toyo Keizai Shinposha, Tokyo.

Nihon Denshi Kikai Kogyokai (Electronic Industries Association of Japan) (1999) "*Handotai shinjigyo keitai ni kansuru chosa kenkyu hokoku* (Research report on new semiconductor business model)." Report by Handotai Iinkai, Handotai Shinjigyo Keitai Chosa Kenkyukai (Semiconductor Committee, New Semiconductor Business Model Survey Research Group). Nihon Denshi Kikai Kogyokai, Tokyo.

Nihon Keizai Shinbun (Nihon Economic Newspaper) (1992a) "*Kanrishoku 9,000 nin shokyu enki—Hitachi yakuin hoshu mo katto* (9,000 managers face suspension of salary raise—Hitachi cuts top executives' salaries)." 31 March, morning, p. 1.

——— (1992b) "*Handotai bumon no jugyoin 60 nin, Hitachi, Hinojiko ni haken* (Hitachi's 60 employees in semiconductor section dispatched to Hino Motors)." 18 June, morning, p. 1.

——— (1993a) "*Handotai kokusai kyoso no shin kozu (II): Kuzureru kosuto yui, endaka shinko, semaru kankoku* (New developments in semiconductor international competition (II): Losing cost advantage, yen appreciation, and Korean catch-up)." 16 June, morning, p. 11.

——— (1993b) "*Dainibu shiko sakugo to kuno—makikaesuka NEC (4) Rienjiniaringu no kensho* (Chapter 2: Trials, errors and struggles—can NEC revive? (4) Examining reengineering)." 15 October, morning, p. 7.

——— (1993c) "*Genkai mieta genryo keiei (II) Seme no risutora kyumu—'tettai' shiya ni minaoshi* (Limitations of cost reduction measures (II) Urgent needs for aggressive restructuring—reformulating strategies with 'withdrawal')." 12 May, morning, p. 17.

——— (1994) "*Handotai kaihatsu, nikkan gurupuka senmeini—NEC, Sansei Denshi tono teikei goi kakunin* (Conspicuous groupings among Japanese and Korean companies for semiconductor development—NEC and Samsung Electronics confirm cooperation agreement)." 2 March, morning, p. 12.

——— (1995) "*Jisedai memori, kankoku kigyo ga kakaku shudoken—ryosan de senko nesage kosei* (Korean companies lead prices in next-generation memory—early production entry and lower prices)." 10 May, morning, p. 1.

——— (1996) "*DRAM seisan tettai—Nihon IBM, Bei ni shuyaku, kokunai wa kofukakachihin ni* (IBM Japan withdraws from DRAM production—IBM to integrate DRAM production in U.S.; only high value-added goods to be produced in Japan)." 6 April, morning, p. 1.

——— (1998a) "*Handotai kara Shin Nittetsu tettai, ikinokori kake 'takakuka' shuen* (Nippon Steel withdraws from semiconductor business for survival: end of diversification)." 29 September, morning, p. 13.

——— (1998b) "*Hanyo DRAM jigyo, Mitsubishi Denki–Oki Denki tettai e—256M toushi o dannen* (Mitsubishi Electric and Oki Electric withdraw from all-purpose DRAM business—giving up on 256M investment)." 17 February, morning, p. 1.

——— (1998c) "*Sharp, Mitsubishi Denki, handotai no shiyo o toitsu, pin no haichi ya keijo—gyokai hyojun nerau* (Sharp and Mitsubishi Electric unify semiconductor specifications for shape and allocation of pins, aim to establish standard)." 15 September, p. 13.

——— (1998d) "*Hitachi Seisaskusho—Sogogata keiei o bappon kaikaku (5 nengo karute)* (Hitachi Corporation—radical reform of all-purpose management (how it looks five years later)." 18 May, p. 47.

——— (1998e) "*Daiichibu motto mae e (2) Hitachi ga honsha o kaitai suru hi* (Chapter 1: Moving further forward (2): The day Hitachi dismantles its parent company)." 16 April, morning, p. 1.

——— (1999a) "*Fujitsu, risutora oowaku kanryo, hanyo DRAM ryosan kara tettai—joho sabisu jigyo kyoka* (Fujitsu completes overall framework for restructuring, withdrawing from all-purpose DRAM mass production—strengthening information service business)." 11 January, morning, p. 13.

——— (1999b) "*Hitachi, Tonan-A de sentan DRAM, Singaporu kyoten kogaisha-ka—handotai fukken e kosei* (Hitachi establishes Singapore subsidiary to produce advanced DRAM in Southeast Asia—action for recovering semiconductor leadership)." 31 March, morning, p. 11.

——— (1999c) "*NEC, 15,000 nin sakugen—kokunai 9,000 nin, saiken e 3 nen keikaku* (NEC reduces 15,000 employees—9,000 in Japan for rebuilding within 3 years)." 20 February, morning, p. 1.

——— (1999d) "*Matsushita, Toshiba, beisha ga teikei: Memori kado kaihatsu* (Matsushita, Toshiba, and U.S. firm align to develop memory card)." 25 August, morning, p. 11.

——— (1999e) "*Sanyo, Hitachi, Fujitsu ga teikei—keitaidenwa riyo no ongaku haishin* (Sanyo, Hitachi, and Fujitsu align to deliver music through mobile telephones)." 9 December, morning, p. 11.

——— (2000a) "*Matsushita, handotai bumon fukkatsu e—shisutemu LSI ni shojun* (Matsushita revives semiconductor division—focusing on system LSI)." 16 February, morning, p. 8.

——— (2000b) "*Toshiba ga keitai tanmatsu senmon soshiki, kaihatsu kyoka, kenkyusha 250 nin tonyu* (Toshiba to develop special organization for mobile terminals, strengthen development, and assign 250 researchers)." 25 August, morning, p. 15.

——— (2001a) "*DRAM tettai, Toshiba, kokusai saihen tatare ketsudan—doitsusha to togo fuchoni, gyoseki koten mikomezu* (Toshiba fails to develop international alliance and decides to withdraw from DRAM—negotiations to integrate with German com-

pany and improve future performance bog down).'' 19 December, morning, p. 13.
——— (2001b) ''*Toshiba jimae shugi o dannen—kokunai 17,000 nin sakugen, gurupu 25 sha sakugen* (Toshiba gives up internal production by eliminating 25 group companies, reducing 17,000 employees).'' 28 August, morning, p. 3.
——— (2001c) ''*Fujitsu 4,600 nin sakugen, konki gokei 21,000 nin—tokubetsu sonshitsu 3,500 oku en ni* (Fujitsu reduces 4,600 employees, totaling 21,000—special loss of 350 billion yen).'' 25 October, morning, p. 11.
——— (2001d) ''*Matsushita-Hitachi ga kaden teikei, 'shiromon' sogo ni seisan itaku—dejitaru bunya, kyodo de kaihatsu* (Matsushita and Hitachi align to mutually produce 'white goods'—jointly develop digital area).'' 21 May, morning, p. 1.
——— (2001e) ''*Dai 3 sedai keitai, Matsushita, NEC teikei happyo—sofuto gijutsusha 5,000 nin kesshu* (Matsushita and NEC announce joint development of third generation mobile telephone—allocate 5,000 software engineers).'' 22 August, morning, p. 11.
——— (2001f) ''*Sony kanpani-sei saihen—keitai, shuryoku bumon ni kakuage* (Sony reorganizes in-house companies—mobile telephone upgraded to main business).'' 29 March, morning, p. 11.
——— (2001g) ''*Hitachi kaden jigyo o bunsha e—'datsu sogo' no uneri utsusu* (Hitachi spins off home appliance business, reflecting movement away from comprehensive production).'' 1 October, morning, p. 7.
——— (2002a) ''*NEC 14,000 nin sakugen konki sosu* (NEC reduces a total of 14,000 employees this fiscal year).'' 1 February, morning, p. 11.
——— (2002b) ''*Hitachi soki taishoku 9,000 nin—Toshiba 8,000 nin, tomo ni yoso kosu* (Hitachi and Toshiba have 9,000 and 8,000 early retirees respectively, more than expected).'' 9 April, morning, p. 11.
——— (2002c) ''*Dejitaru kaden sofuto toitsu, NEC nado 22 sha kaihatsu—kokusan OS saiyo, kosuto osaeru* (22 companies including NEC jointly develop unified digital home appliance software based on Japanese OS to cut costs).'' 23 June, morning, p. 1.
——— (2002d) ''*Matsushita, digitaru kaihatsu ryoku kyoka. Gurupu saihen—'mochikabu kaisha koso' e zenshin.* (Matsushita strengthens digital device development by reorganizing group, advancing holding company concept).'' 27 April, morning, p. 11.
Nikkei Sangyo Shinbun (Nikkei Industry Newspaper) (1992) ''*Fujitsu, shinsotsu saiyo 2/3 ni—raishun 2,400 nin, chutosaiyo mo toketsu* (Fujitsu reduces new graduate hiring to 2/3—2,400 employees and no intermediate career employees next spring).'' 18 September, p. 31.
——— (1993a) ''*Hitachi, suteppa jigyo kara tettai, nito o owazu shorai ni kakeru—EB sochi kaihatsu ni shuchu* (Hitachi to withdraw from stepper business to concentrate on developing EB equipment, a choice for the future).'' 10 August, p. 9.
——— (1993b) ''*Genba ni miru—Toshiba LSI Gijutsu Kaihatsu Honbu, 'deru kugi' sodateru doryoku (ureru mono tsukuri)* (Looking at workplaces—Toshiba LSI Technology Development Divisional Headquarters, making efforts to nurture 'talent' to make hit products).'' 29 March, p. 8.
——— (1994) ''*Kyosoryoku kaifuku e no chosen sekai shea yuragu Nihon (4) Handotai—memori tayori, Bei ni okure* (Challenge to recover competitiveness from shrinking Japanese market share (4) Semiconductors—memory dependence puts industry behind U.S.).'' 6 June, p. 2.
——— (1995) ''*R&D saizensen (28) Sony/Beikoku Risachi Rabo—saijyuyo bunya o mora* (R&D frontlines (28) Sony/U.S. Research Laboratory to cover most important

areas)." 17 January, p. 8.

——— (1996) "*Mitsubishi Denki shuryoku kojo de 16 mega seisan chushi, memori izon no ayausa yomitoru* (Mitsubishi Electric halts 16M production at main factory; sees danger in relying on memory)." 5 June, p. 28.

——— (1997a) "*1 giga DRAM kaihatsu, Toshiba, 4 sha taisei o henko—johokaiji no ninshiki ni zure* (Toshiba changed four-company alliance for 1 gigabit DRAM development: Discrepancies in approaches to information disclosure)." 14 August, p. 8.

——— (1997b) "*Sugao no Toshiba (3) Baransu keiei no handotai—RISC bankai kyumu (sogo denki no kuno)* (True face of Toshiba (3): Semiconductor business with balanced revenue—need for quick recovery in RISC (agony of general electric companies))." 2 April, p. 10.

——— (1997c) "*Matsushita ga shanai bunsha seido, eakon nado 4 tsu ni shuyaku* (Matsushita introduces in-house company system and divides into four companies including air conditioner unit)." 13 January, p. 9.

——— (1998a) "*Dai 2 sho, mokeru shikumi kuto suru Nihon kigyo (11) Toshiba (II) Soshiki no ishiki kaikaku* (Chapter 2: Japanese companies, struggling to find profit-making mechanisms (11): Toshiba (II) Changes in organizational consciousness)." 16 December, p. 32.

——— (1998b) "*LSI seihin kaihatsu to seizo bumon o togo, Fujitsu* (Fujitsu to integrate LSI product development and manufacturing)." 7 July, p. 31.

——— (1998c) "*Sony–Fujitsu, jisedai handotai de teikei—tasha no saihen ni eikyo mo* (Sony and Fujitsu to align for next-generation semiconductor, possibly influencing other companies' alliances)." 26 January, p. 9.

——— (1998d) "*2,500 okuen renketsu saishu akaji—dongyu Hitachi okureta kaikaku* (250 billion yen final consolidated deficit—slowpoke Hitachi, late for reform)." 4 September, p. 1.

——— (1999) "*Matsushita koshueki fukkatsu e no chosen (I) Renketsu besu de sentaku to shuchu—Matsushita Denshi o kaitai* (Matsushita's attempt at high profit rate recovery by selection and concentration, based on consolidated accounting—dissolving Matsushita Electronics)." 24 February, p. 8.

——— (2000a) "*Dai 8 bu, konmei suru sochi sangyo (4) Keiretsu meka shonenba (shirikon indasutori no miraizu)* (Chapter 8: Bewildered semiconductor equipment industry (4): *keiretsu* makers face crucial period)." 24 February, p. 8.

——— (2000b) "*Dai 7 bu, Nihon fukkatsu no shinario (10) Mitsubishi Den (II) (sirikon indasutori no miraizu) owari* (Chapter 7: Scenario for Japanese recovery (10): Mitsubishi Electric (II)—future map of the silicon industry—conclusion)." 15 February, p. 9.

——— (2000c) "*Toshiba no handotai kanpani, kaihatsu bumon nimo koritsuka no nami—IT katsuyo, sekkei nado rinki ohen ni* (Toshiba semiconductor company, wave of rationalization even in R&D section: Flexible design making use of IT)." 14 April, p. 7.

——— (2000d) "*NEC kanpanisei shido—Nishigaki kaikaku, tsugi wa gurupu* (NEC starts in-house company system: Nishigaki reform, the group is next)." 4 April, p. 36.

——— (2001) "*Nishigaki kaikaku dai 2 maku, NEC kuju no ketsudan (I) jinin sakugen kieta seiiki—kojo tohaigo ni nayamu* (Second Nishigaki reform, NEC makes difficult decision (I): Employee reductions, a disappearing sanctuary, facing factory mergers and closures)." 6 August, p. 5.

——— (2002a) *"Mitsubishi Denki, gurupu shain 2,100 nin sakugen—konki eigyo akaji ni tenraku* (Mitsubishi Electric reduces 2,100 employees within group, falls into deficit this term)." 1 March, p. 8.

——— (2002b) *"Mezase 'joho no NEC,' handotai jigyo o bunsha—soryushon suishin* (Aiming to be the 'NEC of information' by making semiconductor business independent: Promoting solutions)." 17 May, p. 3.

——— (2002c) *"NEC–Toshiba jisei zairyo, kako yoi ni—MRAM kyodo kaihatsu* (NEC and Toshiba jointly develop MRAM, including magnetic materials for easier processing)." 18 September, p. 3.

——— (2002d) *"Dai 3 sedai keitai, Toshiba–Mitsubishi ga teikei—kyodo kaihatsu, 2004 nen ni shohinka* (Toshiba and Mitsubishi align to jointly develop third-generation mobile telephone to be marketed in 2004)." 14 March, p. 5.

Nishimura, Y. (1996) *Handotai Sangyo no Yukue* (Future Directions in the Development of the Semiconductor Industry). Maruzen Publishing Co., Tokyo.

Okada, Y. (1989) "Technological development and growth of Japanese integrated circuit firms: An exploratory study." Working Paper at the Center for Japan-U.S. Relations, International University of Japan, Niigata, Japan.

——— (2000) Competitive-*cum*-Cooperative Interfirm Relations and Dynamics in the Japanese Semiconductor Industry. Springer-Verlag, Tokyo.

Porter, M.E. (1990) The Competitive Advantage of Nations. The Free Press, New York.

Press Journal (1993–2002) *Nihon Handotai Nenkan* (Japan Semiconductor Yearbook). Press Journal, Tokyo.

Shepherd, W.G. (1997) The Economics of Industrial Organization. Prentice-Hall, NJ.

Spencer, W.J. and Grindley, P. (1993) "SEMATECH after five years: High-technology consortia and US competitiveness." California Management Review 35(4): 9–32.

Tsuda, M. (1984) *Nihonteki Keiei no Daiza* (Base of Japanese Management). Chuokeizaisha, Tokyo.

Whitley, R. (1992) Business Systems in East Asia: Firms, Markets and Societies. Sage Publications, London.

Yoshikawa, M. (Ed.) (2002) *Kaisha Bunkatsu no Senryaku Katsuyo: Homu, Kaikei, Zeimu no Subete* (Strategies of Company Separation: All about Legal, Accounting, and Tax Procedures). Zaimu Shohosha, Tokyo.

Web Pages

http://panasonic.co.jp/corp/news/official.data/data.dir/jn041029-1/jn041029-1.html
http://www.aist.go.jp/ index_en.html
http://www.etl.go.jp/jp/gen-info/history/index.html
http://www.jeita.or.jp/eiaj/japanese/press/pre80.htm
http://www.mhlw.go.jp/general/seido/toukatsu/gaiyou.html
http://www.miraipj.jp
http://www.moj.go.jp/MINJI/minji20.html
http://www.nri.co.jp/ opinion/r_report /m_word/syohokaisei.html
http://www.nttdocomo.co.jp/info/new/release.html
http://www.semiconductorportal.com/GSC/shodescr.cfm?nm=ASPLA
http://www.semiconductorportal.com/GSC/shodescr.cfm?nm=HALCA
http://www.tse.or.jp/english/mothers/index.html
http://www.umtsworld.com/technology /japan_wcdma.htm

Chapter 4

Institutional, Technological, and Strategic Factors in the Global Integrated-Circuit Industry: The Persistence of Organizational Forms

David T. Methé
Kwansei Gakuin University

1 Introduction

Technological change and the globalization of industries are forces fundamentally reshaping relationships among countries. These twin forces also strongly influence the competitive environment in which firms are enmeshed and the role their strategies play in the evolution of economies and industries. Understanding the relational dynamics between technological change and globalization on the one hand and country-based institutional and firm-based strategic responses on the other can provide possible explanations as to why industries have evolved into the structures that exist today, as well as offer insights into how these structures will continue to evolve. In our study we observed recursive ebbs and flows between the technological and globalization factors that conditioned the developmental path of a country's economy, affected the industrial trajectory and competitive environment existing in the integrated-circuit industry, and influenced the survival of firms competing in that industry.

Globalization is made up of many forces—political, social, and economic, among others—that have spun a web of links between countries that is ever tightening. We begin by focusing on one of the forces pushing industries toward globalization. Because of the actions of managers attempting to make their firms more strategically competitive, technological innovation has become a key element driving the process of globalization. Attempts at becoming more competitive within a given national market by introducing new products and processes have resulted in making the two forces of technological innovation and globalization a self-reinforcing process that throughout this chapter we call techno-globalization (Methé, 1992b). The forces of technological change and globalization are inextricably linked. The critical mechanism linking technological change and the globalization of industries is found in the fact that the effort to gain competitive advantage from technological innovation requires substantial and increasing investments in terms of tangible resources, especially human and financial, and intangible resources as well as time. These investments in resources in turn require larger markets to recoup a return, driving firms beyond their own national market to compete in many countries' markets.

As noted, other complex factors separate from technological innovation are at work in the globalization process because as national markets industrialize and develop, the needs of consumers in those separate markets tend to converge and can be satisfied by more standardized products. We will discuss some of these factors below, but a full discussion of them is beyond the scope of this chapter. For now, it is important to recognize that although the degree of convergence varies from country to country because of differences in the macro-environmental and institutional conditions of each country, and the legacies these impart as economies develop and standards of living rise, the demand for various goods converges asymptotically on a global standard.

One outcome of techno-globalization, then, is at the product level. Greater standardization among product attributes is occurring in order to meet converging customer needs, allowing companies to amortize their increasing research and development resource allocations over these markets. Firm managers create organizational forms through the development of strategies. The strategies that are more effective and efficient in accomplishing the tasks associated with the techno-global process result in organizational forms that survive and grow. Over time, the evolutionary mechanisms of variation, selection, and retention are at work on the organizational forms operating in an industry. These mechanisms operate on many levels, and the selection and retention of successful organizational forms is accomplished according to many different criteria.

A key set of environmental selection criteria is applied to the product put forth by the firm. Product selection provides useful informational feedback as well as the necessary revenue for the firm to exist. As a result, another of the outcomes of techno-globalization at the product level is that it often impels firms to confront similar managerial issues concerning resource allocation, creating contexts in which they can adopt similar structures and strategic behaviors—in short, similar organizational forms. The products and applications of high-technology industries, especially the semiconductor industry generally and the integrated-circuit industry more specifically, are fairly standard around the world, and it is possible to talk about a global integrated-circuit industry and global markets for its products.[1] Consequently, if techno-global forces worked unimpeded over time in the semiconductor industry, it could be expected that similar organizational forms would eventually dominate the industry.

Variation has many sources in the broader semiconductor industry and the integrated-circuit industry. The technological innovation process itself is a variation-generating mechanism at both the product and firm levels. However, it can also be expected that the point of origin of a company in terms of the national economy it came from, as well as the timing of entry as the industry evolves along its trajectory of techno-globalization, introduces a set of institutional and strategic differences that modify and enrich the simple homogenization of organizational forms that would be expected from the techno-global forces at work in an industry. Consequently, the institutional environment of the country of origin and the strategic approach taken by firms within that environment at the time of entry into the integrated-circuit industry can introduce variations in the organizational forms that would come to dominate the industry.

The firm as an actor or agent operates in a multileveled macro-environment made up of the techno-global forces at work and the institutional arenas that are generated from the firm's country and time of origin. The strategic approach it selects to meet the challenges of this multileveled environment creates the firm's organizational form. We will return to this discussion in more detail in later sections. For now, it is important to recognize that the organizational form selected by managers at the time of entry and the adjustments in the strategic approach that result in alterations of the organizational form are then selected against by an evolving techno-global and institution-influenced competitive environment. The picture is further complicated because at times the techno-global and institutional forces may be acting in concert, each reinforcing the effects of the other, and at other times working against one another, thus mutating the direct influence of each.

Having discussed, albeit briefly, the techno-global aspect of economic and industrial evolution, we turn our attention to the institutional aspect and its influence on the evolutionary processes. We view institutions as the norms and rules that guide the behavior of individuals and organizations and form the basis for the laws, regulations, and political, economic, and social conventions and habits that govern a society and a national economy. Institutions run the gamut from very macro-societal structures, such as educational or political systems, to the very micro, such as the values and beliefs set inside an individual. They will further range from the tangible, such as codified laws mandating some type of behavior (how to patent an idea, for example), to the intangible, such as attitudes about risk and failure that exist in a societal and psychological milieu (see Methé, 2005, for a discussion of how risk attitudes affect the generation of entrepreneurial ventures in Japan).

Institutions are very firmly embedded in the context of a particular national setting and a particular time and determine the competitive topography of an industry by setting the "rules of the game" for how competition is played in a national economy. For example, companies entering the integrated-circuit industry at various times and from various national economies, as well as incumbent companies adjusting to the changes occurring in the integrated-circuit industry, are presented various options on how to configure their strategic use of resources. The selection they make is strongly influenced by the logic and perspective dominant at that time of how best to use strategic resources to respond to the forces acting on the industry.

These ideas of how a firm should compete, what strategic approach it should take, and how to array its resources to best enhance its chances for survival and growth, in short its organizational form, are often "recipes" or "rules," or, more colloquially, the conventional wisdom of an industry. We will examine the tug and pull of technological change and globalization versus national institutional factors in this chapter. We will also examine the role of a firm's strategy in adjusting to these two forces and its impact on the types of organizational forms in the integrated-circuit industry.

2 Institutions, Strategies, and Technology

2.1 Institutions

Institutions emerge from the interactions of various agents with one another. These agents can be either individuals or organizations, attempting to coexist and meet the challenges of everyday existence. Their rules of behavior are developed to facilitate these interactions. Over time the rules become institutions, or the accepted way of conducting activities, for the agents. Eventually the institutions take on "lives of their own" separate from the agents that generated them and thus become an outside force or factor that agents must contend with in order to carry out their daily activities. An environment is created where agents and institutions exist and interact. Human agents interacting may perceive institutions as "outside" their interaction and consequently constituting their environment, but these institutions are the result of these human interactions.

In examining institutional factors, we find it interesting that several meta-rules or norms can form the lattice on which a large variety of behavioral responses can be generated when individuals confront a situation. So from a simple set of a few rules, very complex behavioral patterns can emerge. An example from the integrated-circuit industry would be Moore's Law, a statement of how the number of transistors on a single silicon chip will increase over time. This simple statement provides guidance for a vast array of decisions concerning technology choices, human and financial resource allocation decisions, and the relationships between various actors in and around the integrated-circuit industry. To the cognoscenti, these meta-rules offer insight into the intricacies of the workings of the techno-global and institutional arenas, but they also can obfuscate because they offer no concrete sets of advice on how to select or adjust an organizational form strategically to those intricacies. Consequently there is as much "art" as "science" to the interpretation of these meta-rules, and experience is often a key ingredient to their proper interpretation.

Meta-rules can operate at the level of the individual, such as a belief that all humans are basically good. They can operate at the level of an organization, which is a collection of individuals operating with a common purpose or goal that they could not accomplish by themselves as individuals, such as a belief in wealth maximization for shareholders. They can operate at the level of an industry, usually a collection of organizations, with a belief, for example, that to service customers properly, vertical integration across the value chain is necessary. They can also operate at the level of a society, a collection of individuals and organizations, with a belief, for example, that democratic processes are good.

We are primarily interested in institutional frameworks or regimens operating at both the macro- and micro-levels; that is, both outside the individuals and organizations and within each.

These institutional frameworks operate at the macro-level of laws and regulations and the mechanisms to enforce them. The institutional frameworks operate inside individuals in the belief and value systems that are inculcated into them through the socialization process (Pascale, 1985). Organizations also exhibit value and belief systems that are often displayed in documents like vision or mission statements and manifest themselves in broader concepts such as "organizational culture," or "organizational ethos" (Sackmann, 1992; Smircich, 1983). This organizational culture, or ethos, is made up of important elements that are infused into the organizational form selected by managers.

In essence, institutional regimens or frameworks help individuals and organizations understand their identity—that is, who or what they are and where they fit into the overall scheme of life. These institutional frameworks also aid in understanding their purpose or their reason for being—simply put, their raison d'etre. The link between identity and purpose at the agent level and the institutional framework is crucial in understanding, for example, the roles that firms are legitimately expected to play and the different concepts of capitalism that exist (Hall and Soskice, 2001).

2.1.1 Strategic Behavior as a Link Between Institutions and Agents

We must draw a distinction between institutions and agents that will assist us in understanding how these two elements are linked. Quoting from Sackmann (1992), "What differentiates collective sense making or cultural cognitions from individual ones is that the former are commonly held by a group of people in a given organization even though members of the same cultural group may not be aware in their daily activities of what they hold in common. In the process of enculturation, cognitions become rooted in the group and ultimately exist independently of any individual group member, even though individuals are the carriers of culture (White, 1959)." Hence the differences observed to exist between the collective sense making of groups (and in this study we can mean groups writ large, such as whole countries) and the sense making of individuals put values, beliefs, conventions, and norms—that is, the elements of institutions—outside of and above individuals.

As noted, institutions are the broader rules that determine the framework within which agents operate. Also as noted, agents can be either individuals or organizations. The issue of which comes first, institutions or agents, is important to address because this linkage gets to the heart of the issue of institutional change. This study views this recursive relationship as one where agents are embedded in institutions, but are not passive (Dacin, Goodstein, and Scott, 2002; Hodgson, 1998). Agents thus embody the rules and norms of an institutional regime, but in reacting to environmental exigencies, they attempt to survive. Their survival may be in accordance with the "rules of the game" as laid out by the institutional regime in which they are embedded—that is, single-loop change. Or they may alter the rules of the institutional game—that is, engage in double-loop change. Over time, then, the institutions themselves can be changed.

At this juncture it may be helpful to draw an analogy between social systems and games (Aoki, 2001). The game of chess as played in the West has an institutional regimen. The rules concerning the movement of the pieces, even the number of pieces and their placement on the board, are given. How many players can play, the order of engagement, and how the endgame stage is reached and a winner determined are also part of the institutional regimen. The behaviors of the various players, agents in our terms, flow from the strategies of each player. This situation is the same for other board games, such as the game of go. The rules are there concerning the number of pieces and their placement, as well as the number of players, types of moves, and the endgame stage of winner determination. Agents, through the use of strategies, operationalize these rules.

2.1.2 Strategic Behavior as a Channel for Institutional Change

The two games are different in terms of the strategies and therefore the behaviors of the players. In chess, it is a good strategy to try to control the center of the board, whereas in go, it is a good strategy to control the edge of the board. For the agents playing these respective games, each understands the institutional framework and the underlying strategy to win the game. As long as each player stays within the same game, the behaviors make sense and the players can be quite creative and display a large variety of behaviors as exhibited in the combinations of moves. This is an example of single-loop change. Exhibiting creative and diverse behavior within the rules of the game in a way further reinforces the rules of the game.

If you understand the game you are playing, you understand the strategies you can employ. If, however, you think you are playing the game of chess when you are actually playing the game of go, you are at a serious disadvantage. Or suppose one player can alter the situation in some way so that the game being played morphs from chess to go. That agent is then engaging in double-loop change, that is, in behavior that attempts to "change the rules of the game" (Buaron, 1981; Foster, 1986; Mann, 1987). We borrow this idea of single-loop and double-loop from the work that Argyris (1976, 1992: 8–12) did on organizational learning and change.

Single-loop learning relates to the detection and correction of an error without bringing into question or altering the underlying values of the system. This type of change operates on one level of the system, similar to the functioning of a thermostat, and we term it homeostatic change, or single-loop change. Double-loop learning occurs when the underlying values of the system are examined and altered as part of the process of correcting an error. This type of learning brings about double-loop change, which occurs at more than one level of a system, and we term it heterodynamic change. The idea of types of change being bipolar also has a long history in the field of organization study (see one early example in Tushman et al., 1986; for an interesting review of change-related studies see Barnett and Carroll, 1995). We will revisit these issues related to bipolar types of change when we discuss technology and technological innovation.

The double-loop type of change often requires that deinstitutionalization occurs before a new institutional regimen can be put in place to replace the first (Dacin et al., 2002). The analogy of board games does break down here somewhat, because it is unlikely that chess players would suddenly start playing the game of go against their opponents. However, in economic, social, or political situations, it is possible to change the rules in certain circumstances. In fact, often the first key to success is determining the game that is being played and understanding when to play within the rules and when to exert force to change the rules. In such a case the debate may move up to a discussion of the rules, about how the rules of the game can be changed. Again we may find ourselves in a self-referential loop, with the institutionalization of rules on how to change them and so on, moving up some never-ending spiral.

This leads us to ask, what are the channels through which change is initiated and sustained? Are these channels outside the institutional framework, or are we forever caught in an ever-spiraling loop upward concerning rules of change? Agents are the conduits by which change is brought about. New laws, regulations, and ways of manufacturing, making decisions, distributing goods, and so on are not generated by the blind force of history, but by agents of change acting in conjunction with other forces or levers of change. Individuals or organizations, either alone or operating in alliances or coalitions, initiate and sustain change either in novel ways that support the rules or by changing the rules themselves.

Researchers have studied these other sources that exert pressure on institutions to change (Oliver, 1997). Three sources of institutional change have been identified: functional pressures resulting from performance gaps, political pressures resulting from shifts in interest or power distribution, and social pressures that emanate from the introduction of divergent or heterogeneous belief and value systems. One important way of characterizing an institutional regimen is the extent to which it tolerates deviation from its fundamental or core conventions. The extent to which it encourages or discourages variety generation is an important element in determining how well the institutional regimen can absorb and respond to the pressures exerted.

Another important way of characterizing an institutional regimen is the selection criteria that it puts in place for determining what is legitimate and what is not. Simply put, these criteria define what is appropriate and therefore encourages and retains behavior, and what is inappropriate and therefore discourages and extinguishes behavior. Consequently, the type (single-loop change or double-loop change), pacing, and amount of change are determined by the mechanisms put into place by an institutional regimen to foster variety and to select, from among those that created variety, that which is legitimate and hence to be retained, and that which is to be discarded (Campbell, 1965).

Why do institutional regimens need to create variety and select among alternatives? For two basic reasons: first, the limited information-processing capabilities of the human mind, and second, the fact that institutions are part of a larger environment. As for the first reason, Herbert Simon noted that human beings make decisions under the condition of bounded rationality. Our ability to comprehend our world and process information about its condition is limited by the cost of searching for that information and the availability of the information itself. We are often not fully aware of the characteristics of the problems we confront, the possible range of alternatives available, and the consequences of these alternatives. Often, we human beings operate in a state of ignorance because of the uncertainty surrounding our lives.

To clear up this "fog of uncertainty," we engage in search patterns to generate information that is then converted into solutions. We tend to limit our search for information because of the cost of that search, and as a result we tend to "satisfice" or accept, the first available alternative that meets some minimal level of evaluation criteria (Simon, 1991). This type of search often results in the exploitation of existing knowledge and ways of solving problems or confronting challenges (March, 1990), thus applying single-loop learning and creating inertia within organizations. It has been shown that this inertia can channel organizations along constrained product development trajectories and thus affect their chances of survival and growth (Methé et al., 1997).

Human beings also have developed numerous ways to cope with decision making under conditions of uncertainty, such as the use of heuristics, emotions, and intuition (Simon, 1987). The proper use of these coping mechanisms is often gained only through the experience of using them. However, historical events, upon which much of our experience is based, are derived from very small sample sizes, often only one. While individuals and organizations have compensatory mechanisms to extract as much information as possible from an event and attempt to accumulate knowledge by pooling that information across diverse contexts (March et al., 1991), faulty information processing often leads to judgments based on biased perceptions (Beyer et al., 1997) and superstition. Often the way in which a choice is framed or interpreted will affect the decision outcome even when the alternatives and their attendant probabilities are known (Tversky and Kahneman, 1991). These interpretations change and evolve with the flow of a historical event and are linked to where the individual is in the change process itself (Isabella, 1990).

There can be many false starts and blind alleys that occur in confronting an environmentally induced change event, especially when the event is precedent-setting or the unfolding of its impact is ill defined and unstructured. It may be that an alternative solution needs to be created de novo because none exists, or it may be that many exist but all are untried and are terra incognita to the individual or organization that must select from them. Consequently, the more variety of search patterns applied in a particular situation, the greater the likelihood of stumbling onto an appropriate solution. Institutional arrangements that foster greater variety may enhance their chances of finding solutions to problems. These types of search patterns often involve the exploration of new knowledge and ways of solving problems (March, 1990) and engage the organization in double-loop learning. This type of activity usually results in the modification of existing organizational forms or the development of new organizational forms (Methé, 1995a, 1995b, 1997; Methé and Penner-Hahn, 1999).

Institutions, and organizations as the agents of institutions engage in search activities to generate a variety of paths to select from when making decisions. As noted above, they do so because institutions are embedded in a larger environment, an extra-institutional environment beyond the boundaries of the one that created the interaction of institutions and organizations. Part of this environment may be made up of other institutional regimens, which may interact in some way to form a meta-institutional regimen. Early on in human existence this may have been limited to the interactions of certain hunter-gatherer groups and later to tribes in a village structure, and still later to cities, until today we talk about the nation-state. Migration, war, trade, and other forms of social intercourse make up the meta-institutional regimen of our globalizing world. The other part of the environment is made up of the physical world around us. Ecological systems (including other living organisms ranging from viruses all the way across to other mammals), climate and weather, natural resource distributions, and such make up our physical world. Disease, inter-species competition for resources, climatic change, and such make up elements of the larger environment with which organizations must contend.

Although few of us who live in post-industrial societies give much daily thought to our survival in the physical world, it is in reality not a benign place to live, as seen by the number of people who die from disease, natural disasters, and weather-related phenomena. The recent problems posed by SARS were but one example of the impact the physical world can have on the economic, social, and political fabric of agent–institution relationships (Bradsher, 2003). This larger world is continuing to change, and to meet the variety that is created, institutional regimens must also create a requisite amount of variety or be overwhelmed (Ashby, 1952). It is becoming recognized that extra-institutional factors such as demographics, global integration, and technological innovation, among others, will influence both types of institutional change (Lewin et al., 1999). One area of particular interest, especially since it can foster functional, political, or social pressures that may result in alterations of institutional regimes, is change in technology (Burke, 1978; Methé, 1991a; Nelson, 1994).

2.1.3 Technology and Institutions

It is important to pick a starting point because the relationship between technology, institutions, and firm strategy is recursive and nonlinear. Over time, through feedback loops, each of these factors affects the others. This is a process that has no doubt been going on since before written records. Hence the choice of where to start the discussion is as much a philosophical question as it is an empirical one, and it is somewhat arbitrary. The progress of humankind has been inextricably linked to the development and use of tools—that is, technology (Burke, 1978).

It has been asserted that change in a social system begins with technological invention: the trigger effect (Burke, 1978: 1). The technological invention precedes changes in the social system that in turn supports further changes in technology. The movements from hunter-gatherer-based societies to ones based on villages were possible because of agricultural technology. The further movements to towns and cities were predicated on the development of ceramic and metallurgical technologies (Burke, 1978: 7–13). The role that technology and technological innovation plays in the development of modern society and as a wellspring of economic growth has been recognized for some time (Mensch, 1979; Solow, 1957; Schumpeter, 1936).

In its modern manifestation, the relationship between technology, institutions, and strategy has been characterized as a co-evolutionary one (Nelson, 1994). Institutional conventions will set up various incentives and disciplinary constraints, which firms will incorporate into the strategic decisions they make concerning resource acquisition and allocation among products and markets. These strategic decisions by firms on product-market combinations affect choices concerning the technologies used to design and produce the products. These choices alter the technological options available, since some technologies are chosen for further development and others are not. Those chosen for development open up alternative paths for economies and societies to follow. The paths that a society moves along in turn guide the decisions that institutions make concerning incentives and disciplinary constraints.

2.2 Technology

Before proceeding further with the dynamics of this relationship, it is important to understand what technology means in this study (this section draws on the works of Methé, 1985, 1991a, and the collected works cited within these two studies). Technology is the way in which uncertainty is reduced through the application of knowledge concerning the design, development, and use of tools that meet a particular need or solve some particular problem for an individual or group. As such, technology is both a process and a state.

The state is often represented by the set of tools that exists, and the processes are the understanding of how to develop, build, and use the tools. Thus technology is made up of a stock of tools and a stock of knowledge. The tools are often embodied in the capital equipment or products that make up a modern capitalist economy. The stock of knowledge is often found embodied in engineers and scientists. These two stocks are enhanced through flows of finance and information. Flows of finance or money are used to add to the capital stock of tools. Flows of information, in the form of learning, are used to add to the stock of knowledge and understanding of engineers and scientists about the tools.

From the perspective of the user, then, technology is a matching process between a set of problems or opportunities and a set of solutions embodied in tools. How well the tool reduces the uncertainty caused by the problem or opportunity will determine the usefulness of the tool. This may seem like a straightforward system, but in modern capitalist societies the designers and builders of the tools are not often those with the problem or opportunity that are creating a heightened level of uncertainty.

It is also often the case that the designers of the tools and the builders of the tools also make up two separate communities (Cross, 1986; Freeman, 1986). The producers of the tools and the users of the tools must communicate in order to develop a set of tools that will actually meet the latter's needs. Each set of agents, i.e., a community, has a mindset based on a similar but not identical set of institutional conventions. This mindset is derived from their respective knowledge and experience in using the technology to solve problems and confront challenges. We will return to this issue of mindsets and communities when we explore the distinction between industries and markets.

2.2.1 Technology and Knowledge

Technology incorporates knowledge applied to problem solving through the use of tools, which are usually in some material form. It is easiest to think of this in terms of a hammer, a simple tool. In the hands of a skilled craftsperson, the hammer can be used to build complicated structures to live in. In the hands of a two-year-old, the hammer can be a very destructive and dangerous object. The difference, in this case, is the rules or the knowledge of how the hammer can be used. The relationship between the tool (usually something physical or material) and the knowledge governing its design, development, and use exists for all technologies, even software programs.

The combination of the physical tool and the knowledge component makes technology a quasi-public good. This means that it is subject to market failures because externalities exist. For a public good, the consumption of the good by one person does not prohibit it from being resold by that consumer to another consumer; that is, there is joint consumption and non-exclusion. In terms of technology, it is usually the knowledge part, the rules concerning the design, development, and use of the physical tool, rather than the tool itself, that fall prey to externalities. In other words, once someone learns the design, development, or use rules for a tool, that knowledge can be simultaneously passed on to many others and used by all without the original inventor's permission; that is, there is joint consumption and non-exclusion of the knowledge related to the physical tool. A market for knowledge cannot develop without the introduction of some extra-market institutions that define how to appropriate the rights to that knowledge. As an institutional regimen, these are called intellectual property rights (IPR) in the modern capitalist system.

The key distinction among IPR regimens is the extent to which they favor the invention or the spread of technology—that is, the creation of a new technology versus the diffusion of the technology. These issues are often phrased in terms of questions as to the extent IPR regimens provide "strong" protection or "weak" protection for the inventor. IPR regimens make up only one element of the variety-generating aspect of technology. It is also the case that there are often multiple technical or engineering routes to the same end product or tool. This allows for cloning to occur through the process of reverse engineering.

Technological variety generation, then, is affected by the IPR regimen and by the imitability, through reverse engineering, of the original design. Cloning strategies are obviously easier under weak IPR regimens, but not impossible under strong IPR regimens. Cloning becomes a matter of how many other resources an organization is willing to devote to the process. Other resource elements include the availability of financing and people who have expertise in the technology.

The access to financing is crucial in securing the buildings, equipment, and other "capital goods" necessary to carry out business activities. Access to capital is particularly difficult for newly entering firms, or start-ups, and the special needs of these firms require special capital arrangements, often called venture capital (OECD, 2003; JSBRI, 2002). Access to people, particularly engineers and technical staff for a technology-intensive start-up, is also of crucial importance. The type and philosophy of educational system as well as the expectations of workers entering the workforce determine the potential pool of recruits for a start-up (OECD, 2003; JSBRI, 2002). These taken together make up the instructional predisposition toward institutional entrepreneurship (Garudet al., 2002).

Some institutional frameworks are more benign toward technology-induced institutional change, and others are more hostile. The greater the access to financial resources and qualified people, the more easily start-ups are able to enter. This, in turn, creates opportunities for new types of organizational forms to enter, and with these the introduction of new agent–institution relationships. The importance of the entry of new organizational forms is that economic and social progress derives not only from the technology itself, but also from the new agent–institution relationships that emerge from attempts to improve the technological base. Certain organizational forms are more likely to generate certain kinds of technological improvements that range from radical to incremental. New organizational forms are more closely associated with radical types of innovations that redefine existing relationships and are more likely to come from entrepreneurial start-ups than from incumbent firms (Methé et al., 1996). We will turn our attention to issues concerning organizational forms below. For now, suffice it to say that the introduction of new forms of organizations becomes an important, albeit not the only, element in determining the sources of variety generation that an institutional regimen needs for creating the variety necessary to match the changes in its environment.

2.2.2 Invention and Innovation

Technology changes through the process of invention and innovation (Schumpeter, 1936; Sahal, 1979). Simply put, invention is the development of a new concept or machine. Innovation is the putting to use of the invention in society. The impact of the innovation depends on the diffusion of the invention throughout an economy or society. The importance of these distinctions can be simply illustrated by the example of the facsimile machine (see Flatow, 1992, for a more detailed and colorful description). The actual invention of the fax machine occurred in 1843, when the first patents for the basic principles and a working model were introduced, and innovation occurred when a fax transmission system was introduced between Lyon and Paris, France in 1865–70. The diffusion of the innovation was slow, since its use was discontinued after several years. It took more than 100 years and continuing refinement and improvement on the basic principles to arrive at the modern facsimile that we use today.

Invention can take on a number of levels in terms of the disruption that it causes to the status quo. Studies examining technological innovation have spawned numerous typologies concerning technical change, including references to competence-destroying/competence-enhancing change, frame-breaking/frame-bending change, radical and incremental change, modular and architectural change, and references to technological paradigms, technological trajectories, innovation envelopes, and dominant designs (Sahal, 1979, 1981a, 1981b; Adler, 1989; Methé, 1985, 1991a: 6–7; Henderson and Clark, 1990). In this study, for the sake of simplicity, we will adopt the convention of terming these disruptions as radical or incremental.

Depending on the degree of disruption, invention-innovation can lead to the creation of whole new industries when it is radical, to new products or product classes when it is architectural, or to changes in existing products through improvements in the processes of making these products when it is incremental. The special nature of these process improvements will be discussed below in terms of the innovation envelope. For now, it is important to consider what impact these types of invention-innovation categories can have on the existing relationships between agents and institutions and what changes in these relationships can lead to the rise or fall of organizations. Previous research has indicated that the greater the probability of radical technological change, the greater the potential for change in the relationship between the relevant agents, which in turn leads to a greater likelihood of the emergence of new organizational forms (Tushman and Anderson, 1986; Henderson and Clark, 1990; Methé et al., 1996). These new forms in turn generate new agent–institution interactions that may put pressure on existing organizational forms. The degree of coexistence between the new and incumbent forms is affected not only by the amount of environmental munificence, but also by the institutional rules governing the legitimacy of new forms. This issue will be taken up in more detail when we discuss the role of firms in industry settings.

2.2.3 The Innovation Envelope: On Industry, Markets, and Organizational Forms

The social/economic space where the diffusion of both technological innovation and organizational forms takes place is what is termed an industry or market. Recall our discussion above of mindsets and the matching that must take place between the knowledge of the needs of the technology users and the solution or technical knowledge of the producers of that technology. One standard definition of an industry is that of a group of firms producing roughly similar products so that these products are more or less substitutable for each other. For example, the makers of refrigerators have a wide variety of products with the similar function of keeping food cool or frozen in order to preserve it. This corresponds to the consumers' perspective that the various types of refrigerators all have common attributes, the most important of which is to keep food fresh. These common attributes make up the demand side of the economic equation. Often this is referred to as a market.

The producers of refrigerators, however, may also produce air conditioners, humidifiers, washing machines, clothes dryers, convection ovens, and microwave ranges. This may be because these items share some similar technical characteristics either in their design, the materials they use, or the way in which they are manufactured or perhaps even distributed and maintained after sales. This is the supply side of the economic equation. Often this is referred to as an industry. The firm is at the nexus of these two sides of the equation. The consumer would be highly unlikely to attempt to substitute a washing machine for a refrigerator, but the firm may decide to do so by exiting the refrigerator industry and entering the washing machine industry.

Since the firm is at the nexus of these two definitions, some scholars have argued that these conceptualizations of an industry or market make little sense (Freeman, 1995). Rather, they see firms' competition for a common set of resources as more important. In Freeman's words:

> Many firms are not in a single industry, nor are they participating broadly in any industry.... Business firms, even small ones, operate in a resource space that includes a conventional market, but also includes political support, information, and access to social networks. Securing the resources that are needed at any moment in time is the fundamental strategic issue for all firms.... By examining the pattern of availability of these critical resources over time, we can identify the resource levels at which a particular kind of organization prospers (Freeman, 1995: 224–225).

According to this research, the firm is a member of a population's resource niche—that is, the combination of these market-political-information-social networks that provide the resources needed to survive. In essence, the combination of resources necessary for a firm's survival and the firm's ability to acquire them defines the niche and thus the industry that the firm competes in for those resources. The term "resources" covers a wide range of elements that the firm needs to exist. In this view, customers are considered a resource because they buy the firm's products. As we noted above, resources are also the human and financial inputs needed to conduct research and development as well as production and sales. Beyond these tangible resources, other more intangible elements, such as access to political, social, and educational networks and the firm's legitimacy and reputation, would also be included. Consequently, not only the techno-global environment, but also the institutional environment will directly affect the availability and necessity of many of the resources the firm will seek to acquire. This is particularly true of technology and the resources necessary to carry out invention-innovation (hereafter referred to simply as innovation).

The firm is also at the nexus of the technological innovation process, since it must match the technical characteristics of a product to the desired attributes of the product required to fulfill the needs of customers. Changing the technical characteristics of the product to better meet the required attributes of the customers is a function of altering various elements of the product, such as its design, materials, and manufacturing processes. Changes in one of the elements that go into a product may require and/or stimulate changes in other elements. For example, changing the design of the product to add new features may require the addition of new materials and thus the development of new manufacturing equipment. Thus innovation in one focal product is often the result of innovations in the inputs going into that product. The technology trajectory of the focal product forms an innovation envelope for the elements needed to design and make that focal product. Further, the potential for innovation in the focal product is a function of the cumulative potentials of the elements that make up the innovation envelope for that product (Methé, 1985, 1991a; Sahal, 1981a).

Securing access to innovations in the input elements of a particular product that make up one of the critical resource networks that comprise a firm's population niche is fundamental to a firm's strategy and thus to its organizational form. However, these resources often reside in firms that are in different industries, in the traditional sense of that term, from the one producing the product in question. So, for example, steel, aluminum, and chemical firms supply not only critical inputs, but also innovations in those inputs to automobile makers and other users of those materials. The inputs allow for current production of automobiles as a product, but innovation in the inputs allows for potential innovation in the automobiles as a technology. How a firm arranges the links among the various technologies that make up a focal product's innovation envelope can impact the pace and direction of the focal product's technology trajectory. A firm's organizational form is directly affected by how it arranges its relationship to these resources in the innovation envelope.

2.2.4 Strategy, Firms, and Organizational Forms

A firm is a bundle of resources focused to accomplish a goal (Grant, 1991). The adopted strategy shapes the resource requirements and also their configuration within the firm. Since firms may operate in any of several industry/market combinations (hereafter referred to as product/market; we will view this as a defining element of the resource niche that a firm occupies), it is easier to classify them by the organizational form they adopt (Freeman, 1995; Carroll, 1993). These organizational forms are usually classified in terms of their degree of specialization within a population's resource niche and range from very specialized types to generalist types (Carroll, 1985). The degree of specialization is a strategic choice that guides the firm in terms of what resources it will acquire and how it will structure these resources to survive in the environment. The concept of organizational form also argues that firms adhering to a similar strategy that is often shaped at founding (Stinchcombe, 1965; Tucker et al., 1990; Eisenhardt and Schoonhoven, 1990) will often suffer a common or shared fate.

The environmental conditions at founding, and most important the institutional conditions, have a direct effect on the form the organization will take. It is very difficult for the firm to change form over its lifetime (Boeker, 1989; Amburgey et al., 1993). Firms changing their strategy and consequently altering their organizational form, which means altering the way they utilize resources or their organizational routines, often become uncompetitive and have to exit a niche (Delacroix and Swaminathan, 1991). Other researchers have argued, however, that organizations do change and adapt to their environment and continue to survive (Brown and Eisenhardt, 1997; Romanelli and Tushman, 1994; Greve, 1995).

The type of change, environmental conditions at the time of the change, and institutional support for the change are all factors that can alter the draconian rule that change leads to a diminution of survival chances and, in the extreme, to exit. It has been shown that the degree of change in the organizational routines, and hence the necessity of unlearning the old while simultaneously learning the new and carrying out competition against organizational forms that are already using the new routines, has an impact on survival. The pacing of the change is also important. The longer an incumbent must adjust, either because of slow entry and diffusion of the new routines or because it has many resources it can expend in adjusting, the less likely it will be for the incumbent to have to exit (Hrebiniak and Joyce, 1985; Burgelman, 1994; Levinthal and Myatt, 1994; March, 1996; Peng and Heath, 1996).

3 Technology, Innovation, and Organizational Forms in the Integrated-Circuit Industry

Sales volume in the integrated-circuit industry was $140.5 billion in 2002. This was down from its peak of $204.4 billion in 2000 (McClean, 2003). The integrated circuit (IC) is a device that is a type of semiconductor. A semiconductor is an element, such as silicon or germanium, whose electrical conductivity lies between a conductor, such as copper, and an insulator, such as glass. It has the property to either hold an electrical charge or let it pass through. As such it can act as a switch by being on or off. From our discussion of technology it is important to remember that this technical characteristic of being an electrical switch must be matched with various customer needs for the technology to be embodied into a product.

The need for switches is quite large; hence the demand for integrated-circuit products has been growing. The semiconductor industry we know today began with the invention of the solid-state transistor on December 23, 1947, at AT&T Bell Laboratories. The integrated circuit industry that exists today began with the invention of the integrated circuit in 1958. Both of these inventions are considered radical inventions because they created whole new industries that opened up the opportunity for the entry of collections of firms sharing common organizational forms different from those used by incumbent firms. Although not as radical as the two previous inventions, the invention of two particular types of integrated circuit—the dynamic random access memory (DRAM) device in 1970 and the microprocessor in 1974 by Intel—also fundamentally shaped the competitive topography of the integrated-circuit industry.

Both of these devices became industries in and of themselves within the broader integrated circuit industry, again creating the dynamics necessary for the entry of new firms into the industry for each integrated-circuit device. Furthermore, and perhaps more remarkably, both devices have been important initiation points and test beds for the development of innovations in the process and design aspects of integrated-circuit technology. The innovations in these two devices, and in the family of memory and logic devices related to them, have been fundamental in powering the dynamics of the techno-global forces shaping the integrated-circuit industry because these two devices give material expression to Moore's law. This has created an innovation dynamic that is both predictable in its timing and vexingly complex in the combination of design and process technologies necessary to carry it out. We will discuss in detail the dynamics of this type of techno-global innovation in a later section.

3.1 Technology

The switching function that integrated circuits perform has allowed these devices to be used in almost every conceivable electrical product. The market for these products is vast in terms of the scope of applications, ranging from telecommunications to automobile control systems, to consumer electronics that range from games to entertainment systems such as televisions, and to computers. The fate of the integrated-circuit industry is directly tied to the fate of the electronic-systems industry. As this industry grows, so does its need for integrated-circuit devices. The electronic-systems industry stood at $972 billion in the year 2000 and fell to $790 billion in 2002 (McClean, 2003). There are two drivers of the relationship between the electronic-systems industry and the integrated-circuit industry.

The first is simply that the growth rate in one industry, electronic systems, affects the growth rate in the integrated-circuit industry. The second driver is a substitution effect. Integrated-circuit switches have been replacing switches based on other types of technology in products ranging from consumer electronics, computers and telecommunications, to automobiles. The percentage of the value of an electronic system that is derived from semiconductors increased from about 5% in 1974 to a peak of 21% in 1995. It had fallen back to about 18% in 2002. This works out roughly to about half a percentage point a year of growth related to substitution over the 1974–2002 period (McClean, 2003).

3.2 The Invention/Innovation Trajectory

This substitution effect has taken place because the applications that integrated circuits can carry out have been increasing. This is a result of the underlying technological dynamic of the innovation process of the integrated circuit. This dynamic has been termed Moore's law, after Gordon Moore, who first articulated it in the 1960s. At the time he first talked about it, Moore stated that the number of components (now often measured in terms of the number of transistors) on a single integrated-circuit chip would double every year. The rate of this doubling began to slow in the mid-1970s, but has held constant since then at about a doubling of components every 18–24 months. It is projected that Moore's law will continue to be valid for at least the next 15 years.

As the number of transistors on an integrated-circuit device increases, the functions that the device can perform also increase. Since the semiconductor can be either on or off, it can take a 0 or 1 state, which is the underlying Boolean logic of programmable computers. These devices can thus not only do simple tasks such as store information, they can be programmed to carry out very complex tasks such as adjusting the fuel-air mixture for an automobile's internal combustion engine in real time (see Methé, 1992a, for a more detailed discussion of the impact of these relationships on one particular device type, the DRAM).

The ability of integrated-circuit firms to put more transistors on an integrated-circuit device is driven by the technologies that go into the design and manufacture, or fabrication, of these devices. The driving goal has been and continues to be to put more and more components onto the integrated-circuit device. This can be accomplished in a number of ways. One is to increase the size, referred to as the die area, of the device. There are limits to this, of course, since to increase the die area continually would result in the world's biggest microchip. If you cannot increase the die size of the device, you must reduce the size of the components that go onto it. This has been the fundamental approach to increasing the number of components on an integrated-circuit device. One way that this size has been measured is by calculating the width of the circuits on the device. A DRAM device, in the late 1980s, that could store about 1 million bits (1 megabit, or 1 Mb) of information had a circuit width of just less than 1 micron. The current DRAM devices that can store about 1 billion bits (1 gigabit, or 1 Gb) of information have circuit widths of about 0.13 micron.

3.3 The Semiconductor Equipment Technology Trajectory

The requirement to continually reduce circuit width drives the need to innovate new equipment for making the integrated-circuit device. There are many types of equipment used in fabricating an integrated-circuit device. A key type is photolithographic equipment, which is needed to project the circuit design onto the silicon material of the device itself. This width reduction has required changes in the types of photolithographic equipment used in the integrated-circuit fabrication process (Methé, 1985, 1991a). While this has had a tremendous impact on the photolithographic industry in terms of the organizational forms of the firms that represent it (see Methé, 1985, 1991a; Henderson and Clark, 1990), from the perspective of the integrated-circuit device makers, what is important about these changes in the photolithographic technology base is that the cost of the machines keeps increasing. When added up, the cost of fabricating integrated circuits has increased from about $50 million per facility in the mid-1970s to about $100 million in the mid-1980s to about $1 billion in the mid-1990s (Methé, 1985, 1991a). It was expected that the cost of a state-of-the-art fabrication facility would be about $2.4 billion by 2005 (McClean, 2003). Most of the cost for these fabrication facilities, about 70%–80%, comes from the cost of equipment that goes into the facilities, the rest being the cost of the land and the building.

3.4 The Integrated-Circuit Innovation Envelope

To support the capital investment necessary for these fabrication facilities, The sales of integrated-circuit devices must continue to grow. Likewise, the firms themselves must continue to grow. If the market for devices grows fast enough, the number and the types of firms in terms of their organizational forms remain stable (Methé, 1992a). The relatively fast growth of the integrated-circuit industry, about 14% per year during the period from 1981 until 1991, has been enough to support an increasing number of firms. The growth rate has begun to slow in recent years, however, with the average annual growth rate for the period 1991–2001 at about 10% (McClean, 2003). As noted above, the growth rate has been negative over the period from 2000 to 2002.

More important, the volatility of the growth rate has changed. Four of the past six downturns in the semiconductor industry have occurred in the past 14 years, in 1991, 1996, 1998, and 2001. Making the situation even more difficult has been the fact that the 2001 downturn was the worst decline in the recorded history of the semiconductor industry. The decline in the market value of semiconductors in 2001 as measured in dollars was 32%, far surpassing the 1985 downturn of 17% (McClean, 2003).

The industry has become more costly because of the continued innovation drive in its technology base. This is related to links between the electronic systems industry as users of integrated-circuit technology and the semiconductor equipment manufacturers as suppliers to the integrated-circuit technology base. This relationship forms an innovation envelope for the integrated-circuit industry (Methé, 1985, 1991a). This innovation envelope describes the innovative potential of the integrated-circuit industry in terms of the underlying changes in the electronic systems technology base and the semiconductor equipment technology base. The changes in the innovation envelope of the integrated-circuit industry have strong implications for the organizational forms that can be supported in the various integrated-circuit resource niches (Methé, 1991b).

3.5 Integrated-Circuit Industry Organizational Forms

It is important to begin this discussion with a brief outline of the types of organizational forms that exist in the integrated-circuit industry. We will work from a more generic description of these forms to one more suitable to the integrated-circuit industry. In all industries, the breadth of a firm's involvement in the focal industry and other industries can array the types of organizational forms that a firm can take. The firms with the most breadth that also may have involvement in other industries would be classified as generalists and those that concentrate their resources and strategic attention on the single focal industry would be classified as specialists (see Carroll, 1993 for a more detailed discussion of these classifications).

Thus a firm like Hynix, a Korean integrated-circuit firm that makes and sells logic and memory devices and also provides foundry services, would be a generalist compared to one such as LSI Logic, a U.S. firm that makes only logic devices, or Taiwan Semiconductor Manufacturing Company (TSMC), a Taiwanese firm that provides only foundry services; the latter two would be considered specialist firms. Furthermore, a company like LSI Logic, which designs, makes, and sells a wide range of logic devices, is less of a specialist than one like Nvidia, a U.S. start-up, which only designs and sells logic devices for communication applications.

In classifying firms by their degree of specialty, we will adopt the term "system houses" to describe those integrated circuit firms that are strongly linked to the electronic systems industry; "integrated device manufacturers (IDMs)" for those integrated-circuit firms that design, make, and sell integrated circuits; "fabless" design integrated-circuit firms for those that only design and sell integrated-circuit devices; and dedicated "foundries" for those integrated-circuit firms that provide fabrication services by manufacturing integrated-circuit devices but do not design or sell devices of their own. We must make a further distinction within the foundry category between pure-play foundries, those integrated-circuit firms that provide only foundry services, and IDM foundries, those that are IDMs or system houses and that also provide foundry services. For example, IBM Microelectronics, another U.S. firm, makes logic and memory devices and provides foundry services as well as being linked through the parent company IBM to electronic systems. We can also classify the organizational forms selected by firms according to their geographical origin, the U.S., Japan, Korea, Taiwan, or Europe.

Another way of classifying these firms is in terms of how long they have been in the industry. We describe established firms—those already in the industry at a given time—as incumbents and those just coming into the industry at that time as new entrants. We also classify how the new entrants entered, that is, whether they just started up to make and sell integrated circuits, or whether they diversified in from some other industry (see Methé et al., 1996 for further elaborations of these concepts). We can combine these two types of classification systems to understand change in the integrated-circuit industry. Thus we can observe whether a generalist or specialist firm is newly entered or an incumbent, and whether these firms were start-ups or diversifying entrants.

We will now examine what types of firms exist in the integrated-circuit industry and what impact the changes in the innovation envelope have had on the composition of these firms' organizational forms. We begin our examination of the integrated-circuit industry by looking at the top 10 rankings of integrated-circuit firms in terms of their sales worldwide at about the midpoint of each decade beginning with the 1970s. We are interested in those firms and their respective organizational forms that occupy the center of the industry. In this sense we are not attempting to understand the complete population dynamics of birth, change, and exit. We are interested in the entry, change, and exit of firms at the center of the industry.

The firms that occupy the center are those with the largest amount of sales, with the top 10 firms holding a market concentration of 60%–90%, depending on the category of semiconductor and the country's market under discussion. These firms often dominate not only in sales, but also in research and development expenditures, employment, and impact on financial markets. They also have a strong influence on the institutional arrangements that exist for the industry. As we trace the evolution of the industry, we are concerned with the entry, change, and exit of firms at the center of the industry rather than at its periphery. As such we are concerned more with issues of selection and retention than with issues of variety generation per se. For the convenience of data presentation, we initially divide up the integrated-circuit industry roughly by decades, from the 1970s until today, using selected years to represent the presence of various organizational forms in the industry. We then examine the type of organizational form that was dominant in terms of sales in the industry in each of those years. Data are available for more years than are presented in this chapter, but for the convenience of presentation only selected years are shown.

4 Organizational Forms in the Integrated-Circuit Industry

4.1 The Global Integrated-Circuit Industry[2]

As seen in Table 4.1, in the mid-1970s the leading firms worldwide in terms of sales were Texas Instruments (TI), Fairchild, Signetics, National, Intel, Motorola, NEC, Hitachi, Rockwell, and RCA. Six of these firms—TI, Hitachi, Motorola, NEC, Rockwell, and RCA—were electronic systems houses, and two others, Fairchild and Signetics, were transitioning from being system house-connected to becoming a more IDM-type organizational form. Those having entered with the IDM organizational form were National and Intel. By the mid-1980s the top firms were TI, NEC, Hitachi, Motorola, Fujitsu, Intel, National, Toshiba, AMD, and Matsushita. Again, system houses predominated among the top 10 firms, with 7 using this organizational form, and 5 of the top 10 were Japanese firms.

Table 4.1 Top 10 Semiconductor Firms in the World Industry for Selected Years

Rank	1976	1985	1990	1995	2000	2002
1	**TI**	**TI**	**NEC**	*Intel*	*Intel*	*Intel*
2	*National*	**NEC**	**Toshiba**	**NEC**	**Samsung**	**Samsung**
3	***Fairchild***	**Hitachi**	**Hitachi**	**Hitachi**	**TI**	**TI**
4	**Motorola**	**Motorola**	*Intel*	**Toshiba**	**NEC**	***STMicro***
5	*Intel*	**Fujitsu**	**Motorola**	**Samsung**	**Toshiba**	TSMC
6	**NEC**	*Intel*	**Fujitsu**	**TI**	**Motorola**	**Motorola**
7	***Signetics***	*National*	**TI**	**Motorola**	***STMicro***	***Infineon***
8	**Hitachi**	**Toshiba**	**Mitsubishi**	***IBM***	**Hyundai**	**NEC**
9	**RCA**	*AMD*	**Philips**	**Mitsubishi**	**Hitachi**	**Toshiba**
10	**Rockwell**	**Matsushita**	**Matsushita**	**Hyundai**	***Infineon***	**Hitachi**

Key:
BOLD: Diversifying Entrant with Electronic Systems Connection
ITALICS: Start-up as an Integrated Device Manufacturer
STANDARD: Start-up as a Fabless Design Firm or Foundry
BOLD ITALICS: Shifting from Electronic Systems to Integrated Device Manufacturer
Sources: Foster, 1986; ICE Status, various issues; ICE Profiles, various issues; IC Insights Strategic Reviews, various issues

Three IDMs were extant at this time: Intel, AMD, and National. The importance here is not just that the predominant firms are Japanese, thus indicating the increasing internationalization of the industry, but that they had very special relationships not only with electronic-systems products, but also with equipment suppliers, many of whom were Japanese (Methé, 1985, 1991b; also see Okada, 2002). As shown in these other works, one of the main reasons for the ascendancy of Japanese system houses during this period was their vertical linkage back into the equipment industry (Methé, 1985, 1991b).

Again, as seen in Table 4.1, by the mid-1990s the top 10 firms were Intel, NEC, Hitachi, Toshiba, Samsung, TI, Motorola, IBM, Mitsubishi, and Hyundai, and the dominance of system houses is quite evident. The emergence of two Korean companies signals a change, however. The most obvious implication of these two companies' appearance is that a set of players from a new national institutional setting has emerged. These two companies were in competition for some time before entering the top 10 worldwide, and their emergence signals a shift in the competitive topography of the globalizing integrated-circuit industry. A more subtle implication is that the two Korean companies, Samsung and Hyundai, are system houses because they are linked forward into the electronic systems industry, but neither has linkages back to semiconductor equipment manufacturers in the way that the Japanese firms did and still do (see Okada in this book and Wakabayashi and Sumita, 1993). A change had occurred in the relationship between the equipment industry and the integrated-circuit industry. We will return to this in the next section.

Again, as seen in Table 4.1, by 2002 the top 10 firms were Intel, Samsung, TI, STMicro, TSMC, Motorola, Infineon, NEC, Toshiba, and Hitachi. By this time, about 5 of the firms—Intel, TI, STMicro, TSMC, and Infineon—were IDMs, and the other five were still system houses. It is important to note that we see the reemergence of European firms back into the top 10 slots. One of these firms is a spinoff from its system house; Siemens spun off Infineon in April 1999. The other, STMicro, is the result of merger activity between two European system houses (IC Insights Strategic Reviews, 2003; Fisher, 2002). This occurred in June 1987 when Thomson Semiconducteurs, part of the microelectronics business of the French state-controlled company Thomson-CSF, and SGS Microelettronica, the microelectronics business of STET-Societa Finanziaria Telefonica, the Italian state-controlled telephone company, were spun out of their respective companies and merged to form SGS-Thomson Microelectronics. It was renamed STMicroelectronics (STMicro) in May 1998. The other important change is the emergence of a Taiwanese firm, TSMC. This is important not only because it is in Taiwan, but also because it is a pure-play foundry firm. TSMC was founded in 1987 as one of the first pure-play foundries in the semiconductor industry and reportedly held 56% of the 2002 pure-play foundry market. It is the largest semiconductor foundry company worldwide. TSMC was created as a joint venture between the Taiwan government (21%), Philips Electronics (28%), and other private investors. As of March 31, 2002, Philips continued to own 22% of TSMC, with the ROC Development Fund owning 10%. Private investors, including employees through stock option plans, owned the remainder (IC Insights Strategic Reviews, 2003).

The legacy of the past is quite obvious in this analysis of the firms entering the worldwide top 10 as presented in Table 4.1. In spite of the changes occurring at the national institutional level and at the techno-global level, system houses, which were diversifying entrants when they entered the integrated-circuit industry, are the most powerful agents in terms of sales. It is only recently, as readily seen in the 2002 data, that we see the IDM form take over half the slots in the top 10. However, we can see indications that change is occurring at a number of different levels.

First, the emergence of U.S. and European, and then Japanese, Korean, and Taiwanese, firms indicates that the technology of this industry and its innovation envelope has been driving the globalization process and that the growth in sales has been able to support that globalization process. Each emergence of firms based on a given national institutional setting was conditioned on the techno-global phase of the industry and had implications for the competitive dynamics of the integrated-circuit industry. The competitive topography of the integrated-circuit industry also influenced upstream and downstream industries and set the conditions for the next set of firms to emerge.

Second, the agent–institution relationships that each of these economies developed created firms that had organizational forms that could cope with entry into an industry already populated with very strong incumbents. In the case of the Japanese firms, these were system houses coming in as diversifying entrants with strong backward links to Japanese semiconductor equipment suppliers. The Korean firms were also system houses coming in as diversifying entrants, but without the strong vertical links backward into equipment suppliers. It is with the entrance of the Taiwanese firms that we notice a deviation from the system house trend. Most Taiwanese firms entered as IDMs. Furthermore, the Taiwanese firm TSMC entered as a start-up, albeit a different form of start-up from the organizational form most often associated with Silicon Valley. Rather than entering as a venture capital-based start-up, it entered with the backing of the Taiwanese government and a major system house firm. Still, the emergence of TSMC is a further deviation from the trend of system house domination because it is a pure-play foundry.

Third, the reemergence of the two European firms indicates also that the momentum toward specialization is becoming stronger. Both were more strongly linked into system houses throughout the entire period. Their reemergence as specialized IDMs further supports suggestions that the direction of change is toward specialization. Although not shown in this data set, when the breakdown is done according to each economy—U.S., Japan, Korea, Taiwan, Europe—this trend is even more pronounced. This indicates that incumbents can under certain conditions readjust their strategic resource configuration or organizational form to meet the changes brought about by the interaction of techno-global and institutional forces.

Another important point that emerges from the analysis presented above concerns the relationship between the semiconductor equipment industry and the integrated-circuit industry. As noted earlier, the continued advance of the integrated circuit along its technology trajectory is largely dependent upon the technological advances made in semiconductor equipment, such as photolithography. As discussed in other works (Methé, 1985, 1991a), the rise of the Japanese integrated-circuit industry was closely supported by the development of a home-grown semiconductor equipment industry. These two industries' fortunes moved in tandem. Japanese firms' replacement of the U.S. and European integrated-circuit firms was mirrored in the replacement of the U.S. and European semiconductor equipment firms by Japanese firms (Methé, 1991a). The special relationship among the Japanese firms led to a strongly idiosyncratic form of technological innovation in integrated circuits. Each semiconductor firm, for example NEC or Hitachi, worked very closely with a specific set of equipment firms, with the resulting equipment highly customized to that semiconductor firm's fabrication process. Unless one was a member of the club, it was difficult to receive the most advanced semiconductor equipment. Confronted with this situation, the U.S. agent–institution relationship changed with the founding of SEMATECH.

It is important to note that the founding of SEMATECH was a result of the pressures exerted by the techno-global environment on the agent–institution relationship concerning cooperative research among U.S. integrated-circuit firms. In this case, changes in technology and the globalization process, especially the emergence of Japanese firms and their subsequent domination of the DRAM industry, led to the establishment of SEMATECH. Its original purpose was as a way of enhancing the survival of U.S. firms. Although this original purpose for the establishment of SEMATECH was essentially conceived of in the context of the bipolar competition between the U.S. and Japan, its actions set in motion a number of important agent–institution relationship changes in other country settings. Flowing from its original purpose, an important accomplishment of SEMATECH was to begin standardizing the development of semiconductor equipment technology and to make progress along the various technology trajectories that make the equipment industry more transparent and open. An unintended consequence of this more transparent and open equipment development was that it facilitated the emergence of the Korean firms in the integrated-circuit industry, allowing them to acquire state-of-the-art equipment even without the parallel development of Korean equipment makers. As the Korean integrated-circuit firms grew, they became more important customers for European and U.S. equipment makers, allowing these firms to survive through the late 1980s and early 1990s. This process continued with the emergence of the Taiwanese firms in the early to mid-1990s. Again, Taiwanese firms were able to gain access to leading-edge semiconductor equipment technology as they needed it. This access became vital to the development of dedicated foundries, which, as we will discuss below, had an effect on the fate of U.S. fabless design firms.

The relationships described above show the importance of serendipity in the co-evolution of the agent–institution relationship in response to changes in the extra-institutional environment. It is a given that the combination of technological opportunities that open with each new generation of integrated-circuit device allows new entrants using new organizational forms the chance to enter the industry. However, as noted in the creation of SEMATECH, the alteration of competitive strategy among U.S. firms in response to the entrance of Japanese firms, and the subsequent alterations in the agent–institution relationship that existed in the U.S., had implications beyond the U.S. firms. It allowed for the growth of new forms in Korea and Taiwan and for a greater variety of relationships among those forms. One part of that variety was across industry boundaries as first Korean and then Taiwanese integrated-circuit firms became customers for U.S. and European equipment firms. Another part relates to the connections among fabless firms and foundries.

The U.S.-based LSI Computer Systems entered as the first fabless firm in 1969. Although the initiation of the fabless organizational form occurred early in the life history of the integrated-circuit industry, few firms adopted it as a legitimate mode of entry, since the conventional wisdom prevailing in the industry was for firms to design and make ICs. Not until the early 1980s, when fabless firms began entering the integrated-circuit industry in large numbers, did the conventional wisdom concerning this agent–institution relationship change. The period 1982–1983 marks the beginning of the period when multiple entries of fabless firms occurred annually.

These firms came in as fabless design firms because of three overriding techno-global environmental factors. The first was the continuing increase in the cost of fabrication. For an IDM to enter at that time, the cost was around $55 million, whereas entry as a fabless firm it was closer to $2 million or $3 million. Entry as an IDM required an investment in fabrication facilities and capabilities, which at that time required about $50 million. Entry as a fabless firm required only an investment in design and marketing capabilities. This illustrates the shift in techno-globally driven selection choices between organizational forms that came into being in the early 1980s.

Until the early 1980s, as noted above, the conventional wisdom was to enter as a company that fully integrated the value chain functions—that is, either as a diversifying system house organizational form or as a start-up IDM organizational form. Emanating first from the U.S. institutional environment, the fabless design IC organizational form was initially a response to the increasing cost of investment needed to enter the semiconductor industry. This phenomenon arises entirely out of the innovation process of the integrated-circuit industry, as described above. Many entrepreneurs had ideas about meeting emerging market needs or birthing some pioneering semiconductor process or design technology, but the investment necessary to both design and to fabricate the devices was growing beyond the initial carrying capacity of these specialized markets. Even though the entrepreneurial impulse was strong and strongly supported within the U.S. institutional regimen, without access to the greater cash flow available in broader-based markets, the "burn rate" of entering with the IDM organizational form was becoming prohibitive.

The second techno-global influence was the emergence of the Japanese firms. As very powerful competitors in the mainstream memory markets, especially in DRAMs, Japanese firms made it difficult to follow a broad-based IDM-type strategy for newly entering firms. Many established U.S. firms were already in the process of exiting the DRAM segment of the integrated-circuit industry in the early 1980s, and this process accelerated with the entrance of Japanese system house IC firms (Methé, 1985, 1992a, 1992b). Firms that could find product-market niches in small areas such as mobile telecommunications, digital signal processors, or analog-to-digital processors could enter with less fear of immediate head-to-head competition with the large Japanese incumbents. However, these market segments were usually small and would not generate the sales revenue volume needed to maintain a continuous investment in fabrication facility capabilities.

The third techno-global influence was the recessions that occurred in the integrated-circuit industry in 1981 and again in 1985, which freed up a lot of manufacturing space among the system house IC and IDM IC manufacturers. With newly created fabrication facilities lying idle, the fabless entrants could find enough fabrication capacity to meet their needs. The system house IC and IDM IC firms were happy to fill in their capacity needs at the margin with the demand from the fabless firms, at least while they had idle fabrication capacity. The constant ebb and flow of demand for the IC devices produced by these system house IC and IDM IC makers often put the fabless design houses in a pinch for fabrication capacity, however. When times were bad for the system/IDM IC makers in the mainstream memory and logic IC markets, fabrication capacity was freed up for the fabless design firms, but when demand for the system/IDM IC firms' products rose in these mainstream markets, the fabless firms found themselves in a squeeze for fabrication capacity.

It took until 1987, with the founding of TSMC as the first pure-play foundry, to fully legitimize the fabless design organizational form and with it the dedicated foundry organizational form. With the founding of TSMC, a firm for the first time created fabrication space dedicated to the needs of the fabless IC firms. Emanating from the Taiwanese institutional environment, the dedicated foundry organizational form benefited from a strong link with the U.S. institutionally based fabless design house organizational form and from the more open and transparent process of semiconductor equipment development, fostered by SEMATECH, which was then taking hold. The relationship between the fabless organizational form and the dedicated foundry organizational form grew and developed over a 15-year period after the emergence of TSMC. It was not until 2002, when TSMC entered into the top 10 global IC firms, that the fabless and foundry relationship became a mainstream sustainable strategy and, with symbiotically organized resource sharing, simultaneously legitimized both the fabless and the foundry as organizational forms. Prior to the founding of TSMC, a fabless design house was limited in its growth potential in sales and profits unless it transitioned into an IDM organizational form.

After the founding of TSMC, fabless firms were no longer on the margin in terms of fabrication capacity considerations. The dedicated foundry organizational form likewise has no meaning if fabless firms shift to an IDM type organizational form. The emergence of the dedicated foundry organizational form gained momentum as several other firms, first in Taiwan and later in other institutional environments, entered as foundries or shifted over to dedicated foundry applications in order to meet the needs of fabless design firms. We will examine these trends more closely as we look in more detail at the emergence of organizational forms in each of the national institutional settings.

4.2 The U.S. Integrated-Circuit Industry[3]

It is not surprising that the American domestic semiconductor industry has been the dominant single-country market for the world semiconductor industry since its beginnings. This is because the industry began essentially with the invention of the transistor at Bell Laboratories and with the pioneering work on integrated-circuit design at both Intel and Texas Instruments as well as the pioneering processing technology work at Fairchild. It was that pioneering work with respect to both product and process technology development that wrested industry momentum away from the early vacuum tube manufacturers who had diversified into the emerging semiconductor transistor industry in the mid-1950s, as can be seen in Table 4.2. By the late 1960s, the firms that would come to

Table 4.2 Top 10 Semiconductor Firms in the U.S. Industry for Selected Years

Rank	2002	1995	1992	1989	1985	1980	1975	1969	1968
1	*Intel*	*Intel*	*Intel*	**TI**	**TI**	**TI**	**TI**	**TI**	**TI**
2	**TI**	**TI**	**Motorola**	**Motorola**	**Motorola**	*National*	*National*	**Motorola**	**Motorola**
3	**Motorola**	**Motorola**	**TI**	*Intel*	*National*	**Motorola**	***Fairchild***	**Fairchild**	**Fairchild**
4	***IBM***	**IBM**	*National*	*National*	*Intel*	Intel	**Motorola**	*Signetics*	*Signetics*
5	*Micron*	*Micron*	*AMD*	*AMD*	*AMD*	***Fairchild***	*Intel*	*National*	*National*
6	*AMD*	*AMD*	**AT&T**	**AT&T**	***Signetics***	***Signetics***	***Signetics***	*AMI*	**Raytheon**
7	***Agere***	*National*	***Harris***	***Harris***	***Fairchild***	***Mostek***	**RCA**	**Raytheon**	**Sylvania**
8	Nvidia	***AT&T***	*LSI Logic*	*LSI Logic*	***Mostek***	*AMD*	*Mostek*	**NRMEC**	**RCA**
9	Qualcomm	*LSI Logic*	*Analog*	***Western Digital***	**RCA**	**RCA**	*AMD*	**Sylvania**	**ITT**
10	*Analog*	*Cirrus Logic*	*Micron*	*Micron*	**Harris**	**Harris/GI**	**GI**	**RCA**	**General Motors**
11								**Philco-Ford**	**GI**
12								Sprague	***Amelco***
13								**ITT**	**Radiation**
14								**GI**	**Philco-Ford**
15								**Radiation**	*Transitron*

Rank	1955 (Vacuum Tube)	1955 (Transistor)
1	**RCA**	**Hughes**
2	**Sylvania**	*Transitron*
3	**GE**	**Philco**
4	**Raytheon**	**Sylvania**
5	**Westinghouse**	**TI**

Key:
BOLD: Diversifying Entrant with Electronic Systems Connection
ITALICS: Start-up as an Integrated Device Manufacturer
STANDARD: Start-up as a Fabless Design Firm or Foundry
BOLD ITALIC S: Shifting from Electronic Systems to Integrated Device Manufacturer
Sources: ICE Status, various issues; ICE Profiles, various issues; IC Insights Strategic Reviews, various issues; Foster, 1986

dominate the semiconductor industry had already begun to enter. Even though at one level there was continuity in terms of the organizational form of both the diversifying entrants and the start-ups, the older vacuum tube companies were being replaced by a new breed of diversifying entrants and start-ups.

The new diversifying entrants, Motorola, Texas Instruments (TI), and

Fairchild, were all companies that had some connection to the electronic systems industry and as such followed closely behind the vacuum tube manufacturers who also had such ties. The emergence of another set of firms, however—start-ups dedicated to the design and fabrication of semiconductors—introduced a new organizational form, the integrated device manufacturer (IDM). The earliest was Transitron, a company started up in 1952 in Melrose, Massachusetts, to sell transistors. Later companies, such as Fairchild Semiconductor (founded in 1957), National Semiconductor (1959), Signetics (1961), AMI (1966), Intel (1968), AMD (1969), and many others were started up as IDMs dedicated to the design, development, fabrication, and sale of semiconductors, especially integrated-circuit devices.

Most, of these firms, but not all, were founded in the San Jose region of northern California, which is now called Silicon Valley. The firms founded there, initially with the IDM start-up organizational form and later the fabless design house organizational form, are the result of an extraordinary mixture of human, financial, and other tangible and intangible resources that has not been duplicated elsewhere in the world. This story is all the more remarkable, since it was accomplished in as close to a self-organizing system as one could expect to find. Government played no direct overarching or orchestrating role in the creation of the Silicon Valley phenomenon, although government policies on procurement, R&D funding, IPR protection, and such did influence aspects of firm strategy (Methé, 1985; Tilton, 1971). This extraordinary entrepreneurial milieu is still actively generating new start-up firms even today after having sustained several boom and bust cycles in its existence.

As can be seen in the table, in the late 1960s and early 1970s the dominant organizational form was the diversifying entrant with system house connections, some of which were even the older vacuum tube manufacturers. Firms like TI and Motorola represented the newer diversifiers, and Raytheon, Sylvania, RCA, and North American Rockwell Micro Electronics (NRMEC) represented the older diversifying entrants. Signetics and National were IDM start-ups. Fairchild Semiconductor, which originated as an IDM form, in 1965 had been purchased by its main investor, Fairchild Camera and Instrument, for $3 million and was transitioning from the IDM form to the system house form. By 1975, the situation had further shifted in favor of the IDM start-ups. From the table it can be seen that 4 of the top 10 companies were using the IDM organizational form, and 4 were using the system house diversifying organizational form. Joining National were Intel, Mostek (founded in 1969), and AMD. TI, Motorola, RCA, and General Instrument (GI) followed the system house form. One other firm, Signetics, joined Fairchild in transitioning from the IDM form to the system house form. Signetics, which had started as an IDM form, had been acquired by North American Philips and as such came under the system house organizational form. Fairchild Camera and Instrument, with the Fairchild Semiconductor division, was bought by Schlumberger in 1979 and continued as an IDM within a system house organizational form.

Change again can be seen in the 1980s portion of the table. In 1980, 4 firms,

TI, Motorola, RCA, and Harris/GI, were following the system house organizational form, and 2 firms, Intel and AMD, were following the IDM form. Mostek was acquired by United Technologies in 1980 and sold to SGS-Ates in 1981; thus it was a transitioning organizational form going from an IDM to a system house form. In 1985, TI, Motorola, RCA, and Harris were system house organizational form companies. Signetics, Fairchild, and Mostek were transitional organizational forms. Intel and AMD were the only companies of the IDM organizational form to remain in the top 10 companies for the U.S. semiconductor industry in 1985.

In 1989, the U.S. semiconductor industry had changed yet again. TI, Motorola, and Harris still remained in the top 10 as system house organizational forms, but AT&T had joined them. AT&T had had substantial captive semiconductor capacity and had turned into a merchant company by selling its semiconductor devices in the open market. Western Digital, which had started out in 1970 making chips that controlled computer drives, had now diversified into making the drives themselves and is represented as a transitioning organizational form, but one that was doing so through internal organic growth rather than through acquisitions. Intel and National, which had acquired the semiconductor operations of Fairchild in 1987, AMD, LSI Logic (founded in 1981), and Micron (founded in 1978) joined the IDM organizational form. At the end of the decade of the 1980s, the competitive topology of the U.S. domestic semiconductor industry looked like this: 4 system house organizational form companies led the top 10, followed by 5 IDM organizational form companies and one transitioning organizational form company.

By 1992, the domestic industry had begun to change again. Motorola, TI, Harris, and AT&T were representing the older system house organizational form. But for the first time, a firm representing the IDM organizational form, Intel, had become the leading company in the top 10; with the addition of National, AMD, LSI Logic, Analog Devices, and Micron, the IDMs now made up the majority of the top 10 companies. Intel occupied the top spot in 1990 and has hung onto it since. The previous transitioning company organizational forms were no longer present on the top 10 companies list. By 1995 TI and Motorola were still representing the system house organizational form. IBM had joined them much in the same way that AT&T had entered the merchant market in 1988. IBM had been producing semiconductors going back to the early years of the industry, but had done so only for internal use and as such had remained a captive company. It began selling its IC devices in 1992, turning from its captive position into a merchant company using the system house organizational form. Intel remained the leading company in 1995 and along with Micron, AMD, LSI Logic, and Cirrus Logic, which was founded in 1984, rounded out the top 10 companies utilizing the IDM form.

In 2002, the domestic industry was again undergoing change with the introduction, for the first time, of a new organizational form into the top 10 positions. TI, Motorola, and IBM represented the older system house organizational form. The dominant form once again was the IDM form represented by Intel,

Micron, AMD, and Analog Devices. AT&T had become Lucent Technologies in 1996 and still maintained a system house organizational form. Agere was a transitioning company, having been spun out of Lucent Technologies in 2002 and taking on a more IDM-type organizational form because its product focus was on semiconductor devices. The listings of Nvidia and Qualcomm represent the emergence of a new organizational form on the top 10 list: the fabless semiconductor organizational form. As noted above, this form was initiated in the late 1960s and began entry in earnest in the early 1980s. Firms have been entering the U.S. domestic semiconductor industry using this form ever since. However, it took some 20 years for this form to move into the top 10 listing for the U.S. domestic semiconductor industry.

There are several trends that are apparent from the above analysis. First is the persistence and resilience of the system house organizational form. From the very inception of the semiconductor industry until the present time, organizations that have adopted this form, albeit not the same companies, have been present in the semiconductor industry in the U.S. Second, the IDM form, while quickly establishing itself as a viable alternative organizational form, did not come to dominate the industry until the late 1980s, more than 30 years after its first appearance. Third, the newest organizational form to emerge into the top 10 list of companies in the U.S. institutional setting, the fabless semiconductor design firm, has taken about 30 years from its first appearance to even enter this area of dominance. Fourth, in the earlier years firms were transitioning from the IDM form to the system house form, often because of difficulties that a company had in the market with an IDM form, as with the Philips acquisition of Signetics and the Schlumberger acquisition of Fairchild, or because a company with a system house form was looking for a quick entry into the semiconductor industry, as with the United Technology acquisition of Mostek. Fifth, the most recent trend in transitioning appears to be the movement from a system house organizational form to an IDM form, as in the case of Agere and to a lesser extent IBM Microelectronics and Motorola, which have all spun out their semiconductor operations into separate divisions with more autonomy, if not into separate companies.

The sixth trend concerns the innovation envelope relationship between equipment suppliers and semiconductor firms in the U.S. The basic relationship was governed by market forces of price, delivery, and quality and was organized as a loose network of these market-based contracting relationships. The origin for this configuration of the innovation envelope is found in the self-organizing processes at work in the early development of the semiconductor industry in the U.S. Like most of the semiconductor industry, the equipment supplier firms began as spinoffs and start-ups. The relationship was important, since advances in semiconductors could only be made if equipment was available to mass-produce the devices. In the early years, the center of process innovation lay more closely with the semiconductor companies. Robert Noyce's development of the Planar process for fabrication while at Fairchild is perhaps the best example of this. This put the equipment companies in a less than advantageous position relative to the semiconductor companies, which led to a less than cordial relationship from time to time.

Add to the above the ordering practices that existed between the electronic systems users of ICs and the semiconductor firms, and between the semiconductor firms and the equipment suppliers, and at times the relationship could be downright hostile. Electronics firms would often double- or triple-book semiconductor orders in order to be assured an adequate supply during good times. This would lead to overestimations of demand by the semiconductor companies and over-ordering of equipment from equipment makers. When demand for electronic systems slowed, the double orders were dropped and the demand for semiconductors evaporated, causing the semiconductor companies to cancel their orders for equipment. Since the semiconductor equipment was expensive and not many units were sold, the loss of even a few orders would cause the equipment companies to have difficult times maintaining technology development momentum. It was once remarked that if the electronics companies got the sniffles, the semiconductor companies caught cold and the equipment companies suffered pneumonia.

This market-contract-based, loosely governed network worked until the mid-1970s to late 1970s, when it began to compete against the more tightly linked relation-based club arrangement that existed in Japan. U.S. equipment suppliers were slower in developing the latest equipment needed to produce high-quality semiconductors in volume, especially DRAMs. The DRAM was special because it was a commodity semiconductor device, so its design was similar within each generation, and it was produced in such volume that it literally drove advancements in the processing technology needed to fabricate it and any other semiconductor device. The Japanese semiconductor companies were able to dominate in DRAMs, partly because of the closer ties that existed between the equipment suppliers and the semiconductor companies. These closer ties allowed for a more efficient use of resources in developing each new generation of DRAM (Methé, 1985, 1991, 1992a). It is not surprising that as U.S. semiconductor companies began to exit the DRAM segment of the semiconductor industry, so too did U.S. equipment suppliers. The sense of crisis that this generated spurred the various actors connected to the semiconductor industry to act.

The establishment of SEMATECH was part of the U.S.'s institutional answer to the crisis. The impact of SEMATECH and various other initiatives related to semiconductors that sprang from the government or from the semiconductor industry itself—such as the Semiconductor Research Corporation (SRC), which helped foster better university-industry relationships—was not just in reviving the U.S. equipment firms and IC firms, but also in enhancing the technological forces that were globalizing the semiconductor industry.

These techno-global forces lay in the increasing capital cost of semiconductor equipment accompanied by the decreasing unit cost of the semiconductor devices themselves. The decreasing unit cost meant that semiconductor devices were finding their way into myriad applications because of the cost advantages they gave over other non-electronic switching devices. As such, any electronic systems company needed a supply of semiconductor devices in order to compete in its respective market. As the electronics industry globalized, especially to other parts of Asia, this need spread as well. SEMATECH's work on equipment technology facilitated the growth of Korean and Taiwanese firms by providing better information about equipment technologies. Although the cost of equipment continues to rise, the greater information on the direction and pacing of innovation along various equipment trajectories allowed for market-based transactions to occur and reduced uncertainty in evaluating the alternatives offered for new equipment innovation. The changes in the semiconductor industry wrought by these techno-global dynamics have come full circle in their influence on institutional responses such as SEMATECH, which recently lost its U.S. government financial backing and has evolved into International SEMATECH (ISEMATECH) and begun to accept non-U.S. firm participation. We will discuss these issues in the final sections of this chapter.

The U.S. equipment suppliers were aided, then, by two market-related developments. The first was the emergence of the microprocessor and later other logic devices, such as application-specific integrated circuits (ASICs) that could be made in enough volume to drive processing technology. The second was the breaking of the bipolar orientation of the global semiconductor industry away from a U.S.–Japan axis with the emergence of South Korean and later Taiwanese semiconductor companies. Both of these developments created virtuous cycles between the non-Japanese equipment suppliers and the non-Japanese semiconductor companies. The standardization of equipment technology and the more open and transparent evaluations that could be performed on it made it more readily available to new entrants. The emergence of new customers for the non-Japanese equipment suppliers drove their gradual reascendance in the market.

4.3 The European Integrated-Circuit Industry[4]

System houses that have diversified into the technology by setting up divisions or subsidiaries, some as joint ventures with U.S. companies and some entirely on their own, have dominated the European semiconductor industry. Rather than take this year by year, as we did in examining the U.S. semiconductor industry, we will examine the European industry on a firm-by-firm basis.

In 1978 the dominant companies were Philips and Siemens. Their semiconductor operations were company divisions and had begun early; Philips started in 1964 with its Components Division. In 1991 a separate product division, Philips Semiconductor, was created out of the Components Division in order to focus activities on semiconductors. Siemens began research on semiconductors in 1949 and was producing integrated circuits in 1963. In 1988 the Siemens Semiconductor Group was established as a self-standing unit within Siemens AG. In 1999 this group was spun out as Infineon.

ITT Semiconductor was a subsidiary of the ITT Corporation in the U.S. that was formed in 1952 in Germany as Intermetall GmbH to sell germanium transistors and diodes. SGS-Ates was the merger of Ates, a subsidiary of the Italian

Table 4.3 Top 10 Semiconductor Firms in the European Industry for Selected Years

Rank	2002	1995	1992	1989	1985	1983	1978
1	***STMicro***	***SGS-Thomson***	**Philips**	**Philips**	**Siemens**	**Philips**	**Philips**
2	***Infineon***	**Philips**	***SGS-Thomson***	***SGS-Thomson***	**SGS-Ates**	**Siemens**	**Siemens**
3	**Philips**	**Siemens**	**Siemens**	**Siemens**	**Philips**	**SGS-Ates**	**ITT**
4	**Bosch**	***TEMIC***	**GEC Plessey**	**Plessey-Ferranti**	**Thomson**	**ITT**	**SGS-Ates**
5	*Micronas*	**GEC Plessey**	**ITT**	**ITT**	***Inmos***	**Thomson**	**Thomson-CSF**
6	**Alcatel**	**Ericsson**	**Ericsson**	**Telefunken**	**ITT**	**Ferranti**	**Plessey**
7	***AMS***	**Alcatel Mietec**	**MHS Semi**	**Matra Harris**	**Ferranti**	**Inmos**	**Ferranti**
8	**Ericsson**	***Austria Mikro***	**Telefunken**	***Austria Mikro***	**Plessey**	**Plessey Telefunken**	
9	X-Fab	**ITT Semi**	**Mietec**	**ABB Hafo**			
10	Melexis	***EM Micro Elec***	***Austria Mikro***	**Marconi**			

Key:
BOLD: Diversifying Entrant with Electronic Systems Connection
ITALICS: Start-up as an Integrated Device Manufacturer
STANDARD: Start-up as a Fabless Design Firm or Foundry
BOLD ITALIC S: Shifting from Electronic Systems to Integrated Device Manufacturer
Sources: ICE Status, various issues; ICE Profiles, various issues; IC Insights Strategic Reviews, various issues

telecommunication company STET (Societa Finanziara Telefonica) that was set up in the 1950s, and SGS, which was set up by Olivetti also in the 1950s. SGS had entered the semiconductor industry through a joint venture with Fairchild in 1960. Fairchild withdrew from the joint venture in 1968, and it reverted back to SGS. In 1971 SGS-Ates was formed through the merger of the two companies by the Italian government. In 1981 SGS-Ates acquired Mostek from United Technologies Corporation, and in 1987 it was merged into Thomson to form SGS-Thomson. Thomson-CSF is the parent company of Thomson Semiconducteur and is part of the larger Thomson SA group in France. The Thomson group has continued to develop semiconductors for the military.

Plessey Semiconductors began in 1966 as a part of Plessey, Inc., an electronic systems house. It was merged with Marconi and acquired by GEC in 1990. Ferranti Semiconductor was a part of Ferranti, Ltd., an electronic systems house that was one of the first companies to build computers in the 1950s. It was merged with Plessey in 1988. Ferranti developed the gate array, 10 years before LSI Logic in the U.S. exploited it commercially. AEG-Telefunken, or simply Telefunken, was part of the Daimler-Benz group when it entered the semiconductor industry. Telefunken acquired 50% of Matra Harris Semiconductor (MHS) in 1989. Telefunken was itself folded into TEMIC, which was formed in 1992 when the Daimler group and Deutsche Aerospace set up a joint venture.

Inmos, which joined the top semiconductor vendors in 1983, was established in 1977 through a $50 million investment from the UK government. It developed some unique microprocessor designs such as the Transputer. Inmos was sold to Thorn EMI in 1984 and later sold to SGS-Thomson in 1988. Matra Harris Semiconductor, later just MHS, was formed in 1979 as a joint venture between Matra SA of France and Harris Semiconductor of the U.S. This joint venture was set up as one of several the French government encouraged to bring in semiconductor technology from abroad through a program called Plan Circuits Intégrés. The French government at the time owned Matra SA, and it was privatized in 1988. The company became a subsidiary in 1992 of the TEMIC organization, and is responsible for semiconductor operations in France. Austria Micro Systems (AMS) was established in 1981 as Austria GmbH. It was originally a joint venture between American Micro-Systems Inc. (AMI) and VOEST-Alpine AG. In 1987 it changed its name to Austria Mikro Systeme as AMI was withdrawing. It changed its name to Austria Micro Systems in 2001 and has become a privately held company with Aspern Industrie Beteiligungs AG holding 98% of the company's stock.

ABB Hafo was originally established in 1934 as a private research institute; it began to focus on semiconductor research in 1954 and was part of the ASEA group. It became a part of the Asea Brown Boveri Group in 1987. A Canadian firm, Mitel, acquired ABB Hafo in 1996. Mietec was formed in 1983 as a joint venture between Bell Telephone Manufacturing Co., a subsidiary owned by ITT, and GIMV, a Flanders regional investment company. In 1987 the telecommunications activities of ITT were merged into Alcatel's operations and Mietec went with them. In 1990 Alcatel purchased all the remaining shares of Mietec, and the name of the company was changed to Alcatel Mietec. In 2002 Alcatel sold its semiconductor operations to STMicro.

EM Microelectronic-Marin was founded in 1975 as a division of the Swiss Ebauches Electronics SA, which was part of ASUAG, a larger group of Swiss watchmaking companies. Ericsson Microelectronics was the semiconductor division of the Ericsson electronics company. It began operations in the early 1970s, and much of its activity was captive. It moved into the merchant market more in the 1990s. In 2002 it sold off much of its semiconductor operations to Infineon, which was the semiconductor operations unit of Siemens. As noted above, Infineon was spun off from Siemens in 1999, but it is still majority-owned by Siemens at about 19%. It is, however, seen as a system house organizational form transitioning into an IDM form.

Micronas has a more complex history, since part of it was founded in 1980 as a subsidiary of Nokia, and then in 1989 Crosstec Engineering AG acquired it. The Micronas name was kept, and in 1992 it became an independent company. Micronas acquired the semiconductor operations of ITT Semiconductor in 1997, and then went through a restructuring in 1998, selling off the remains of the old Nokia division; therefore we are classifying this as an IDM start-up. X-Fab is a pure-play foundry company formed in 1999 when Belgium's Elex NV combined three of its semiconductor facilities into one company. Melexis is also part of the Elex NV organization and a major customer of X-Fab. We classify X-Fab as a foundry start-up. Melexis Microelectronic Integrated Systems originally was established in 1988 and produced primarily ASICs. It is part of the Elex NV holding company along with X-Fab and Thesys Mikroelektronik GmbH. We have classified this company as an IDM start-up.

Several trends can be identified from the analysis presented above. First, the role of the large system houses in establishing semiconductor operations in Europe dominates all other organizational forms. IDM start-up forms did occur, but few became large or remained independent in the European institutional environment. The system house organizational form has dominated from the beginning of the European semiconductor industry. This industry was highly fragmented by national markets throughout much of its history, and much of the European demand for semiconductors—more than 60% in many years—was filled either by Japanese or U.S. firms. Even if generous amounts of venture capital had been available, it would have been difficult to support these newly entering firms.

Second, governments played a much more direct role in establishing and shaping the topography of the European semiconductor industry. This is seen in the active participation of various national governments in the establishment of semiconductor companies. This governmental activity went further when it was recognized that national markets would not sustain the operations of national champions. Cross-border mergers were set up between various national champions. Many began occurring in the late 1980s in preparation for the 1992 unification of European markets. Governments also played a more traditional role. The various governments comprising Europe established research institutes and funded research consortia concerning semiconductors and electronic systems. BRITE and ESPRIT were two formed during the 1980s, and Interuniversity MicroElectronics Center (IMEC) is a current research consortium. Unlike previous consortia that focused on a limited set of objectives, IMEC is an ongoing consortium of university, business, and government researchers carrying out midterm research focused on advancing semiconductor fabrication technology.

Third, when start-up companies began as IDM organizational forms or later as fabless/foundry organizational forms, these companies often drew their financial resources from either holding companies or regional development companies, or from the participation of system houses. The line demarcating the IDM start-up and system house organizational forms is less clear in the European institutional setting than in the U.S. institutional setting. Philips and Siemens were true system houses because these two companies were connected to multiple electronics markets. Many of the European system houses were diversifying entrants from the military or industrial electronics/computer markets. The domination of the system house form also had an impact on the human resources necessary for starting up a firm. Moreover, most of the downstream customers of the semiconductors produced in Europe were the very same system houses.

Fourth, merger and acquisition activity took place in the U.S., but in Europe the effect was more marked because the industry has been experiencing consolidation throughout its history. According to some estimates, the top 2 firms accounted for 87% of the semiconductor output in Europe in 2003. This high level of concentration was exhibited throughout the history of the European market, where the top 2 or 3 firms controlled anywhere from 70% to 90% of the market. In the U.S. the continued entry of new firms has muted the consolidation effect of mergers and acquisitions. This consolidation around a few large firms and the lack of continual renewal through start-up entry is one explanation why some years have fewer than 10 firms in the top list.

The fifth trend is seen emerging in the last year of the data: movement to the independent IDM organizational form with STMicro, Infineon, and the emergence of companies like Micronas and Melexis and the foundry X-Fab into the top list. The European semiconductor topology is beginning to resemble that of the U.S. in its mix of organizational forms, with system houses, IDMs, and foundry organizational forms coexisting. Two caveats need to be interjected concerning this recent trend. It is just appearing, and in its nascent form may be blunted or redirected by other environmental or institutional factors; also, the level of concentration, as noted, is higher in Europe than in the U.S., which has a substantial impact on the distribution of the resources necessary for a firm representing a particular organizational form to get established and survive.

The sixth trend concerns the configuration of the innovation envelope for the European semiconductor industry. Most of the semiconductor industry equipment firms in Europe were spun off from semiconductor companies, but the connection was tighter than in the U.S. case because of the connection of the semiconductor companies to the larger system houses, which in turn were often connected to larger industrial groups. Furthermore, because the European semiconductor companies often served small fragmented markets and supplied mainly domestic electronics firms, few process innovations originated in Europe relative to the U.S. and Japan. The European manufacturers were slow to move from bipolar process technology to MOS process technology and often lagged by as much as six months to a year behind their U.S. and Japanese counterparts. Because of the techno-global forces driving the semiconductor industry, those equipment firms that became competitive, such as Kulicke & Soffa and Schlumberger, did so in the less technologically advanced equipment areas and established their presence early in the U.S. or Japanese markets.

4.4 The Japanese Integrated-Circuit Industry[5]

In the Japanese situation, as in Europe, the dominance of large diversifying system houses is evident. Unlike the European situation, the Japanese system houses were more like Philips and Siemens with connections to multiple downstream electronics markets. Although the Japanese semiconductor industry has been well covered in this volume (see Okada's chapters) as well as in other works (see Methé, various works), several key trends should be given additional attention. The first is that the Japanese semiconductor system houses were not all equal in terms of access to resources. There is an important distinction that

Table 4.4 Top 10 Semiconductor Firms in the Japanese Industry for Selected Years

Rank	2003	2002	1995	1992	1989	1985	1983	1978
1	***Renesas***	**NEC**	**NEC**	**Toshiba**	**NEC**	**NEC**	**NEC**	**NEC**
2	**Toshiba**	**Toshiba**	**Hitachi**	**NEC**	**Toshiba**	**Hitachi**	**Hitachi**	**Hitachi**
3	***NEC Elec***	**Hitachi**	**Toshiba**	**Hitachi**	**Hitachi**	**Toshiba**	**Toshiba**	**Toshiba**
4	**Sony**	**Fujitsu**	**Mitsubishi**	**Fujitsu**	**Mitsubishi**	**Fujitsu**	**Fujitsu**	**Mitsubishi**
5	**Fujitsu**	**Mitsubishi**	**Fujitsu**	**Mitsubishi**	**Fujitsu**	**Matsushita**	**Matsushita**	**Fujitsu**
6	**Matsushita**	**Matsushita**	**Matsushita**	**Matsushita**	**Matsushita**	**Mitsubishi**	**Mitsubishi**	**Matsushita**
7	**Sharp**	**Sony**	**Sanyo**	**Sharp**	**Sharp**	**Sanyo**	**Sanyo**	**Sanyo**
8	*Rohm*	**Sharp**	**Oki**	**Sony**	**Sanyo**	**Oki**	**Oki**	**Sharp**
9	**Sanyo**	**Sanyo**	**Sharp**	**Sanyo**	**Oki**	**Sharp**	**Sharp**	**Oki**
10	**Oki**	*Rohm*	**Sony**	**Oki**	**Sony**	**Sony**	**Sony**	**Sony**

Key:
BOLD: Diversifying Entrant with Electronic Systems Connection
ITALICS: Start-up as an Integrated Device Manufacturer
STANDARD: Start-up as a Fabless Design Firm or Foundry
BOLD ITALIC S: Shifting from Electronic Systems to Integrated Device Manufacturer
Sources: ICE Status, various issues; ICE Profiles, various issues; IC Insights Strategic Reviews, various issues

must be made between system houses like NEC, Hitachi, Toshiba, Fujitsu, Oki, and Mitsubishi Electric, the *sogo denki* makers, who made industrial electronics and computers as well as consumer electronics, and companies like Matsushita, Sony, Sharp, and Sanyo, who focused on consumer electronics. Further, it was the *sogo denki* makers of semiconductors who were included in government-sponsored research consortia, the most famous of which was the Cho LSI Kenkyu Kumiai (VLSI Research Cooperative) (Methé, 1985).

Second, the institutional environment changed over the history of the Japanese semiconductor industry from one of "catch-up" to one of "integration" and back to "catch-up." This can be seen in the role of the government and the various sponsored consortia that changed as a result of the shift from the bipolar competition between the U.S. and Japan to the multipolar global industry that exists today. The effect of these consortia can be debated, but the VLSI Research Cooperative was credited with much of the success of the Japanese semiconductor companies in overtaking the United States, at least in the minds of U.S. policy makers and the leaders of the various industry associations linked to the U.S. industry. Efforts were made by the U.S. side to open up access to these Japanese government-sponsored research endeavors, and for both policy and practical reasons the Japanese government allowed foreign access to various electronics-related research programs, as seen in the SELETE program. The focus also shifted within these programs away from the more practical aspects of readying the technology to launch the next generation to more long-term or basic research-oriented goals. This process shifted again in the late 1990s as the Japanese firms found themselves behind the Koreans and Taiwanese in memory and fabrication technology and unable to match the U.S. companies in the heavily design- and market-oriented logic areas. Recent research consortia such as ASPLA, ASUKA, and others have attempted to remedy this situation.

Third, many companies in the Japanese semiconductor industry, especially the *sogo denki* makers, were connected not only downstream to various electronics markets, but also upstream to various semiconductor equipment companies through the innovation envelope. These relationships could be as wholly owned subsidiaries or as in-house production units, but more often than not they were the equity relationships known as vertical *keiretsu* ("business group"). The impact of these upstream linkages with equipment companies was important in the early years because they enabled the Japanese semiconductor companies to catch up and then surpass their U.S. counterparts in fabrication process technology (Methé, 1985, 1991a). The relationship between the equipment companies and the semiconductor companies was tighter than in the U.S. or European cases and was relation-based—that is, based on long-term mutual commitments to co-develop fabrication technology and refine it for the primary contractor. The character of this relationship shifted from facilitator to inhibitor as the context of the semiconductor industry began to change around the end of the decade of the 1980s and early 1990s.

During the period when the global semiconductor industry was bipolar in terms of market contenders, from roughly the late 1970s (1978) until the early 1990s (1993), with Japanese and U.S. companies in heavy competition, the strong links between equipment companies and semiconductor companies that existed in Japan helped the Japanese to gain and then maintain their lead in fabrication process technology. This was evident in the DRAM market that drove innovation in this technology, especially in the decades of the 1970s and 1980s. Japanese semiconductor and equipment makers could co-develop new fabrication process technology faster than their U.S. counterparts could.

Furthermore, the Japanese equipment makers would continually fine-tune the equipment after it was in place to the exact specifications of the Japanese semiconductor maker in order to increase the yield from the fabrication line. As noted, U.S. semiconductor companies had more loosely linked network relationships with their equipment suppliers, and these were governed by market-based contracting as opposed to the more relation-based contracting of the Japanese. One outcome of the bipolar competition between the U.S. and Japan was the creation of SEMATECH, which worked to advance and standardize fabrication process technology, thus diffusing advanced process technology more rapidly out into the industry. U.S. equipment suppliers could then add customized software solutions to the technology with the hope of gaining advantages over their equipment rivals.

With the emergence of a multipolar semiconductor industry, the Japanese equipment and semiconductor companies were now faced with an entirely different industry situation. The advantage of closely linked innovation envelope relationships that had been so important in the 1970s and early 1980s began to fade in the late 1980s as equally good or better fabrication technology became available. Further, as Japanese semiconductor companies lost momentum in the DRAM segment of the semiconductor industry to the new Korean competitors, their ability to fund the increasing demand for capital needed for new equipment faltered. This started to drive the Japanese equipment manufacturers to search for new customers. The Achilles' heel of Japanese electronics firms in general has always been in the area of software development and systems integration. With the growing importance of software-controlled fabrication equipment, the Japanese equipment makers were at a disadvantage, and one that could not be compensated for by the sharing of information with Japanese semiconductor firms, which were equally as deficient. The advantage of a tightly linked innovation envelope had now become a disadvantage.

To understand further why the Japanese began to lose momentum in the DRAM industry, we find it important to note a macro-institutional event that occurred in 1985. The Plaza Accord raised the value of the yen substantially against the dollar. This agreement between the Japanese government and the other OECD member governments was not aimed specifically at the semiconductor industry, but it had an impact on it nevertheless. We will discuss the Korean semiconductor industry more fully below, but the Plaza Accord opened the door for the Koreans to come in with lower priced DRAMs, in dollar terms, than the Japanese. The 1985 Plaza Accord put an effective floor under the price of Japanese DRAMs relative to Korean and U.S. companies. The heavy dependence of Japanese semiconductor companies on DRAMs for much of their revenue as well as volume placed a considerable burden on them in terms of financing the further development of new processing technology. This burden was magnified by the slowdown in the growth of the Japanese economy overall after the bursting of the "Economic Bubble" in 1990 and in the slowdown in consumer electronics within Japan.

The Japanese semiconductor companies were part of the system house operations of the Japanese electronics companies. Much of the volume production of semiconductors was driven by the growth of the consumer electronics industry. Japanese system houses and the *sogo denki* makers in particular were more dependent on the domestic Japanese market than were the other electronics companies, such as Sony, Matsushita, Sharp, and Sanyo. Consequently, as demand for consumer electronics began to wane in the Japanese domestic market, price competition intensified and this affected the margins of all electronics companies. The situation of the PC industry in particular had an impact on the *sogo denki* makers, especially NEC and Fujitsu, after the arrival of viable foreign competitors (Methé et al., 1998a, 1998b).

These broader institutional, economic, and specific consumer electronics industry related factors put differential pressure on the various system house forms that supplied semiconductors and set in motion the fourth trend evident in the table above. The *sogo denki* system house form, as represented by NEC, Hitachi, Toshiba, and Mitsubishi Electric, began to withdraw from segments of the semiconductor industry, such as DRAMs. Hitachi and NEC created a joint venture for their DRAM operations called Elpida, which later absorbed the DRAM operation of Mitsubishi. Toshiba sold off its DRAM operation to Micron, a U.S. IDM. NEC further streamlined its semiconductor operations by spinning off its logic device operation as NEC Electronics in November 2002. NEC Electronics went public in July of 2003, although NEC is still the largest single shareholder after the initial public offering (IPO). This accounts for the system house shifting to the IDM designation as its organizational form in Table 4.4. The same can be said for Renesas, the joint venture for logic devices that is a combination of Hitachi's and Mitsubishi Electric's logic operations. Currently, Hitachi has 55% of the equity and Mitsubishi Electric 45%. Renesas has yet to have its IPO, but one is planned. These two firms, NEC Electronics and Renesas, are concentrating much of their efforts on what has become the system-on-a-chip (SoC) segment of the semiconductor industry, an outgrowth of the older ASIC segment. This trend of shifting to an IDM organizational form with a focus on the SoC will most likely continue as companies like Fujitsu, Toshiba, Matsushita, Sony, and other system house firms that made semiconductors continue to have difficulties competing in the market. It remains to be seen if this strategic approach will be successful or not. As noted above, the Japanese electronics firms have had problems in developing their capabilities in software development and engineering. This is particularly troubling because success in the SoC segment requires, among other capabilities, sophisticated software engineering for embedding the software on the chip itself.

In the DRAM area, only Elpida remains. It is not listed in the table because its operations are not large enough to qualify, but it is also indicative of the movement toward the IDM organizational form that is evident in the cases of NEC Electronics and Renesas. Elpida has had a difficult time of it but was able to move toward a successful IPO on April 28, 2005. Rohm, which first appeared on the top supplier list in 2002, was established in 1958. It began producing integrated circuits in 1981 and has a more focused strategy when confronting the selling of them in the merchant market. Although it is not a semiconductor start-up per se, it is much more akin to the IDM form than to the system house form, since semiconductor devices generate about 85% of its revenue and the company does not produce any electronic systems products, only components. It is a focused operation that has carved out competitive positions in selected segments of the semiconductor industry, such as signal processing and control chips for multimedia applications, and is a leading company in nonvolatile memory devices. It represents an alternative organizational form to the more dominant system house form and appears to be more profitable.

A fifth trend is seen more in its absence because few other companies in Japan have emulated Rohm's success. As a result of the barren environment in terms of human, financial, and other resources necessary for entrepreneurial start-ups to begin and grow, few such start-ups have entered the Japanese market (Methé, 2005; Methé and Bracker, 1994; Bracker and Methé, 1994). This lack of start-up organizational form support is deeply ingrained in the Japanese economic system and has inhibited the birth and growth of even the fabless organizational form. It should be remembered that this form originated in the U.S. as a counter to the high cost of entering with a fabrication facility. There have been no foundry start-ups either. Some of the system house forms have diversified into foundry operations, however. The alliance in 2000 between Hitachi and UMC in creating Tricenti was such a diversification. This alliance ended in 2002, however, because Hitachi bought out its UMC partner and later transferred the Tricenti operations to Renesas in 2003. Renesas has closed down the foundry operation, converting it into a leading-edge production fab for Renesas.

4.5 The Korean Integrated-Circuit Industry[6]

Anam Industrial, one of the Korean *chaebol* (large industrial group), initiated the Korean semiconductor industry with the development of contract services in 1968. Through its connections with Amkor, a U.S. firm that still offers services in the area of packaging and testing, Anam Industrial began offering assembly and testing services in Korea. Throughout the 1970s and into the 1980s, both Anam and Amkor did much of the spadework to promote the front end, or fabrication process, and the back end, or assembly and test process, in Korea. In the 1980s, European and U.S. firms—partly in response to the challenge coming from Japanese producers—availed themselves of the lower labor costs and skilled and increasingly knowledgeable engineering talent in Korea (Kim, 1997). However, the Korean semiconductor industry did not really begin to take off on its own until the early to late 1970s as the government set semiconductor technology as one of the key areas for future growth.

Drawing on the engineering talent that was graduating from the Korean Advanced Institute of Science and Technology (KAIST), the government set forth in its fourth five-year plan the specific target of developing an indigenous semiconductor industry in Korea. In the early 1980s the focus of this development plan became the DRAM segment of the semiconductor industry. Through a combination of government promotion and the astute strategic moves of several of the large Korean *chaebol*, the semiconductor industry grew rapidly throughout the late 1980s and into the 1990s. The *chaebol* were tapped early for the development of semiconductor technology in Korea, and with the entry of Korean *chaebol* firms such as Samsung Electronics in 1983, Hyundai Electronics Industries in 1983, and Goldstar Electron in 1989 (the latter being a combination of the semiconductor operations of Goldstar Company and Goldstar Semiconductor that had begun in the early 1980s), a critical mass of financial and human resources was quickly created.

Of these three *chaebol* players, Goldstar, which changed its name to LG Electronics, was the weakest and would in 1999 lose most of its semiconductor operations to Hyundai. Daewoo, which began its electronic systems operations in 1974, also entered into the semiconductor industry in the early 1980s, but did not develop into a strong enough contender to take its place within the Korean

Table 4.5 Top 10 Semiconductor Firms in the Korean Industry for Selected Years

Rank	2002	1995	1992	1989	1987	1985	1983
1	**Samsung**	**Samsung**	**Samsung**	**Samsung**	**Samsung**	**Samsung**	(LITTLE sophisticated semiconductor production done by indigenous Korean firms)
2	***Hynix***	**Hyundai**	**Hyundai**	**Hyundai**	**Hyundai**	**Hyundai**	
3	***Anam/Dongbu***	**LG Semi**	**Goldstar**	**Goldstar**	**Goldstar**	**Goldstar**	
4					**KEC**	**KEC**	

Key:
BOLD: Diversifying Entrant with Electronic Systems Connection
ITALICS: Start-up as an Integrated Device Manufacturer
STANDARD: Start-up as a Fabless Design Firm or Foundry
BOLD ITALIC S: Shifting from Electronic Systems to Integrated Device Manufacturer or Foundry
Sources: ICE Status, various issues; ICE Profiles, various issues; IC Insights Strategic Reviews, various issues

domestic semiconductor industry and then displace Japanese firms in the DRAM industry as Samsung, Hyundai, and Goldstar did. Many of the human, technological, and financial resources of the *chaebol*, as seen in the LG Electronics case, were recirculated among the remaining *chaebol*, rather than out into entrepreneurial start-up firms.

The combination of focused firm strategy and government policies that supplied both financial and human resources helped to shape the Korean semiconductor industry. Korea is a latecomer both to industrialization and to the high-technology world of semiconductors. As such, it has experienced both the benefits and the costs of the techno-global forces that have been driving the global semiconductor industry. The competition between the Japanese and U.S. segments of the semiconductor industry opened up opportunities for the Korean companies to gain valuable technological knowledge, especially as U.S. equipment firms were looking for new markets for their fabrication equipment. Furthermore, the Korean industry's proximity to Japan opened up opportunities to secure technology either through strategic alliances or by paying for moonlighting Japanese engineers to come to Korea periodically to help with various design and production problems. Although Korean semiconductor companies make a wide variety of semiconductor types, both logic devices and memory devices, the focus on DRAM production made the acquisition of knowledge easier.

The Korean semiconductor industry is also a captive of its latecomer industrialization roots in terms of the institutional environment in which it was born and grew up. The government supplied financial resources through various grant and loan programs. These had traditionally gone to members of the *chaebol*, and those aimed at the semiconductor industry were no different. Likewise, the government's efforts to supply good engineering talent were met with the demand from the *chaebol*. The best engineering talent competed for positions with Samsung, Hyundai, LG, and Daewoo. This left little for smaller *chaebol* or companies not fully connected to these industrial giants, let alone anything for entrepreneurial start-ups.

Furthermore, this engineering talent was young and inexperienced in semiconductor fabrication. However, the fact that many Korean nationals had emigrated to the U.S. and had worked in the U.S. semiconductor industry helped to bring seasoned talent into the companies in areas such as project management. Again, the larger *chaebol* members were able to attract the best overseas talent to return to Korea in order to work for them. Many of these returnees ended up managing critical elements of each *chaebol*'s entry into sophisticated integrated-circuit production. They provided the necessary managerial and project experience that was lacking with the younger homegrown engineers, and this enabled these companies to grow rapidly.

These factors explain why only 3 or at most 4 firms are listed as the top companies for the various years in Korea. It also explains why most of these are essentially of the diversifying system house organizational form. Each of the companies occupying a top position—and the concentration ratio in the Korean semiconductor industry is around 80%–90% of production with these top 3 or 4—is a member of one of the large industrial groups that still dominate the Korean economy. Only in the past few years, beginning with the financial crisis of 1997 and followed by the collapse of the semiconductor industry in 2001, have we seen the emergence of different types of organizational forms.

The Korean government's attempts to reign in the power of the *chaebol* took a serious turn after the financial crisis of 1997. The recognition that the Korean economy was very top-heavy with the *chaebol* occupying the best positions in many industries, coupled with the sudden loss of economic growth that followed the Asian financial crisis, brought about a different policy environment concerning the future activities of the *chaebol*. Furthermore, the *chaebol* were not always run with the best of managerial decision-making algorithms. Samsung's move into the automobile industry was not based on sound economic and financial reckoning, but more on the chairman's interest in the auto industry in general and automobiles in particular. Daewoo's drive to become large in terms of market share often left it with a lot of debt and not the most efficient operations. As a result the government ordered that the *chaebol* members rationalize their operations. This had an impact on the semiconductor industry because LG's semiconductor operation, LG Semicon, was sold to Hyundai in October 1999. In taking over the LG semiconductor operation, the Hyundai group also had to assume the debts of LG. The new company was called Hynix.

The creation of Hynix came when the DRAM segment of the semiconductor industry was moving through a rapid series of peaks and troughs, culminating with the worst downturn in the industry's history in 2001. Hynix has been in near bankruptcy since then and has been under considerable pressure to separate its memory from its non-memory operations. This saga still continues today with no clear end in sight. Although Hynix is more focused—having spun off its telecommunications and liquid crystal display (LCD) operations—than its predecessor, conforming more closely to an IDM organizational form, it is still an open question, given the ownership issues to be determined, whether it will adopt a true IDM form. The role of the Korean government became an issue with Hynix as well because the company was hit with 57% tariffs by the U.S. for receiving subsidies from the Korean government. These subsidies kept the company afloat during 2001 and 2002 by allowing Hynix to sell its DRAMs below cost.

Several important trends can be observed from the Korean semiconductor case. First is the role of the techno-global aspects of the semiconductor industry. Knowledge and skills were gained because of the industry's globalization through the flow of people and equipment. Further the bipolar axis of the industry between the U.S. and Japan during much of the 1980s opened up opportunities for the diversifying Korean entrants to gain access to knowledge from both contenders. Second, as noted above, the broader institutional factor of the Plaza Accord in 1985 created a price floor below which the Japanese producers of DRAMs could not go. This allowed the Korean suppliers of DRAMs to compete on price at a time when they were still untested as suppliers of this important commodity device. Third, the institutional latecomer environment clearly shaped the size of the Korean industry and the organizational forms that were able to enter. The diversifying system house organizational form dominated from the industry's inception and throughout the 1980s and 1990s.

Fourth, the very narrow focus of the Korean semiconductor companies on DRAMs facilitated their entry, but put them in a trap. The DRAM industry is a commodity industry and one that is subject to business as well as silicon cycle fluctuations. Furthermore, the drive of the Korean semiconductor companies to outperform the Japanese led them to invest in capacity beyond what would have been economically feasible had the institutional support of the Korean government not been available. As a result, the overcapacity created by the Korean manufacturers and their over-reliance on DRAMs has also led to their being hurt more than others when this industry turns down. Some fabless design houses and IDM organizational form companies have entered in non-memory areas, especially in the middle to late 1990s as the Korean government has attempted to open up the economy to more domestic competition, but none of these firms has achieved any significant global market presence as yet.

Fifth, in terms of the innovation envelope, the volume generated by the focus on DRAMs has created an environment out of proportion to the number of device companies. As a result the equipment segment of the industry includes foreign firms from the U.S., Japan, and Europe as well as the indigenous Korean semiconductor equipment suppliers. Most of the Korean suppliers, however, were established to serve the Korean semiconductor companies and must work harder to develop a global presence. This is especially true because the number of Korean companies in the DRAM industry has declined.

A sixth trend, which is just emerging and is not evident from the table or our discussion to date, but it is quite evident from visiting the Web site of the Korea Semiconductor Industry Association (KSIA) and from discussions with Korean semiconductor engineers and managers, is the recent entry of fabless design house IC firms. Their number is not great, but several of these firms adopting the fabless organizational form have entered since the middle to late 1990s. It is too early to tell if these firms will have a measurable impact on the semiconductor industry in Korea, but they are indicative of the techno-global dynamics of innovation driving the integrated-circuit industry.

4.6 The Taiwanese Integrated-Circuit Industry[7]

The Taiwanese semiconductor industry is also a true latecomer to the global semiconductor industry, but its story, though bearing some resemblance to the Korean one, is remarkably different (Hu, 1997). As a latecomer, it features the same agents, or players, but they are configured differently. The regular players were the government, indigenous companies, emigrants returning from the U.S., foreign semiconductor companies, and foreign semiconductor equipment companies. The beginnings of the semiconductor industry in Taiwan go back to action taken by the Taiwanese government in setting up the Industrial Technology Research Institute (ITRI) in 1971. Concern for electronics first manifested itself within the ITRI organization with the establishment of the Electronics Research Service Organization (ERSO). The activities within ERSO resulted in the spin-out of the United Microelectronics Corporation (UMC) in 1979. This event set the difference in tone between Taiwanese semiconductor industry efforts and those of either Japan or Korea.

UMC began in 1980 as an IDM start-up and went public with an IPO on the Taiwan Stock Exchange in 1985. It moved from the IDM organizational form to the foundry organizational form in 1995, though it had had some foundry operations after 1982. It was the first semiconductor company to do so. In 1987 another company was spun out of ITRI, Taiwan Semiconductor Manufacturing Company (TSMC). As noted in a previous section, this company had financial support that was about equally divided among the Taiwanese government, Philips, and private investors. TSMC was the first pure foundry start-up in the world. In 1994 another company, Vanguard International Semiconductor Corporation (VIS), started up as an IDM organizational form focusing initially on memory devices, especially DRAMs. Since then, ITRI and even ERSO have largely withdrawn from active support of the semiconductor companies and moved on to other emerging technological areas.

These companies were nestled in a newly created science park in the city of Hsinchu. The park was set up through the National Science Council and has received government funding, but a Park Administration runs it with about 89% of its funding coming from private sources. Foreign companies can set up in the park, and about 53 of the 335 companies currently in the park are from other countries. It is also the home of a wide variety of technology-related companies, not just semiconductor companies. As of 2002 the park had 136 companies related to the semiconductor industry. Of these, 75 were fabless design start-ups and 14 were IDM types. The Park Administration offers a variety of services, but one that was important to returning engineers was the establishment of schools within the park. The National Experimental High School was set up in 1983 and runs programs in English and Chinese from kindergarten through high school. This educational service eliminated a major stumbling block for returnee

Table 4.6 Top 10 Semiconductor Firms in the Taiwanese Industry for Selected Years

Rank	2002	1995	1992	1989	1987	1985
1	TSMC	TSMC	UMC	UMC	UMC	(LITTLE sophisticated semiconductor production done by indigenous Taiwanese firms)
2	UMC	UMC	TSMC	TSMC	*Quasel*	
3	*Winbond*	*Winbond*	*Winbond*	**Hualon**	*Mosel*	
4	*Nanya*	**TI-Acer**	**Hualon**	*Winbond*		
5	*Mediatek*	*Mosel-Vitelic*	*Holtek*			
6	VIA	*Macronix*	*Macronix*			
7	ProMOS	Hualon	*Mosel-Vitelic*			
8	*Macronix*	**Acer Labs**				
9	*SiS*	*Holtek*				
10	*Powerchip*					

Key:
BOLD: Diversifying Entrant with Electronic Systems Connection
ITALICS: Start-up as an Integrated Device Manufacturer
STANDARD: Start-up as a Fabless Design Firm or Foundry
BOLD ITALIC S: Shifting from Electronic Systems to Integrated Device Manufacturer
Sources: ICE Status, various issues; ICE Profiles, various issues; IC Insights Strategic Reviews, various issues

engineers and managers from the U.S., many of whose children had been educated in U.S. school systems.

Other companies have been established in and around the Hsinchu Science Park. Companies such as Winbond and Macronix began as IDM start-ups in 1987 and 1989, respectively, and Mosel and Vitelic, two privately held companies, began in 1983 as IDM start-ups and later merged. Mosel or MOS Electronics Taiwan was a Taiwanese start-up, and Vitelic was a U.S.-based start-up. Some were fabless start-ups such as VIA Technologies and SiS, both of which began in 1987. Others were diversifying entrants such as Hualon Microelectronics, which was established in 1984 as an assembly operation and began fabrication operations in 1987. It was part of the Hualon Group, a multibillion-dollar conglomerate at the time.

Another diversifying entrant was Acer Laboratories Inc., which began as an independent research and development company for the Acer Group in 1987 and became a fabless design house called ALi in 1999. Nanya Technology was founded in 1995 as a diversifying entry for the Formosa Plastics Group. Foreign companies have also been involved. TI set up a joint venture with Acer called TI-Acer in 1989 and Mitsubishi Electric set one up with Taiwan's Umax-Elite Group called Powerchip Semiconductor in 1994. Another, ProMOS Technologies, was initially a joint venture between an existing Taiwanese semiconductor company, Mosel-Vitelic, and Infineon. In a different entry pattern, the company

Holtek began as a fabless design form in 1983 and added a fabrication facility in 1989, but reverted back to its fabless organizational form in 1998. The variety of organizational forms entering and moving into the top listing of semiconductor companies in the Taiwan semiconductor industry is seen in only one other region, the United States. In some respects the Taiwanese industry is dominated more by the IDM and fabless/foundry start-up organizational forms than is any other region, including the U.S.

Several trends can be seen in this latecomer to the semiconductor industry. First, although the role of government was important in the formative years of developing a critical mass of semiconductor-related technology and knowledge, this role changed in terms of how that knowledge was diffused. The government chose to spin out companies as venture operations and then basically withdrew. Market forces were allowed to shape the development of the semiconductor industry in Taiwan. This is not to say that the Taiwanese government plays no continuing role in the semiconductor industry. This role, however, is not the direct role of subsidies and funding, but of tax incentives and the education of engineering and managerial talent. The Taiwanese government has not directly stepped in to rescue a failing company.

Second, electronic systems houses did exist, such as Acer and Hualon, but with the exception of these two and later Formosa Plastics, few moved into the semiconductor industry as diversifying entrants. By the time the larger industrial groups, such as Formosa Plastics, took an interest in the semiconductor industry, the IDM and fabless/foundry start-up organizational forms had become well established and difficult to dislodge. Part of the answer may lie in the fact that UMC began essentially as a proving ground for whether semiconductor technology could take root in Taiwan. Much of the technology was imported from the U.S., and many of the people at UMC had had some experience working in the U.S. semiconductor industry. In the early 1980s the semiconductor industry was a risky place for companies that were engaged in relatively simple electronic systems assembly. The investments and the skills and people resources needed were not readily available, and profits could be made by further investment in electronic systems operations.

Third, the Taiwan semiconductor industry has been an active source of new entrepreneurial start-up activity. The growth in the numbers of new entrants and the variety of semiconductor segments has a much broader base than in the growth in Korea. This is reflected in the top listing of semiconductor companies in Taiwan, which includes many fabless, foundry, and IDM companies. The 1987 founding of TSMC using the pure foundry organizational form set in motion forces that have affected both the Taiwan semiconductor industry and the world semiconductor industry. By legitimizing the fabless design house strategy, the yoke of ever-increasing capital investment was lifted from the neck of any engineer who had an idea for a new semiconductor device. This has opened up more opportunities for latecomers and mature countries alike if they have the institutional environment to support such entrepreneurial activities. However, the foundry/fabless nexus has had other impacts on the industry that may not be as beneficial.

Fourth, in the period running from the 1970s through about the early 1990s, there were several downturns. The silicon cycle of boom, overinvestment, bust, and underinvestment followed by a new boom has been repeated throughout each downturn. In the semiconductor industry of the periods throughout 1970–1990, memory and logic market segments were complementarily linked. Semiconductor companies focused on either logic or memory or both, and each used an IDM format even if the company itself was part of a system house. That is, all semiconductor operations were integrated to include design through fabrication and sales. If one company had a difficult time or even if the entire industry was confronted with an economic downturn, the fortunes of individual companies varied. The linking of many previously separated market segments occurs through the fabless/foundry nexus. From about the 1990s through the present, the global semiconductor industry has gone through another series of downturns that have been far more devastating in terms of their troughs than previous cycles and that have occurred closer together. Although it is difficult to establish a clear causal link between the emergence of the fabless/foundry strategy and the worsening of these cycles, the circumstantial evidence asks to be explored further.

Fifth, as with Japan and Korea, the innovation envelope tying the semiconductor industry to the equipment industry is in full activity in Taiwan. The role that equipment companies played and are continuing to play is that of diffusers of fabrication technology. The growth and strength of the Taiwanese semiconductor industry has altered the balance that existed before. Reinforcing the trend begun in Korea, the existence of another market outside the U.S.–Japan axis has freed up equipment companies to compete more on technical and market merit that emphasizes clear and transparent adherence to standards than on a customized approach that depends on intense company-to-company interaction. Although the Taiwanese semiconductor industry supports both indigenous and foreign equipment companies, the leading companies are still either Japan- or U.S.-based semiconductor equipment companies. Further, with the catching up to and surpassing of world semiconductor fabrication standards by Taiwanese companies such as TSMC, another node has been added to the global network of companies and research institutes developing next-generation semiconductor technology.

5 Some Observations on the Change Mechanism Role Played by the Interaction of Institutional and Techno-Global Forces on Organizational Forms

We have examined the theoretical and conceptual literature concerning the relationship of institutions to agents and the potential that this relationship brings for institutional change. We have seen that not only is there an endogenous source of change that can exist between institutions and agents as functional, political and social pressures are exerted, but that extra-institutional elements, in particular technology, can exert considerable influence for change. These change factors we termed techno-global; they are balanced by various institutional regimens that exist within the domestic national markets that were examined. How do these two forces interact in the integrated-circuit industry?

The change mechanisms that work endogenously within a current agent–institution relationship tend to be single-loop changes, that is, those that would continue to support the basic relationship and help buffer it against the extra-institutional environment. The development of SEMATECH was one such example. The founding firms were all U.S. incumbents in the integrated-circuit industry. They represented the already established system house IC and IDM IC organizational forms. The more recently emerging fabless design IC and foundry organizational forms were not part of the original SEMATECH organization. The development of new-process technology helped the established U.S. system house and IDM organizational forms to continue competing against Japanese system house organizational forms.

We also observed that whether intended or not, the combination of continuing extra-institutional change and the adjustments of the agents and institutions within a relationship can bring about a double-loop change. Continuing with the SEMATECH example, this occurred as SEMATECH began to change its original response to the techno-global pressure being exerted, from a response of developing process technologies related to specific integrated products to one of a more generic approach to innovation and standardization of semiconductor process technology. As noted above, this shift facilitated the emergence of both the Korean and Taiwanese semiconductor industries. It also facilitated the legitimization of the fabless and foundry organizational forms.

It is also interesting to note that the relationship between agents and institutions can change in terms of direction. Again as illustrated by the example of SEMATECH in the U.S., the government went from essentially a "let the market adjust" attitude, which it exhibited from the mid-1960s through the 1970s, to one of active government involvement beginning in the early 1980s. The post-SEMATECH era, as that organization has transitioned into International SEMATECH or ISEMATECH, is also a marker for a shift in government policy away from direct involvement in integrated-circuit technology innovation processes. This pattern of changes appears among the Japanese institutions and agents. The period beginning in the 1970s and culminating in the establishment of the VLSI Research Cooperative in the early 1980s marked a time when the Japanese government was actively exerting influence on the techno-global forces driving the innovation process in the integrated-circuit industry. During the later 1980s and into the 1990s the Japanese government had withdrawn from such active participation in the process. With the reemergence of research cooperatives such as SELETE, ASPLA, ASUKA and others, an attempt is being made to duplicate the pattern exhibited earlier with the hope that government involvement will again create conditions conducive to a Japanese semiconductor industry rebirth. The openness of these consortia to international participation may have a telling effect on their success.

It is an open question whether the earlier attempts exhibited by the VLSI Research Cooperative were essential to the emergence of the Japanese as dominant players in the integrated-circuit industry in the 1980s (see Methé, 1985, 1991a, for comments on the success or lack thereof in the activities of the VLSI Research Cooperative). It is also an open question whether the efforts of the newly formed cooperative research consortia will be of much help, or whether the strongest support for any rebirth will emanate from the restructuring of the Japanese companies themselves. Likewise it is still an open question whether the initiation of SEMATECH and its activities can be completely credited with the revival of the U.S. semiconductor industry in the late 1980s and early 1990s. It is well beyond the scope of this chapter to attempt to definitively answer those questions. It is enough to note that the institutional responses to these techno-globally driven changes were similar, in spite of the different institutional histories of the U.S. and Japan. The activities of these consortia and the firms themselves have been to develop vectors that have multiplied the knowledge bases for semiconductor innovation around the world. It is important that we understand the vectors by which techno-global change has exerted its influence on various institutional settings.

The vectors for channeling techno-global forces, as we have seen, in part work through and in part are shaped by the innovation envelope that exists within the semiconductor technology. The relationship between the semiconductor technology and the processing technologies required to fabricate each generation of devices sets up mechanisms for both innovation and diffusion of the innovation across different countries' institutional boundaries. We have observed that the role that equipment firms played in moving the latest technology from its point of origin, whether that was in the U.S., Japan, Europe, or now Korea or Taiwan, to semiconductor firms working in other countries has been in existence from the beginnings of the semiconductor industry through today. The fact that neither Korea nor Taiwan has developed a strong presence in the semiconductor equipment industry has made the "globalization" role of the extant U.S., Japanese and European firms all the more important today.

Another vector for channeling techno-global forces exists in the direct movement of people, especially engineering and managerial talent, from the U.S. institutional environment to other institutional environments. This is not to downplay the indigenous efforts of the Japanese, Europeans, Koreans and Taiwanese in the development of their respective domestic semiconductor industries, which were substantial in scope. But another important element was the training received at U.S. companies in the U.S. by a core group of engineers who later went on to head the domestic development of integrated-circuit technology within their respective countries. Many Japanese engineers who headed the drive towards dominance in the DRAM industry had for a time worked at Bell Labs in the late 1950s and 1960s. Likewise, many of the engineers who headed efforts at Samsung, Hyundai or LG in Korea, or who went on to found firms such as TSMC in Taiwan, had work experience at U.S. firms in the U.S. before taking on leading roles in their current firms.

Another vector observed was the direct movement of companies in entering each other's institutional environments, either through green field establishment of overseas wholly owned subsidiaries, the acquisition of companies, or strategic alliances that included the sharing of financial or knowledge resources through capital and/or technological investment. We observed the intensive use of this vector in Europe, both among European companies from various countries within Europe, and by U.S. companies entering Europe in the early 1960s. This vector also played a role in the early years of the Korean and Taiwanese efforts to develop their domestic semiconductor industries.

The use of mergers and alliances continues as a vector for developing and moving resources to meet the needs generated from the dynamics of techno-global change. Institutional forces have affected the use of these mechanisms, however. Mergers and acquisitions as well as divestitures appear more likely to occur within an institutional regimen, such as Texas Instruments' purchase of Burr-Brown, the creation of Elpida and Renesas in Japan, the folding of LG's semiconductor operations into Hynix in Korea, and the creation of STMicro in Europe. Alliances among firms through the sharing of financial and technological resources are common both within and between institutional regimens. Systematically organized alliances, as seen in research consortia in the early decades of the development of the semiconductor industry, were more likely to be limited to firms within an institutional regimen, such as the VLSI Research Cooperative in Japan, SEMATECH in the U.S., ESPRIT and BRITE in Europe, and the fourth five-year plan in Korea as well as its successor, the HAN project (Methé, 1995b). Although each was successful in some respect, as the semiconductor industry has become more global, limiting membership to firms from one institutional regimen may not be the best way to organize current or future consortia. As illustrated by the more open membership rules of the Hsinchu Science Park, IMEC in Europe, and ISEMATECH in the U.S., participation by international companies may now be a prerequisite for the success of these national-base institutional initiatives. This is because the knowledge bases for innovation have multiplied around the world. Likewise the earlier consortia were limited, either by design or by accident, to specific organizational forms, mostly system house IC organizational forms and some IDMs. The more recent cooperative endeavors are more open to various types of organizational forms. This more open attitude towards membership may in part derive from recognition that the dynamics of techno-global innovation place more emphasis on capability than on institutional or organizational form pedigree.

We found that each individual country began with the same general set of institutional and company actors, but established a different configuration of these respective actors, resulting in differences in the types of firms that have entered and dominated their respective national markets. The effect of institutional forces on the composition of the firms comprising each country's integrated-circuit industry is readily apparent. Although the contrasts among the U.S.,

Europe, and Japan are stark enough, the disparity between the two latecomer countries, Korea and Taiwan, is profound in illustrating how differences in the configuration of players and policies can result in a differing mix of organizational forms at the time of the founding of the industry in each country.

The difference in institutional regimens between Korea and Taiwan was evident from the beginning in terms of the types of firms that received government assistance to enter their respective integrated-circuit industries. Established system houses diversifying into the IC industry were chosen for Korea, and IDM start-ups were chosen for Taiwan. The initial mix of organizational forms could not have been more different. We have also found that the oldest organizational form, the diversifying electronic systems house, has had remarkable staying power. Although individual firms may have come and gone, the organizational form itself has lasted throughout the entire history of the semiconductor industry and has existed within each country's local institutional context. We have further found that the techno-global forces at work are pushing the global semiconductor industry into a new set of dominating organizational forms.

It appears that at the beginning of the 21st century, the dedicated IDM organizational form and the fabless and foundry organizational forms are about to finally push the venerable system house form out of the top tier of the global semiconductor industry. This is particularly evident in the U.S. and Taiwanese integrated-circuit industries, but is also becoming apparent in the European, Japanese, and Korean industries. First, it is important to point out that some firms will most likely continue with a system house organizational form. In the U.S., IBM appears to be continuing to use this form. In Europe, Philips has continued to keep its integrated-circuit operations closely tied to its systems operations. The same appears to be so with Samsung in Korea. There are strong technological and economic reasons for linking system house and IC operations in one organizational form. Astute management can capture potential economies of scale and scope and can focus research and development efforts to take advantage of both a large internal market as well as the external merchant market.

Second, it is also important to recognize that the exit of the system house organizational form from the top position in the industry is not simply through some blind selection force that has begun to erase this organizational form from existence. Instead, the system house organizational form is declining through the strategic choice of the firms that had adopted it in the first place. Many system houses are spinning out their semiconductor operations to become more standalone companies, albeit with some equity connection back to the parent company. The actions in Japan of Hitachi and NEC in forming Elpida, of Hitachi and Mitsubishi Electric in forming Renesas, and of NEC Electronics and Elpida in becoming more freestanding companies within the NEC group are one set of illustrations of the developing IDM organizational form. In Europe the creation of Infineon and STMicro are also examples of spinouts from system houses of their integrated-circuit operations. The same can be said of Hynix within the Hyundai group; it is more independent than its predecessor Hyundai Electronics was. The same techno-global driving forces are also at work in the move of Motorola to spin out its semiconductor operations into an independent company.

The IDM organizational form is perhaps best suited to respond to the changes in the merchant market and also has sufficient resources and links between design and process activities to continue to pioneer technological innovations. Moreover, the focused strategy of the IDM organizational form may be easier to manage, in tracking both the upswings and the downturns of sales and profit performance in semiconductors, than the more broad-based system house form. However, strategic choices by managers using the IDM form may make the IDM form more of a blended form itself. Many IDM companies are beginning to reduce their commitment to the fabrication aspect of semiconductor technology. Even firms newly adopting the IDM organizational form, like Motorola, NEC Electronics, Elpida, and others, regardless of their country of origin, as well as some system house forms like Philips, are beginning to adopt a "fab-lite" strategy. With the fab-lite strategy, the IDM company devotes some human and financial resources to fabrication technology, but it also begins to rely on the dedicated foundry companies such as UMC and TSMC. IDM companies that adopt this strategic approach may eventually evolve into a collection of fabless design houses under one company name as each of their various IC divisions sheds its fabrication capability and relies on dedicated foundries for production. Or each division may be spun out as a separate fabless company. It remains to be seen if this strategy will be lasting and what direction it will take, but the techno-global forces of increasing resource needs for each succeeding semiconductor generation and the worldwide diffusion of fabrication skills are driving it.

From discussions with senior managerial and engineering personnel at many companies mentioned in this report, it appears that a consensus is forming around the belief that the fabless organizational form is the wave of the future. We have seen that it has been in existence since the late 1960s and came into prominence as a preferred mode of entry in the early 1980s. Its growing importance as a mode of entry emerged in response to certain features of the techno-global innovation dynamics driving the integrated-circuit industry. The emergence of the dedicated foundry legitimized the fabless organizational form. The combination of these two organizational forms into a symbiotic link could be considered a new organizational form in its own right. Whether considered so or not, the fabless/foundry nexus has had a growing impact on the integrated-circuit industry, as is evident from the emergence of TSMC into the global top 10 in 2002[8]. It should be noted, however, that no fabless firm by itself has yet entered the global top 10 semiconductor firms. Some, such as Nvidia and Qualcomm, have entered the top 10 semiconductor producers in the U.S., and there are also VIA and ProMOS among the top 10 companies in the Taiwanese semiconductor industry. It is possible and in fact very likely that some firm that has adopted the fabless organizational form will enter the global semiconductor industry's top 10 rankings. Given the relatively narrower customer focus adopted by these firms, however, the fabless form is by no means the most likely organizational form to have the organizational resources necessary to dominate over the IDM form. It is also an open question whether the new entries into the semiconductor industry from China using the dedicated foundry organizational form will be as successful as the initial firms that adopted that form. The level of concentration of foundry services has been about 80% for the top 3 firms. However, it does appear that the dedicated foundry organizational form, along with its symbiotic partner, the fabless organizational form, is a legitimate form within the global semiconductor industry and one that will not disappear soon.

6 Conclusion

We have examined the influence of techno-global and institutional forces on the birth, development, change, and exit of organizational forms within the global semiconductor industry and within the major country segments of the industry. We have found that the earliest entering organizational form, the system house IC form, has had remarkable staying power. It does appear, however, to finally be on its way out of the global industry, at least as a dominant form occupying the center of the industry. The IDM form, which also entered early in the development of the semiconductor industry, seems also to have remarkable staying power and is poised to become the dominant form for the foreseeable future. However, it will share the stage with the fabless and foundry forms.

It is important to note that these two new forms entered roughly midway through the development of the semiconductor industry, if we measure this from the early 1960s until today. As we observed, all the various organizational forms including the fabless form and then the dedicated foundry form had entered by the 1980s. No new organizational forms have emerged from the techno-global dynamics of the industry since the 1980s. It is possible that after more than 40 years of existence, the techno-global dynamics of the semiconductor industry have entered or are entering a period of maturation of the technological and globalization forces that have given birth to these various organizational forms. The exiting of the system house organizational form from the industry may also be an indicator of this passage into a more mature phase of development. It is quite clear that the competitive dynamics that result in the turnover of individual firms will continue, however. The strategic adjustment by integrated-circuit firms using the system house organizational form to move to an IDM form, and by those firms using the IDM form to move to a "fab-lite" strategy, is indicative of the ability of incumbents to sustain their positions in the industry. Strategic choices, both in terms of the organizational form adopted during entry into the semiconductor industry and in terms of the changes that managers make to that organizational form, are important transmission mechanisms for selection and adaptation to the techno-global and institutional forces at work in the semiconductor industry.

This study has also shed some light on the processes of change and continuity in an industry that is considered a technology-intensive industry and thus one that is characterized by a volatile environment. We do not dispute the characterization of the semiconductor industry's environment as volatile. It has undergone many recessions, several quite severe, as well as many technological changes both in underlying technology and in product classes, such as DRAMs and MPUs. It is important to note that some changes, such as the development of the semiconductor and the integrated-circuit themselves, were radical (double-loop or heterodynamic changes) and that others, such as the movement along the integrated-circuit technology trajectory, were more moderate and predictable (single-loop or homeostatic changes). Although the radical changes did open up the industry to many new entrants, they did not open it up to many new organizational forms. The commercialization of semiconductor technology resulted in the first two types of organizational form, the system house and the IDM, but it was the more routine technology progression along the IC innovation envelope that created the conditions for the development of the fabless and dedicated foundry types of organizational form. It appears that single-loop change at one level of the system resulted in double-loop change at another level of the system. Likewise, the diminution in the number of firms holding to the system house organizational form in recent years does not appear to be the result of fundamental or double-loop technological change. The tremendous decline in the market that occurred in 2001 does seem to have hastened the decline of the system house form, but it does not appear to have initiated it. The dynamics of the techno-global and institutional forces at work in the semiconductor industry have created an intricate nested system of relationships. We have explored some aspects of those relationships, and it is hoped that this study will stimulate and inform discussions on these important issues. It is obvious, but still needs saying, that further study is warranted in order to develop a deeper understanding of the processes described in this work.

Notes

1 We recognize that the integrated-circuit industry is part of the semiconductor industry, but that the semiconductor industry includes a broader range of solid-state physics-based products such as discrete transistor smf diodes. In this chapter we are primarily interested in the integrated-circuit industry, but given the time frame involved for the study, i.e., from the 1950s to today, we will refer to the semiconductor industry and integrated-circuit industry interchangeably.

2 Data for this section are derived from various McClean Reports 2002–2003, ICE Status reports 1968–1999, and various ICE Profiles reports and IC Insights Strategic Reviews. Information was also gathered from the Web sites of companies mentioned in the text and organizations related to the semiconductor industry, such as the Semiconductor Industry Association (SIA), Korea SIA (KSIA), Taiwan SIA (TSIA), Fabless Semiconductor Association (FSA), and Semiconductor Equipment and Materials International (SEMI). Additional information was collected at various semiconductor-industry-related meetings, such as the Industry Strategy Symposium (ISS) sponsored by SEMI, and in particular ISS Korea 2001, ISS Taiwan 2002, and ISS Japan 2001–2003. Information was also collected through interviews conducted at these symposia and at other times in Taiwan, Korea, and Japan during the period 2001–2003. Information for Korea was also obtained from annual interviews conducted during the period 1991–1996 through grants

from the University of Michigan's Center for International Business Education and for Japan from interviews conducted periodically from 1983 to 2000.

[3] Data for this section are derived from various McClean Reports 2002–2003, ICE Status reports 1968–1999, and various ICE Profiles reports and IC Insights Strategic Reviews. Information was also gathered from the Web sites of companies mentioned in the text and organizations related to the semiconductor industry, such as SIA, SEMI, Fabless Semiconductor Association, and International SEMATECH (ISEMATECH). Additional information was collected at various semiconductor-industry-related meetings, such as the ISS sponsored by SEMI, in particular ISS Korea 2001, ISS Taiwan 2002, and ISS Japan 2001–2003. Information was also collected through interviews conducted at these symposia and at other times in the U.S. during the period 2001–2003. Information is also used from interviews conducted in the U.S. periodically from 1983 to 2000.

[4] Data for this section are derived from various McClean Reports 2002–2003, ICE Status reports 1968–1999, and various ICE Profiles reports and IC Insights Strategic Reviews. Information was also gathered from the Web sites of companies mentioned in the text and organizations related to the semiconductor industry, such as SIA, SEMI, SEMI Europa, and Interuniversity MicroElectronics Center (IMEC). Additional information was collected at various semiconductor-industry-related meetings, such as the ISS sponsored by SEMI, in particular ISS Korea 2001, ISS Taiwan 2002, and ISS Japan 2001–2003. Information was also collected through interviews of European participants conducted at these symposia during the period 2001–2003.

[5] Data for this section are derived from various McClean Reports 2002–2003, ICE Status reports 1968–1999, and various ICE Profiles reports and IC Insights Strategic Reviews. Information was also gathered from the Web sites of companies mentioned in the text and organizations related to the semiconductor industry, such as SIA, SIA Japan, SEMI, and SEMI Japan. Additional information was collected at various semiconductor-industry-related meetings, such as the ISS sponsored by SEMI, in particular ISS Japan 2001–2003. Information was also collected through interviews conducted at these symposia and at other times in Japan during the period 2001–2003. Further information about Japan was obtained from interviews conducted periodically from 1983 to 2000.

[6] Data for this section is derived from various McClean Reports 2002–2003, ICE Status reports 1968–1999, and various ICE Profiles reports and IC Insights Strategic Reviews. Information was also gathered from the Web sites of companies mentioned in the text and organizations related to the semiconductor industry, such as SIA, KSIA, SEMI, and SEMI Korea. Additional information was collected at various semiconductor-industry-related meetings, such as the ISS sponsored by SEMI, in particular ISS Korea 2001. Information was also collected through interviews conducted at these symposia and at other times in Korea during the period 2001–2003. Information for Korea was also obtained from annual interviews conducted during the period 1991–1996 through grants from the University of Michigan's Center for International Business Education.

[7] Data for this section are derived from various McClean Reports 2002–2003, ICE Status reports 1968–1999, and various ICE Profiles reports and IC Insights Strategic Reviews. Information was also gathered from the Web sites of companies mentioned in the text and organizations related to the semiconductor industry, such as SIA, TSIA, Fabless Semiconductor Association, SEMI, and SEMI Taiwan. Additional information was collected at various semiconductor-industry-related meetings such as the ISS sponsored by SEMI, in particular ISS Taiwan 2002. Information was also collected through interviews conducted at these symposia and at other times in Taiwan during the period 2001–2003.

[8] This issue of whether to consider the fabless/foundry as an organizational form in and of itself or the fabless and foundry companies as separate organizational forms is emerging in a current debate among various market research organizations over how to count the production figures of each. Our use of sources to construct the tables in this chapter should in no way be construed as an endorsement of a particular source in terms of its position on this production-counting debate or its usefulness as a market forecasting tool. Our concern in choosing data sources was to be as consistent as possible over the time frame involved in this study.

Bibliography

Adler, P.S. (1989) "Technology strategy: A guide to the literatures." Research in Technological Innovation, Management, and Policy 4: 25–151.

Amburgey, T.L.; Kelly, D; and Barnett, W. (1993) "Resetting the clock: The dynamics of organizational change and failure." Administrative Science Quarterly 38: 51–73.

Aoki, M. (2001) Toward a Comparative Institutional Analysis. MIT Press, Cambridge, MA.

Argyris, C. (1976) "Single- and double-loop models in research on decision-making." Administrative Science Quarterly 21(3): 363–375.

——— (1992) On Organizational Learning. Blackwell Publishing, Inc., Cambridge, MA.

Ashby, W.R. (1952) Design for a Brain. Wiley, New York.

Barnett, W.P. and Carroll, G.R. (1995) "Modeling internal organizational change." Annual Review of Sociology 21: 217–236.

Beyer, J.M.; Chattopadhyay, P.; George, E.; Glick, W.H.; Ogilvie, D.; and Pugliese, D. (1997) "The selective perceptions of managers revisited." Academy of Management Journal 40: 717–737.

Boeker, W. (1989) "Strategic change: The effects of founding and history." Academy of Management Journal 32(3): 489–515.

Bracker, J. and Methé, D.T. (1994) "A cross-national study of planning characteristics of U.S. and Japanese entrepreneurs." International Journal of Management 11(2): 634–640.

Bradsher, K. (2003) "SARS is disrupting worldwide business: Disease hits wide variety of industries." International Herald Tribune. 4 April, pp. 1 and 4.

Brown, S.L. and Eisenhardt, K.M. (1997) "The art of continuous change: Linking complexity theory and time-paced evolution in relentlessly shifting organizations." Administrative Science Quarterly 42: 1–34.

Buaron, R. (1981) "New-game strategies." McKinsey Quarterly (Spring): 21–40.

Burgelman, R.A. (1994) "Fading memories: A process theory of strategic business exit in dynamic environments." Administrative Science Quarterly 39: 24–56.

Burke, J. (1978) Connections. Little, Brown and Company, Boston.

Campbell, D.T. (1965) "Variation and selective retention in socio-cultural evolution." In: Barringer, H.R.; Blanksten, G.I.; and Macks, R.W. (Eds.) Social Change in Developing Areas: Reinterpretation of Evolutionary Theory. Schenkman, Cambridge, MA, pp. 19–48.

Carroll, G.R. (1985) "Concentration and specialization: Dynamics of niche width in populations of organizations." American Journal of Sociology 90(6): 1262–1283.

——— (1993) "A sociological view on why firms differ." Strategic Management Journal 14: 237–249.

Cross, N. (1986) "The changing design process." In: Roy, R. and Wield, D. (Eds.) Product Design and Technological Innovation: A Reader. Open University, Philadelphia, pp. 36–47.

Dacin, M.T.; Goodstein, J.; and Scott, W.R. (2002) "Institutional theory and institutional change: Introduction to the special research forum." Academy of Management Journal 45(1): 45–57.

Delacroix, J. and Swaminathan, A. (1991) "Cosmetic, speculative, and adaptive organizational change in the wine industry: A longitudinal study." Administrative Science Quarterly 36: 631–661.

Eisenhardt, K.M. and Schoonhoven, C.B. (1990) "Organizational growth: Linking founding team, strategy, environment, and growth among U.S. semiconductor ventures, 1978–1988." Administrative Science Quarterly 35: 504–529.

Fisher, L.A. (2002) "STMicroelectronics: The metaphysics of a metanational pioneer." Strategy+Business, Issue 28. Booz Allen Hamilton, New York.

Flatow, I. (1992) They All Laughed... From Light Bulbs to Lasers: The Fascinating Stories Behind the Great Inventions that Have Changed Our Lives. HarperCollins, New York.

Foster, R.N. (1986) Innovation: The Attacker's Advantage. Summit Books, New York.

Freeman, C. (1986) "Successful industrial innovation." In: Roy, R. and Wield, D. (Eds.) Product Design and Technological Innovation: A Reader. Open University, Philadelphia, pp. 29–33.

Freeman, J. (1995) "Business strategy from the population level." In: Montgomery, C. (Ed.) Resource-Based and Evolutionary Theories of the Firm: Towards a Synthesis. Kluwer Academic Publishers, Boston, pp. 219–250.

Garud, R.; Jain, S.; and Kumaraswamy, A. (2002) "Institutional entrepreneurship in the sponsorship of common technological standards: The case of Sun Microsystems and Java." Academy of Management Journal 45: 196–214.

Grant, R.M. (1991) "The resource-based theory of competitive advantage: Implications for strategy formulation." California Management Review 33(3): 114–135.

Greve, H. (1995) "Jumping ship: Diffusion of strategy abandonment." Administrative Science Quarterly 40: 444–473.

Hall, P.A. and Soskice, D. (Eds.) (2001) Varieties of Capitalism: The Institutional Foundations of Comparative Advantage. Oxford University Press, New York.

Henderson, R.M. and Clark, K.B. (1990) "Architectural innovation: The reconfiguration of existing product technologies and the failure of established firms." Administrative Science Quarterly 35: 9–30.

Hodgson, G. (1998) "The approach of institutional economics." Journal of Economic Literature 36: 166–192.

Hrebiniak, L.G. and Joyce, W.F. (1985) "Organizational adaptation: Strategic choice and environmental determinism." Administrative Science Quarterly 30: 336–349.

Hu, G.J. (1997) "Perspectives of the Taiwan semiconductor industry." Business Briefing ASEAN: Semiconductor Manufacturing Technology. World Market Research Centre, London.

ICE Status (1968–1999) A Report on the Integrated Circuit Industry. Integrated Circuit Engineering Corporation, Scottsdale, AZ.

ICE Profiles (1991–1994, 1996, 2000) A Worldwide Survey of IC Manufacturers and Suppliers. Integrated Circuit Engineering Corporation, Scottsdale, AZ.

IC Insights Strategic Reviews (2000–2003) Extensive Profiles of the World's IC Manufacturers and Fabless Suppliers. IC Insights, Inc., Scottsdale, AZ.

Isabella, L.A. (1990) "Evolving interpretations as a change unfolds: How managers construe key organizational events." Academy of Management Journal 33(1): 7–41.

JSBRI (2002) White Paper on Small and Medium Enterprises in Japan: The Age of the Local Entrepreneur: Birth, Growth, and Revitalization of the National Economy. Japan Small Business Research Institute (JSBRI), Ministry of Economy, Trade and Industry, Tokyo.

Kim, C.L. (1997) "The Korean semiconductor industry." Business Briefing ASEAN: Semiconductor Manufacturing Technology. World Market Research Centre, London.

Levinthal, D. and Myatt, J. (1994) "Co-evolution of capabilities and industry: The evolution of mutual fund processing." Strategic Management Journal 15: 45–62.

Lewin, A.Y.; Long, C.P.; and Carroll, T.N. (1999) "The coevolution of new organizational forms." Organization Science 10(5, Sept.-Oct.): 535–550.

Mann, C. (1987) "Protection and retaliation: Changing the rules of the game." Brooking's Papers on Economic Activity, Issue 1, pp. 311–335.

March, J.G. (1990) "Exploration and exploitation in organizational learning." Organization Science 2(1): 71–87.

——— (1996) "Continuity and change in theories of organizational action." Administrative Science Quarterly 41: 278–287.

March, J.G.; Sproull, L.S.; and Tamuz, M. (1991) "Learning from samples of one or fewer." Organization Science 2(1): 1–13.

McClean, W.J. (Ed.) (2002) The McClean Report 2002. IC Insights, Inc., Scottsdale, AZ.

——— (Ed.) (2003) The McClean Report 2003. IC Insights, Inc., Scottsdale, AZ.

Mensch, G. (1979) Stalemate in Technology: Innovation Overcomes Depression. Ballinger, Cambridge, MA.

Methé, D.T. (1985) Technology, Transaction Costs, and the Diffusion of Innovation: The Evolution of the United States and Japanese DRAM Industries. University of California, Irvine.

——— (1991a) Technological Competition in Global Industries: Marketing and Planning Strategies for American Industry. Quorum Books, New York.

——— (1991b) "The effect of innovation on market structure." Engineering Management Review 19(4): 18–30.

——— (1992a) "The influence of technology and demand factors on firm size and industrial structure in the DRAM market—1973–1988." Research Policy 21: 13–25.

——— (1992b) "Techno-global competition in the integrated circuit industry." In: Foster, L.W. (Ed.) Advances in Applied Business Strategy, Vol. 3. JAI Press, Greenwich, CT, pp. 145–201.

——— (1995a) "Basic research in Japanese electronics companies: An attempt at establishing new organizational routines." In: Liker, J.; Ettlie, J.; and Campbell, J. (Eds.) Engineered in Japan: Organization and Technology. Oxford University Press, Oxford, UK, pp. 17–39.

——— (1995b) "Moving into the technological fast lane: From reverse to forward engineering through the establishment of innovation communities in Korea." Proceedings of the IEEE Engineering Management Conference, Singapore, 28–30 June.

——— (1997) "Living on the edge: Basic research and knowledge creation in Japanese electronics companies." In: McIntyre, J.R. (Ed.) Japan's Technical Standards: Implications for Global Trade and Competitiveness. Quorum Books, Westport, CT, pp. 47–63.

——— (2005) "Continuity through change in Japanese management: Institutional and strategic influences." In: Haak, R. and Padelko, M. (Eds.) Japanese Management—The Search for a New Balance between Continuity and Change. Palgrave, London.

Methé, D.T. and Bracker, J. (1994) "A cross-national study of perceptions of the business environment by U.S. and Japanese entrepreneurs." International Journal of Management 11(1): 599–603.

Methé, D.T.; Miyabe, J.; and Toyama, R. (1997) "Product development strategy and organizational learning: A tale of two PC makers." Journal of Product Innovation Management 14(5): 323–336.

——— (1998a) "A tale of two PC industries: Technology, environment and managerial action in shaping the Japanese and US personal computer industry." RIEB Kobe University Discussion Paper Series No. 89, Kobe University, Kobe, Japan.

——— (1998b) "Overcoming a standard bearer: Challenges to NEC's personal computer in Japan." RIEB Kobe University Discussion Paper Series No. 90, Kobe University, Kobe, Japan.

Methé, D.T. and Penner-Hahn, J. (1999) "Globalization of pharmaceutical research and development in Japanese companies: Learning and the parent-subsidiary relationship." In: Beechler, S. and Bird, A. (Eds.) Japanese Multinationals Abroad: Individual and Organizational Learning. Oxford University Press, Oxford, UK, pp. 1–42.

Methé, D.T.; Swaminathan, S.; and Mitchell, W. (1996) "The underemphasized role of established firms as the sources of major innovations." Industrial and Corporate Change 5(4): 1181–1203.

Nelson, R. (1994) "The co-evolution of technology, industrial structure, and supporting institutions." Industry and Corporate Change 3: 417–419.

OECD (2003) OECD Economic Survey: Japan. Vol. 2002, Supplement No. 2, January. OECD, Paris, France.

Okada, Y. (2002) "Decline of the Japanese semiconductor industry: Institutional restrictions and disintegrated techno-governance." Working Paper, Institute of Comparative Culture, Sophia University, Tokyo.

Oliver, C. (1997) "Sustainable competitive advantage: Combining institutional and resource-based views." Strategic Management Journal 18: 697–713.

Pascale, R. (1985) "The paradox of 'corporate culture': Reconciling ourselves to socialization." California Management Review 27(2): 304–316.

Peng, M.W. and Heath, P.S. (1996) "The growth of the firm in planned economies in transition: Institutions, organizations and strategic choice." Academy of Management Review 21(2): 492–528.

Romanelli, E. and Tushman, M.L. (1994) "Organizational transformation as punctuated equilibrium: An empirical test." Academy of Management Journal 37(5): 1141–1166.

Sackmann, S.Z. (1992) "Culture and subcultures: An analysis of organizational knowledge." Administrative Science Quarterly 37: 1–22.

Sahal, D. (1979) "A theory of evolutionary of technology." International Journal of Systems Science 10(3): 259–274.

——— (1981a) "Alternative conceptions of technology." Research Policy 10(3): 2–24.

——— (1981b) Patterns of Technological Innovation. Addison-Wesley, Reading, MA.

Schumpeter, J.A. (1936) Business Cycles: A Theoretical, Historical and Statistical Analysis of the Capitalist Process. McGraw-Hill, New York.

Simon, H.A. (1987) "Making management decisions: The role of intuition and emotion." Academy of Management Executive 1(1, February): 57–64.

——— (1991) "Bounded rationality and organizational learning." Organization Science 2(1): 125–134.

Smircich, L. (1983) "Concepts of culture and organizational analysis." Administrative Science Quarterly 28: 339–358.

Stinchcombe, A.L. (1965) "Social structure and organizations." In: March, J.G. (Ed.) Handbook of Organizations. Rand McNally, Chicago, pp. 142–193.

Solow, R.M. (1957) "Technical change and the aggregate production function." Review of Economics and Statistics 36: 312–320.

Tilton, J.E. (1971) International Diffusion of Technology: The Case of Semiconductors. Brookings Institution Press, Washington, DC.

Tucker, D.J.; Singh, J.V.; and Meinhard, A.G. (1990) "Founding characteristics, imprinting and organizational change." In: Singh, J.V. (Ed.) Organizational Evolution: New Directions. Sage Publications, Newbury Park, CA, pp. 182–200.

Tushman, M.L. and Anderson, P. (1986) "Technological discontinuities and organizational environments." Administrative Science Quarterly 31: 439–465.

Tushman, M.L.; Newman, W.H.; and Romanelli, E. (1986) "Convergence and upheaval: managing the unsteady pace of organizational evolution." California Management Review 29: 29–44.

Tversky, A. and Kahneman, D. (1991) "Loss aversion in riskless choice: A reference-dependent model." Quarterly Journal of Economics 106(4): 1039–1061.

Wakabayashi, H. and Sumita, M. (1993) "South Korea's semiconductor industry." NRI Quarterly, Summer. Nomura Research Institute, Tokyo.

White, A. (1959) "The concept of culture." American Anthropologist 61: 227–251.

Chapter 5

Industrial Environment, Institutional Changes, and Technological Innovations in the Japanese Telecommunications Industry

Yuzo Murayama
Doshisha University

1 Introduction

The Japanese telecommunications industry provides an interesting example by which we can understand the relationship between changes in the industrial environment, institutional changes, and technological innovations. Since the end of World War II, the environment surrounding Japanese telecommunications has changed drastically. Japan's telephone network was heavily damaged by the war, and it became the government's major goal to install a modern telephone network throughout Japan. This task was completed in the 1970s. By that time, however, a new competitive environment was being created by the deregulation of the worldwide industry. Moreover, as digitization of the telecommunication networks advanced, the telecom and computer industries started to merge, producing a new industrial environment. The governments of advanced countries were beginning to privatize and divest traditional public telephone and telegraph companies in order to adjust to this new environment. Deregulation and globalization of the industry were further advanced by the diffusion of the Internet in the 1990s. This so-called IT (information technology) revolution is now creating a totally new environment for the telecommunications industry.

The research and development institutions supporting the Japanese telecommunications industry have also changed drastically. Until 1952, when the U.S. occupation of Japan ended, telecom services were run by the Japanese government. In 1952, Nippon Denshin Denwa Kosha (Nippon Telegraph and Telephone Public Corporation, NTTPC), the main engine for Japanese telecommunications R&D, was launched as a public corporation. Since NTTPC itself did not have a manufacturing division, it closely cooperated in telecommunications R&D with such companies as NEC, Fujitsu, Hitachi, and Oki, all of whom manufactured NTTPC-related equipment. The R&D framework thus consisted of NTTPC and the so-called NTTPC family (or Denden family, from the company's Japanese acronym, Dendenkosha). These manufacturers comprised the main institutions that led to innovations in the telecommunications industry.

NTTPC was privatized in 1985 and renamed NTT. As a result, the Japanese telecommunications industry was deregulated and institutional arrangements were also significantly altered. New entrants came into the Japanese telecommunications industry and for the first time were providing both services and equipment. In 1999, NTT was partially divested and deregulation was further promoted. Eventually it became a holding company with two local companies and one long-distance company under its umbrella.

The Japanese government encouraged the deregulation process and implemented policies reflecting recommendations by governmental committees. These policy changes in telecommunication services significantly affected institutional R&D arrangements. NTT, the giant that had once dominated the research and development of Japanese telecommunications equipment, was reduced in its importance, and telecom manufacturers were expanding their own capabilities. Furthermore, as part of the globalization of this industry, foreign companies were entering the market and beginning to play a certain role.

Under the changing institutional framework outlined above, various innovations have emerged. Initially, NTTPC put an emphasis on transmission technologies, especially in the optic-related area, and produced such innovations as VAD (vapor-phase axial deposition), a new method of manufacturing optic fiber. NTTPC was also quick to respond to the digitization of telecommunications. For instance, it developed a series of DIPS (Dendenkosha Information Processing System) computers, which was NTTPC's own family of computers for telecommunication purposes. This was in response to the need for telecommunications companies to go into the data processing area. A recent example of successful innovation in the industry is "i-mode," which is a wireless connection to the Internet by mobile telephone. This technology was developed by NTT DoCoMo, a spinoff company from NTT that originated in 1992. The i-mode has become one of the biggest successes in Japan's Internet field.

It is an interesting yet challenging task to understand the interrelationship among these three elements—environment, institutions, and innovation—and then to identify the Japanese patterns of innovation. As was pointed out by Richard Nelson, a professor of evolutionary economics who also has done extensive studies of technological development patterns, the co-evolution of institutions and technologies is one of the major elements in understanding patterns of technological evolution (Nelson, 1994). Moreover, such an understanding is essential for assessing the competitiveness of the industry from an institutional perspective.

This chapter begins with an explanation of the postwar history of Japan's industrial environment, its institutions, and innovations within the telecommunications industry. Section 2 describes conditions in the telecommunications industry after World War II up through the 1960s. During this period, the goal of the industry and the Japanese government was to install a telephone network throughout Japan as fast as possible, and institutions were established to serve this purpose. Section 3 describes conditions in the Japanese industry during the 1970s and 1980s, when worldwide deregulation and privatization were taking place. Here, the focus is on the privatization of NTTPC and its impact on R&D institutions and innovation patterns. Section 4 covers the period when the Internet was diffused throughout the Japanese market, bringing a number of changes to the industry. Changes in telecommunications policy are explained in detail, along with a discussion of the most successful innovation of this period: the i-mode.

Section 5 further explains the success of the i-mode as well as recommendations by the Telecommunications Council (Denki Tsushin Shingikai). The discussions in this section explain newly emerging patterns of R&D that have the potential to break the deadlock Japan's telecommunications industry is now facing. Here, the focus is on new patterns of competition, moves toward a more open R&D system, and the newly emerging concept referred to as *ba*. In the final section, 6, relationships among the environment, institutions, and innovations are discussed and the implications of the success of the i-mode are analyzed from an institutional perspective.

2 The Closed System Era: 1950s–1960s

2.1 Environment

The history of postwar telecommunications in Japan actually began seven years after the end of World War II, when the occupation ended and NTTPC was established. Since telecommunication services were operated by the government before that year, there were debates over what form of management the new telephone company should take. Four options were available: (1) a nationalized corporation, (2) a privatized corporation, (3) companies divided into nationalized parts (to handle long-distance, international, and telegraph operations, respectively) and a privatized part (to handle local telephone operations), and (4) a public corporation (Inoue, 2000: 51).

There was a strong argument for a privatized company, since the prewar, nationalized form of telephone operation was inefficient and could not meet society's needs. On the other hand, there was also an argument that telecommunication was a natural monopoly-type business and had a strong public aspect. More important, it was predicted that a private company would face difficulties in obtaining the kind of investment capital and government financial support that would be necessary to install a nationwide telecommunications network. Having considered these points, the government decided on a public corporation that would try to incorporate the advantages of governmental support coupled with the strengths of a private management style (Inoue, 2000: 52–53).

The telephone network of Japan was heavily damaged by the war. At the end of the war, the number of telephones was only 540,000, half the prewar level, and the rate of telephone diffusion among residential users was less than 1% (Kashiwabara, 1987: 19). Even though public demand for the installation of telephones was high, NTTPC could not keep up with the orders, and by the end of 1952, its first year of operation, only one-third of the orders were filled. It was not unusual for users to wait one hour to make a telephone call from Tokyo to Osaka, and in the worst case a caller had to wait for two hours and forty minutes. Even local calls took a long time to connect, and it was a common joke that riding a bicycle was faster than telephoning (Hiramatsu, 1980: 4). In view of these circumstances, the newly established NTTPC set two major goals of operation: one, to eliminate the telephone installation backlog, and two, to install a nationwide direct dialing system. Having established these goals, NTTPC launched its first five-year plan in 1953.

2.2 Institutions and Innovative Activities

These goals reflected the research and development priorities of NTTPC. Hence, the goal of R&D was not new innovations, but to install a telecommunications network utilizing existing technologies. According to a publication by NTTPC entitled *The 25- Year History of NTT Public Corporation*, the slogan at the time was "to reconstruct facilities lost during the war as quickly as possible by introducing new technologies that integrate the capabilities of Japan's technological institutions" (Nippon Denshin Denwa Kosha 25-Nenshi Henshu Iinkai, 1977: 295). At that time it was said that Japanese telecommunications technology was 20 years behind the United States and Europe; therefore it was natural for NTTPC to look to foreign technologies as new sources for reconstructing Japan's network (Hiramatsu, 1980: 150).

Takeshi Kajii, the first president of NTTPC, traveled to the United States and Europe to inspect the state of telecommunication technologies there and to determine what needed to be introduced to Japan to catch up to foreign technological levels. NTTPC then decided to send engineers to technologically advanced countries for training, and what followed was the very active importing of technologies from the United States and Europe. NTTPC decided to introduce the Kellogg crossbar switch, a U.S. product by an ITT subsidiary, after examining several central-switch models. NTTPC also imported microwave communications technology from STC of the United Kingdom and coaxial cable technology from ISE of the United States and SH Corporation of West Germany (Hiramatsu, 1980: 150–51).

NTTPC reverse engineered these imported technologies, thereby developing indigenous capabilities. For instance, after importing the crossbar switch from Kellogg in 1953, NTTPC succeeded in producing an indigenous version in 1956 and finally developed an improved version of the switch, the C-400, in 1966. It is said that the improvements in the C-400 led to a 30% reduction in cost and that installation space was reduced by 40%–50% (Hiramatsu, 1980: 150–51). During this period, as this example shows, NTTPC's basic R&D strategy was reverse engineering. By studying technologies, NTTPC developed and enlarged upon those technologies to produce indigenous models that would be compatible with the Japanese telecommunications market. This strategy served a dual purpose: NTTPC was able to increase its own technological capabilities and was also able to speed up the installation of a modern, nationwide telecommunications network.

According to the Nippon Telegraph and Telephone Public Corporation Law (Nippon Denshi Denwa Kosha Ho), NTTPC's business was limited to such operations as installation of the telecom network, research and development, acquisition and maintenance, and training. The manufacture of related equipment was not permitted. Therefore telecommunications equipment researched and developed by NTTPC had to be manufactured by private companies from whom NTTPC then acquired the equipment (Inoue, 2000: 70–71). It was out of this legal restriction that the "NTTPC family" (Denden family) was born.

A close relationship between the government-run phone service and the telecommunications manufacturers existed in the prewar period. In particular, five companies—NEC, Oki, Hitachi, Fujitsu, and Anritsu—monopolized the telecommunications market, jointly controlling 100% of it. This arrangement was partially revived after the war with the establishment of NTTPC, but under the postwar system, Anritsu became less important, with NEC, Oki, Fujitsu, and Hitachi becoming the core of the NTTPC family. This is because these four manufacturers were engaged in the central switch business, which was the most important of the telecom-equipment products. They were sometimes referred to as "A-makers." In addition to these A-makers, there were several hundred companies that supplied cables, construction services, and telecom equipment parts. In a broader sense, these companies, too, were part of the NTTPC family.[1]

Table 5.1 shows the demand structure for telecommunications equipment in 1966. As can be seen, NTTPC dominated the Japanese market with 58.1% of the total demand for telecom equipment: 73.6% of this for telephones, 82.8% for central switches, and 80.4% for transmission equipment. Obviously it was lucrative to secure contracts with NTTPC, thereby penetrating the biggest telecommunications market in Japan. For instance, in the case of NEC (the leading company among all the family members), nearly half of its sales came from NTTPC in the mid-1960s (Fransman, 1995: 332).

NTTPC itself was also a fast-growing market. The total value of contracts with NTTPC in telecom equipment grew from 16,286 million yen in 1953 (the year NTTPC started its first five-year plan) to 83,595 million yen in 1963, an increase of more than 5.13 times in 10 years (Table 5.2). The value of contracts for central switches grew even faster during the same period, from 5,985 million yen to 35,027 million yen, an increase of 5.85 times. Another important item for NTTPC, transmission equipment, grew by a factor of 13.4 during the same 10 years.

The contract system with NTTPC was in itself attractive for NTTPC family manufacturers. To begin with, since entry into the market was controlled by a family-type relationship between NTTPC and its manufacturers, competition was limited. Moreover, NTTPC's acquisitions proceeded according to five-year plans, and thus orders to manufacturers were predictable. Payments to manufacturers were made based on cost-plus profits: After adding all the costs for materials,

Table 5.1 Demand Structure of Telecom Equipment, 1966 (%)

	Telecom Equipment	Cable Equipment	Wireless Equipment	Telephone	Central Switches	Other Phone Equipment	Telegraph Equipment	Transmission Equipment	Cable Parts
Total Orders	100%	100%	100%	100%	100%	100%	100%	100%	100%
Public Demand	68.7	72.8	49.4	75.5	86.1	31	48.6	86.9	52.6
NTT	58.1	67.5	14.1	73.6	82.8	23.3	36.8	80.4	45.8
National Railroad	1.9	1.8	2.2	0.7	1.4	2.5	3.4	2.8	1.2
Japan Defense Agency	4.1	0.6	20.2	0.2	0.2	0.3	1.5	1.6	0.4
Police Agency	0.5	0.3	1.8	0.1	0.3	0	1.2	0.3	0.2
Local Government	0.9	0.5	2.5	0.2	0.4	2.3	0.5	0.8	0
Others	3.2	2.1	8.6	0.7	1.0	2.6	5.1	1.1	5
Private Demand	23.5	21.1	34.8	18.4	9.2	48	49.6	7	43
Electricity	1.8	1.3	3.7	0.2	0.9	0.9	0.6	3.9	0.8
Broadcasting	0.9	0.2	4.3	0.1	0.1	0.6	0.1	0.2	0.5
Finance	1.7	2	0.2	0.8	1.5	0.2	18.7	0.1	0.1
Transportation	2.6	0.8	10.8	0.3	0.5	0.9	5.6	0.4	0.2
Agr, Forestry, Fishery	2.7	2.2	5.1	0.1	0.1	26.8	0.5	0	0
Others	13.9	14.5	10.8	16.9	6.1	18.6	24.1	2.4	41.2
Foreign Demand	5.5	3.4	15.3	2.3	3.7	1.6	1.6	6.1	1.9
Demand via Agencies*	2.3	2.7	0.4	3.8	1.0	19.4	0.2	0	2.4

* Demand coming from sales agencies; not possible to identify type of customers.
Source: Tsushin Kikai Kogyokai, 1968, p. 50.

Table 5.2 Growth of NTT Contracts, 1953–63 (million yen)

	1953	1954	1955	1956	1957	1958	1959	1960	1961	1962	1963
Telecom Equipment	16,286	17,272	15,574	22,982	22,009	28,622	36,564	47,151	60,446	65,172	83,595
Telephone	2,380	2,666	2,742	3,112	1,938	2,757	3,352	3,894	3,946	5,214	4,724
Central Switches	5,985	5,786	5,140	6,779	7,898	8,844	13,123	16,442	24,903	25,577	35,027
Telegraph Equipment	339	530	521	615	576	449	439	823	1,223	1,206	1,576
Transmission Equipment	1,238	1,546	2,111	3,621	3,068	4,937	6,137	8,668	10,229	12,344	16,535
Major Parts	676	484	408	1,276	812	1,032	1,695	2,412	2,815	3,178	4,705
Wireless Equipment	1,010	1,880	1,107	1,405	1,899	2,701	1,820	1,567	2,510	3,090	4,392
Others	4,658	4,380	3,545	6,183	5,818	7,866	9,998	13,345	14,820	14,563	16,636
Cable Equipment	17,333	10,497	12,784	22,402	11,742	15,320	26,441	31,385	37,649	37,689	41,268

Source: Tsushin Kikai Kogyokai, 1968, pp. 33–34.

manufacturing, management, sales, and so on, transportation costs and profits were added and payments were made to manufacturers accordingly. Furthermore, cost calculations were adjusted according to the rate of inflation. One more advantage for the manufacturers was the advance payment system: When manufacturers needed cash for development or for acquiring necessary materials or parts, NTTPC made advance payments of up to 60% of the contract price.

In short, the NTTPC market was a huge, fast-growing market for manufacturers. Moreover, because of this family-type arrangement, profits from NTTPC's telecom business were assured and business risks for manufacturers were greatly reduced. There is no doubt that NTTPC family members were strongly attracted to the NTTPC market and had powerful incentives to maintain this advantageous, institutionalized arrangement (Hiramatsu, 1980: 112).

The NTTPC family system served NTTPC's operational goals very well. As mentioned earlier, NTTPC's goal in the 1950s and 1960s was to install a modernized, nationwide telecom network as fast as possible. NTTPC could fully utilize Japan's industrial and technological resources by including all the major makers of telecom equipment in the NTTPC family. By integrating its manufacturers in this way, NTTPC could work on co-development projects and share knowledge about telecom technologies. It could also avoid the overlapping of R&D. After the completion of vital equipment, the diffusion of technology was rapid, a process that also helped facilitate the standardization of telecom networks. Further, since several makers who cooperated at the R&D stage had to compete over prices at the manufacturing stage, NTTPC was able to reduce acquisition prices to a certain extent (Fransman, 1995: 236).

During this closed R&D system period, centered on the NTTPC family, there were clear targets to aim for and necessary technologies to acquire in foreign countries that helped generate the system. Under these circumstances, it could be said that the closed system worked well, facilitating network installation as well as providing benefits for NTTPC and its family members.

3 The Era of Deregulation and Digitization: 1970s–1980s

3.1 Environment

By 1977, NTTPC had accomplished its goal of eliminating the installation backlog, and by 1978 automatic dial calling was a reality nationwide (Inoue, 2000: 163). By the time NTTPC achieved these goals, however, two new trends in the industry were emerging. One was deregulation within the worldwide telecom industry, and the other was the digitization of telecommunication services.

The United States initiated and controlled these new trends. In 1963, Microwave Communications, Inc. (MCI) filed a request with the FCC to build a microwave communications system between St. Louis and Chicago that would offer a variety of telecom services. These services would be in competition with telecom services offered by AT&T, and so AT&T opposed MCI's request. However, in February 1966 the FCC ruled that MCI was technically, legally, and financially qualified to undertake these services, and after holding hearings on the issue the commission affirmed its decision in August 1966. This marked the beginning of competition in the long-distance telecom market (Brock, 1981: 211).

Deregulation also advanced in the terminal equipment area. In December 1948 Hush-a-Phone Corp. had filed a request with the FCC to sell the Hush-a-Phone, a cup-like device that snapped onto a telephone mouthpiece to provide speaking privacy and to shield out surrounding noises. The court affirmed Hush-a-Phone's position and private use of the device was allowed if no public harm resulted (Brock, 1981: 238). In June 1968 the FCC decided that AT&T could not prohibit the connection of a Carterphone, a device that could connect a mobile radiotelephone system to the telephone network, provided that the device met the standards established by AT&T (Brock, 1981: 240–42). The Carterphone decision advanced the deregulation of terminal equipment, and the trend was further accelerated by an FCC decision in July 1978 to allow private branch exchanges (PBX), key telephone equipment, and telephones to connect to AT&T's telephone network. By the 1980s, terminal equipment makers had considerable freedom to manufacture and connect their devices to AT&T networks—a far cry from the situation 20 years earlier (Brock, 1981: 247–52).

Rapid technological progress started to blur the boundaries between the telecommunications and computer industries, bringing previously unrelated products and services into competition. It was the digitization of telecommunications that gave birth to this new trend. The major difference between telephones and computers is that telephones are designed to transmit voices in analog form, but computers process digitized data. However, technological progress made it easy to convert analog messages into digital form, and computer technology was increasingly used in telephone systems. On the other hand, computers were beginning to increase the usage of telephone lines to transmit data. These changes brought the two industries into close interaction (Brock, 1981: 254–70).

A major legal problem caused by this interaction was that telephone service was a regulated industry, but the computer industry operated in a purely private market. This complex situation forced the FCC to establish a new legal framework in 1971. Thus the FCC promulgated its first computer-related rule, which divided services into four categories: data processing, hybrid data processing, hybrid communications, and communications. The FCC decided that communications and hybrid communications were to be regulated and that hybrid data processing and data processing were to be unregulated. In 1980, a second computer rule was established stipulating that all terminal equipment was to be deregulated and that telephone sets by AT&T or General Telephone & Electronics Corp. (GTE) could be provided only through a separate, unregulated subsidiary—not as a part of basic telephone service. Only basic transmission would remain regulated, a clear move toward deregulation (Brock, 1981: 270–73).

In 1984, AT&T was divided into seven regional Bell operating companies, and the new AT&T handled the long-distance market. It also conducted R&D (at Bell Laboratories) and manufactured telecom equipment (at Western Electric). In return, AT&T was allowed to enter such businesses as data processing, information services, and cable TV through separate subsidiaries. The breakup of AT&T greatly facilitated competition in the telephone service and terminal equipment industries. Moreover, competition across the telecommunications and computer industries became more severe in an integrated and unregulated environment.

Deregulation-led competition in the telecom industry, and the process of digitization, spread to other parts of the world. In Great Britain, British Telecom was privatized in 1984 and began to compete with Mercury Communications, a newly established telecom company. By the 1970s and 1980s, the world telecom market was transforming itself from a monopolized, heavily regulated market into an increasingly competitive one.

3.2 Institutions

The number of computers installed in Japan began to grow in the 1970s, which increased the demand for computer services over the telephone network. Accordingly, the same legal questions that had arisen in the U.S. regarding the framework for new competition emerged in Japan in the context of the Public Telecommunication Law (Koshu Denki Tsushin Ho). In 1971, the law was amended and a new legal framework allowed the connection of computers and other terminal equipment to NTTPC's public telephone network. In return, NTTPC was officially allowed to enter the data communications business (Hiramatsu, 1980: 130). However, there were severe restrictions on how to connect terminal equipment to the network, and users were sometimes subjected to inspections by NTTPC and approval by the Ministry of Posts and Telecommunications (MPT) as conditions for using the network for data communications. There were complaints from data communications users over these restrictions and over the unfair competitive environment created by NTTPC's monopoly of telecom operations (Hiramatsu, 1980: 140–44). There was also a recognition that a monopolized system could not meet all the demands of the new era of integration between telecommunications and computers (Fuke, 2000: 4).

The forces of change came from a different direction. The Provisional Commission on Administrative Reform (Rinji Gyosei Chosa Kai, or Rincho) was established in 1981 to examine the roles of various administrations, and one of its focuses was on issues surrounding public corporations. Three public corporations (for railroads, telecommunications, and tobacco) were being criticized for their monopolistic management style, handling of employer–employee relations, and inefficient operations because of the very nature of public corporations. Rincho examined these problems, which included NTTPC-specific issues, with the result that major institutional changes in the telecom market and industry followed (Inoue, 2000: 151–62).

Rincho saw three major problems in NTTPC management: (1) profits from telephone operations were decreasing, and a consequent increase in telephone tariffs in the near future was expected; (2) the major reason for cost increases was labor costs, which were aggravated by the existence of a surplus labor force because of the modernization of telecom facilities and automatic telephone exchanges; and (3) there were problems in employer–employee relations, which included rigid rules and customs that impeded the rationalization of operations. In order to solve these problems, Rincho recommended that (1) NTTPC should be privatized; (2) a new framework for competition should be devised, including the elimination of impediments arising from the monopoly; and (3) NTTPC should be broken up in such a way that it would provide long-distance services, and several other companies would provide local services (the very size of NTTPC was causing management problems). In short, they recommended NTTPC's privatization and breakup, as well as the deregulation of the telecom market (Inoue, 2000: 175–80).

After discussions based on these recommendations, a series of laws was passed by the National Diet in 1984 that changed the institutional framework of Japan's telecommunications market and industry. First, NTTPC was partially privatized into NTT—"partially" because NTT continued to be regulated by the newly legislated NTT Corporation Act (Nippon Denshin Denwa Kabushiki Kaisha Ho). According to the act, the Japanese government was required to hold a third of the NTT shares, and investments from overseas were prohibited. Additionally, NTT's business was confined to the domestic market and only NTT was to be responsible for providing universal service within that market (Fuke, 2000: 5–12).

The breakup of NTTPC recommended by Rincho was not realized. However, the government was required to address the breakup issue by reexamining various aspects of NTT after privatization and then implementing proper measures within five years. It was said that the Ministry of Finance opposed the breakup because it would prolong the schedule for selling NTT shares on the market, which would affect financial revenues to the ministry. Moreover, NTT (both management and the labor union) was against the breakup and had a degree of influence on the decision (Inoue, 2000: 184–85).

This "partial" aspect of its privatization affected NTT's pattern of R&D. According to the NTT Corporation Act, "[NTT is required to] contribute to the creative development of telecommunications and promote the general public welfare through promotion of research and diffusion of its results." Thus NTT was forced to open up and transfer the results of its R&D activities to the public. Although this is an obvious responsibility of a public corporation, there remained a degree of opaqueness in NTT's R&D activities because the privatization was "partial" (Fuke, 2000: 10). According to the president of NTT, Hitoshi Kojima, "The position of NTT's research laboratories is, in actuality, between a nationally operated corporation and a privately operated one" (Nonaka, 1996: 86).

Rules for new entry into the Japanese telecom market were established by the Telecommunications Business Act (Denki Tsushin Jigyo Ho). This act designated two types of telecommunication carriers: type-I carriers that operate a telecommunications business using their own facilities, and type-II carriers that operate without such facilities. The act established different procedures for obtain-

Table 5.3 Construction Investments and Central Switch Orders by NTT, 1965-80 (billion yen)

	1965	1966	1967	1968	1969	1970	1971	1972
Construction Investments	356.3	421.3	483.4	542.3	597.5	716.6	892.9	1,070.5
Central Switch Orders	47.16	56.24	62.52	68.45	75.92	84.76	99.56	125.99
	1973	**1974**	**1975**	**1976**	**1977**	**1978**	**1979**	**1980**
Construction Investments	1,168.1	1,340.5	1,418.1	1,361.8	1,624.7	1,639.8	1,666.4	1,709.0
Central Switch Orders	125.85	116.47	122.23	102.55	118.1	117.1	118.54	134.64

Source: Denki Tsushin Nenkan, 1982, p. 776.

ing entry permission and for registration depending on the type of carrier. Three major companies, Daini Denden Inc., Japan Telecom Company, and Teleway Japan Corporation, entered the long-distance market, and for the first time competition began in Japanese telecommunications (Fransman, 1995: 361).

Real competition had also begun in the terminal equipment market. The Telecommunications Business Act deregulated the market and users were able to connect a variety of telecom and computer terminal equipment provided they met the technical standards set by the government. After the privatization of NTTPC, various manufacturers, in addition to manufacturers within the NTTPC family, began to enter the telecom terminal equipment market, resulting in a severely competitive environment.

Besides the changes created by privatization, a fundamental transformation of the NTTPC family was going on in the 1970s and 1980s. NEC, the most representative NTTPC family manufacturer, depended on NTTPC for nearly half of its revenues in the mid-1960s; however, that share declined through the 1970s and 1980s, diminishing to 32% in 1974, and further reduced to 13% in 1985, the year of NTTPC's privatization (Fransman, 1995: 333). There were two major reasons for this decline. The first one was the stagnation of NTTPC's procurement budget. During the active construction period of Japan's telephone network, demand for telecom equipment increased dramatically, as was shown in Table 5.1. However, this growth rate started to decline in the mid-1970s. The value of NTTPC orders for central switches is shown in Table 5.3. According to this table, orders grew by an average annual rate of 15.2% from 1965 to 1973; however, that declined to 1.3% over the next eight years. Because of NTTPC's shrinking procurement budget, the dependence of telecom makers on NTTPC declined, and NTTPC came to play a less important role in the growth of the major telecom manufacturers (Hiramatsu, 1980: 113-14).

The "A-makers" of the NTTPC family, such as NEC, Fujitsu, Hitachi, and Oki, were not pure telecom equipment makers; they were integrated electronics companies that also operated in such businesses as computers, semiconductors, and home electronics. These other businesses, especially semiconductors and computers, grew at a much faster rate in the 1970s and 1980s and became leading sectors of these companies. Even within the telecom equipment market, the commercial market (as opposed to the NTTPC market) significantly increased in importance. These changes in the growth prospects of various businesses further reduced the importance of NTTPC's procurement market. It can therefore be said that the once tightly knit NTTPC family began to disintegrate during this period, and manufacturers started turning toward more commercial markets, including those overseas.

3.3 Innovations

The innovation record of NTTPC during the 1970s and 1980s was mixed. On one hand, some of the R&D behind its technology was successful, not only because NTTPC gained a share of the world market but because its technology helped to set world standards. On the other hand, there was R&D and resulting technology that, despite the investment of huge amounts of money, could not be diffused at all, even in the Japanese market.

NTTPC's most successful area of innovation was in optic technologies.[2] Here it gained a high world market share in such optic-related areas as optic fiber, optic connectors, and arrayed waveguide gratings (AWG) (NTT, 2001). As explained in the previous section, the goal of postwar Japanese telecommunications was to install modern nationwide networks as fast as possible, and in order to achieve this goal it was necessary to increase the speed of transmission. From the beginning, therefore, NTTPC focused strongly on transmission technology, assimilating the most advanced U.S. and European technologies and adapting them to indigenous technology (Katsumi, 2001: 31–32).

Overseas, the first news of the successful development of optic fiber was an announcement by Corning in 1970. It was very important news for NTTPC, which decided to focus its R&D on optic fiber technology in the hope of dramatically improving transmission speed. At first, NTTPC researchers tried to reproduce Corning's optic fiber based on available information and on trial and error where information was not available (Katsumi, 2001: 36–44). They did make some progress, but the performance of the optic fiber they developed was below Corning's level (Fransman, 1995: 216).

Bell Laboratories was another source of information. A researcher at that company successfully developed an optic fiber production method called MCVD (modified chemical vapor deposition). This method enabled optic fiber transmission over a distance of 30,000 meters, compared to only 1,000 meters by the Corning method (Katsumi, 2001: 44). NTTPC researchers were shocked to learn of the MCVD method and proceeded with further research on this method, using pure silica instead of compound glass for the fiber (Fransman, 1995: 219).

NTTPC finally succeeded in developing its own method of producing optic fiber in 1976 and announced it at an international conference on optic fiber in 1977. The method, called vapor-phase axial deposition (VAD), was original in the sense that soot is deposited on the bottom of the glass preform, which is rotated and moved upward. Unlike other methods, no target rod or mandrel is required. As the process of developing the VAD method shows, it was an incremental innovation. The advantage of this method was that longer fibers could be produced, thus enabling longer distance transmission without connectors. Also, production costs were low because of the continuous formation of the glass preform (Fransman, 1995: 219–23). VAD became one of the major methods of producing optic fibers, demonstrating that NTTPC had reached the cutting edge of technological development in the optic fiber field by the mid-1970s.

NTTPC's record in the data communications field was not so bright, and a number of projects failed. The DIPS computer project was a typical example. Seeing new commercial opportunities in data communications in the late 1960s, NTTPC decided to develop its own computer system. In order to construct a data communication system for customers, NTTPC needed computer technologies as well as telecommunications technologies, the latter in which NTTPC already had some competence. NTTPC embarked on a project to develop DIPS computers in 1968 and made a joint development contract with NEC, Fujitsu, and Hitachi, the major players in the NTTPC family. The project started in 1969 (Joho Shori Gakkai Rekishi Tokubetsu Iinkai, 1998: 183–93).

The DIPS computer project created difficult problems for NEC, Fujitsu, and Hitachi. These companies, which already had their own computer businesses, were now required to develop a new DIPS operating system. At first, it looked as though the project would provide mutual benefits for NTTPC and the manufacturers because NTTPC could utilize the manufacturers' existing computer hardware for DIPS, while the manufacturers could gain software competence and increased sales of their computers.

It eventually became apparent, however, that the DIPS project would actually cause the computer companies to compete with NTTPC in the data communications market. NTTPC, through its Data Communications Division, marketed integrated telecom and computer systems. The customers to whom NTTPC sold its DIPS computers were also important marketing targets of the computer divisions of NEC, Fujitsu, and Hitachi. Therefore these companies had to compete with NTTPC in the end-user market while at the same time cooperating with NTTPC in the DIPS project. This conflict of interest was so serious that the companies gradually lost any incentive to put further innovative efforts into the DIPS project. Moreover, these computer makers were also members of a computer development project under the auspices of the Ministry of International Trade and Industry (MITI), whose purpose was to implement policies for the information-processing industry. Thus they were placed in a difficult position, politically speaking, between MPT, which oversaw NTTPC, and MITI (Fransman, 1995: 156–58; Joho Shori Gakkai Rekishi Tokubetsu Iinkai, 1998: 188–91).

In addition to the competition between NTTPC and the computer makers, NTTPC had difficulties with its software. As mentioned, the DIPS project had to develop an operating system that was unique to the DIPS system. However, the industry standard for computers at that time was the IBM operating system. Therefore NTTPC was forced to rewrite its popular application software, which was based on the IBM system, into a format that would be compatible with the DIPS system. This considerably raised the cost of using the DIPS system. To solve this problem, NTTPC tried to promote the Multivendor Integration Architecture (MIA) Project, which was to develop new architectural interfaces with different types of computer hardware. This project began in 1988 and included IBM and DEC. Although the goal was to develop an open computer system, it did not progress well, and the DIPS computer system itself ceased to exist in 1992 (Fransman, 1995: 156; Joho Shori Gakkai Rekishi Tokubetsu Iinkai, 1998: 304–05).

Companies in the NTTPC family (NEC, Fujitsu, and Hitachi) were forced to develop two different operating systems because of their relationship with NTTPC. The same kind of problem arose when these companies tried to enter the international market in digital switches. NEC, a leading switch maker, entered the U.S. market in May 1979, a late date compared with such competitors as Northern Telecom of Canada, which had already introduced its digital switches in October 1977. According to Martin Fransman, a researcher of the Japanese telecommunications switch industry, this delay was caused by NTTPC's hesitation to go digital. Fransman quotes Koji Kobayashi, then president of NEC: "Because NTTPC was our biggest customer, we could not make the decision ourselves regarding entry into digital switching. We had to follow the policy of NTTPC. At this stage NTTPC had not yet decided to begin R&D on digital switching." NTTPC at that time was preoccupied with driving down the cost of its space-division switch, which was introduced in 1972. Under these circumstances, NEC was forced to develop a different digital switch model for the U.S. market. Therefore it had no choice but to enter the U.S. market without first testing, debugging, or improving the switch through trials in the Japanese market, which was the usual path taken by Japanese companies before entering foreign markets. Furthermore, NEC had to develop and maintain two different digital switch systems, one for domestic use and the other for the foreign market (Fransman, 1995: 61–71).

As a result, NEC's effort to enter the U.S. market did not succeed, having gained a mere 0.1% share of that market 10 years after introducing its digital switches (Fransman, 1995: 70). During the 1970s and 1980s, the once solid and well-organized NTTPC family system began to create a variety of problems for the manufacturers and institutions that had made the rapid installation of a domestic telecom network possible during the previous period. They were now faced with a new set of challenges created by digitization and internationalization.

4 The Era of the Internet: 1990s to the Present

4.1 Environment

The most dramatic environmental change that the world telecom industry experienced in the 1990s was the diffusion of the Internet. During the period from 1993 to 1997, the number of Internet domains increased from 26,000 to 1,301,000 (Beikoku Shomusho, 1999: 16). Because of this incredible rate of diffusion, the interdependence of countries and populations was greatly enhanced, and telecom companies whose operations were confined to domestic markets in the past now extended their operations beyond their countries' borders.

The technology of the Internet itself is not new. The first successful experiment with the Advanced Research Projects Agency Network (ARPANET), predecessor of the Internet, was carried out in 1969, when an SDS-940 computer at the Stanford Research Institute was connected with a Sigma-7 computer at the University of California, Los Angeles (UCLA). By 1976 there were only 63 connecting points, and by 1985 the count was still only 1961. However, by 1990, the spread of personal computers greatly raised the network's potential, and this, in combination with a decrease in the price of telecommunication service, provided the basis for using the network at an affordable cost. Furthermore, such technological innovations as the World Wide Web, Mosaic, and Netscape Navigator increased the ease of use and the utility of the Internet, leading to a sharp rise in the number of Internet users in the 1990s (Murayama, 2000: 49).

The Internet brought dramatic changes to the industrial environment. Companies such as Microsoft and Intel, which established industry standards for the Internet, recorded phenomenal earning growth rates. For instance, Microsoft recorded an average of 47% annual profit growth from fiscal 1994 to 1999, and Intel recorded a 22% growth rate from fiscal 1993 to 1998 (Murayama, 2000: 163–64). New companies created by the Internet revolution, such as Cisco Systems (routers) and Netscape Communications (browsers) became leaders in the diffusion of the Internet. Along with these new companies, old computer and telecom companies such as AT&T and IBM restructured their businesses to fit in this new environment. Furthermore, this rapid diffusion created a variety of other companies that utilized the merits of the Internet. These waves of change originated in the United States, and governments and industries in other countries were forced to adjust to the new environment (Murayama, 2000: 164–71).

4.2 Institutions

Japanese institutions and industries were hard-hit by the changes created by the Internet and were late to adjust to the new industrial environment. To explain the institutional changes in Japan in the 1990s and early 2000s, we must start with the legacy of NTTPC's privatization into NTT in 1985. As explained earlier, the NTT Corporation Act required that the government reexamine changes in the industrial environment and take necessary measures to reform NTT's corporate structure. The Telecommunications Council was established in 1988 for this purpose and made recommendations to MPT in 1990 (Yuseisho Denki Tsushin Shingikai, 1990: 1).

The main purposes of the reexamination by the Telecommunications Council were to improve the efficiency of NTT management, to preserve fair and effective competition, and to promote research and development (Yuseisho Denki Tsushin Shingikai, 1990: 1). The main recommendations made by the council were: (1) to privatize long-distance operations after separating them from local telecom operations; (2) to allow local telecom operations under one company system; and (3) to separate mobile communication operations from NTT and privatize that service (Yuseisho Denki Tsushin Shingikai, 1990: 11). There was strong opposition to the Telecommunications Council's recommendation to break up NTT, especially from the Ministry of Finance and MITI. A political compromise was therefore made to the effect that the mobile communication division would be separated within two years, and the separation and privatization of NTT's long-distance operations would be examined once again in five years (Fransman, 1995: 385–90).

The basic framework for research and development established by the NTT Corporation Act in 1985 was upheld by the recommendations of the Telecommunications Council. The council recommended that it would be desirable for NTT's R&D functions to be administered as one body and that a local telecom company should inherit these R&D operations. By maintaining this framework, the council said it would be possible to meet the obligations of NTT as stipulated by the NTT Corporation Act to open and transfer the results of its R&D activities to the public. Furthermore, it was recommended that each separated NTT company should share in the cost of the basic aspects of R&D carried out by NTT (Yuseisho Denki Tsushin Shingikai, 1990: 15).

Thus the ambiguity of NTT's R&D functions, that is, whether they were for public or private purposes, was left unresolved. The Telecommunications Council recommended that NTT continue to widely diffuse the results of its R&D and try to implement a system for incorporating the opinions of other telecom operators, manufacturers, and users (Yuseisho Denki Tsushin Shingikai, 1990: 20). In principle, therefore, it was possible for competing telecom operators such as DDI and Japan Telecom to use the capabilities and results of NTT's R&D for a price. However, not a single company attempted to use this public aspect of NTT's R&D activities for the company's own operations (Yuseisho Denki Tsushin Shingikai, 2000: 12).

The next set of recommendations by the Telecommunications Council concerning NTT's breakup was submitted to MPT in February 1996. This report pointed out the need for a second stage of information and telecom reform. The first reform had been carried out in 1985 when NTTPC was privatized and competition was introduced in the market; however, the report cited Japan's need for a second reform because of the rapid pace of technological innovation, the multimedia trend, globalization, and the growing sophistication of consumer needs (Yuseisho Denki Tsushin Shingikai, 1998: 2–4). In order to adjust to these new environmental conditions, the council made these recommendations: (1) to reorganize NTT into one long-distance telecom company and two local telecom companies, and to privatize the long-distance company in such a way that it could enter such markets as international telecom, local telecom, CATV, and other content-related operations, and (2) to maintain these local companies as special companies that could compete in other local-carrier markets and to target these companies for privatization in the future.

There were pros and cons voiced regarding the recommendations made by the Telecommunications Council; after heated discussions, a political compromise was finally reached at the end of 1996, resulting in the following breakup plan. First, NTT would reorganize itself into a long-distance telecom company and two local telecom companies, as the Telecommunications Council had recommended. However, a holding company that controlled all three companies would also be established. Second, the long-distance telecom company would be privatized completely. This meant that the NTT Corporation Act would no longer apply to the company and that NTT Communications, the new long-distance company, could offer international telecom services. Third, the two local telecom companies would remain as special companies regulated under the NTT Corporation Act, with their areas of operation divided into east Japan (Higashi Nihon) and west Japan (Nishi Nihon).

Under this arrangement, the holding company would be in charge of basic research and development, while applied research more closely connected to telecom service would be carried out by the local telecom companies. This R&D was covered by the NTT Corporation Act; hence the requirement to open up and diffuse the results of R&D remained in effect. An interesting aspect of the new arrangement was how basic R&D would be financed within this framework. A portion of it would be useful for such privatized companies as NTT Communications (the long-distance telecom company), NTT DoCoMo (a mobile telecom company), and NTT Data (a data communications company). Because of the interdependence of R&D among these NTT companies, an arrangement was made whereby the privatized ones would pay for part of the basic R&D carried out by the NTT holding company (Yuseisho Denki Tsushin Shingikai, 2000: 3–9). Therefore, even though NTT was reorganized in response to environmental changes in the telecom market, a portion of NTT's R&D activities was regulated under the NTT Corporation law, which stipulates a public commitment. Moreover, even the privatized NTT companies were partially responsible for this regulated basic R&D.

The next Telecommunications Council was organized in July 2001 to make recommendations on competitive policies for the telecom market in order to promote the "IT Revolution." The Council submitted its first report in December 2001 and its final report in February 2002. The main assignment of this Council was to examine competitive policies in the new era of the Internet and globalization of the telecom market. Three subcommittees on Competitive Policy, Universal Service, and International Competitiveness were created under the council. The first subcommittee examined the issue of competition in the telecom market and submitted recommendations that would promote competition in the market, although no structural changes in NTT were recommended. It was the third Subcommittee on International Competitiveness that examined and tried to resolve the ambiguous role of NTT's research and development.

The subcommittee acknowledged that by international standards it was highly unusual that one telecom company would be required by the government to promote and diffuse its research results to the public. Therefore the subcommittee recommended that this requirement be abolished in the future. It also clearly recognized that research institutions belonging to the government were the ones responsible for basic research. The subcommittee therefore recommended that the government should maintain Japan's overall capabilities in basic research by ensuring that the abolition of the requirement for NTT regarding basic research would not hurt those capabilities. If this recommendation were accepted, NTT would be able to concentrate on R&D for its own sake without having to worry about the public aspect of its R&D. Such government-related research laboratories as the Communication Research Laboratory, the Advanced Telecommunications Research Institute International, and the Telecommunications Advancement Organization would be responsible for strengthening the country's basic research (Soumusho, Joho Tsushin Shingikai, 2002: 116–18).

The recommendations by the Subcommittee on International Competitiveness should also be looked on from an industrial policy perspective as well. During Japan's closed-system era of the 1950s and 1960s, the main goal was to install a modern nationwide telecom network, and the primary means of achieving that goal were the importation of foreign technologies, reverse engineering, and internalization of those technologies. As discussed earlier, the Japanese government, NTTPC, and the NTTPC family companies cooperated closely and achieved this goal during the 1970s. Under this closed system, foreign companies played a role as providers of technologies, while the Japanese maintained an inward-looking attitude that focused on how best to utilize those technologies for domestic purposes.

In contrast to this closed system, the recommendation made by the subcommittee was that Japanese R&D should transform itself into an open system. The reason is that in the telecommunications area, international standards based on interconnections are very important; in order for Japan to develop international standards, including de facto standards, Japan's R&D system would have to be open to international players. Therefore the subcommittee recommended that Japan should become a *ba*, or gathering place, for telecom R&D and encourage participants from foreign countries to gather in Japan to do research cooperatively. It is worth noticing how different this new industrial policy, based on the open *ba* concept, truly is. It represents a fundamental revision of the policies carried out during the era of the closed system (Soumusho, Joho Tsushin Shingikai, 2002: 111–13).

The companies in the NTTPC, and later the NTT family, further reduced their dependence on NTT procurement in the 1990s. Some of the lower-ranked companies that supply NTT with parts such as wires and cables and that are in charge of construction-related work still depend heavily on NTT. But the so-called A-makers (NEC, Fujitsu, Oki, and Hitachi) have greatly reduced their dependence. It is obvious that these electronics companies no longer survive merely by fulfilling NTT's demands, and in order to sell in other markets, domestic and foreign, they will have to develop their own R&D capabilities. For instance, Oki's sales to NTT started to decline in 1996, and sales in 1999 dropped to a 10-year low (Oki Denki, 2000: 2).

The Telecommunications Council accepts public comments after it releases a draft of its recommendations. There were no public comments from telecom manufacturers expressing opinions against the council's recommendation that the regulation requiring NTT to disclose its R&D results be abolished. By this time the NTT family's dependence on NTT had become so weak that the report by the Subcommittee on International Competitiveness itself commented that "the dependence of telecom companies on NTT has been reduced, and NTT's R&D system has changed from a system to develop hardware for central switches by working with domestic companies, to a system to develop software by cooperating with a broad range of foreign and domestic companies and universities." The report also said that because of this change, "the industry's expectations toward NTT have also been changing" (Soumusho, Joho Tsushin Shingikai, 2002: 117–18). It should be noted that the trend toward an open system is also advancing in terms of the relationship between NTT and manufacturing companies.

4.3 Innovations

The innovation record during this period has not been a bright one for Japan. The United States has led the IT Revolution through the rapid diffusion of the Internet, and the U.S. has also dominated the development of Internet-related equipment, software, and standards. To be more specific, Cisco Systems occupies the major world share in routers, which are switches for the Internet; browser software is dominated by such companies as Microsoft and Yahoo. Computer languages as well, including Java and VRML (Virtual Reality Modeling Language), were developed in the United States (Nihon Keizai Shinbun, 1996). Latecomers to the Internet world, Japanese companies could not enter these markets fast enough and as a result lost significant opportunities to increase their share of them.

The one exception is the i-mode, a technology that makes it possible to access the Internet from a small, mobile telephone (*keitai*). The i-mode was developed by NTT DoCoMo, which was spun off from NTT in 1992 on the recommendation of the 1990 Telecommunications Council. In an effort to expand its *keitai* service to non-voice applications, such as data communications, NTT DoCoMo created a special project team in 1997. This team recruited talent from outside, an unusual practice for a company that used to be a division of the conservative NTT. The team succeeded in developing the i-mode, the first technology in the world that allowed continuous and therefore instant wireless access to the Internet from a mobile telephone. The i-mode also accommodates a variety of content that users can enjoy, and charges are based on the volume of data sent and received, not on usage time, thereby reducing the cost for users. Invoicing is done through telephone bills, a system that assures that providers of information will receive their usage fees (Murayama, 2001: 363–64).

Because of these advantages, the i-mode grew explosively and the number of users surpassed 10 million by August 2000, only a year and a half after the i-mode's introduction. By the end of fiscal year 2001, the number of users had passed the 30 million mark (NTT DoCoMo, 2002: 316). The ramifications of the success of the i-mode are dynamic and point to a new trend in Japan's telecom industry.

5 An Emerging R&D System

The success of NTT DoCoMo and the recommendations by the Telecommunications Council in 2002 suggest major changes in the Japanese telecom industry's system of R&D. Let us discuss three of these emerging trends.

5.1 From Controlled Competition to Direct Competition

As mentioned in section 3, controlled competition was the main characteristic of R&D in Japan's telecommunication sector. That is, NTTPC and a group of telecom manufacturers formed a family-type organization that cooperated on R&D. These manufacturers competed with each other at the manufacturing stage, which contributed to cost reductions. However, this system ran into difficulties with the advance of deregulation and globalization, as exemplified by the failure of the DIPS computer project.

The success of the i-mode was based not on the above type of controlled competition, but on direct competition by NTT DoCoMo in the mobile telephone market. When NTT DoCoMo was spun off from NTT in 1992, the company was running a deficit, with bankruptcy a real possibility considering the severe competition in this market (Oboshi, 2000: 2). The main reason for this was that Japan's penetration rate for mobile phones was, in 1991, a mere 0.7%, compared to 6.2% in Sweden, 2.5% in the United States, and 2.0% in the United Kingdom (Oboshi, 2000: 87).

In a search for reasons for the low diffusion rate in Japan, Koji Oboshi, then president of the newly-launched NTT DoCoMo, came up with three: (1) telephone conversations were frequently cut off because of deficiencies in the wireless network; (2) user fees were too high, especially the initial contract fee for mobile services; and (3) mobile phones were bulky and the batteries did not last long enough. In order to solve these problems, Oboshi began an aggressive investment program to extend a seamless mobile telecom network. He also abolished the initial contract fee and lowered the price for using mobile phones. Equally important, NTT DoCoMo and its manufacturers succeeded in miniaturizing and reducing the weight of the phones so that by 1996 they weighed less than 100 grams.[3] Although aggressive advance investment and reduced prices were risky steps for a deficit-running company, the outcome was indeed favorable, not to mention prescient. Users of mobile telephones started to increase, and by 1996 the penetration rate grew to 10% (Oboshi, 2000: 149). This in turn led to a further decrease in user fees.

An extended wireless network, low prices, and a miniaturized *keitai* terminal handset all provided DoCoMo with the necessary infrastructure to make a business of i-mode. Oboshi foresaw that since penetration of the *keitai* was so rapid, market saturation would soon occur. He therefore decided to establish a new project team that would search for new business opportunities using the *keitai*. He perceived that business based on value should follow business based on volume and saw a bright future in wireless data communications. The result was the development of the i-mode. This new kind of service would not have started off so smoothly without an infrastructure in place and some quick decision making. Nor would DoCoMo's entry into data communications have been possible if it had remained a part of NTT, unable to face the tough competition of the market. As Oboshi (2000: 149) said, "It is the destiny of fast-changing industries such as ours to always think of and plan new businesses."

Competition, then, was one of the driving forces behind these changes. Because NTT DoCoMo was separated from the giant NTT, DoCoMo had little choice but to earn its own profits. Prior to separation, even if the division had run deficits, it would not have paid any mind to the possibility of going bankrupt because NTT's other, more profitable businesses would have absorbed the loss. After separation from NTT, however, it became a matter of survival. As Oboshi (2000: 73) personally admitted, DoCoMo was a new company that could all too easily go bankrupt. Oboshi further said that since DoCoMo did not have the advantages of scale of a giant like NTT, as a small company it would have to increase the speed of its decision making in order to advance faster than its competitors. This kind of thinking was not part of NTT's mindset, and it can be said that the legal requirement that threw DoCoMo into a competitive market is what led to the company's success (Oboshi, 2000: 114). In fact, the Japanese mobile phone market became the most deregulated wireless telecommunications market in the world by the mid-1990s (Oboshi, 2000: 135). In 1994, MPT liberalized the wireless market, in which such companies as DDI, IDO, and TU-KA competed vigorously with NTT DoCoMo to increase their share of this fast-growing market. This direct-competition mentality can also be seen in the recommendations by the 2002 Telecommunications Council. The council recommended that NTT be completely privatized and therefore freed from regulatory requirements, meaning that NTT would have to face its competitors on an equal footing. Further, by clarifying that basic research would be in the hands of the government and that NTT would pursue R&D for its own sake, the council gave a complete endorsement to the trend toward direct competition.

In short, controlled competition is giving way to direct competition in the Japanese telecommunications sector, both in terms of company strategy and governmental policy. This change also reflects the transformation from a closed system of innovation to an open one, which will be discussed next.

5.2 From a Closed System to an Open System

The old R&D system of the Japanese telecom market was a closed one; that is, NTTPC and its family of manufacturers formed a solid relationship that neither domestic nor foreign companies could easily penetrate. Under this closed system, NTT and its family cooperated in fulfilling the needs of the domestic market and building Japan-specific telecom equipment.

However, it was under the open system that replaced the old closed system that the development of the i-mode succeeded. From the beginning, the members of the i-mode project team were recruited under the open system, and project leader Keiichi Enoki was given full autonomy to recruit his staff as he wished. He accepted applicants from inside the company as well as specialized talent from the outside. Engineers from telecom manufacturers were also added (Oboshi, 2000: 151–53).

Those members who were recruited from outside brought much needed new blood to the project. Mari Matsunaga, the chief editor of a job information magazine before she joined DoCoMo, was a prime example. Her principal contribution to the i-mode's success was in presenting the i-mode concept and building the i-mode's information content. To implement her ideas, Matsunaga organized brainstorming meetings that included outsiders. She even asked the company to designate one room especially for the purpose of gathering people together to freely discuss possible concepts and functions of the i-mode. It was in this open atmosphere that the i-mode was born. The concept that was finally agreed on was the "hotel concierge" model; that is, users should be able to access any necessary information through the i-mode. A further contribution made by Matsunaga to the i-mode was in the nature of the content it would provide to its users. As a past editor of a job information magazine, Matsunaga had extensive knowledge of the needs and interests of potential users and used her knowledge and ability in developing the content of the i-mode (Matsunaga, 2000: 84–91).

Another good example of outside talent was Takeshi Natsuno. Natsuno was a young entrepreneur who was running Internet start-ups before he joined DoCoMo. His main contribution was to set up a billing method whereby DoCoMo would receive commissions for providers of content to the i-mode. Users could be charged through telephone bills for the use of information made available by DoCoMo-licensed content providers. In an interview with Business Week, Natsuno said: "People say the Internet has to be free, but we're charging for it," and "This is a model for the mobile Internet that others now want to emulate." (Business Week, 2000: 19) As these examples show, the open system of recruiting project members enhanced the possibility of developing new ideas, concepts, and business models. This would have been impossible under the old, closed system.

The basic technology adopted for the i-mode was also based on the open system. The operating system (OS) of the Japanese mobile telephone was based on TRON (The Real-time Operating System Nucleus), developed by Ken Sakamura of Tokyo University. NEC engineers, who were engaged in developing software for the *keitai*, tried various operating systems available on the market, but the response times of these systems were not quick enough to be useful for *keitai* software. Several tens of seconds elapsed from switch-on time to the time that conversation could start. They then tried TRON, which had been around since the mid-1980s, and succeeded in significantly cutting response time. Today almost all the operating systems for *keitai* used in Japan are based on TRON; as of the end of 2001, more than 70 million mobile telephones were using TRON technology (Nihon Keizai Shinbun, 2002).

TRON is suitable for the *keitai* environment because it is designed for a microcomputer that can be inserted into various types of equipment used in daily life. Also, these computers can be connected with one another through networks. The term "ubiquitous computing" is often used to express this concept. The TRON concept was already developed by the mid-1980s; the TRON project started up in 1984 through an alliance between universities and industry (Sakamura, 2001: 87). However, the project did not succeed at that time because the micronization of computers was still too radical a concept during the era of mainframe computers, which was dominated by IBM.[4] But TRON resurfaced with the *keitai* and finally became a major operating system.

TRON was designed as an open-technology system. The basic thinking was that in order for everyone in this information-based society to have access to information technology, a specific organization should not monopolize that technology. It should be open to any individual or organization. Therefore the TRON concept is that any entrepreneur or company who is interested in it is free to use TRON and develop products and businesses based on it. The Japanese *keitai* uses TRON as its OS; therefore, any company interested in the *keitai* business can adopt TRON without charge and develop products utilizing it (Sakamura, 2001: 71–72). The open TRON-based *keitai* system is a major departure from the old closed system in which the number of companies that could develop telecom technologies was limited. Moreover, such companies tried to develop equipment that was specific to the Japanese market. This openness is one of the main reasons companies like Matsushita, Kyocera, Sony, and Sharp, as well as such foreign companies as Nokia and Ericsson, all of which were outside the NTT family, could enter DoCoMo's *keitai* market and make the *keitai* business extremely competitive.

NTT DoCoMo continues to gravitate toward an open system. In 1996 DoCoMo succeeded in developing W-CDMA, a third-generation mobile telephone technology that makes it possible to send moving pictures via the Internet. DoCoMo has made this technology openly available to other companies, and through negotiations with foreign governments and companies is seeking the global standardization of W-CDMA technology (Oboshi, 2000: 68). Asia and the EU have already adopted this third-generation technology.

The basic open-concept strategy for a third-generation *keitai* consisted of three parts: (1) developing mobile multimedia capability; (2) offering a global system; and (3) promoting an open R&D environment (Oboshi, 2000: 69). In fact, Oboshi (2000: 222) stated in his book, "We will open up all information regarding new technologies. In return let us all work together." In the spirit of this principle, DoCoMo has built a research institute at Yokosuka Research Park which promotes international cooperation in telecom research.

The 2002 Telecommunications Council's recommendation also advocated an open system, and it was pointed out that Japanese R&D should move in this direction in order to participate in the setting of global standards. This conclusion was an outcome of the council's recognition that Microsoft and Intel (collectively dubbed "Wintel") had succeeded in setting standards that created an unfavorable environment for the Japanese R&D system. The strength of Japanese technology is based on incremental innovations, not on major breakthroughs. It is true that Japanese companies have achieved incremental innovations through continuous improvement. However, because of the closed environment created by Wintel, this process has not worked when applied to existing information technologies. In other words, Microsoft, the provider of Wintel's basic software, and Intel, the provider of its hardware (semiconductors), got together and established the global standards for information technology. Since Wintel successfully protected their technologies through strong enforcement of intellectual property rights to their products, companies other than Wintel could not improve on these technologies. Because of the closed, or black-box, characteristics of the Wintel standards, Japan's incrementally innovative R&D system, whereby a product is constantly improved, could not be utilized.

Based on these realities, the Telecommunications Council recommended that Japan's telecom R&D activities be opened to the world, a process that would include cooperation with foreign researchers and companies. By adopting this new direction, Japan could participate in the process of setting global standards and through this process promote incremental innovations that would put Japan at a comparative advantage. In short, the council's logic was that an open R&D system would enable Japan to gain competitiveness in the telecom sector.

5.3 From Family to *Ba*

The third element of change is the introduction of the *ba* concept to research and development. The concept of *ba* is closely related to the open R&D system discussed above. Under the old family system, such as the NTTPC family, members cooperated with each other and their relationship was therefore important in R&D, but this was a closed concept that restricted family membership to a few companies. By comparison, *ba* is an open concept that accepts anyone into the system who has an interest in it. It is an open gathering space (both real and virtual) in which to conduct R&D.

The *ba* concept puts an emphasis on relationships. Ikujiro Nonaka, who introduced the *ba* concept to management theory and has tried to construct a new concept of knowledge creation, writes, "The power of creation does not exist within individuals, but comes out of relationships between individuals and relationships between individuals and environments; in other words, it is born from *ba*" (Itami et al., 2000: 45–46). Nonaka thinks that the Japanese pattern of knowledge creation is distinctly different from the Western style, which tends to emphasize the talent and ability of individuals. But knowledge is created within *ba* that generates a variety of productive relationships.

A company that is very conscious of the concept of *ba* is NTT DoCoMo. As mentioned above, DoCoMo opened a research institute in Yokosuka Research

Park for international cooperation in R&D. In the words of President Oboshi (2000: 222–223), it is "a *ba* for international cooperative research," and the goal is a Silicon Valley-type environment where universities and start-up companies can gather together and share intellectual innovations at the international level. For Oboshi, the i-mode became popular because it was conceived through an "open *ba*" system culminating in a highly attractive, high-content product. Moreover, the i-mode functions as "an open *ba* where participants cooperate and share profits by providing information, without DoCoMo monopolizing the profits" (Oboshi, 2000: 58).

One might thus say that the 2002 Telecommunications Council's unique contribution is its recommendation that "Japan should function as a *ba* and an open R&D environment" (Soumusho, Joho Tsushin Shingikai, 2002: 222–23). We can see the transformation of the Japanese government's industrial policy from one based on a family system to one based on *ba*. As mentioned, council members recognized that without internationalizing R&D, it would be extremely difficult for Japan to set global standards. It is interesting to note that Japan's response to the globalization of R&D is the *ba* concept, which is in fact based on traditional Japanese philosophy. For instance, Nonaka took the thinking of Kitaro Nishida, a notable Japanese philosopher, and applied it to management theory to construct a new theory.[5] In this new era of globalization, it is important to note how the traditional *ba* concept has emerged as an effective way of conducting new patterns of R&D.

6 Environmental Changes, Institutional Changes, and Innovations

In this final section, the relationship between environmental changes surrounding the telecommunications industry, institutional changes, and technological innovations will be discussed. The first part of the section addresses the relationship between environmental and institutional changes, followed by an analysis of the relationship between institutional changes and their effects on innovation. Finally, the implications of the success and limitations of the i-mode are discussed from an institutional perspective.

6.1 Linkages between Environmental and Institutional Changes

The industrial environment and its institutional framework were well suited for the closed-system era of the 1950s and 1960s. After the destruction of Japan's telecom facilities during the war, the first priority of the Japanese government was the reconstruction of a modern, nationwide telecom network. Japan's government, industries, and universities made tremendous efforts toward this end, and the result was an institutional framework that supported high-speed telecom installation. This institutional arrangement was a closed system. In order to utilize existing technologies, which at the time were available only in foreign countries, NTTPC and its equipment-family members cooperated closely in importing foreign technologies. They then reverse-engineered those technologies that best suited Japanese needs.

The standardization of the telecom network, as well as the focused use of scarce technological resources, led to the rapid installation of telecom facilities.

However, the closed system soon became obsolete with the telecom industry's deregulation, which started in the United States. From that point on, the telecom market became competitive. The trend toward digitization, which merged the computer and telecom industries, also facilitated this process. In 1984 the Japanese government decided to privatize NTTPC into NTT, a landmark decision reflective of the deregulatory trend. In consideration of the fact that AT&T was divested and British Telecom was privatized in 1984, this was a remarkably swift move by the Japanese government.

The Provisional Commission on Administrative Reform (Rincho) that debated the privatization issue in the early 1980s also recommended the breakup of NTTPC. However, debate over the latter issue continued until the second half of the 1990s before the government finally decided on a partial breakup of NTT under a holding company system in 1996. The actual breakup took place in 1999.

A question one might ask is, why did it take so long to break up NTT? The question is vital because it touches on the issue of linkage between environmental changes and responses by the R&D institutions of Japan's telecommunications industry. It was right (judging by world telecom industrial trends) for the Japanese government to privatize NTTPC, introduce competition, then break up NTT to further promote competition. However, while it was relatively easy to privatize the company, it was more difficult to break it up, and took much longer.

To answer this question, we have to explore the decision-making process of telecommunications policy. Under the Japanese system, when an issue concerning the telecommunications industry needs special attention, MPT establishes a Telecommunications Council, and this council discusses the issue and makes recommendations to the ministry. Council membership typically consists of university professors, industry representatives, researchers from think tanks, and journalists, all of whom are selected by MPT. After receiving their recommendations, the ruling political party, usually the Liberal Democratic Party, examines them and makes a final decision. Laws and regulations are implemented after they have been passed by the National Diet.

Compromises are usually arrived at through the process of accommodating the various interests of concerned groups. However, the decision to privatize NTTPC was a rare case where the majority of those interest groups favored privatization. According to Teruyuki Inoue, a scholar who has done extensive studies of the political aspects of Japan's telecommunications industry, there existed seven interest groups involved with the issue of NTTPC's privatization (Inoue, 2000: 80–85). Rincho, whose role was to examine the functions of various governmental administrations and evaluate levels of efficiency, was the major force behind privatization. Privatization of the national railroads and the tobacco public corporation was already under way, but privatization of the NTTPC was a new and attractive idea. It would appeal to the public on the grounds that the world was becoming an "information society," and by privatizing and raising the efficiency of NTTPC, Japan could become one of the major players in the increasingly competitive information and telecom market (Inoue, 2000: 181).

The Ministry of Finance (MoF), one of Japan's most powerful ministries, also favored the privatization idea because MoF would obtain considerable revenues by selling shares of the privatized NTT. MPT was at first hesitant about the idea because it feared it might lose control over NTT. However, MPT finally accepted the idea and then pushed for privatization on the belief that the ministry could thereby exert an overall influence on the telecommunications industry. NTTPC management was also in favor of privatization because it would obtain more freedom and flexibility in dealing with the new types of telecom business now made possible by digitization. Privatization would also benefit NTTPC's labor union in the sense that wage levels would be decided on separately from other public corporations (i.e., railroads and tobacco). The telecommunications industry was a growing business compared to these other public corporations; thus the labor union anticipated that wages would increase more rapidly through privatization. Telecom equipment manufacturers were also in favor of privatization because they could expect new NTT orders. Their rationale was that NTT would have more freedom in business management, which meant moving toward digitization of the telecom network. For smaller-scale manufacturers, however, there were mixed blessings because while they could expect increased demand, they would also have to face more severe competition after privatization. Generally, however, Japanese industries expected positive effects from privatization. Liberalized use of the NTT network would increase flexibility to the benefit of business operations, and decreases in telecom user charges could also be expected. Certain industries might also realize major business opportunities arising from a liberalized telecom market.

Although there were interest groups that opposed NTTPC's privatization, they were minor forces compared with the seven groups mentioned above. The global trend toward small government at that time (the 1980s), pushed by such political leaders as Ronald Reagan and Margaret Thatcher, also helped to escalate the privatization initiative.

By contrast, it took almost 15 years to achieve NTT's breakup because of the powerful forces that opposed it. MoF had supported the privatization of NTT but opposed its breakup. After all, the ministry's interest as a major shareholder in NTT would be jeopardized: A breakup would decrease the value of NTT's shares and thus decrease revenues to MoF from the sale of those shares. MITI, another powerful ministry, also opposed the divestiture. A major turf battle between MPT (in charge of the telecommunications industry) and MITI (in charge of the computer industry) was building up as the two industries began to merge in the wake of increasing digitization. MITI was afraid that if MPT increased its policy-making power, MITI's power to implement industrial policies for the construction of a high-tech-based information society might be reduced.

Of the government agencies, the only one that supported NTT's breakup was MPT. The intention of MPT throughout the telecom debates was to increase the policy-making power of the ministry. MPT supported privatization in the expectation that it would enhance its power to implement policies that would apply not only to NTT, but to the overall telecom market. Breakup was also expected to increase the political power of MPT by reducing the influence of NTT, which traditionally had its own strong political allies (Fransman, 1995: 380).

Both management and the labor union of NTT were opposed to divestiture. Management was opposed because a breakup would surely increase the competitive threat from other companies, and integrated operations in both telecom service and R&D might be hurt. Telecom services, whether long-distance or local, depended on similar technologies and competencies, and it did not make sense to break up these operations and reduce the integrated character of the telecom network (Fransman, 1995: 380). NTT's union was concerned that a breakup would lead to reductions in employment. After all, the company's largest cost factor was labor, and reducing this expenditure would be one of the most important elements in increasing NTT's efficiency. The union was also concerned that a breakup would weaken its position through a fragmentation of its membership, with increased inequality in wages and employment conditions depending on the nature of the divested companies (Fransman, 1995: 381).

Thus although Rincho, MPT, and the Telecommunications Council argued for the breakup, the two most powerful ministries and NTT itself (both management and labor) opposed it. It was this conflict that resulted in a five-year postponement of Rincho's 1984 recommendation to break up NTT, followed by another five-year postponement of the 1990 recommendation by the Telecommunications Council that long-distance and local operations be separated and privatized. The Telecommunications Council's recommendation in 1996 that NTT be separated into one long-distance and two local companies was also opposed, but a compromise was finally reached at the end of 1996, and a holding company system was chosen.

This type of gray-area compromise decision represents a clear contrast with comparable cases in the United States. As explained in section 3, deregulation and liberalization of the telecom market advanced swiftly in the U.S. through court decisions that were based on the principles of fair competition and anti-monopolistic behavior. As such, there was little room for various political factors to influence the decision. As a result, clear-cut, black-and-white decisions were made in the U.S.

In Japan, however, various interests come into play. To begin with, the main decision-making body, the Telecommunications Council, is under the influence of MPT, since members of the council are chosen by the ministry. However, since the council members consist of representatives from a variety of sectors, including academics, business people, journalists, and consumer groups, MPT does not have total control over the council's recommendations. In fact, there is room for interest groups to wield a certain amount of influence through council members and MPT officials.

As the preceding discussion shows, decisions and recommendations made by the Telecommunications Council are by no means final. Based on the council's recommendations, the ruling political party discusses them and to a certain extent can change them.[6] During this process, there is room for influence on final decisions by political alliances and interest groups. As a result, decisions under this system tend to be based on compromises among influential interest groups, and radical institutional change is difficult to achieve unless there is strong political leadership that outweighs the interest groups' influence.

In short, the reason it took so long to break up NTT (even a breakup that itself was not a clear-cut solution) can be found in the decision-making mechanism of Japanese telecommunications policy. Decision making through compromise slows down institutional changes that are needed in order to respond to environmental changes.

6.2 Linkages Between Institutions and Innovation

Let us now turn to the linkage between institutional arrangements and innovations. During the closed era of the 1950s and 1960s, Japan did not need major innovations to achieve its goal of installing a modern, nationwide telecom network and related industry. Japan imported the necessary technologies from foreign countries and improved on these technologies to serve domestic purposes. Through this process, Japan increased its indigenous technological capabilities, and a number of notable innovations resulted. A good example of this in the optic communications field was optic fiber, where the innovation evolved out of the needs of the Japanese domestic telecom market to increase transmission capabilities.

The transition to a globally open, digitized telecom system in the 1970s and 1980s caused problems. As was explained above, Japan was slow to adjust to the new environment and necessary changes were essentially compromised by partial solutions. The first problem was the digitization trend. NTTPC, which had dominated the telecom market, began to enter the data communications and computer fields. However, these were areas where the NTTPC family manufacturers, such as NEC and Fujitsu, competed vigorously in the domestic market. Therefore these NTTPC family companies were obliged to cooperate with NTTPC in terms of the NTTPC market while they still had to compete with NTTPC in the private market. Since efforts by these manufacturers to develop NTTPC computers would only create more competition in the private market, they lost their incentive to work closely with NTTPC in such areas as data communications and computers; in short, the old NTTPC family system was malfunctioning, and this hurt the competitiveness of NTTPC.

The second problem arose from globalization. The postwar legal framework confined NTTPC's business to domestic telecom operations while Kokusai Denshin Denwa (KDD) was given charge of international operations. This division of services between the domestic and foreign markets was a source of trouble. NTTPC was responsible only for the domestic market and therefore installed a telecom network that took only the domestic market into account. The standardization of telecom services was also suited only to the needs of the domestic market. Because NTTPC could not sell its products and systems on the foreign market, its attitude of focusing heavily on the domestic market was understandable. However, this was a great source of trouble for the NTTPC family companies who, while depending on NTTPC for their telecom equipment sales, were trying to gain international competitiveness by selling their products on foreign markets.

The typical strategy of integrated electronics companies in Japan was to first reduce costs as much as possible while accumulating experience by selling their products on the domestic market, and then to penetrate the foreign market using the advantages thus created. This is precisely the way Japanese manufacturers of such consumer products as television sets and videocassette recorders, as well as producers of semiconductors, gained international competitiveness. However, this strategy did not work in the case of telecommunications because domestically developed equipment, with its different standards, systems, and software, could not be sold on the foreign market. Consequently, these companies sometimes had to develop two different sets of equipment, one for the domestic market and the other for the foreign market. This redundancy in development unquestionably hurt their international competitiveness, as the example of the central switching business discussed in section 3 shows. The institutionalized division of foreign and domestic telecom markets was unfortunately perpetuated until the late 1990s, long after the privatization of NTTPC.

Government requirements regarding NTTPC's R&D also impeded the progress of these companies. The NTT Corporation Act of 1984 required that the newly privatized NTT diffuse the results of its R&D to the public. So while NTT became a private company, it retained a public responsibility vis-à-vis R&D. The ambiguity of NTT's R&D functions must have hurt the company's R&D efficiency, since it could not concentrate on R&D for only NTT's benefit.

The period of the 1970s and 1980s was a golden era for Japanese technology. Automobiles, semiconductors, machine tools and a variety of other consumer and commercial products gained international competitiveness in markets throughout the world. The one exception was the telecommunications equipment industry. Although it was typical of the kind of high-tech industries that launched Japan into worldwide competitiveness, its potential to obtain shares of the world market (especially the more competitive U.S. market) could not be utilized. The analysis here suggests that the institutional framework introduced to establish Japan's domestic telecom market after the war remained in place long after the era of digitization and globalization began, and that institutional adjustment delays in this industry had a major negative impact on its R&D functions.

6.3 The i-Mode from the Institutional Perspective

It is interesting to note that the most successful innovation of the 1990s did not come from NTT or from old members of the NTT family of manufacturers; it came from a company that was able to distance itself from the old institutional framework. NTT DoCoMo, a company that was legally forced to separate from NTT, was consequently free to operate outside the old institutional framework.

As explained in an earlier section, the business model created by NTT DoCoMo fit well with emerging models of innovation. DoCoMo was faced with direct competition by virtue of its separation from NTT, but the resulting stimulus was a key element in the development of the i-mode. Critical to this development was an open system that allowed for the recruiting of outside personnel and the use of operating software. Furthermore, the i-mode's success was closely associated with the concept of *ba*.

Not only was DoCoMo free from the constraints of old institutions, it was also able to choose its manufacturers. These included the old, experienced NTT family members as well as new entrants to this business, such as Sony and Sharp. Although DoCoMo had to pay certain basic R&D fees to the NTT holding company, it did not have an obligation to disclose the results of its own R&D to the public.

One challenge that DoCoMo has not yet overcome is the institutional legacy created by the domestic-international division of telecom services, which continues to impede penetration into foreign markets. Despite the i-mode's phenomenal success in Japan, its success in foreign markets has been limited. DoCoMo succeeded in standardizing its operating system for third-generation mobile telephones in Asia and Europe and invested in European and Asian telecom companies in order to diffuse the i-mode there. However, these investments produced huge investment losses rather than benefits. The accumulated valuation loss from overseas investments in the first half of fiscal year 2002 reached $125 billion, or 80% of the value invested. This huge loss can be partially attributed to the bursting of the IT bubble; however, it cannot be denied that DoCoMo's inexperience in the foreign market, exacerbated by the old institutional legacy (the foreign-domestic division of markets), is also a factor.

On the other hand, DoCoMo's business in the Asian market is developing positive signs. It was pointed out that a distinct characteristic of the *keitai* in Japan is that its diffusion rate is quite high among teenagers as compared with Western countries. These youths generally use the *keitai* for non-purposive reasons: merely to greet their friends, for example (Hakuhodo Seikatsu Sogo Kenkyusho, 2001: 44–46). It is also considered fashionable to use the *keitai* on city streets, and as such it has become an important part of Japanese youth culture.

This kind of youth culture is equally accepted in such Asian countries as Singapore, Taiwan, and China, where teenagers tend to emulate Japanese *keitai* culture.[7] If DoCoMo can exploit this cultural aspect of the Japanese *keitai*, it will surely help DoCoMo, as well as the Japanese *keitai* manufacturers, to develop their Asian markets.

It has been a great challenge for DoCoMo to break through the barriers created by the old institutions. The most difficult one for DoCoMo seems to be the barrier of foreign business development. The question now is whether the legacy of the old institutions will continue to impede development overseas or whether DoCoMo will be able to utilize the youth culture, among other technological advantages, and succeed in penetrating the foreign market. These elements appear to be critical in any assessment of the current competitiveness of Japan's *keitai* -related industries as well as of their future prospects from the institutional standpoint.

Notes

1 Those smaller companies that supply cables and telecom parts and do construction work for NTT are often called "B-makers." For details, see Inoue (2000: 283–331).

2 See Suzuki (1999: 1098–1103).

3 For details, see Oboshi (2000: 86–128).

4 It was also unfortunate that TRON was designated an unfair trade barrier by the U.S. Trade Representative for reasons that were not made clear. TRON lost momentum in its diffusion because of this political incident. For details, see Sakamura (2001: 88).

5 For example, see Nonaka and Takeuchi (1995).

6 However, politicians cannot totally change or ignore recommendations by the Telecommunications Council. If it becomes difficult to achieve a compromise, the deadline for a conclusion is frequently extended.

7 For example, see Nikkei Bijinesu, 15 January 2001.

Bibliography

Beikoku Shomusho (U.S. Department of Commerce) (1999) *Dijitaru Ekonomi* (The Emerging Digital Economy), translated by Yasuhiro Murota. Toyo Keizai Shinposha, Tokyo.

Brock, G. (1981) The Telecommunications Industry: The Dynamics of Market Structure. Harvard University Press, Cambridge, MA.

Business Week (2000) "Amazing DoCoMo." 17 January, p. 19.

Denki Tsushin Nenkan (1982) Annual Report of Telecommunications. Sancho, Tokyo.

Fransman, M. (1995) Japan's Computer and Communication Industry: The Evolution of Industrial Giants and Global Competitiveness. Oxford University Press, Oxford, UK.

Fuke, H. (2000) *Joho Tsushin Sangyo no Kozo to Kisei Kanwa: Nichi-Bei-Ei Hikaku Kenkyu* (The Structure of the Information and Communication Industry and Deregulation: A Comparative Study of Japan, the United States and the United Kingdom). NTT Shuppan, Tokyo.

Hakuhodo Seikatsu Sogo Kenkyusho (Hakuhodo Institute of Life and Living) (2001) *Keitai Seikatsu Hakusho* (White Paper on Mobile Phone Life). NTT Shuppan, Tokyo.

Hiramatsu, H. (1980) *Denwa no Muko wa Konna Kao* (The Face on the Other End of the Telephone). Saimaru Shuppankai, Tokyo.

Inoue, T. (2000) *Denden Mineika Katei no Kenkyu* (Study of the Privatizing Process of Nippon Telegraph and Telephone Public Corporation). Eruko, Tokyo.

Itami, H.; Nishiguchi, T.; and Nonaka, I. (2000) *Ba no Dainamizumu to Kigyo* (Businesses and the Dynamism of *Ba*). Toyo Keizai Shinposha, Tokyo.

Joho Shori Gakkai Rekishi Tokubetsu Iinkai (Special Committee on History, Information Processing Society of Japan) (1998) *Nihon no Konpyuta Hattatsushi* (The History of Computer Development in Japan). Omusha, Tokyo.

Kashiwabara, H. (1987) *Denden wa Koshite Kabushikikaisha ni Natta* (The Way Nippon Telegraph and Telephone Public Corporation Became a Private Company). Tokuma Shoten, Tokyo.

Katsumi, A. (2001) *Hikari no Mirai ni Kaketa Kenkyusha Supiritto* (Researchers' Spirit for Future Optics). Daiyamondosha, Tokyo.

Matsunaga, M. (2000) *Ai-Modo Jiken* (The Case of i-Mode). Kadokawa Shoten, Tokyo.

Murayama, Y. (2000) *Tekuno-Shisutemu Tenkan no Senryaku: San-Kan-Gaku Renkei e no Michisuji* (Strategy of Techno-System Transformation: The Alliance of Industry, Government and Universities). NHK Shuppan, Tokyo.

——— (2001) "Creolization in business management: The internet and responses of Japanese companies." In: Matsuda, T. (Ed.) The Age of Creolization in the Pacific: In Search of Emerging Cultures and Shared Values in the Japan-America Borderlands. Keisuisha, Hiroshima, pp. 347–375.

Nelson, R. (1994) "The coevolution of technologies and institutions: Recent research bearing on the coevolution of technology and institutions." In: England, R.W. (Ed.) Evolutionary Concepts in Contemporary Economics. The University of Michigan Press, Ann Arbor, pp. 139–156.

Nihon Keizai Shinbun (Nihon Economic Newspaper) (1996) "*Denno shakai ikinuku tenbo o* (Vision needed for survival in a computer-driven society)." 17 January, morning, p. 25.

——— (2002) "*Fukkatsu TRON Uindozu o utsu* (Revived TRON shoots Windows)." 3 January, morning, p. 1.

Nikkei Bijinesu (Nikkei Business) (2001) "*Daitoa atsuzoko kyoeiken* (Common culture and prosperity in East Asia)." 15 January, pp. 27–41.

Nippon Denshin Denwa Kosha 25–Nenshi Henshu Iinkai (Editorial Committee of the 25-Year History of Nippon Telegraph and Telephone Public Corporation) (1977) *Nippon Denshin Denwa Kosha 25-Nenshi Jokan* (The 25-Year History of Nippon Telegraph and Telephone Public Corporation, Vol. I). Denki Tsushin Kyokai, Tokyo.

Nonaka, J. (1996) *NTT Gurupu* (NTT Group). Nihon Jitsugyo Shuppansha, Tokyo.

Nonaka, I. and Takeuchi, H. (1995) The Knowledge-Creating Company: How Japanese Companies Create the Dynamics of Innovation. Oxford University Press, New York.

NTT (2001) "*NTT ni okeru R&D no kangaekata to kiso kenkyu ni tsuite* (NTT's point of view on R&D and basic research)," Paper for the Ministry of Public Management, Home Affairs, Posts and Telecommunications, Telecommunications Council. (http://www.soumu.go.jp/joho_tsushin/policyreports/joho-tsushin/it/pdf/010417_1_2.pdf). 17 April.

NTT DoCoMo 10-Nenshi Hensan Jimukyoku (Editorial Office of the 10-Year History of NTT DoCoMo) (2002) *NTT DoCoMo 10-Nenshi: Mobairu Furontia e no Chosen* (The 10-Year History of NTT DoCoMo: Challenging the Mobile Frontier). NTT DoCoMo, Tokyo.

Oboshi, K. (2000) *DoCoMo Kyuseicho no Keiei* (DoCoMo's Rapid Growth and Management). Daiyamondosha, Tokyo.

Oki Denki (Oki Electric Industry) (2000) "*Denki tsuhin shingikai/denki tsushin gijutsu shingikai godo hiaringu setsumei shiryo* (Paper for joint hearing by the Telecommunications Council and Telecommunications Technology Council)." (http://www.soumu.go.jp/jpho_tsusin/policyreports/japanese/telecouncil/it/PDF/001023d21107.pdf). 19 October.

Sakamura, K. (2001) *Joho Bunmei no Nihon Moderu: TRON ga Hiraku Jisedai IT Senryaku* (The Japanese Model of Information Civilization: IT Strategy for the Next Generation Developed by TRON). PHP Shinsho, Tokyo.

Soumusho, Joho Tsushin Shingikai (Ministry of Public Management, Home Affairs, Posts and Telecommunications, Telecommunications Council) (2002) *IT Kakumei o Suishinsuru tame no Denki Tsushin Jigyo ni okeru Kyoso Seisaku no Arikata ni tsuite no Dai 2-Ji Toshin* (The Second Report on Competition Policy to Promote an IT Revolution in the Telecommunications Business). 13 February. Soumusho Joho Tsushin Shingikai, Tokyo.

Suzuki, S. (1999) "*NTT ni okeru rekishi ni nokosubeki gijutsu* (Technologies that should be bequeathed to history by NTT)." Denki Joho Tsushin Gakkaishi (Journal of the Institute of Electronics, Information and Communication Engineers) 82(11): 1098–1103.

Tsushin Kikai Kogyokai (Communications and Information Network Association of Japan) (1968) *Tsushin Kogyo 20-Nen no Ayumi* (The 20-Year History of the Telecommunications Industry). Tsushin Kikai Kogyokai, Tokyo.

Yuseisho Denki Tsushin Shingikai (Ministry of Posts and Telecommunications, Telecommunications Council) (1990) "*Nippon Denshin Denwa Kabushiki Kaisha-Ho Fusoku Dai 2-Jo ni motozuki kozuru beki sochi, hosaku nado no arikata* (Measures that should be taken based on Supplementary Provision II of the Nippon Telegraph and Telephone Corporation Law)." 2 March. Yuseisho Denki Tsushin Shingikai, Tokyo.

——— (1998) "*Nippon Denshin Denwa Kabushiki Kaisha no arikata ni tsuite* (How Nippon Telegraph and Telephone Corporation should be)." 29 February. Yuseisho Denki Tsushin Shingikai, Tokyo.

——— (2000) "*Denki tsushin jigyo ni okeru kenkyu kaihatsu taisei no arikata ni kansuru genjo to kadai* (Status and problems of research and development systems in the telecommunications business)." 19 September. Yuseisho Denki Tsushin Shingikai, Tokyo.

Chapter 6

Transition in Japan's Biotechnology Sector: Institutional–Organizational Co-Evolution

Kazuhiro Asakawa
Keio University

1 Introduction

Research and technological standards vary from nation to nation. The creating, diffusing, and leveraging of intellectual capital is closely linked to a nation's innovation system and the capabilities of organizations (such as universities, governments, research institutes, and ventures) within the system (Freeman, 1987; Hollingsworth, 1996; Lundvall, 1992; Nelson, 1993; Casper et al., 1999). Because each system is deeply rooted in its own historical and social patterns (Freeman, 1987; Lundvall, 1992), changing one is obviously not easy. However, a radical technological breakthrough may trigger change in the whole innovation system.

Japan's biotechnology sector represents such a case. A major technological revolution in genome research has made the traditional system of innovation in chemistry-based pharmaceutical research obsolete, but the resilience of the old innovation system appears to impose constraints on potentially innovative actions to be taken by players within the system.

Some of the technological differences between traditional pharmaceutical drug development and genome-based drug development are as follows (Nakazawa, 2000):

- Traditional pharmaceutical drug development is largely based on experience and serendipity, but genome drug development is a much more rational process based on human genome information.
- The intent of traditional pharmaceutical drug development is to target all sick people regardless of their physical differences. Effectiveness and safety can therefore vary among individuals. Genome drugs, on the other hand, are tailor-made to match each patient's genome information.

- In pharmaceutical drug development, there have been about 400 target discoveries, and further discovery of new lead chemical compounds is difficult. In genome drug development, there are around 3,000 to 10,000 target discoveries, and many new discoveries, including orphan receptors, have become possible.
- In the pharmaceutical field, the development of antibiotics is basically incremental, i.e., a process of building on existing technological bases. In the genome field, antibiotic research is basically a process of radical innovation (i.e., competence-destroying) based on newly emerging genome research.
- Although traditional pharmaceutical research has been directed toward enzymes and receptors, genome research is directed toward identifying messenger ribonucleic acid (mRNA) and deoxyribonucleic acid (DNA).
- Although drug research in the traditional pharmaceutical field is rather closed, genome research is much more open and has much greater potential for further scientific advancement.
- There is no need to process huge amounts of data to conduct pharmaceutical drug development. By contrast, genome drug development requires bioinformatics to process huge amounts of data from the medical, particle biology, genomic, and structural biology fields. Such high-tech tools as microarray technology (the DNA chip and complementary DNA chip), combinatorial chemistry, and high-throughput screening—including structure-based drug design (SBDD) and computer-aided drug design CADD—continue to serve as powerful engines for genome drug development.

We consider today's situation a transitional phase, because a radical shift from the development of traditional pharmaceutical drugs to new genome-based drug development has not yet taken place. Here the coexistence of two different logics is inevitable.[1]

As of today, Japan is still behind in such areas as conserving genome resources and related basic research, maintaining an intellectual base for accumulating and sharing data, financing R&D-intensive firms, and collaborating among industry, academia and government (Government of Japan, 1999).

More specifically, Japan's weaknesses in these areas arise from the following factors:

- Substantial numbers of basic patents have been filed by Western universities and firms, while Japan lacks notable patents even in the more applied technological domain. Moreover, Japan's shortage of patent attorneys who specialize in biotechnology is a serious problem.
- The number of university students majoring in biology has been quite low compared with Western universities, resulting in a low number of researchers in the field of life science.[2]
- The difference in the amount of R&D funding is huge (Japan Biotech In-

dustry Conference Committee, 1999). The total amount of investment by the Japanese government in the life science field in 1998 was merely a quarter of that by the U.S. government.

- One obstacle to the creation of venture firms in Japan was that the concept of risk money was not sufficiently understood until recently, and assistance from financial "angels" involving such risk money has only recently emerged. Banks are reluctant to lend money to start-up venture firms with weak capital assets.
- In human resources, the low mobility of personnel between companies is a significant bottleneck for start-up biotech firms. The lack of employee stock options in Japan is another major handicap for Japan's venture companies because they cannot attract capable scientists from large, well-established institutions that can assure stable job positions and reasonable levels of compensation.

As indicated above, Japan's institutional environment did not provide the biotechnology sector with favorable initial conditions, and changes are now taking place at multiple levels. Although some changes are driven by the government's public policies, others are initiated by individual firms. How are changes at these different levels interrelated? In other words, how do changes at the macro-institutional and micro-organizational levels evolve? This paper focuses on the co-evolution of macro-institutional changes and micro-organizational changes.

In accord with Nelson's (1993) assumption "that since we do not presently have an adequate theory on how institutions, firms, and technologies co-evolve, we are not yet at a stage whereby we can test a set of formal hypotheses which flow from some well-defined model" (Hollingsworth, draft, p. 2), we have made an inductive study of the co-evolution process of Japan's biotechnology industry and have drawn several insights concerning the logic of macro- and micro-driven processes.

Instead of conducting extensive surveys or field interviews, we have analyzed relevant data that are publicly available regarding macro-institutional changes. Public documents were examined extensively to capture other dimensions of change, such as those at educational institutions, at financial institutions, and in inter-organizational collaboration. Recent trends in company-level strategies were also identified by studying original and published data, including our own. Additional interviews were conducted whenever necessary to clarify and expand upon particular points of interest.

Inasmuch as our primary intention was to analyze the way macro- and micro-level changes influence each other, this was a preliminary attempt to reflect on what can be concluded from the data we have. Further efforts are necessary to enrich our data by conducting more interviews and surveys on a systematic basis.

2 Theoretical Background of Institutional Change: A Shift from Static Macro-Micro Determinism to Dynamic Co-Evolution

Institutional theory has traditionally provided more insights into institutional stability than change (Seo and Creed, 2002; Barley and Tolbert, 1997; Oliver, 1991; Scott, 1991). What is less well explored in this field is the issue of "deinstitutionalization," or "the process by which institutions weaken or disappear" (Scott, 2001). Only recently has institutional theory begun to incorporate the change dimension much more explicitly, as represented by research on deinstitutionalization (Dacin et al., 2002).

Prior investigations into institutional change have been conducted either from a macro or a micro viewpoint. The former tends to be at the national institutional level, and the latter at the individual firm level.

The macro view argues that institutional changes affect micro business systems. Whitley (1992), while shedding light on business system levels, made it explicitly clear that "the relationship between the institutional setup and the business system is unidirectional." Lundvall (1998) reiterates by describing "the direction of causal relationships as going from culture and institutions to the business system."

Although the role of rational actors (or agents) guided by their self-interest is partially incorporated into this theory, there is a dilemma in the sense that the actors and their interests are themselves institutionally constructed (DiMaggio and Powell, 1991). The direct incorporation of a strategic choice perspective (Child, 1972) into institutional theory contradicts the premise of the theory (Goodrick and Salancik, 1996). Holm (1995) asked this: "How can actors change institutions if their actions, intentions, and rationality are all conditioned by the very institution they wish to change?" (p. 398, cited in Seo and Creed, 2002: 223).

On the other hand, the micro view argues that individual and organizational actions influence macro-institutional changes. The importance of the role played by micro-level rational actors guided by their self-interest in changing macro-institutional systems is discussed by DiMaggio (1988). He introduces the concept of institutional entrepreneurship, "whereby agents deploy the resources at their disposal to create and empower institutions" (Dacin et al., 2002). Garud et al. (2002) studied the role of Sun Microsystems, which acted as the primary sponsor of Java technology for the Internet. The company destroyed existing taken-for-granted standards and constructed new rules governing competition in the software industry. The authors explored the complex mixture of cooperative and competitive practices employed to craft common standards to govern a technology (Dacin et al., 2002).

Even though it was a major improvement for institutional theory to shed light on changes in institutional systems, a change in theorizing exclusively at either the national/institutional level or the firm level is not sufficient. More recently, an integrated view of institutional change is emerging. For example, Murmann's (1998, 2003) research illustrates the dynamics of co-evolution between institutional change and individual firm performance. While institutional endowments provide the initial conditions under which a particular type of technological activity takes place, successful firms surrounded by a dynamic global environment may engage in collective action to modify their institutional conditions to enhance their innovativeness.[3] Such a view is consistent with the following point made by Seo and Creed (2002): "Contradiction between isomorphism at the macro-institutional level and divergent interests at the micro-organizational level is a source of institutional change."

As represented by Murmann (1998, 2003), macro and micro changes are dynamically interrelated. Seo and Creed (2002: 233) argue that "the presence and degree of misaligned interests increase the likelihood and the scope of praxis for institutional change by generating potential change agents." They further argue that such institutional contradictions as inefficiency, nonadaptability, interinstitutional incompatibilities, and misaligned interests generate institutional crisis, which, in turn, generates reflective shifts in consciousness, actor mobilization, and collective action. The whole process will then lead to institutional change (Seo and Creed, 2002).

In the following sections, we first look at a concrete case of institutional change in Japan's biotechnology sector at both the macro and micro levels. Our focus then shifts to the way macro- and micro-level changes influence each other in a dynamic manner.

3 Institutional Changes in Japan's Biotechnology Sector

As discussed in the previous section, Japan's institutional environment did not provide its biotechnology sector with favorable initial conditions. What are the reasons behind Japan's weakness in this area?

First, the Japanese government did not put priority on strengthening the R&D capability and productivity of Japan's pharmaceutical industry. Japan was known much more for industrial policies that targeted a few selected industries, such as the electronics and semiconductor industries (Freeman, 1987). Not until the late 1990s did the pharmaceutical and biotechnology industries become a part of the pattern. The vertical division of labor among government ministries was another barrier to promoting such emerging new industries as biotechnology, which typically cut across different fiefdoms of the ministries.

Second, under the traditional system of innovation within Japan's universities, professors were not particularly interested in filing patents or commercializing their research findings. They tended to look down on the more applied ends of research, preferring to stick to pure science in the interest of protecting their prestige as academics. The evaluation of performance in Japanese academia is largely based on scientific publication, and the filing of patents has not been considered an index of academic achievement. Since filing patents would require academics to delay the timing of conference presentations and journal submissions, they are often discouraged from considering it.

Furthermore, as government employees, national university professors were forbidden to serve as officers or external board members of private companies, a situation that prevented the smooth transfer of technology from universities to industry. Nor until recently was there any official institutional arrangement to facilitate such a transfer.

Third, investment in venture firms was a concept that did not exist under the old innovation system.[4] Japan's culture of "high uncertainty avoidance" (Hofstede, 1980) discouraged investors from taking high risks, thus impeding the emergence of venture capitalists. Financial institutions, such as banks and securities houses, were not enthusiastic about collecting data on highly uncertain research domains, and potential investors therefore had little information to act on.

Fourth, there has been a huge gap in the amount of investment between Western firms and their Japanese counterparts. Accordingly, the technological level and research capacity of Japan's biotechnology industry has lagged far behind that of the West. Human genes are limited in number (80,000–100,000), and they have already been patented by foreign firms. As a result, Japan's biotechnology industry has incurred huge drug development expenses arising from the application of genome knowledge patented by foreign firms. Moreover, Japan's conservative and protective agricultural policies have delayed the development of DNA agriproducts, resulting in an increased reliance on imports. Also, a heavy reliance on existing technology has done much to deter radical innovation in DNA technology.

Fifth, Japan's pharmaceutical firms often looked for products that were very close to market, but their interest would often evaporate if the product required significant development or was too innovative (Hammond, 2000). Hammond also noted a significant lack of interest on the part of Japanese university researchers in collaborating with Japanese companies. Under the old system, pharmaceutical firms had a preference for in-house R&D, and university-industry relationships were not particularly strong, at least on a formal basis. University faculty or staff had the right to apply for patents on their inventions, but they usually passed these rights informally on to companies that contributed to their research budgets or employed their students (Kneller, 2000).

Sixth, Japan's universities, research institutes, financial institutions, and pharmaceutical firms have long been embedded in the traditional socio-cultural norms of the country. Until the recent surge in biotechnology research, there were no institutional contradictions (Seo and Creed, 2002) to resolve and therefore no need to change the system.

Recently, various efforts have been made to overcome such problems. First, the nature of government involvement in fostering biotechnology has changed.

Inter-ministry collaboration was initiated in 1999 among one agency and four ministries (the Science and Technology Agency, the Ministry of Education, the Ministry of Health and Welfare, the Ministry of Agriculture, Forestry and Fisheries, and the Ministry of International Trade and Industry)[5] (Government of Japan, 1999), and legal measures facilitating technological transfer between universities and industry—such as the Technology Licensing Organization (TLO) Law in August 1998 and the Japanese equivalent of the Bayh-Dole Act[6] in 1999 —have been put into place.[7]

Second, Japan's educational institutions have shown some improvement. A new trend is becoming evident in these institutions: Clearer incentives are being given to university scientists to file patents and to commercialize their research findings. In the wake of the TLO legislation of 1998, followed by the Japanese version of the Bayh-Dole Act in 1999, interaction between university scientists and industry has been more intensive.

Third, Japan's financial institutions have undergone some changes. Recent trends include the introduction of stock options after the establishment of venture firms and the founding of the NASDAQ Japan[8] (in 2000) and Tokyo Stock Exchange MOTHERS[9] (in 1999) markets, institutions that laid the groundwork for capital inflow to selected biotech ventures.

Fourth, Japan's technological environment is gradually changing as well. Because of the strategic focus on life science innovation at the national and the corporate and industrial levels, several emerging fields are attracting attention as potential Japanese strengths. The most outstanding area is bioinformatics, which combines two distinct fields of innovation, biology and information technology.[10]

Fifth, inter-organizational relations show some changing patterns. In 1998, a law was promulgated that authorized the establishment of university-affiliated TLOs that could transfer royalties back to inventors and universities. In the biomedical field, the number of companies with close academic ties has been growing. Although only about 1–4 such firms existed in 1990, as many as 20–40 with close academic ties had emerged by the year 2000 (Kneller, 2000).

Sixth, changes are also appearing at the organizational level. For example, market mechanisms are gradually being introduced in Japanese universities.[11] More and more universities are beginning to consider patent and business applications as a factor in performance evaluation. Moreover, the limitations of conducting in-house research in biotechnology have been recognized. Japan's pharmaceutical firms, having focused on low-particle chemical compound research, failed to accumulate competence in high-particle research. Biotechnology innovation is by nature "competence-destroying" (Tushman and Anderson, 1986), and earlier research in the pharmaceutical domain cannot easily be leveraged. The locus of biotechnology innovation resides within inter-firm networks (Powell et al., 1996; Liebeskind et al., 1996), and this has forced Japanese pharmaceutical firms to enter alliances with small biotech venture firms in the U.S. and Japan.

4 Co-Evolution of the Macro/Micro Innovation System

In this section, two different patterns of evolution are described: institutionally-driven change and organizationally-driven change. We shall try to show that changes at the macro and micro levels do not take place independently, but instead have an interdependent relationship.[12] The remaining part of this chapter is devoted to an examination of this relationship.

4.1 Dynamics of Institutionally-Driven Change

Macro-level change began with the onset of the national government's concern over the weakness of Japan's biotechnology research (Lehrer and Asakawa, 2004 a, 2004b). In contrast with the electronics and automobile industries, which were granted certain competitive advantages (Porter, 1990), the pharmaceutical and biotechnology industries were at the weaker end of the spectrum. Recognizing that life science would become a key source of national innovativeness, the Japanese government began taking actions to ameliorate the situation. Designating biotechnology as a strategic core technology for the 21st century, it implemented a number of concrete measures.

In 2000, the Japanese government launched a national project, the Millennium Project, to raise the standards of key industrial sectors, including life science and biotechnology. In July 2002, the government set up a biotechnology panel to enhance the standards of Japanese biotechnology research and its commercialization. The Biotechnology Strategy Council (Baio Senryaku Kaigi) was headed by Dr. Tadamitsu Kishimoto, president of Osaka University. The council's members included Prime Minister Junichiro Koizumi, ministers in charge of ministries related to the field,[13] and twelve experts from the medical, academic, and business fields. A set of strategic principles drawn up by the panel for the development of biotechnology included an action plan for technical development and a plan for the appropriate use of genetic engineering in food products, to be implemented by 2010. These strategic principles include the following:

- To attain a 25 trillion yen market in biotech-related industries
- To create new demand by over one million people by 2010
- To double the government's R&D budget within five years

Tax breaks for start-up companies and large research projects, either public or private, were also suggested.[14]

These initiatives by the government to bring the Japanese biotechnology sector up to par with Western countries were linked to another, broader initiative: the establishment of a Council for Science and Technology Policy within the Cabinet Office in 2001. The aim of this council is to strengthen competency levels in science and technology, to link academia and industry, and to promote key high-tech industries. Its objectives include producing 30 Japanese Nobel Prize winners within the next 50 years as well as fostering industrial, academic, and governmental linkages. University reform (including private universities which comprise 80% of the universities in Japan) has also been emphasized. The council has called for several summits to facilitate networking among industry, academia, and the government. A significant number of regional summits have also been held to foster mutual networking. It has also requested reform within all three sectors, including overcoming such obstacles as the government's tendency to engender sectionalism among ministries, which impeded the creation of new industries, including biotechnology. These governmental initiatives are consistent with the policies of the Millennium Project launched in 2000.

Macro-level change has been prompted by the government's clear recognition that Japan's current techno-governance system cannot cope with today's radical innovations in the field of biotechnology research. A crisis in national competitiveness arises when a country's existing socio-technical system is unable to cope with competence-destroying innovation. A proper understanding of the deficiencies of the national techno-governance system is the first, and most necessary, condition for successful institutional change.

The points below summarize the ways in which measures at the macro level are generating more micro-level changes.

First, the TLO legislation of 1998, followed by the Japanese Bayh-Dole legislation of 1999, facilitated interaction on an official basis between university scientists and industry. Before this time, the underlying norm was for university professors to grant patent rights to companies in exchange for receiving substantial research budgets and securing future job positions for currently enrolled students. The introduction of new legislation has raised awareness on the part of university professors of the value of filing patents, and working with TLOs should minimize patent-filing workloads for the academics. Thus the market mechanism is gradually being introduced in Japanese universities, more and more of whom are beginning to consider patent and business applications a factor in performance evaluation.

Second, a law for strengthening industrial technological capabilities (Sangyo Gijutsuryoku Kyoka Ho) was passed in 2000, allowing national university professors to be appointed as outside directors by the firms that use their research output. By enabling them to assume such positions at private corporations, the deregulation of national university professors paved the way for closer industry-academic interaction.

Initiatives by the Ministry of Education, Culture, Sports, Science and Technology (MEXT) to foster university-based innovation include support for creating university spinoff ventures, joint R&D between universities and firms through matching funds, and the creation of intellectual clusters for university-industry collaboration. As of August 2002, a total of 424 university spinoff venture firms had been created, a 68.9% increase over the previous year. A typical example is Anges MG, a firm created in 1999 as a result of its spinoff from the University of Osaka.

Third, the creation of the NASDAQ Japan and Tokyo Stock Exchange

MOTHERS markets has laid the groundwork for considerably more capital inflow into the biotechnology sector. Moreover, the availability of venture capital has removed a barrier and increased incentives for start-up ventures.

4.2 Limits of Macro-Driven Change

Macro-driven change does not take root easily because there are forces of resistance to institutional change. Zucker (1991: 105) wrote that "Institutionalized elements become embedded in networks, with change in any one element resisted because of the change it would entail for all the interrelated network elements." Seo and Creed (2002) wrote that although institutionalization is an adaptive process, once in place, institutions are quite likely to be both psychologically and economically locked-in and, in a sense, isolated from or unresponsive to changes in their external environments. Points of institutional inertia in Japan include the following.

First, the TLO, in practice, is not functioning as well as it might (Nakamura, 2002) because there is no obligation for university-based technology to be transferred to companies through this type of organization (i.e., direct contact between the universities and companies is possible). Second, the Japanese equivalent of the 1980 Bayh-Dole Act, though passed in 1999, still needs to be diffused much more widely across the various government ministries. Third, the financing system for fostering biotech ventures is insufficient. Fourth, the incentive system at universities is insufficient, mainly because academic publication in refereed journals remains the top priority for academics. Fifth, the fundamental values of academics remain conservative. In other words, the new system cannot change basic values.

Macro-level change does not automatically lead to micro-level change at the organizational level. Macro-micro "spillover" is effective only when organizations act as agents or rational actors that consider change to be beneficial. For example, TLO legislation becomes effective only when such micro actors as knowledge providers (i.e., university scientists) and technology adopters (i.e., companies) find it beneficial to use TLOs as mechanisms for university-industry technology transfer, because, as mentioned, neither side is legally obliged to go through a TLO. Similarly, the diffusion of the Bayh-Dole Act involves much more than simply passing a law in the National Diet. The variety of responses to identical institutional changes on the part of different biotech venture firms (e.g., the difference between Sosei and Anges MG) personifies this view. This institutional-change dimension has been largely ignored by neo-institutionalists (DiMaggio, 1988), but has received much attention from old institutionalists with a more "micro" focus (Selznick, 1949, 1957). More-recent writers on institutional change have begun to observe this phenomenon more carefully.

The most significant limitation of the macro perspective lies in the lack of an explanation for the differing strategies of various biotech venture companies. Although biotech venture firms are heavily influenced by the turbulence of their surrounding environment, what remain unanswered are the reasons why these firms respond so differently to identical external stimuli. The following section sheds some light on the strategic choices these firms make.

5 Dynamics of Organizationally Driven Change

The macro-institutional changes described above could become a catalyst for change, but more immediate measures will be needed to trigger the process. In the changes that have taken place so far, strategic choices made by certain firms have also played an important role. Instead of waiting for the government to act as the guardian of change in the institutional environment, some firms have taken action on their own to overcome their home-country disadvantage. Here are some examples.

First, some firms (e.g., Eisai, Yamanouchi, and Fujisawa) have opened overseas R&D laboratories and are conducting state-of-the-art research there. It generally takes a long time for such global R&D approaches to mature, and to date the influence on Japan's national innovation system has been minimal.[15] However, such overseas relocation of basic research activities has the potential to stimulate change in the national system of innovation in the following way: Firms become free to bypass Japan's scientific base by tapping into overseas resources. Such bypassing may undermine the research standards of Japanese universities and the competitiveness of the national innovation system.

Second, many pharmaceutical firms have formed R&D alliances with universities, research institutes, and biotech ventures outside of Japan. According to one report, 55% of Japanese firms (compared to 25% of U.S. and European companies) got major benefits from collaboration with higher education institutions, mainly with those in the U.S. and Europe (Murphy, 1999). Transnational linkages in high-tech research would make the national innovation system less significant as long as the firms involved could get strategic benefits from such alliances. In reality, many Japanese pharmaceutical firms invest much larger amounts of money into U.S. (and European) universities and biotech ventures than into their Japanese counterparts. Although such company-level strategies do not directly lead to the transformation of innovation systems at the national-level, the Japanese government recognizes the problem of intellectual hollowing out and has drafted a series of legislative acts to enhance Japan's competitiveness in the biotech/life science sector (as pointed out in an earlier section). The above is a typical scenario of indirect organizationally driven institutional change.[16]

Third, Japanese biotech venture companies are also forming alliances with overseas R&D organizations. The biotech venture firm Sosei, for example, has a unique strategy for leveraging its extensive global R&D network. The firm's president, Shinichi Tamura, oversees this network from London's BioScience Innovation Centre, and such leading scientists as the Nobel Prize laureate Dr. Baruch S. Blumberg, Sir Mark Richmond of Genentech and Roche, and Drs. Jeff Robinson and Brian Morgan of SmithKline Beecham have all served on Sosei's Scientific Advisory Board (SAB). Sosei also has R&D alliances with partners in the U.S., U.K., South Korea, India, and Israel as well as Japan (Asakawa and Osada, 2003). Anges MG, another Japanese biotech venture firm that was originally a spinoff from Osaka University, also collaborates with overseas units in the U.S. and U.K. (Nakamura, 2003). These two companies demonstrate the importance of differing strategies.

Fourth, individuals sometimes play a major role in initiating institutional change. For example, the activities of Dr. Yoshihiro Otaki of Bio Frontier Partners, who has made a lifelong commitment to nurturing biotech ventures in Japan, have attracted tremendous attention.[17] He has participated in many governmental committees on promoting life science businesses, and his influence is considerable. Hence the role of individuals in transforming the national innovation system cannot be underestimated.

In summary, initiatives for change can be undertaken by individual organizations within a system when they clearly recognize the limitations inherent in the existing national techno-governance system. When they notice a huge gap between world and domestic standards, they often resort to cross-border solutions, i.e., co-opting first-class overseas competencies. If there is no benchmark organization within one's own country, one might as well look for it abroad. Several of Japan's pharmaceutical firms (such as Eisai) and a number of biotech venture firms (such as Sosei) have launched R&D collaborations with overseas research organizations in order to tap into state-of-the-art R&D activities. This kind of "prospector strategy" (Miles and Snow, 1978) can take time to gain legitimacy within a country whose antiquated techno-governance regime is tightly embedded. Alternatively, Japanese firms that share a "crisis mentality" have jointly formed an interest group called the Bio Industry Association (Baio Sangyojin Kaigi) to reinforce the nation's biotechnology research standards and to facilitate commercialization.

Institutional theory often assumes that strategic choices at the individual and organizational levels may result in contradictions that put the underlying premise of the theory at risk in the sense that actions and interests are shaped by the institutions they belong to (DiMaggio and Powell, 1991; Friedland and Alford, 1991; Goodrick and Salancik, 1996; Holm, 1995). However, our data show that clear initiatives may be taken by individuals and organizations based on their rational interests and visions. Individuals and organizations are not simply "locked-in" to existing routines (Arthur, 1989), but rather serve as stimuli for change. According to Seo and Creed (2002), the contradiction between isomorphism at the macro-institutional level and divergent interests at the micro-organizational level is itself a source of institutional change.

6 Conclusion

We have explored the ways in which institutional changes are taking place within the national innovation system in Japan in relation to the country's growing biotechnology sector. A careful investigation into the phenomenon has revealed that institutional changes in the biotechnology sector are the result of the co-evolution of macro innovation policy at the national level and micro R&D and venture strategies at the organizational level. Co-evolution consists of change in a variety of ways: recent policies in favor of life science research promulgated by the Japanese government, the fostering of university-industry technology linkages, growing incentives for biotech venture companies in biotechnology research because of the financial deregulation of capital markets, shifting business and R&D strategies in favor of life science research, and cross-border research alliances. Through an analysis of the Japanese biotechnology industry, we have provided a framework for a dynamic approach to the understanding of institutional change at multiple levels.

This study sheds light on institutional change from the following perspectives: (1) it examines elements of institutional change at different levels, ranging from macro-national to micro-organizational levels, and (2) it captures macro- and micro-level factors not independently but interactively. Japan's relative lack of competitiveness in biotechnology research and innovation has prompted calls for change at the national and the organizational levels. Macro-driven institutional changes require the endorsement of organizations and individuals acting as self-interested agents. Micro-driven changes require the endorsement of a national authority (the Japanese government) to gain legitimacy.

Figure 6.1 Macro-Micro Interactions in Institutional Change

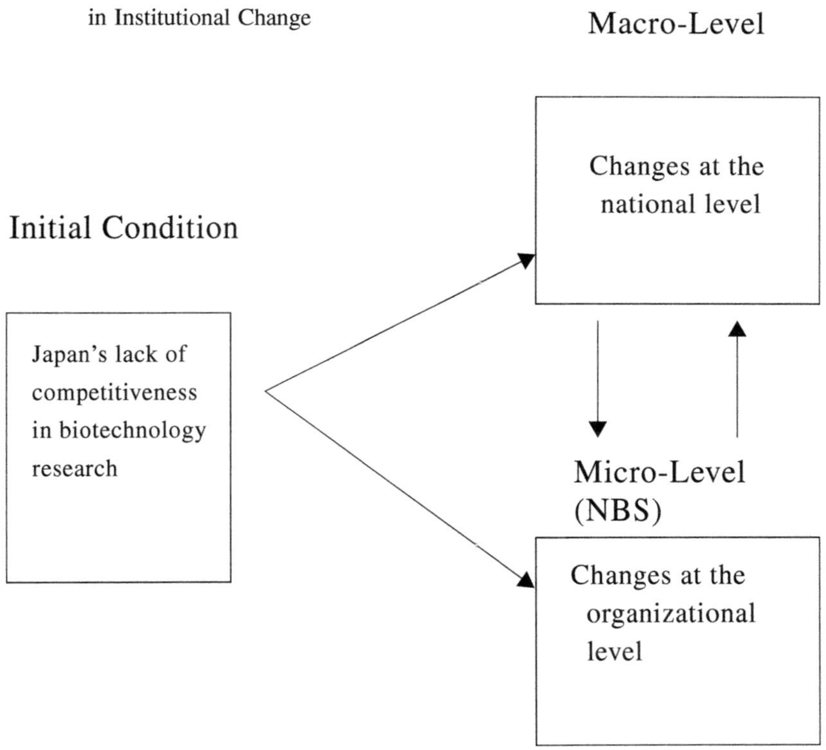

By combining these perspectives, we believe we have provided a framework for understanding multilevel institutional change. It is generally said that institutional theory provides more insights into institutional stability than change (Seo and Creed, 2002; Barley and Tolbert, 1997; Oliver, 1991; Scott, 1991). Less well explored is the issue of deinstitutionalization, "the process by which institutions weaken or disappear" (Scott, 2001). The weakening of one set of beliefs is associated with the arrival of new ones (Scott, 2001).

Recent developments in institutional theory incorporate the change dimension much more explicitly, and such improvements have rendered moot the familiar criticism that the theory is static and exclusively focused on converging patterns. The growing research focus on deinstitutionalization represents such a trend (Dacin et al., 2002). Our study was also intended to capture changes in institutional arrangements along this line.

Unfortunately, in the field of biotechnology in Japan, institutional change has just begun to take place, and sufficient data for a close examination of this change are not yet available. Further study will be called for when a new innovation system is institutionalized in the Japanese biotechnology industry in the near future.

Notes

[1] In pharmaceutical drug development, the forecasting of drug targets is followed by chemical source screening in which low-particle compounds are identified and evaluated by clinical testing. In genome drug development, the forecasting of drug targets is followed by protein engineering, which then progresses to rational drug design and/or protein drug development (Nakazawa, 2000).

[2] For example, there are about 60,000 university graduates per year with biology degrees in the U.S., but only 2,000 per year in Japan. In 1996, there were roughly 6,000 Ph.D.s in biology in the U.S., but only about 200 in Japan (Nakazawa, 2000; Japan Biotech Industry Conference Committee, 1999).

[3] Here we can recall early institutional theory, which highlights the interaction between institutions, the individual self, and character (Cooley, 1956; Dacin et al., 2002).

[4] What we mean by the "old" system is the system of innovation in traditional-chemistry-based pharmaceutical R&D prior to the advent of the era of biotechnical science (Zucker and Darby, 1997). The old system continues to prevail at the initial stage of biotechnological research. The new innovation system pertains to the recent biotechnology era and is not an extension of the old system. What follows is a series of changes taking place at the levels mentioned above.

[5] The agreement was concluded among the four ministers and the director-general of these ministries and agency, respectively. Ministry and agency names are as of 1999.

[6] The Bayh-Dole Act of 1980 is significant because it allowed ownership of federally sponsored inventions to be taken from the public and sold to corporations.

[7] Other legislation includes the following: a law facilitating the creative activities of small- and medium-sized firms (1995); introduction of an "Angel Tax System" (1997) allowing a 20% tax waiver to venture firms; and implementation of the Small Business Innovation Research (SBIR) system (1998) to allocate greater amounts of R&D funding to small- and medium-sized firms and to provide them with special subsidies for promoting

the commercialization of research.

[8] The NASDAQ Japan stock market was renamed Nippon New Market—Hercules as of 16 December 2002 because the NASDAQ Stock Market of the U.S. had pulled out of Japan (Wall Street Journal, 2002).

[9] "MOTHERS" stands for Market of the High-Growth and Emerging Stocks.

[10] Adding to Japan's strength are the following domains: electronics, mechanics, and optoelectronics essential for high-throughput screening tests. Antibiotic substances and the fermenting of alcohol, soy sauce, and miso are also of great potential (Oishi, 2001).

[11] Such a trend can also be regarded as an institutional-level change, since it relates to the educational system as part of an institution.

[12] These two levels are conceptual, and the criteria for dividing issues between these levels remain an empirical question. The national system of innovation also includes inter-organizational networks, and company strategies include external environmental management (alliances vis-à-vis governments, universities, and other institutions). Thus while the distinction may not be altogether clear-cut, we find these to be useful conceptual dimensions.

[13] These include the Ministry of Education, Culture, Sports, Science and Technology (MEXT), the Ministry of Economy, Trade and Industry (METI), and the Ministry of Health, Labor and Welfare (MHLW).

[14] MEXT has also set the following targets (Endo, 2001): (1) 15 times as many patent filings by universities within 10 years; (2) 10 times as many talent-search programs by universities within five years; (3) a 10-fold research budget increase provided by firms to consigned universities within 5 years; and (4) creating more than 10 Japanese "Silicon Valley" locations within 10 years.

[15] Yamanouchi, for example, has decided to close down its basic research lab at Littlemore Hospital near Oxford Science Park after a decade of basic research operations.

[16] Although it is generally not the case that company-level strategies serve as direct change factors in national-level institutions, the former may act as a catalyst for change at the latter level.

[17] Dr. Otaki, besides being a venture capitalist, is an expert on biotechnology and life science. He holds a position as visiting professor at the University of Tsukuba.

Bibliography

Arthur, W.B. (1989) "Competing technologies and lock-in by historical events: The dynamics of allocation under increasing returns." Economic Journal 99: 116–131.

Asakawa, K. and Osada, E. (2003) "Sosei (A)/(B)." Case study. Keio Business School, Japan.

Barley, S.R. and Tolbert. P.S. (1997) "Institutionalization and structuration: Studying the links between action and institution." Organization Studies 18: 93–117.

Casper, S.; Lehrer, M.; and Soskice, D. (1999) "Can high-technology industries prosper in Germany: Institutional frameworks and the evolution of the German software and biotechnology industries." Industry and Innovation 6(1): 5–20.

Child, J. (1972) "Organization structure, environment, and performance: The role of strategic choice." Sociology 6(1): 1–22.

Cooley, C.H. (1956) Social Organization (1902). Free Press, Glencoe, IL.

Dacin, M.T.; Goodstein, J.; and Scott, W.R. (2002) "Institutional theory and institutional change: Introduction to the special research forum." Academy of Management Journal 45(1): 45–57.

DiMaggio, P. (1988) "Interest and agency in institutional theory." In: Zucker, L. (Ed.) Institutional Patterns and Organizations: Culture and Environment. Ballinger, Cambridge, MA, pp. 3–21.

DiMaggio, P. and Powell, W.W. (1991) "Introduction." In: Powell, W.W. and DiMaggio, P. (Eds.) The New Institutionalism in Organizational Analysis. University of Chicago Press, Chicago, pp. 1–38.

Endo, H. (2001) "*San-kan-gaku renkei no saranaru kasoku ni mukete* (Toward the promotion of industry-government-academia collaboration)." Unpublished report at Daiikkai San-gaku Renkei Samitto (First Summit on Industry-Academia Collaboration) (http://www.meti.go.jp/kohosys/press/0001939/0/011005sangakukan.pdf).

Freeman, C. (1987) Technology Policy and Economic Performance: Lessons from Japan. Pinter Publishers, London.

Friedland, R. and Alford, R.R. (1991). "Bridging society back in: Symbols, practices, and institutional contradictions." In: Powell, W.W. and DiMaggio, P. (Eds.) The New Institutionalism in Organizational Analysis. University of Chicago Press, Chicago, pp. 232–263.

Garud, R.; Jain, S.; and Kumaraswamy, A. (2002) "Institutional entrepreneurship in the sponsorship of common technological standards: The case of Sun Microsystems and Java." Academy of Management Journal 45(1): 196–214.

Goodrick, E. and Salancik, G.R. (1996) "Organizational discretion in responding to institutional practices: Hospitals and cesarean births." Administrative Science Quarterly 41: 1–28.

Government of Japan (1999) "*Baiotekunoroji sangyo no sozo ni muketa hoshin* (Basic policy toward creation of biotechnology industry)." Interministerial Agreement, 29 January.

Hammond, S.M. (2000) "Collaboration between the Japanese pharmaceutical industry and European academic researchers." GOR Report 2(2, Summer): 38–45.

Hofstede, G. (1980) Culture's Consequences: International Differences in Work-Related Values. Sage Publications, Beverly Hills, CA.

Hollingsworth, J.R. (1996) "Idea-innovation networks: Integrating institutional and organizational levels of analysis." Mimeo. University of Wisconsin, Madison.

——— (Draft) "Doing institutional analysis: Implications for the study of innovations." Mimeo. University of Wisconsin, Madison.

Holm, P. (1995) "The dynamics of institutionalization: Transformation processes in Norwegian fisheries." Administrative Science Quarterly 40: 398–422.

Japan Biotech Industry Conference Committee (Nihon Baio Sangyojin Kaigi) (1999) "*Baio sangyo gijutsu senryaku* (Technology strategy of biotechnology industry)." Report, 24 November.

Kneller, R. (2000) "University-industry cooperation in biomedicine." Presentation. University of Tokyo.

Lehrer, M. and Asakawa, K. (2004a) "Rethinking the public sector: Idiosyncrasies of biotechnology commercialization as motors of national R&D reform in Germany and Japan." Research Policy 33: 921–938.

——— (2004b) "Pushing scientists into the marketplace: Promoting science entrepreneurship." California Management Review 46(3): 55–76.

Liebeskind, J.P.; Oliver, A.L.; Zucker, L.; and Brewer, M. (1996) "Social networks, learning and flexibility: Sourcing scientific knowledge in new biotechnology firms." Organization Science 7(4): 428–443.

Lundvall, B-A. (Ed.) (1992) National Systems of Innovation: Towards a Theory of Innovation and Interactive Learning. Pinter Publishers, London.

——— (1998) "National business systems and national systems of innovation." International Studies of Management and Organization 29(2): 60–77.

Miles, R.E. and Snow, C.C. (1978) Organizational Strategy, Structure, and Process. McGraw-Hill, New York.

Murmann, J.P. (1998) Knowledge and Competitive Advantage in the Synthetic Dye Industry, 1850–1914. Ph.D. Dissertation, Columbia University.

——— (2003) Knowledge and Competitive Advantage: The Coevolution of Firms, Technology and National Institutions. Cambridge University Press, Cambridge, UK.

Murphy, I.D. (1999) "The role of universities in the pharmaceutical sector." GOR Report, 1(1): 46–54.

Nakamura, H. (2002) "*San-gaku renkei no kadai to kyoka no tame no teigen* (Issues of industry-academia collaboration and proposal for strengthening it)." Report. Japan Patent Agency.

——— (2003) "Anges MG." Case study. Keio Business School, Japan.

Nakazawa, Y. (2000) "*Genomu soyaku to kongo no iyakuhin gyokai* (Genome drug development and the future of the pharmaceutical industry)." October. Tokyo-Mitsubishi Securities, Tokyo.

Nelson, R.R. (Ed.) (1993) National Innovation Systems: A Comparative Analysis. Oxford University Press, Oxford, UK.

Oishi, M. (2001) "*Kagaku gijutsu men kara mita baio bijinesu no kongo no doko*" (The future trend of biotechnology businesses from the viewpoint of science and technology). Presentation. Kazusa DNA Institute.

Oliver, C. (1991) "Strategic responses to institutional processes." Academy of Management Review 16: 145–179.

Porter, M. (1990) The Competitive Advantage of Nations. Free Press, New York.

Powell, W.W.; Koput, K.W.; and Smith-Doerr, L. (1996) "Interorganizational collaboration and the locus of innovation: Networks of learning in biotechnology." Administrative Science Quarterly 41(1): 116–145.

Scott, W.R. (1991) "Unpacking institutional arguments." In: Power, W.W. and DiMaggio, P. (Eds.) The New Institutionalism in Organizational Analysis. University of Chicago Press, Chicago, pp. 164–182.

——— (2001) Institutions and Organizations. Sage, Thousand Oaks, CA.

Selznick, P. (1949) TVA and the Grass Roots. University of California Press, Berkeley.

——— (1957) Leadership in Administration. Row and Peterson, Evanston, IL.

Seo, M-G. and Creed, W.E.D. (2002) "Institutional contradictions, praxis, and institutional change: A dialectical perspective." Academy of Management Review 27(2): 222–247.

Tushman, M.L. and Anderson, P. (1986) "Technolcgical discontinuities and organizational environments." Administrative Science Quarterly 31: 439–465.

Wall Street Journal (2002) "Japan market gets Hercules name" (Eastern edition), New York, NY. 16 December: C.18.

Whitley, R.D. (1992) European Business Systems: Firms and Markets in their National Contexts. Sage, London.

Zucker, L.G. (1991) The Role of Institutionalization in Cultural Persistence. In: Powell, W.W. and DiMaggio, P. (Eds.) The New Institutionalism in Organizational Analysis. University of Chicago Press, Chicago, pp. 83–107.

Zucker, L.G. and Darby, M. (1997) "Present at the revolution: Transformation of technical identity for a large incumbent pharmaceutical firm after the biotechnological breakthrough." Research Policy 26(4): 429–447.

Conclusion

Yoshitaka Okada
Sophia University

Since technological innovation is considered one of the leading factors in maintaining industrial dynamics and national development, this issue remains extremely important for companies, governments, and many other technology-related actors, especially when global market competition becomes severe and when the competitiveness of a country is weakening. Technology is understood not simply as mechanical information, but rather as a certain kind of knowledge embodied in people. Hence to understand technological innovation, we have to take into consideration the influence of diverse factors, such as social norms, product-market conditions, regulations, and the quality of education. The techno-governance approach focuses on the way in which innovation depends on the harmonization of diverse technology-related actors, and on the relationship of innovation to the aforementioned institutional and non-institutional contingencies. This approach allows us to examine the dynamic interactions between organizations (as actors) and institutions. These interactions are particularly affected by drastic changes in product-market conditions and by efforts to revive weakening industries by transforming the old techno-governance structure into a new one. Such a comprehensive approach is considered crucial to a proper understanding of the transformation of industries in a turbulent and path-disturbing environment, something that has become a recurrent situation in such high-tech industries as the semiconductor, telecommunications, and biotechnology industries.

Since new technological ideas and inventions have to be turned into products and successfully marketed, the most important actors are companies that develop intra- and inter-firm relations suitable for high-tech innovation and production. Companies, however, are not the sole players in the technological innovation process. Technology-supporting organizations (TSOs) and governments play vital roles in providing technological assistance, the stimulation and promotion of innovation and the dissemination of technological information. Some TSOs even engage in leading-edge research activities by themselves, while government R&D subsidies and various other policies provide opportunities for innovation and risk-and-cost sharing. As these technology-related actors eventuallydevelop a repeated and harmonized pattern of behavior vis-à-vis high-tech innovation and production, the pattern evolves into a techno-governance structure. But as the behavior of technology-related actors changes and disturbs their harmony, the structure is transformed. Thus the concept of the techno-governance structure captures, on the one hand, actors' behavior and their repeated patterns of behavior, and on the other hand, changes in the elements that constitute this structure, including (1) companies' choices of intra- and inter-firm relations, (2) companies' choices of relations with governments and TSOs, and (3) relations between governments and TSOs (see Fig. 1.1).

What differentiates actors' behavior and companies' choices, and what stimulates or restricts the changes they undergo, depends on the contingencies underlying the structure. These consist of institutions and non-institutional factors such as market conditions and historical incidents. Institutions, understood as the rules of games and the enforcement characteristics of these rules—extending to broader and more general characteristics of repeated human behavior—are highly persistent and difficult to change, and therefore they often function to restrict the range of behavior and enforce harmonization. In contrast, market conditions and historical incidents are fluid, inconsistent, and sporadic, sometimes disrupting the harmonized techno-governance structure and forcing changes even in institutions. Thus market conditions and historical incidents trigger changes in the behavior of technology-related actors, especially companies, forcing them to reformulate their micro-level strategies and even inducing the development of collective macro-level strategies among companies, often involving TSOs and governments. They generate changes in the old techno-governance structure and influence the direction of these changes. In this process of transformation from an old techno-governance structure to a new one, changes in institutions may become unavoidable or even indispensable. Such changes involve companies' collective actions and macro-level strategies as well as government actions to change the rules of the game and their enforcement characteristics. This book has therefore tried to elucidate the interrelations among (1) the turbulent and path-disturbing contingencies of product-market conditions and historical incidents, (2) changes in relations among diverse technology-related actors, and (3) changes in institutions—in other words, to shed light on the co-evolution of market conditions and historical incidents, the techno-governance structure, and institutions.

The old Japanese techno-governance structure evolved with a strong awareness that technological innovation was one of the key factors enabling Japan to develop its industries, and that an institutional legacy of cooperation and an emphasis on human relations and cooperative learning were quite useful in harmonizing diverse actors. Japan's emphasis on cooperative learning in particular facilitated the exchange of information among partners, promoted learning, enhanced capabilities, and fostered highly effective networks, whose extension also formulated complex networks of knowledge generation and dissemination within each industry and between industries.

One core type of network in Japanese industry is inter-firm relations. In particular, vertical *keiretsu* relations between large-sized firms (LSFs) and small- and medium-sized firms (SMFs) were considered the most dynamic element of inter-firm relations in the past, involving technology transfer from the former to the latter and dynamic cooperative learning between them. But these relations tended to be exclusive, requiring very strong commitments, preventing know-how from flowing outside the network, and locking firms into a relation-specific technological trajectory. As this author has argued in Chapter 2, this was especially so in the semiconductor industry, since technological refinements and improvements that enabled firms to increase their yield in DRAM production became the very source of cost advantages and international competitiveness. Closed but dynamic *keiretsu*-type vertical linkages between semiconductor manufacturers and semiconductor equipment manufacturers, involving engineers' craftsman-type refinements, became essential for gaining international competitiveness in DRAM production.

Methé agrees with the importance of Japanese institutions, especially vertical inter-firm relations, in achieving international competitiveness in DRAM production. According to him, the domination of system houses and the later emergence of integrated device manufacturers (IDMs) in the semiconductor industry all over the world suggest that the technological framework itself becomes an extra-institutional restricting force and demands a particular set of necessary factors, irrespective of national and institutional differences. He names this force techno-globalization and refers to the set of necessary factors, including locally available factors, as an innovation envelope. The shift from the system house to the IDM took place largely because of the increased costs of R&D and equipment development and the increased amount of investment in production facilities. Specialization in function-specific devices, such as memory and microprocessors, became necessary to cut these costs, and intra- and inter-firm relations, often quite different from country to country, also became an important part of the innovation envelope in effectively sustaining comparative advantages. Although techno-globalization restricts technological choices, ample options still exist for the selection, implementation and arrangement of local factors in an innovation envelope. Japan's strength in the DRAM sector was clearly an indication that the institutional tradition of cooperation in vertical *keiretsu* relations was a source of comparative advantages, while a strong demand for electronics goods in the Japanese market was an additional factor in its success. In contrast, the EU had a limited market size and a weaker innovation envelope, significantly delaying its shift from the system house to the IDM, while the venture orientation of the U.S. generated more options and gave birth to the next-stage business model in the semiconductor industry.

This author further argues that various TSOs and the national government supported Japanese semiconductor companies in building up their technological capabilities under the old techno-governance structure. National research institutes in particular initiated experiments on the transistor and the integrated circuit (IC), and research cooperatives subsidized by the government helped Japanese companies advance their technological capabilities beyond those of U.S. companies in the 1970s. National research institutes and governmental subsidies functioned to bring competitors together to jointly cultivate and develop technological capability. Regional research institutes, or *kosetsushi*, also helped the

SMFs among equipment manufacturers strengthen their basic technological capabilities. Thus TSOs and the government helped semiconductor companies develop their capabilities especially by promoting cooperation among competitors, and their craftsman-type vertical relations became more dynamic with the support by regional TSOs of equipment manufacturing SMFs. The old techno-governance structure enjoyed a quite effective synergy among semiconductor and equipment manufacturers, TSOs, and the government. This structure was further supported by a traditional and institutional Japanese emphasis on trust, cooperation, commitment, and harmony.

The old techno-governance structure, with its highly cooperative, closed, and dynamic interactions, was even more conspicuous in the telecommunications industry, as Murayama argues. In this industry, the major reason for developing vertical *keiretsu* relations was the monopoly by the Nippon Telegraph and Telephone Public Corporation (NTTPC) in the telecommunications market, a monopoly enforced by Japanese telecommunications laws. In the interests of catching up with Western countries in telecommunications capacity, Japan's telecom research was concentrated at NTTPC, and a limited number of suppliers, such as NEC and Fujitsu, were the recipients of leading-edge technology developed by resource-rich government-owned research institutes. Japanese R&D efforts focused on learning about foreign technology and improving beyond the original to ensure that the technology was not only suitable for and indigenously adapted to Japan, but also reliable for a certain period. The old techno-governance structure of the telecommunications industry was closed, since NTTPC dealt with a limited number of "NTTPC family" equipment suppliers and maintained tight relations with them. The family members sometimes cooperated among themselves with the mediation of NTTPC, and sometimes competed with one another. This form of governance functioned properly to disseminate new technology and to improve it indigenously for the benefit of the public. Once again, the traditional concept of family and the institutional emphasis on cooperation provided a basis for the ready development of such a techno-governance structure.

Asakawa examines the biotechnology sector, following the argument of the national system of innovation. He finds that the Japanese pharmaceutical industry developed quite differently from the semiconductor and telecommunications industries. R&D activities at pharmaceutical companies were strongly in-house oriented and had weak relations with TSOs, since the companies were dependent on existing technology and did not need to engage in radical technological innovation. Consequently, their R&D investments were far smaller than those at Western companies. Universities remained indifferent to corporate activities, and companies engaged in collaborative research with university professors mostly in return for receiving well-trained students as employees. Moreover, unlike its stance toward the electronics and machinery industries, the government did not adopt the pharmaceutical industry as a policy target. Weak inter-firm relations, introverted and isolated intra-firm R&D, weak cooperation with TSOs, and weak government involvement combined to create a highly market-oriented and weakly networked techno-governance structure in the pharmaceutical industry.

A comparison of the old techno-governance structures of these three industries suggests something very interesting. On the one hand, the telecommunications industry evinced a much tighter structure of vertical relations with a strong sense of cooperation and concentrated research activities because of NTTPC's monopoly of that industry. The government exercised tight control through regulation and ownership of techno-governance in the industry. On the other hand, the semiconductor industry, consisting as it did of several competing manufacturers, had a somewhat more fluid and competitive structure, thus requiring an active hand by the government and national TSOs in promoting cooperation among competitors for technological advancement. The TSOs and the government prevented tight lock-ins within cooperative vertical inter-firm relations and promoted technological stimulation and dissemination through joint research projects.

Since the government considered the semiconductor and telecommunications industries crucial to Japanese economic development, it actively supported companies in these industries and developed a harmonized system among companies, TSOs, and the government that fit well with technological and market conditions. By contrast, the pharmaceutical industry enjoyed far less support from the government, partly because its technological base was too weak and partly because its industrial experience was too immature. Given their low level of technological capability, Japanese pharmaceutical companies made use of existing technologies, and the government assigned a low priority to the development of the industry. In other words, where the government got involved in certain industries, it made a drastic difference in nurturing extensive networks and promoting cooperative interaction among related actors, and it produced marked differentiation in the relative complexity of these various techno-governance structures.

Hence, even though the old techno-governance structures in all three industries were greatly influenced by the Japanese institutional tradition of cooperative learning, the failure to develop effective networks in the pharmaceutical industry suggests that a traditional cooperation-oriented institution by itself does not stimulate industrial dynamics. To turn an institution into a dynamic industrial element requires the active participation of technology-related actors driven by their immediate and future needs, appeals to the importance of the synergetic effects generated by adhering to the traditional values of cooperation, and effective facilitation by active and neutral third parties, especially regional and central governments. In this book, we found that the old dynamic techno-governance structure consisted of a complex mixture of organizational actions and institutions and of collective macro-level strategies and individual company-based micro-level strategies, as shown in Cell 1 in Table 1.1. This point became especially clear when we identified organizations as actors separate from institutions, and when we closely analyzed the relations between institutional characteristics and dynamic actions by organizations.

Around the mid-1980s, global markets and technological conditions began changing, and the old techno-governance structures of these three industries became less fit for global competition. All three industries faced serious challenges, though the problems of the semiconductor and telecommunications industries differed from those of the pharmaceutical sector. The former faced the restrictions of well-developed network-oriented structures, while the latter suffered from its lack of such a structure as well as a lack of technological capabilities in biotechnology. How, then, did companies in these industries try to survive, and what types of organizational and institutional transformation took place in the 1990s?

According to Murayama, the most radical changes took place in the telecommunications industry. These changes were spurred by pressures from the digitization and globalization of the industry, the privatization of NTTPC in 1984, and the deregulation of Japan's telecommunications markets. Even though an institutional change in telecommunications regulations stimulated changes in the market, the path-dependent effects of the government's regulatory role and the past function of NTTPC as a public service provider remained as important as before. Despite becoming a private entity, NTTPC (renamed NTT) remained partly owned by the government and was continuously regulated; and it was not allowed to operate internationally. Competition in the domestic telecommunications market was introduced with the entry of new firms, but NTT's division into two companies was postponed for a while because of conflicts among various actors. Despite becoming a private company, NTT was still required to publicly disseminate the results of its R&D, thus making it impossible for NTT "family" members to rely on advanced NTT technology for their own market advantages. Furthermore, the confinement of NTT operations to the domestic market constrained NTT family suppliers from developing their own capabilities for international competition. Some suppliers therefore began operating independently, strengthening their own R&D capabilities in telecommunications and advancing into foreign markets. Even so, the cumulative experience and technology they had acquired with NTT were not competitive enough to gain them a significant share of these markets. Despite Japan's success with general electronic products on the global market in the 1970s and 1980s, it failed in the field of telecommunications, especially telephone-related products, because of path-dependent institutional restrictions that limited these products and the R&D capabilities of their producers. This is an example of how the persistence of old macro-level TSO strategies, even as companies try to develop new micro-level strategies, results in a loss of dynamics because of institutional, governmental, and TSO support restrictions, as shown in Cell 7 of Table 1.1.

Mobile telephone and data processing operations came to be deregulated, and telephone operations remained under governmental regulation, despite their privatization. NTT DoCoMo, a completely private company with no guarantee of either governmental protection or success in the market, had to develop new technology on its own and create a viable business. Mobile telephones were not initially popular because of technical, weight, and cost problems, and the top executives of the company were, for the first time in their careers, confronted with a threat to their company's very survival. NTT DoCoMo needed to develop a radically new way of conducting its business, and quickly. For this purpose, the old management practices inherited from NTT were not only inappropriate, but a hindrance. However, the completely deregulated status of the company provided a favorable legal environment for developing an open system. NTT DoCoMo introduced open personnel recruitment, headhunted leading specialists in the field, and solicited ideas openly both inside and outside the company. It even chose its own suppliers. It could not rely on NTT for technology because that technology still had to be publicly disseminated, which would have reduced the product differentiation capabilities of NTT DoCoMo. Instead, DoCoMo set up its own research facility and developed "i-mode," the world's first breakthrough in mobile telephone-based Internet operations. The company is currently trying to develop an open system for the purpose of defining global standards.

Despite this open and market-oriented approach, Japanese tradition still exerted a significant influence on NTT DoCoMo. Its approach to engaging in research activities and developing ideas was strongly based on the Japanese concept of *ba* (place). Innovative ideas emerge not simply from individual contemplation, but from human interaction in a space conducive to intermingling. This Japanese philosophy became the basis for DoCoMo's business operations and technological innovations. DoCoMo has also made effective use of traditional vertical inter-firm relations, in which one key company exercises a significant influence over related companies. It purchases all its mobile telephones from manufacturers and distributes them to retailers with a rebate, which the retailers use to discount the market price. It engages in close collaboration with portal site providers, through which content suppliers distribute information to users, and it collects charges on behalf of the content suppliers. In other words, DoCoMo developed a new mobile-telephone-company-centered business model based on vertical cooperation (Daiyamondo, 2004). Even in this era of globalization, NTT DoCoMo still found the cultural and social institutions of vertical inter-firm relations important in developing its business model. Although a highly market-oriented approach with a more open system has generated new business dynamics, it was combined with a traditional Japanese philosophy and business model. Market-like mechanisms were mixed effectively with traditional practices. This is a situation in which the withdrawal of old macro-level strategies forced companies to face path-disturbing conditions and compelled them to introduce new micro-level strategies. It resulted in stimulating new company dynamics with little governmental or TSO help under path-disturbing conditions, as indicated by Cell 8 in Table 1.1. Even in this situation, however, institutional factors provided an important foundation for introducing new micro-level strategies.

As this author argues, changes in technological development and market conditions in the semiconductor industry were so gradual that it took a while for Japanese companies to recognize these changes. By then, the Japanese companies had lost their competitive advantage in the global market. They detected the advancement of Korean companies in the DRAM market, to which their response was a strategy of advancing DRAM technology into higher line refinements. However, increasing line refinements in semiconductor production led to stronger demand for the system LSI (or system-on-a-chip), which houses on one chip memory, microprocessor, digital signal processor, and other devices. The U. S. consortium SEMATECH led the way in developing technological capabilities suited to the system LSI. This change caught Japanese companies by surprise; meanwhile, the Korean companies had begun dominating the DRAM market. Moreover, according to Methé, the U.S. modularized production model, which separates electronic design, chip production and foundry operations, has influenced some aspects of the new U.S. advancement toward the system LSI and may even become a dominant new business model in the future, one that Japanese companies find a less-than-perfect fit in the Japanese context. This may augur another unfavorable technological change for Japan amid the techno-globalization of coming years.

This author argues that the failure of Japanese semiconductor companies to respond to change was due to the old techno-governance structure as well as the disintegration of its capacity to stimulate further technological innovation. Japanese companies had a strong belief in cooperative learning and vertical inter-firm relations. The government and TSOs extensively promoted cooperation among competitors in order to reduce costs and risks in basic R&D, while also disseminating information and encouraging competition for innovation among these competitors. This network-oriented techno-governance, however, disintegrated as a result of the U.S.-Japan trade disputes and the high cost of silicon-related R&D. The government and TSOs were forced to refrain from direct involvement in silicon-related R&D because this would further strengthen the market conditions of Japanese semiconductor companies and aggravate trade disputes with the U.S. Consequently, these disputes and the high cost of R&D generated disharmony among technology-related actors and discouraged innovative activities that might produce marketable products, while the vertical relations that remained in place between semiconductor firms and equipment manufacturers entrapped them in perspectives and activities governed by relation-specific technological trajectories. The techno-governance structure began to acquire more of a semiconductor-company-based market orientation, except in its cooperative vertical *keiretsu* relations. Technology-related actors lost the networks that had been effective in disseminating information and making companies alert to changes, and the semiconductor companies became entrapped in very limited, relation-specific technological perspectives. As shown in Cell 2 of Table 1.1, the continuity of traditional micro-level strategies by these companies lost its sense of future direction without proper support from governments, TSOs, or collective strategies.

Meanwhile, cooperation through SEMATECH enabled U.S. competitors to take over global technological leadership of the semiconductor industry by shifting their technological focus from the DRAM to the system LSI, resulting in Japan's loss of technological competitiveness. Japanese craftsman-type vertical cooperation was particularly well suited to the development and production of the DRAM. In contrast, U.S. horizontal cooperation among competitors was especially well suited to the development of low-cost, leading-edge, standardized semiconductor technologies, with each company competing in its own specialized area of system design.

Despite a drastic decline in Japanese semiconductor sales, the need for maintaining the Japanese institutional tradition of lifetime employment, a strong belief in their DRAM-based technological capabilities, and their tradition of tightly developed vertical cooperation delayed efforts by Japanese semiconductor companies to make radical changes in their micro-, corporate-level strategies. This delay exacerbated the situation to the point where traditional vertical inter-firm relations and lifetime employment could not be sustained, as indicated by Cell 5 in Table 1.1.

Market-oriented strategies by semiconductor companies functioned to expand the choices and options available to decision makers, who laid off employees, terminated vertical long-term relations, and divided their companies into several units, either as in-house companies or as spun-off subsidiaries (*bunshaka*), which allowed corporate headquarters to sell these units, combine them in joint ventures, or keep them inside the parent company. The headquarters modularized their operations and separated them into several units to facilitate independent decision making, hiring, and cash flow accounting in each unit. They also required more efficient financial performances of their spun-off subsidiaries through independent fund-raising, stock issuing, investment, and other means.

However, the company separation system and modularization within each company weakened the technological and financial capabilities of each separated unit and induced inter-firm cooperation among competitors. Japanese semiconductor companies, still vertical cooperation oriented but recognizing the importance and effectiveness of cooperative learning, felt it was easier to work with other Japanese competitors rather than with U.S. competitors who did not share a Japanese sense of cooperation. This means that the Japanese traditional sense of inter-firm cooperation restricted their choice of partners, with Japanese companies struggling to achieve effective horizontal cooperation based on their shared values. Moreover, even though the sale of modularized units had become a convenient means for companies to reduce their payrolls, the Japanese government, unlike that of the United States, passed a new law to protect employees in spun-off subsidiaries from being laid off. The law, in principle, guarantees these employees the continuation of lifetime employment, even though such a guarantee may not be effective when those subsidiaries are sold off. These findings clearly suggest that even under path-disturbing conditions, Japanese institutions restricted choices and stimulated a new type of development based on traditionally shared values, though the company separation system basically functioned to facilitate payroll reductions with minimum damage to the legitimacy of lifetime employment and employee morale in the Japanese management system.

However, the struggle to develop horizontal cooperation among Japanese competitors resulted in the competitors intensively cooperating in some product areas while intensively competing in others. These companies have thus created modularized competition in the market. Competition is no longer clearly defined along company lines; the cooperators and competitors vary for each product market. For example, in one product market company A cooperates with company B and competes against company C, and in another product market company A cooperates with company C and competes against company B. This new mix of cooperation and competition has produced complex networks of horizontal cooperation that are quite different from the old vertical inter-firm relations.

Weakened financial and technical capabilities also created an environment that encouraged competitors to cooperate and develop collective measures for rebuilding competitiveness through consortia—some with government subsidies, as in the 1960s and 1970s, and some without subsidies. The latter is a rather new form of collective cooperation, but Japan's long history of collaborative research among competitors has facilitated the rapid and effective formulation of such research consortia. Managers in research cooperatives made use of old practices in a new context of horizontal cooperation, while they introduced diverse new practices to create open and transparent environments.

The implementation of market-oriented mechanisms thus signified the difficulty of maintaining the old techno-governance structure and the need to accept and tolerate changes, creating a basis for finding new ways to solve industry problems. Yet at the same time, these mechanisms were implemented in a manner that minimized damage to the legitimacy of existing values and made full use of certain traditionally shared values as the basis for new developments. Even the reassessment of traditional collective behavior yielded new approaches to collective sharing suitable for the system LSI, and in the market, companies began cooperating in some product areas while competing in others. The consequence was the development of continuous patterns of cooperation and competition that were more open and flexible, but also far more complex than in the past. With collective behavior among companies and the government and TSOs playing a prominent role in the revival of the semiconductor industry, a shift took place from the conditions shown in Cell 5 to those shown in Cell 6 of Table 1.1, and the introduction of new micro-level strategies also suggested a possible shift to the conditions of Cell 9.

The biotechnology sector—with strong governmental assistance—started developing a more effective and dynamic network-oriented techno-governance structure by harmonizing biotechnology-related R&D activities among companies, TSOs, and the government. Asakawa's chapter describes the co-evolution of macro-level strategies by the government to implement national-level innovation policies and micro-level corporate strategies in R&D and venture activities.

Policy-wise, the government actively promulgated the development of the biotechnology industry. Recognizing the widespread applications of biotechnology, it established policy coordination mechanisms for inter-ministry collaboration to prevent vertical ministry splits in policy implementation. Because of the scientific nature of the technology, university-company relations acquired special importance. The government made legal provisions for closer university-industry technology links, stimulating university R&D by increasing the amount of research grants and the number of interns and postdoctoral scholars, allowing university professors to own patents, and shifting patent ownership to universities from the government. The government also launched large collaborative projects at national research institutes in which university professors and researchers from companies and TSOs could participate. To provide financial resources for ventures, the government deregulated capital markets, created tax incentives for angel investors, and established stock exchanges for new ventures. More market-based incentive systems were introduced to stimulate further change. These changes in policy also applied to other industries besides biotechnology.

As for micro-level corporate strategies, companies started entering the biotechnology business, installing executives with biotechnology backgrounds, limiting in-house R&D, building research facilities overseas, developing global linkages and alliances to overcome limitations in domestic capability, and promoting spinoff venture firms. These micro-level changes corresponded well with macro-level collective strategies. Thus the old system came to be deemphasized as new processes began stimulating multilevel transformations. This introduction of both macro-level collective and micro-level company strategies suggests a possible shift to a new techno-governance structure (Cell 9), especially if these two levels of strategy match well with each other as well as with path-disturbing contingencies.

All three industries thus faced turbulent environments caused by historical incidents and market conditions from the mid-1980s to the 1990s. Japan's biotechnology sector in particular suffered from a lack of international competitiveness; the telecommunications industry faced privatization, deregulation, and digitization; and the semiconductor industry lost its technological leadership and global market. The new market orientation adopted to cope with these turbulent conditions sent clear signals and provided incentives for introducing more openness, fluidity, and flexibility into the existing techno-governance structure. In all three industries, this market orientation stimulated the development of venture firms, and biotechnology companies also focused on developing "meta-national" global alliances. NTT DoCoMo engaged in market-based open acquisitions of various resources, and semiconductor companies laid off workers, dismantled vertical *keiretsu* relations, started procuring equipment from external sources, and modularized their production units so that corporate headquarters could sell them to, or form joint ventures with, other companies—especially competitors—or retain them within the company. Market-like mechanisms undeniably generated a greater diversity of options for decision-makers to choose from, introduced openness, and created flexibility for corporations.

Does this mean that the new techno-governance structure has simply become more market oriented? The answer is no. The outcome is far more complex, largely because path-dependent institutions still form an important basis for the judgment of decision makers and because market-oriented mechanisms are not by themselves adequate for developing dynamic industrial capability. Past Japanese experiences in the pharmaceutical and semiconductor industries clearly show that the lack or disintegration of harmonization and networks among diverse technology-related actors weakens industrial capability and creates a dangerous situation. The traditional emphasis on cooperation and harmony remains highly influential.

However, the difficulty of building an effective techno-governance structure is also well recognized. The experiences of the telecommunications and semiconductor industries suggest that too much governmental intervention in the former industry and the lock-in of relation-specific technological trajectories in the latter industry stifled dynamic, marketable, and timely technological developments in both industries.

Diverse path-dependent practices are still also employed. For example, as in the 1960s and 1970s, policies to promote the respective development and redevelopment of the biotechnology and semiconductor industries resulted in the establishment of a significant number of large research cooperatives with government subsidies. Emphasis on the concept of *ba* in NTT DoCoMo's R&D activities is also based on Japanese institutional traditions. However, some new attempts at institution building include the strengthening of university roles in technology development, nurturing effective company-university linkages, and establishing major research cooperatives without government subsidies.

Thus the government played a very important leading role in orchestrating and mobilizing existing resources and technological capabilities at the macro-level, with both the government and private companies making full use of institutional arrangements and innovation networks through associations, national research institutes, and research consortia with and without government subsidies. Meanwhile, companies also implemented their own micro-level strategies. These macro- and micro-level strategies interacted dynamically and co-evolved as indicated in Table 1.1. These findings amply support both the resource orchestration (Casper, 1999) and idea innovation networks (Hage and Hollingsworth, 2000) perspectives.

In conclusion, as Fig. 1.1 indicates, market conditions and historical incidents acted as path-disturbing influences on the old techno-governance structure, introduced more market-oriented approaches, and created openness, fluidity, and flexibility, but the tradition of cooperation and collective approaches also effectively contributed to the building up of basic technological capabilities. The new techno-governance structure seems to be evolving as a complex mixture of competition and cooperation—in other words, of market-oriented approaches and path-dependent institutions. This mixture of cooperation and competition is not at all new in Japan, though the types of market-oriented mechanisms and the nature of cooperation have drastically changed. This also suggests that a transformation is taking place in the rules for how actors cooperate and compete, namely, in the institutions themselves. Companies, techno-governance structures, and institutions are thus co-evolving to cope with turbulent environments and to adapt to the new conditions of the global market.

Bibliography

Casper, S. (1999) "High technology governance and institutional adaptiveness: Do technology policies usefully promote commercial innovation within the German biotechnology industry?" Paper presented at Conference on National Innovation Systems and the Idea-Innovation Chain, held at The Netherlands Institute of Advanced Study in the Humanities and Social Sciences, Wassenaar, The Netherlands, 27–29 January.

Daiyamondo (2004) "*Keitai taikoku ga kawaru!* (The leading mobile telephone country is changing!)." 24 January, pp. 30–43.

Hage, J. and Hollingsworth, J.R. (2000) "A strategy for the analysis of idea innovation networks and institutions." Organization Studies 21(5): 971–1004.

Index

d

e

o

p

q

r

t

y

MIX
Papier aus verantwortungsvollen Quellen
Paper from responsible sources
FSC® C105338

If you have any concerns about our products,
you can contact us on
ProductSafety@springernature.com

In case Publisher is established outside the EU,
the EU authorized representative is:
Springer Nature Customer Service Center GmbH
Europaplatz 3, 69115 Heidelberg, Germany

Printed by Libri Plureos GmbH
in Hamburg, Germany